TAKE THIS PHONE AND *SHOVE* IT!

A Frustrated Senior's Guide to Smartphones

ANNE GOLDBERG

Savvy Senior Tech LLC

Published by:
Savvy Senior Tech, LLC
Boca Raton, FL

ISBN First Edition: 979-8-9920749-0-1

Character illustrations by Denis Vasiluev, used with permission.

The following is a trademark of Anne Goldberg: "Take This Phone and Shove It!"
Artwork: Creative Commons and Anne Goldberg, Material Design Icons

iPhone is a registered TM of Apple, Inc.
Samsung is a registered TM of Samsung Electronics Co., Ltd.
Pixel 3 is a registered TM of Google, Inc.

For bulk sales or to order copies for you or your group or to send as a gift, please contact Anne Goldberg at Anne@TakeThisPHONEandSHOVEit.com

WHAT PEOPLE ARE SAYING ABOUT TAKE THIS PHONE AND SHOVE IT!

From the start, Anne inspires readers to embrace smartphones with curiosity rather than fear, showing how learning new technology can stimulate the brain. Her conversational tone, sprinkled with nostalgic anecdotes, makes the journey enjoyable and accessible. She provides a brief history of cell phones, practical tips for choosing the right device, and a clear, user-friendly guide to essential functions and features. With a deep understanding of her audience, Anne not only teaches smartphone basics but also highlights their potential to simplify and enrich everyday life.

Zeva S., Boynton Beach, FL, 60

Anne Goldberg's friendly guide is perfect for seniors and anyone looking to boost their smartphone skills, blending essentials with advanced features to build confidence. Packed with helpful information, it's a lifesaver for those struggling with technology—like me, when I couldn't figure out how to open the iPhone control center. After endless online searches, I found the simple answer in minutes. Whether reading systematically or looking up specific problems, this book prevents the frustration of wanting to "shove" your phone and is the only resource you need to master smartphones at any age.

Connie S., Chapel Hill, NC, 77

As a practicing attorney for over fifty years who relies on my iPhone daily, I never realized how little I knew and how important an iPhone can be. This book changed not only my practice but my day to day life. I am more efficient and effective. Failing to buy this books is iPhone malpractice. It is as essential as the phone itself.

Frank L., Tom's River, N.J., 77 years

From setting up your phone, to changing the settings, messaging, emails, apps and more, this book is for us. Anne's book makes me feel less dependent on my grandkids and more independent. Nothing makes you feel dumber than asking a twelve-year-old how do you this or that. Well, no more for me. Anne's book makes me feel like I'm young enough to learn how to be self-sufficient with my phone. Thank you. From no longer dazed and confused.

Mark M., Miami, FL, 73

Anne Goldberg has a knack for making learning how to use cell phones easy and fun. Her experience coupled with her ability to communicate makes it possible for everyone to learn how to use (or make better use of) their cell phones. The book is a great reference tool, so if you don't remember something, it's easy to find what you're looking for. I highly recommend this book to any senior (and frankly, anyone else who wants a simple how-to guide for cell phones).

Jenae R., 67

If you, like so many other seniors, are befuddled and often frustrated by the complexity of the space-age communicator commonly called a "smartphone," this book offers some welcome clarity. Written by a senior with years of experience teaching seniors how to comfortably integrate technology into their lives, the book serves bite-sized morsels of guidance that can be dipped into individually for specific questions or taken together as a full meal. It can help you to maybe even teach your grandchildren a thing or two about using their smartphone! Recommended.

Andy R., Chapel Hill, NC, 77

"This is a must-have book for seniors--and anyone seeking to get the most out of their smart phone. I found the basic information presented in clear, concise and readable language and appreciated the informative illustrations. I was also

delighted to find that Goldberg includes some valuable tips for more advanced smart phone users."

Kathy L, Senior community resident in Delray Beach, 82

I found this book easy to read, entertaining, accessible and, above all, USEFUL! I'm a young Baby Boomer and fairly tech-savvy, but I still learned things that have made me even more efficient using my mobile devices. Thanks, Anne, for explaining this area in a way that lessens anxiety and promotes confident use of technology.

Judith K,, Pompano Beach, FL

"Anne Goldberg writes with humor and compassion, making readers feel understood from the start. Her charming reflections on the 'days of old'—like rotary phones and three-channel TVs—bring smiles, while her simple, effective tips for both Android and iPhone users make learning easy. Anne's deep understanding of how seniors learn, combined with her practical advice, transforms the smartphone journey into an enjoyable experience. Take This Phone and Shove It is a must-read for any senior wanting to master their device and embrace the digital age with confidence and fun."

Maxine K., Boynton Beach, FL, 75

"A really great summary of iPhone and Android phones. This book is lots of fun to read! It's a combination of nostalgia and clear concise instructions that will allow you to feel a sense of competence in using this ubiquitous device we call our phone. You will be surprised what you learn even if you consider yourself somewhat savvy with today's phone technology.. but great for whatever level you are at. Highly recommend."

Yona M., Plantation, FL, 72

Fantastic. Finally, an answer to all my questions about my cell phone! The book is laid out so well and is so easy to follow. Besides being informative, it is humorous. Anne has taken a lot from her life and shared it, making the information more relatable. I would recommend this book to anyone who needs help figuring out their cell phone. It has taught me some new things!

Karen R., Plantation, FL, 65

Dedicated to my parents, Nat and Ida Louis, of blessed memory. May they rest in peace knowing they never have to learn how to use smartphones.

Acknowledgments

I could never have attempted or completed this book without the help of a few people who are very dear to my heart. Fleur Heaton, thank you for your constant support and friendship and especially for lending me your Android Samsung Galaxy 21, my source for all the Android pictures throughout the book.

Rabbi Marc Labowitz, for more than twenty years, you have consistently encouraged me to reach for the stars. Thank you, more than I can say, for your constant loving encouragement. And to my dear friends Staci Kessler, Connie Andrews, and Zeva Soroker, thank you for helping me see the best in myself and encouraging me every step of the way. Your believing in me helped sustain me through the writing process.

To my sons, Jake, Rob, and Jaxson, and my granddaughters, Amelia, Ava, and Auralia, you give my life meaning. Nothing is more important to me than you.

To my book coaches, Wendi Weiss and Patricia Wooster, there is no way I would have been able to achieve this level of creativity and professionalism without you both. Your guidance has been invaluable in every step of getting the book ready for publishing and sales and so much more. Thank you. A big thank you to Sushmitha Naroor and the staff at Happy Self Publishing. Wow, you made me look good! To Ron Kaufman, I can't thank you enough for your generous spirit and your invaluable help.

And finally, to my beloved, David Hall, whose daily love, humor, support, and inspiration allowed me to step out of my comfort zone and finish this book. I love you so.

Step-by-step tutorials start on page 393

From the Author

I have to admit that, as a Boomer, it's weird being old. I was born in 1952. You do the math. I am objectively old. As far as my kids are concerned, I've been old for twenty years already! And my young granddaughters are always fascinated by how old I am. It's a number they can't quite fathom. It's so close to 100, they tell me. Yes, it is, I tell them. Yes. It. Is.

Over my seventy-plus years, I have learned that age is just a number. There are those who feel happy and fit at eighty and those who feel crappy and handicapped with pain or illness at sixty. Aging is not a prescription for suffering. And I, for one, am not prepared to suffer from getting older. While I yield to the reality of aging, I refuse to accept it has to stop me. I've written this book because I don't want it to stop you either—at least not when it comes to technology in day-to-day living.

The way we do things is very different from when we were young, but that doesn't mean life has to pass us by. It was a different world sixty to eighty years ago from the world we live in now. Social media has changed

Age should never be a barrier to learning new things, including technology.

the way people interact. It has changed how we do things. In so many ways, it was so much easier when we were kids.

We did things a certain way, based on the technology of the times, and that's where most of us are comfortable. Your habits and ways of doing things have been honed over decades of life. Back in the 1950s to the 1970s, consumer electronics were still in their infancy. Televisions and early computers were bulky, expensive, and limited in what they could do. Telephones had rotary dials and were tethered to the wall. Communication was simpler but much slower than today. Fast-forward to the seventies, and we saw the rise of personal computers. But even then, few of us could have imagined a world where a small device in our pocket could not only make calls but also access the entire world's information, take photos, and connect us instantly to anyone, anywhere.

I sometimes yearn for those times, but that's an exercise in nostalgia that doesn't change the reality of today's world. And I am determined to deal with the *what is the reality* of any situation. In the twenty-first century, the *what is* is that electronics have woven their way into the very fabric of daily life all over the planet. Truly some of the electronic advancements are fantastic, like computers, robotic surgery, and… smartphones. Maybe you don't feel that way now. My deepest wish is that you will feel that way after making your way through this book. Consider yourself in one of my classes as I guide you through this curriculum designed to help you relate to and understand technology and how to use it for convenience, safety, communication, shopping, entertainment, and education. And if you want more support, visit my website: www.TakeThisPhoneAndShoveIt.com. You'll find short tutorials on a variety of subjects.

Whether you want a smartphone or not, your kids and friends want you to have one so they can be in touch with you. And it's great having a phone when unexpected traffic causes a delay. Now we can text or call (pulling off the road or using voice commands) to update them as to our ETA (estimated time of arrival). That's a great convenience and a way to be thoughtful to the person (or persons) waiting. And the benefits of turn-by-turn GPS directions are huge and so appreciated. Clearly, these devices have redeeming features, but I find that most seniors have a love/(mostly) hate relationship with their smartphones. I understand the love/hate. There are times when I want to pound my phone onto the ground, but calm prevails, and I can usually figure out what went wrong.

I'm not a computer geek, but for some reason, using tech comes easily to me. I am naturally curious and learned how to type in high school, so the keyboard didn't scare me. Maybe it's because I worked on an early keypunch computer back in the late seventies and started using PCs in early 1989. And I do love my PC (no offense to Mac users), and I enjoy learning how to do more with it.

But what about you? What's your relationship with your smartphone? I dare ask, "Does your smartphone make you feel dumb?" If the screen suddenly changes to something completely unexpected, do you feel dumb because you're not sure what to do? And what about those annoying bells and bongs the phone makes? Have you got any idea what they are?

Well, consider this. If you feel that technology makes you feel dumb, I invite you to search YouTube for "teenager, rotary phone." There are plenty of hilarious videos of this, and, believe me, those kids look pretty dumb trying to figure out how to make a call. In point of fact, **they are not dumb, and neither are you. They are simply confronted with something they have absolutely no experience using. Rotary phones are foreign to them. You have to learn the language**. And, lucky for you, I cover that in Chapter Six – Gestures, i.e., the language of the smartphone and how you communicate with your device.

This Photo by Unknown Author is licensed under CC BY-SA-NC

You are either on the technology boat...or you miss it.

From entertainment to research to monitoring your heart, technology is ubiquitous, useful, and beneficial. It is an incontrovertible part of the twenty-first century.

And, as time marches forward, it will insert itself into our daily experience in more and more ways. As robotic technology improves, we may all have a Rosie the Robot®, like George and Judy Jetson had in the sixties TV show.

Since their introduction, smartphones have taken over the world and fundamentally changed the way things are done. For many seniors the rapid advancement of technology feels overwhelming and hard to navigate, yet it is here to stay.

Now you are faced with a choice: Do you turn your back on learning anything new, resolutely refusing to consider it, or do you embrace this as an opportunity to challenge your brain and learn new ways of living life, especially about connecting and communicating with loved ones near and far? If you keep your mind open and curious, I will guide you from feeling overwhelmed to understanding how technology has replaced so many common devices and how to do these things yourself with ease.

Whether using an iPhone or Android (Samsung, LG, Motorola, or Google Pixel), you will learn the smartphone basics.

What qualifies me to teach you?

My life as a teacher of tech to seniors began in October 2013 in South Florida. Since then, I have had the honor of teaching computers and smartphones to thousands of seniors, average age eighty-five. I am uniquely qualified to understand the learning needs of my peers and have developed a curriculum that allows them to understand the subject, making learning technology easier and with less frustration.

Also, because I'm in my seventies, I understand firsthand the head-scratching moments that come with learning this stuff. In case you doubt my sincerity on that point, the first time I saw an iPhone in 2007, it was so alien, I was afraid of it. Seriously, the phone was so different, I was anxious at the thought of even trying it! I had a BlackBerry and I loved it. I wasn't going to jump on that smartphone bandwagon! But two years later, the handwriting was on the wall, and I caved in and got a Samsung smartphone. I found that once I understood the logic, the phone was not so complicated. But until that moment, I was having none of it. So, please believe me when I say that mastering this confounded device requires **humor, patience,** and **persistence**.

After nearly a decade of teaching, that little voice inside my head just kept saying, "Write the book, write the book!" There was no escaping it. *Take This Phone & Shove It – A Frustrated Senior's Guide to Smartphones* was created from those words in my head as the most comprehensive beginner's guide for seniors navigating the world of smartphones. It provides you with the knowledge and confidence to make the most of your devices without the urge to toss them out the window!

I strive to make technology fun, accessible, and stress-free, helping you stay connected and engaged in today's digital world. I want you to feel more confident because you now have a guide that will help you to embrace the digital age with ease. After all, *age should never be a barrier to learning new things, including technology.* Throughout this book, you will find clear explanations and illustrations that will help you understand and master the various things you can do with smartphones in a straightforward, step-by-step guide that familiarizes you with the language of smartphones. Whether you prefer to read from start to finish or jump to specific chapters, you will find this to be a flexible and helpful companion.

Who is this book for?

- If you, fundamentally, do not understand how the phone works, this book is for you.
- If you always do what you know you know how to do very well, but can't get past that, this book is for you.
- If you are a regular user but don't take the time to explore deeply into the most common apps, this book is for you.
- If you're constantly calling your kids or grandkids to help you, this book is for you.

I would like to take a minute here to address the technical folks out there reading and reviewing this book. This book is not for the advanced user. Its purpose is to present smartphone basics to people of a certain age for whom this does not come easily. Please don't take me to task for taking professional license regarding how technology works. The metaphors I use to teach these concepts work well for this demographic. While it's true that the technology behind 5G antennas is a different animal from that of rooftop antennas, they are both still types of antennas that send and/or receive signals. That's good enough to get the point across.

And finally, I want to address age and learning. Yes, I know we're not supposed to talk about that. But I'm seventy-three, so I think it's okay for me to address my fellow seniors with a certain degree of authority.

There's a famous story about legendary baseball star Leroy Robert "Satchell" Paige. Satchell was already in his forties when he was recruited by Major League Baseball, and he was wildly successful. At a press conference, a reporter asked, "Satchel, how old are you?" His wise answer… "How old would you be if you didn't know how old you are?"

...old enough to
have a past and
young enough to
have a future...™

I often start my classes with this question. "How old would you be if you didn't know how old you are?" Take a minute and think about it. Personally, I don't feel any age in particular. I am me. I am the same me I've been my whole life. Each age and stage brought with it challenges and pleasures, and this stage is no different.

But people are sensitive to the subject of age, and so was I when I was younger. In fact, as a Baby Boomer, I was horrified at the thought of turning thirty. Thirty! OMG! I was moaning about this to a forty-something woman who said to me, "Anne, what are you worried about? You're ...old enough to have a past and young enough to have a future...™"

It was a revelation! Instantly relieved, I had to admit that I felt a certain pride at being "old enough to have a past" and a certain empowerment in having a future. And forty-three years later, I acknowledge what I've accomplished (and failed at) in my past and look forward to accomplishing more in my future.

I invite you to embrace this for yourself. Age has no boundaries. Only our limited thinking forces boundaries on us. I say, the hell with that. **Be a savvy senior** and agree to move into your future with a commitment to stay with the times, not be left behind, and commit to learning new things.

The idea that we are *young enough to have a future* is the underpinning of this book. This book is the beginning of a movement. A movement of elders who won't be ignored, a movement that affirms we are all young enough to have a future!

How to Use This Book

Take This Phone and Shove It! is not just a smartphone manual. It's part storytelling and part technical instruction. The book is designed to help you understand how we did things in the past and how we do them now; to help you understand the evolution of mobile phones and how we got to this place where technology rules the way things are done. The information builds upon itself to create an understanding of what these devices are and how they work. Some of you will jump directly to the lessons and some of you may want to read it from cover to cover, immersing yourself in the entire narrative and tutorials.

On the next page is a table of contents of the chapters. You will find very detailed tables of contents at the beginning of each chapter, guiding you to find the particular lesson you desire. I have done my best to separate Android and iPhone tutorials. But remember, smartphones have certain commonalities so each chapter begins with information that is applicable to both types of phones. Then it breaks down by Android and iPhone instructions.

I wanted to make it easy for you to use! The colored borders are so you can easily find content while the book is closed, just by opening to the right color. I recommend you keep the book handy, maybe even on your coffee table or nightstand so you always have it available for help.

Finally, and most importantly, learn at your own pace and don't feel that you have to master the whole thing from start to finish. It's best to learn one lesson at a time before you move on to the next. Remember, practice is the key to learning.

However you use it, *Take This Phone And Shove It!* is your personal smartphone guide written by a senior, me, just for you.

Written with great love and respect for all seniors,

Table of Contents

Chapter 1

The Obstacles

Table of Contents

Obstacle #1 - I'm too old to learn

NO, NO…you are NOT too old to learn! I can't stress this enough.

Most people think they lose the ability to learn new things as they age. Assuming you have normal cognitive function (meaning you are always forgetting where you put your purse/watch/phone/keys but otherwise function normally), **you can learn.** Actually, my dad gave the very best description of bad memory vs. dementia. When my father was in his fifties, he came out of the bathroom and forgot to zip his fly. My mom started making fun of him, teasing him that he was losing his marbles. He looked right at her and declared, "Honey, it's not a problem if I forget to zip up. It's only a problem if I forget to zip down!" And that, dear reader, is the essence of the difference between succumbing to the brain disease of dementia versus normal, slightly forgetful, and slower-than-it-used-to-be memory.

Louis Family Photos

I like to make the analogy of filing cabinets. The average eighteen-year-old has memories that fill maybe one five-drawer file cabinet, and the files are loosely arranged in each drawer. But us? We're in our sixties, seventies, eighties, or even nineties. We have a house full of filing cabinets, and each one is stuffed tightly with memories of so many decades of living. So please don't beat yourself up when a memory comes a bit slower to you than it used to. Your brain has to sift through a lot more files before it finds the right one!

You'll be happy to know that the latest research proves we are not born with a fixed number of brain cells. In fact, our brains are designed to expand and contract throughout our lives, based on choices we make. The science is called *neuroplasticity*. Neuro-what? Let me explain.

According to *Psychology Today*[1], in an online article entitled, "How to Create a Durable Memory" by Shahram Heshmat PhD, "*Neuroplasticity* is the brain's …ability …to adapt or change over time, by creating new neurons and building new networks." In other words, the brain is not a fixed thing. It can actually grow and evolve in response to life experiences. The article goes on to explain that the term *plasticity* implies an ability to adapt or change by creating new neurons and building new neural networks.

While it's true our brains do shrink by the time we are in our sixties, constant stimulation through learning new skills (like a smartphone) can help you retrain your brain and expand these important neural pathways. By the same token, lack of stimulation, dehydration, poor nutrition, and a sedentary lifestyle will cause the brain to adapt in a way that is negative to your cognitive health. It will get smaller.

In layman's terms, this means that the brain is not fixed. Its ability to create new memories, *at any age*, is part of human biology. If not, then stroke victims would never learn to walk, talk, or read after parts of their brains were destroyed. This is the "plasticity" part. The brain can form new memories and new skills at any time in a human's life. This is a drastic departure from previous ideas that the number of neurons in the brain was fixed, and if you lost neurons, well, too bad for you.

Learning is the best brain stimulation, and learning something new takes practice and a "can-do" attitude. Here's the thing, though. Forming new memories is not instantaneous. You don't learn something the first time you do it, unless of course you have a photographic memory or are a savant. But most of us do not have these abilities. Did you know how to drive the second time you got behind the wheel? Of course not. When you learn a complicated new game like bridge or chess, will you know how to play after just one game? Certainly not! Well, it's the same with smartphones.

Yes, it's daunting for us seniors to tackle something as unfamiliar as a smartphone or tablet, especially if we feel afraid of it. Now, with respect to this fear, your point of view will impact your ability to learn. If you think you can't, you likely won't learn anything new. However, if you can change your perspective and see tackling this with a can-do approach, you may just surprise yourself.

To sum it up, be the little engine that could. Tell yourself, *I think I can, I think I can,* and you may be delightfully surprised that you do learn.

Still have reservations? Here are three evidence-based tips about memory and learning to help you form new neural networks, i.e., to learn something new:

FIRST, THERE MUST BE OXYGEN TO THE BRAIN.

If you're breathing, you are at this step! To enhance learning, take two or three long, deep breaths, slowly inhaling and very slowly exhaling. Maybe even go for a walk before trying to learn something new to get blood flowing more to the brain.

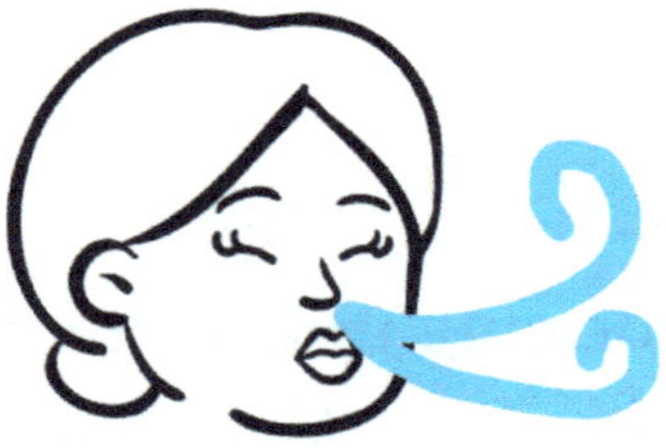

Graphic by Anne Goldberg

A GOOD NIGHT'S SLEEP IS ESSENTIAL.

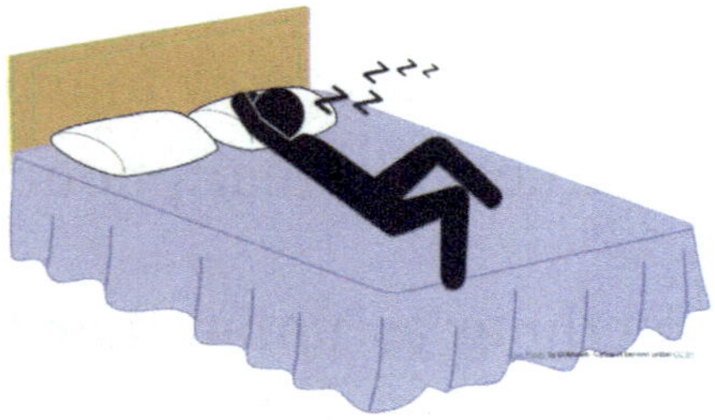

Graphic by Anne Goldberg

Sleep is the time when the brain solidifies its new neural pathways in order for them to become part of the brain's network, i.e., a new skill or memory. The relationship between memory and sleep has been explored for thousands of years. In a fascinating article published by The Perelman School of Medicine at the University of Pennsylvania,[2] it seems "... the first records of the benefits of sleep for memory come from the first century AD. Rhetorician Quintilian stated, 'It is a curious fact, of which the reason is not obvious, that the interval of a single night will greatly increase the strength of the memory.'" The article continues, citing studies over the past hundred years have found that "…sleep improves memory retention and recall by between 20 and 40 percent." I could go on, but I think I've made my point here. There are many health benefits of a good night's sleep, and having a better memory is one of them.

So, start your learning on the right track. Get a good night's sleep. Before you learn something new, take a few nice deep breaths and begin. Then repeat and repeat again and again and again. Do it for about five minutes and then do your lesson. Stop. Do something else. Get a good night's sleep and try again in a day or two. This pulls at your memory and reinforces the pattern. Prepare to be amazed at how you will begin to remember what to do without referring to notes.

PRACTICE MAKES PERFECT!

Photo by Anne Goldberg

My kids studied multiplication in the second, third, and fourth grades. We were constantly going over those flash cards to reinforce the lessons. Musicians, athletes, and actors practice all the time to perfect their craft. It's no different for you to learn technology. As an older adult, the need for repetition in learning is the same as it is for a child. *Neuroscience News*, in an online article published May 25, 2024, notes a key fact from a recent new study by

UCLA and co-led by Rockefeller University on learning published in the journal *Nature*.[3] The study has "shown that repetitive practice not only is helpful in improving skills but also leads to profound changes in the brain's memory pathways." Said more simply, repetition stabilizes memory patterns in the brain, aka you remember things!

I'm a great teacher, and this book has it all laid out for you, but if you don't practice, your brain will not create those new neural connections we call memories. Commit to working on your phone skills a few times a week, using this book as your guide. Start simply with the phone's features in Chapter 5. Pick one thing to learn and just do it. Then do it again. You get it. I believe YOU CAN DO THIS! When you have a can-do attitude, commit to spending time working on your skills, and have no significant cognitive decline, I am confident you will learn how to use your phone.

Obstacle #2

I'M AFRAID I WILL BREAK MY PHONE.

Many seniors are afraid that if they begin tapping around the phone, they will break it. You will not. Just don't change any settings, meaning don't turn anything off or on. If you want to change a setting, my best advice is to write down each step you take. That way, you can recreate your steps and undo what you did. Be mindful when you are making any changes. Read what's on the screen.

But let me be clear…

There are just a few ways to break your phone.

1. You will break your phone if you throw it against a wall in frustration.
2. You will break your phone if you leave it in a hot car. (Note to my Sun Belt readers, please never leave your device in the car on a hot day, even if it's in the glove compartment with the vehicle in the shade.) Heat is the enemy of electronics. If your phone display tells you the phone is in danger of overheating, remove it from its case and place it in a cool, not cold (no refrigerators) place (on top of a cold gel pack or frozen vegetables with a towel on it) and allow it to cool down. Newer phones recover quickly. An older phone may take a bit more time.
3. You will break your phone if it gets wet, but only if your phone is not water resistant. iPhones became water resistant around 2020. iPhone SE and models from the iPhone 7 or newer are rated IP67, which means they will resist water damage if the phone is not in the water for more than thirty minutes and less than three feet deep. Later phones can withstand deeper water. Android phones' water resistance varies according to the manufacturer. Samsung phones have been water resistant since 2014.

If you want to confirm whether your phone is water resistant, you will need to check online. Open the Internet and search for your phone manufacturer and model number and the words "water resistant." You will see quickly if your phone is water tolerant.

If your phone does suffer from water exposure, resist the urge to turn it on to see if it's working. Remove it from the case, dry it off, and stand it up so the charger port is facing down (allowing any moisture to seep out). Do not plunge your phone in rice.

Yes, I know that's been the wisdom for a decade or more, but experts suggest that rice can get stuck in ports. A better solution is to save all those little desiccant packages you get in packaged food, shoe boxes, and vitamin bottles. I have a Ziploc in which I keep mine, pictured here. If my phone were to get seriously wet, I would simply put the phone in the bag for twenty-four hours and allow those little packages to do their thing, which is wicking out the moisture. If you don't have any of these, simply allow your phone to dry out on a counter, out of the sun. Remember to take the case off. Another tip is to put the phone in a bowl of (uncooked) dry instant oatmeal or couscous as these will absorb moisture effectively.

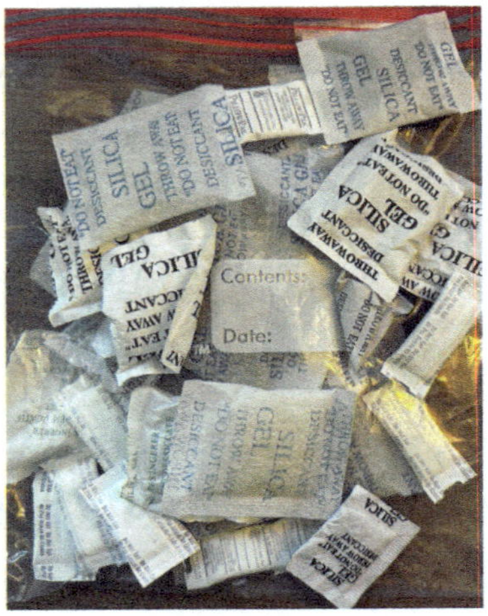

Photo by Anne Goldberg

4. And finally, **you will break your phone if you click on any blue link you receive in a text or email from someone you don't know.** (More about that later when I cover Spams and Scams in Chapter 11). For now, just know that you NEVER, EVER click on any link sent to you unless you know who sent it. NO MATTER

WHO IT'S FROM OR WHAT IT SAYS. If it references your bank account, call or visit your online banking account to see what's really happening. It's the same with Amazon, USPS, Medicare, insurance offers, weight-loss offers, or any other catchy come-on scammers can manufacture to trap you into giving them your money and/or vital information.

Obstacle # 3 - Impatience, Fear & Resistance

Fear of the unknown. Fear you can't do it. Fear, fear, fear. That is the most common emotion I find seniors have towards their mobile devices.

Resistance to anything new, anything different is a big reason so many seniors shy away from technology. I say bunk to that. Let's get on board with something new and stretch ourselves to learn.

Many seniors are simply impatient with the learning process. "I should know this!" or "It shouldn't be so hard to learn!" This self-talk is disempowering. Be patient with yourself. Be kind and compassionate with yourself. It's worth it.

Chapter 2

Then and Now

Table of Contents

Television

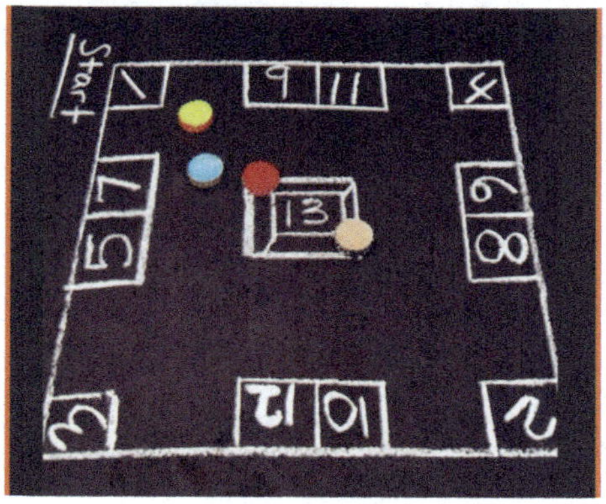

Image 1.1

This Photo by Unknown Author is licensed under CC BY-SA-NC

Like most of you reading this book, I'm a Baby Boomer, born in 1952. My older brother and I grew up in a modest, two-family, mock-Tudor home in Brooklyn. We weren't rich, we didn't live lavishly, but we each had our own room and toys and books to put in it.

Image 1.1a

This Photo by Unknown Author is licensed under CC BY-SA-NC

My brother played stick ball in the street with his friends. Sometimes they played skelly (with bottle tops) (Image 1.1) or stoop ball, throwing a pink Spaldeen™ or Pensie Pinkie™ ball (made by Spalding) against the brick steps leading up to the front door. (Image 1.1a) I, on the other hand, played with my Barbie™ dolls, my baby dolls, and their assorted accoutrements.

This Photo by Unknown Author is licensed under CC BY-SA-NC

In the living room there was a big, boxy piece of furniture with a tiny black-and-white television. (Image 1.2) And there were no remote controls! Someone had to get up and walk to the TV to adjust the volume, change the channel, or adjust the vertical hold knob so the picture would stop scrolling.

Image 1.2

ChatGPT version of 1950s TV

There were three major television stations: ABC, CBS, and NBC. In New York, we also had PBS and local channels WPIX and WOR. And, with just these channels, there was always something interesting to watch! That is, until midnight, when the stations all signed off with the Star-Spangled Banner. Then there were just the call letters of the station, or a white, snowy screen until 6:00 a.m., when programming resumed. (Image 1.3)

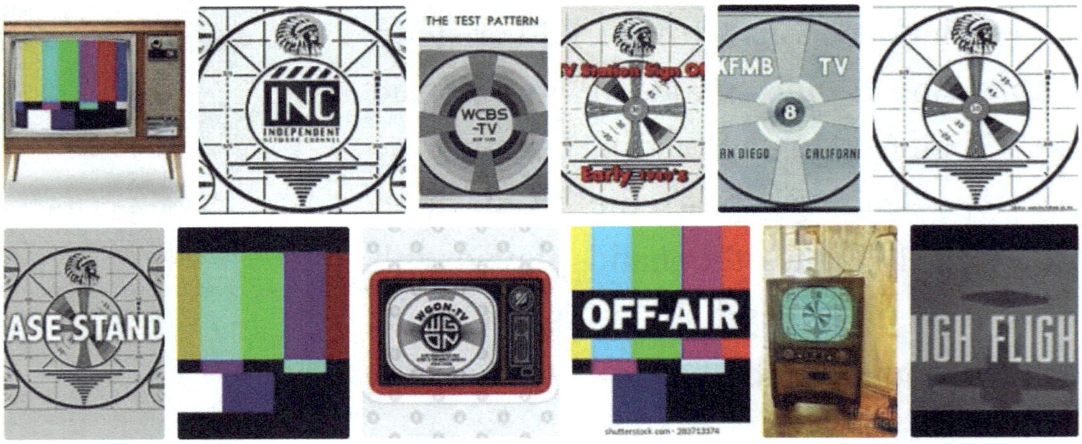

Image 1.3

TODAY, IN THE TWENTY-FIRST CENTURY, THERE'S AN APP FOR THAT.

We can now watch television on the Internet. Every major station has a website and runs episodes online. Sites like Hulu, Netflix, and Prime have a considerable collection of older TV shows that are fun to watch. If you have Xfinity cable service, at a certain plan level you can watch TV in real time and even schedule, watch, and delete from your recordings through the Xfinity account website (aka the Xfinity app).

You have to admit, having hundreds of channels from which to choose programming is a vast improvement over the limited options of the mid-twentieth century.

Antennas

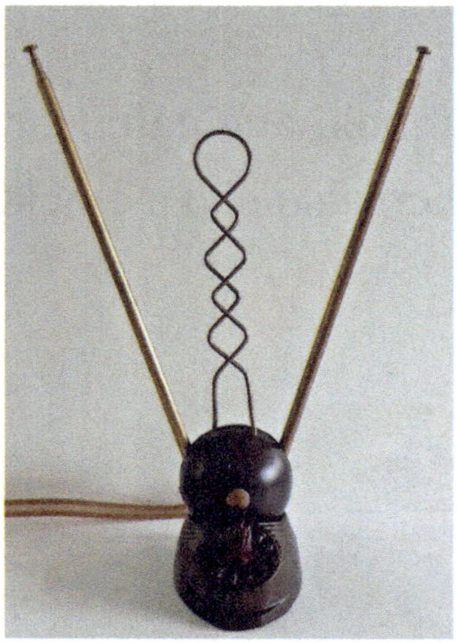

Image 1.4

At first, the TV signal came from those little rabbit ear antennas. (Image 1.4) Then came the big roof antennas. (Image 1.5) I vividly remember my dad up on the roof, twisting and turning the thing until we got a good picture.

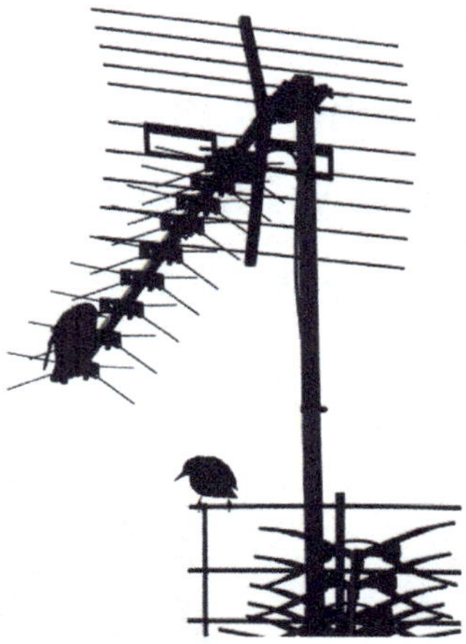

Image 1.5

I was the one who carefully wrapped the tiny wires of the antenna cable around the screws at the back of the TV.

It was commonly understood that the antennas were capturing wireless signals from the TV stations, the way that radio captured its invisible signals. The signals travelled down the wire I connected to our TV so we could watch *Ed Sullivan* on Sunday night. Or, *Howdy Doody* on Saturday mornings. Or *Lassie*, *I Love Lucy*, *The Real McCoys*, and so many other iconic shows of the era.

The Telephone

Oh, the memory of that single rotary-dial phone in the kitchen. (Image 1.6) Ours was a countertop model, but my mother's cousins had the wall version. (Image 1.7) And they all had that awful curly cord!

Right by the phone was an address book, pen, notebook, and calendar. The White and Yellow Pages were nearby. The kitchen also had a clock, a timer, and my mom's cookbooks.

Image 1.6

Image 1.7

The defining characteristic of these phones, at least for me, was that we were tethered to where the phone was. It was hard to have a personal conversation in the middle of the kitchen!

Of course, as the years advanced, so did the phones, and at the age of sixteen, I got a beige Trimline phone in my bedroom! I was so excited. I could finally have some privacy! Some of my friends got Princess phones. Which one did you have? (Image 1.8)

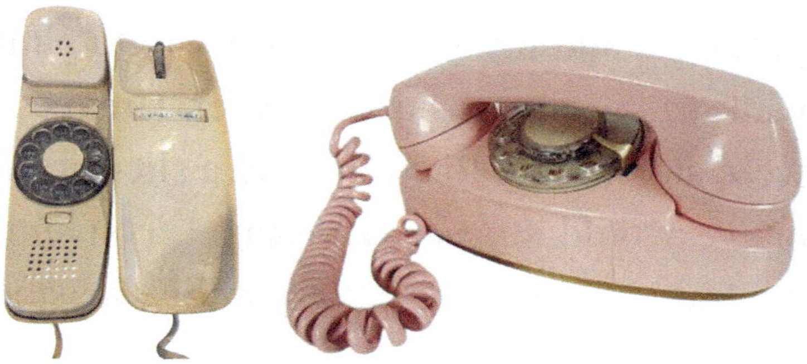

Image 1.8

This Photo by Unknown Author is licensed under CC BY-SA-NC

TODAY...THERE ARE APPS FOR THAT!

Fifty years ago, the idea of talking on the telephone while taking a walk in the park or at a restaurant was preposterous. Complete science fiction. And yet here we are today, talking into our smartwatches, looking just like Dick Tracy! We use the phone app to make and receive calls and texts. Fiction has become fact.

You have to admit that it's pretty fantastic when you can video chat (i.e., FaceTime, Messenger, WhatsApp, etc.) with loved ones living thousands of miles away. It sure beats the expensive long-distance calling we grew up with.

The Movies

Then there were the movies. I remember when I was eleven or twelve years old and my friends and I would gather and take a fifteen-minute walk to the Sheepshead Theater. (Images 1.9, 1.10) If we were early, we'd stop at Bay Pizza and get a slice and a Coke for twenty-five cents, or we would stop at Bay Bagel, conveniently located at the base of the train station, and get a yummy, toasted bagel with butter or cream cheese for twenty cents.

Image 1.9

Image 1.10

Then we'd get to the theater, buy our tickets for seventy-five cents, along with popcorn or ice cream (about fifteen cents each, as memory serves me) at the concession stand. The whole day might have cost $1.00. And there were always TWO movies and sometimes a short feature or cartoon before the *main event* began. It was the best way to spend a Saturday with friends. Those were the days!Those theaters were huge and fancy. (Images 1.9, 1.10) There were matrons who patrolled the aisles, making sure we took our feet off the backs of the chairs. We all giggled and put our feet right back up after they had passed us!

TODAY THERE'S AN APP FOR THAT!

There are many apps to watch (*i.e., stream, which means watching a movie on the Internet*), including Netflix, Apple TV, Max, Xfinity Stream, Prime, and Flixster.

Still and Video Cameras

My dad was an amateur photographer. He had a Leica camera (Image 1.11) for still pictures and a movie camera that used 8mm film. (Image 1.12) We stored the pictures in photo albums and boxes. We also had an 8mm projector and a screen to watch those home movies, and the reels were stored in special boxes. My dad even had a portable darkroom we would set up in the bathroom to develop black-and-white photos. It was magical watching images appear on blank paper.

Image 1.11

This Photo by Unknown Author is licensed under CC BY-SA-NC

Image 1.12

This Photo by Unknown Author is licensed under CC BY-SA-NC

The cameras were brought out for special occasions like birthdays and vacations. Then the family would gather around the screen set up in the living room, and we would watch ourselves silently sightseeing, running, eating, and playing games. I especially loved it when my dad ran the projector forward and in reverse again and again so that we saw ourselves jumping in the water, then "jumping" back out of the water, over and over and over again… It was so much fun!

TODAY THERE'S AN APP FOR THAT!

These photography and video apps native to smartphones have evolved into highly sophisticated cameras, with special effects. They far exceed the quality my dad got with his "state of the art" equipment of the fifties and sixties.

The Mail

When I was growing up, our front door had a covered metal slot near the bottom of the door. The mailman would slide the envelopes through that space, and they landed in a pool of paper on the floor of the foyer.

In many areas, folks had (and have) mailboxes hanging outside, adjacent to the front door. Others had/have to walk to the curb to collect their mail.

In the apartment buildings of Brighton Beach, where my aunts and uncles lived, there were big banks of locked brass mailboxes lining one wall of the main lobby.

Image 1.13

The mail was a big event. Hearing from loved ones who lived overseas or across the country was a treat. (After all, long-distance calls were expensive.) When birthdays and holidays rolled around, we always were excited to get cards (and presents!) in the mail, especially when there was a check or cash in the envelope! And when someone sent pictures, that was a real treat! Do you remember writing, in big, bold letters, on the envelope, "PHOTOS – DO NOT FOLD. HAND STAMP"?How many times did you walk to a nearby USPS mailbox to send something important? They were everywhere, especially in the cities. Now you hardly see mailboxes at all.

You had to plan ahead to send a gift because it took a few days or sometimes a week to get packages delivered. Even a simple letter, in the best of USPS times, took a day for local delivery. Compare that to the immediacy of email and texting.

AND OF COURSE...TODAY THERE'S AN APP FOR THAT!

Email! Since its popularity began in the early eighties, email communication has grown exponentially. The United States Post Office has suffered with fewer letters being mailed each successive year pretty much since then. User-friendly AOL debuted in 1989, which spurred email use among private users of PCs and Mac computers. *You've got mail!*

Listening to Music

Image 1.15

Photo by
Ane Goldberg

Image 1.14

This Photo by Unknown Author is licensed under CC BY-SA-NC

In addition to his photography equipment, my dad always had a hi-fi system (later replaced by a stereo system) to play his collection of 33 1/3 record albums. (He let the old 78s warp in the garage).

And, of course, there were other radios in the house. How many of you had a transistor radio? I have a confession. I still have the transistor radio I listened to when I was twelve! (Image 1.15) I loved Cousin Brucie and Murray the K in New York. Who did you listen to?

TODAY...THERE ARE APPS FOR THAT!

The Internet is filled with ways to listen to music and radio. In fact, ever wonder what a podcast is? Well, essentially, it's radio (audio only) that you listen to over an Internet connection. There are so many apps such as Spotify, Pandora, Amazon Music, Apple Music, your favorite radio stations and talk radio (yep, those podcasts). There are also apps like Yesterday USA Radio Network (yesterdayusa.com) that play music we grew up with. If you want to know about others, open the Internet and search for "online radio stations playing sixties music."

Travel

When I was a young teenager, my parents and I drove to California with some friends. I vividly remember my father going to AAA, where a travel representative put together a Triptik helping him choose the routes that best served our itinerary. Each page was a partial map of the route with a long green line denoting the specific roads to take. All the pages were held together with a spiral binder, so the pages folded flat for ease of use. Instead of Siri calling the directions, it was usually my mom directing where and when to turn. (Image 1.16)

Image 1.16

Of course, if you were planning to fly and stay at hotels, you needed a travel agent. (Image 1.17)

Image 1.17

This Photo by Unknown Author is licensed under CC BY-NC

Travel agents did it all. They booked the flights, car, and hotel. They took care of all the details, and all we did was use them. The airlines, car companies, and hotels paid fees to the travel agents. It cost us nothing extra (other than AAA membership) to use their excellent services. Ah, the old days. There are still many wonderful, reputable travel agents who will help you plan luxurious trips to exotic locations. But most of the world just needs a flight and/or hotel and/or auto for the best price.

And yes…

TODAY THERE ARE APPS FOR THAT!

Expedia, Priceline, Hopper, Google Travel, Kayak, and so many more sites—not to mention each individual airline, cruise line, and hotel—has their own website, allowing you to find rates and deals and book your own trip, often with substantial savings. And yes, you can find a really good travel agency online too.

Books

Unless you had a set of encyclopedias, you had to go to the library for information or to find a great book to read at the beach or park. Local public libraries had all the basics for doing a term paper or a report on the culture of Peru. And if you needed to investigate something deeper, regional libraries were/are treasures of all kinds of books, maps, plus toys for kids to play with.

Today, libraries are facing funding cutbacks as so many people have moved to digital books on a Kindle, a tablet like an iPad, or their phones.

YEP, THERE ARE APPS FOR THAT! (ARE YOU SEEING A PATTERN?)

Libraries even offer a way to borrow books online and read (or listen to) millions of titles in all genres. Sites like Libby, Cloud Library, and Hoopla are just a few apps that work with your local library to provide absolutely free online access to a wealth of reading entertainment. For more information on books and audiobooks for free, go to the library and speak with the librarian or do it online by searching for "(Name of county or city you live in) + library + digital books." That should give you search results about renting digital books.

Games

I have vivid and loving memories of playing gin rummy with my grandmother when I was a kid. Oh, how I loved that time with her. Card games like that filled the hours while she baby-sat for my brother and me. I have taken that tradition with my young granddaughters, and we play war, solitaire and rummy. It's wonderful non-screen time together.

Remember Toys 'R' Us? Oh, it was a wonderland of fun with toys and games galore. For our purposes here, let's focus on games. From Twister to Monopoly to The Game of Life to Headache and so many more, consumers had a field day with fun board games for the whole family.

Image 1.18

Image 1.19

Image 1.20

THERE ARE APPS FOR THAT!

While games for kids have evolved to complex video games, many adults find great pleasure in playing poker, canasta, and bridge online. And let's not forget the fun of solitaire, FreeCell, Wordle, Scrabble, and more games that are so easy to do with a simple online search.

Clocks, Timers, and Stopwatches

Back in the day, we had bedside and travel alarm clocks. In the kitchen, we had timers, and athletic coaches had stopwatches.

Image 1.21

THERE ARE APPS FOR THAT!

The clock is a standard app on every Android and iPhone. It's also a timer, a stopwatch, and an alarm. It's one of my most used apps that helps me arrive at my appointments on time. In fact, I haven't had any hard-boiled eggs explode in the pot now that I have a timer with a loud sound to remind me they are done! Check out Chapter 12 for instructions on using the clock app.

YES, THOSE WERE THE DAYS!

This was the technology that we Boomers grew up with. It is what each of us got used to. We understood the dials and settings on the new washer and dryer, dishwasher, and/or dashboard of our newest car. You might even have been someone who could figure out how to set a DVR (although those of us who could were few and far between!). Even as things modernized, there was a certain sameness to the look and operation of these things. There were recognizable controls, whether switches, dials, or knobs. Acquiring a new appliance did not require an advanced degree to operate it.

Fast-forward some sixty years, and suddenly the world is digitized and *electronicized* and you are supposed to simply know how to adapt to these newfangled ways. It's as though you were dropped in the middle of Greece, where there is no English spoken or written, and you are expected to navigate this different reality. It's not possible. You have to learn the language before you can effectively communicate.

> *The sad reality is that today's technology leaves most seniors feeling stupid. Let me be clear about this. You are not stupid. You are simply uneducated as to language that allows you to communicate with these devices.*

It is unreasonable to expect any adult over the age of sixty-five to pick up electronic technology and automatically know what to do unless, like me, they took to it very early in its development.

The way these devices look and operate is alien to us. But they are not alien to our grandchildren. At three, my granddaughter could find and select her game and then scroll, slide, pinch, and tap like a pro playing it.

Chapter 3

A Brief History of Mobile Technology – How Did We Get Here?

Table of Contents

I'd like to take a few pages to discuss how smartphones evolved. For me, and I hope for you, it's instructive to understand how we got here—how the devices we hold in our hands became so powerful, so essential to modern life, and so unlike the technology we grew up with.

Back in the 1950s, electronics were still in their infancy. Radio, television, and early computers were bulky, expensive, and limited in what they could do. And, oh those telephones with rotary dials that were tethered to the wall. Communication was simpler but much slower than today.

Fast-forward to the seventies, and we saw the rise of personal computers. But even then, few of us could have imagined a world where a small device in our pocket could not only make calls but also access the entire world's information, take photos, and connect us instantly to anyone, anywhere.

The iPhone revolutionized what a phone could do by integrating a touch screen, apps, and powerful software. It was no longer just a communication device but a minicomputer in your hand. In the years since, smartphones have become faster, smarter, and more central to our lives. Smartphones serve as our cameras, planners, libraries, and social hubs. For those of us who didn't grow up with this technology, it can be overwhelming to learn it all. But understanding its history can help you appreciate how far we've come and remind us that technology has always been advancing—we're just adapting to the latest chapter.

A Timeline of Smartphone Development

The evolution of the mobile phone began in earnest in the eighties with the first brick phones—large, heavy, and limited to voice calls. (Image 3.1) As the years passed, phones became smaller, lighter, and capable of texting. By the early 2000s, devices like the BlackBerry were introducing us to mobile email and basic Internet browsing. But it wasn't until 2007 that the modern smartphone, the iPhone, truly arrived.

Image 3.1

This Photo by Unknown Author is licensed under CC BY-SA-NC

CELL PHONES & SMARTPHONES – 1980s

Cell phones, such as flip phones, were a new and exciting generation of small mobile phones generally available to the public in the late 1980s. (Image 3.2) They had a physical keyboard that looked like a telephone keypad.

Cell phones work via specific frequencies over a network provided by companies like Verizon, T-Mobile, AT&T, and so on. Early cell phones could send and receive calls and send texts, take low resolution photos, and had (limited) access to the Internet. (Image 3.3)

Image 3.2

Image 3.3

While the physical telephone keyboard had a certain familiarity when making calls, it was (and is) a pain in the neck when texting. Do you remember trying to type a text on a cell phone? You had to go through several taps of the number one key to move from ***a*** to ***b*** to ***c*** to *capital* ***A*** to ***B*** to ***C*** and so on. And if you passed the letter you wanted, you had to start all over again. They are a pain to use!

Many of my older clients cling to their flip phones, not realizing that a smartphone can be accommodated to a variety of visual, hearing, or touch settings, making them quite easy to use, even for someone with limited skills, assuming their cognitive skills are normal for their age.

Two of the biggest differences between cell phones and smartphones are size and the keyboard.

Smartphone screens are exponentially larger than those on cell phones. Plus, smartphones have **QWERTY** keyboards. A what keyboard? The name QWERTY comes from the first six characters in the top far left row of letters on a keyboard. (Image 3.4, 3.5)

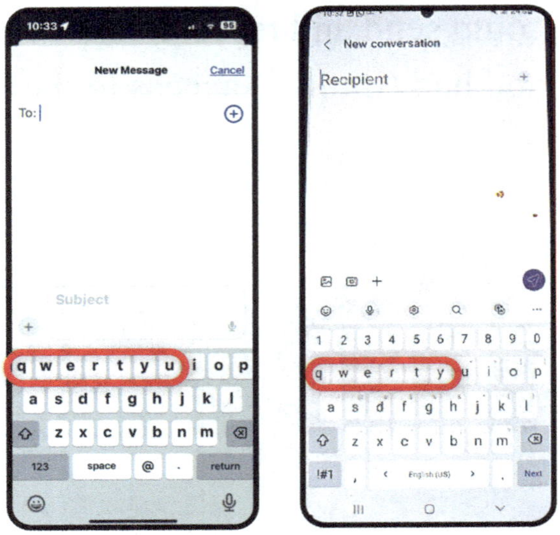

Image 3.4

Image 3.5

QWERTY keyboards are almost the same as our old typewriter keyboards. For those of you who were touch typists, this will feel familiar. Even for those of you who aren't trained typists, QWERTY keyboards are much easier to use than the telephone-like keyboards of cell phones.

Keyboards on Android and iPhone are slightly different. The Android keyboard is more complete. It includes numbers and basic symbols, thus eliminating the need to switch between a letter keyboard and a number or symbol keyboard, such as Apple offers on its devices. It is much easier to use. Apple's keyboard is split into three pieces—a letters screen and two screens for all the symbols—so switching between those keyboards is necessary when typing an address, as an example.

Other Mobile Devices We Loved

PALMPILOT - 1996 TO 2007

Image 3.6

Photo by Anne Goldberg

Remember the **PalmPilot**, the original Personal Digital Assistant (PDA)? It debuted in 1996 and was an instant hit. It was so different from the cell phone. It was an address book, calculator, memo pad, and calendar, and it could do expense sheets. Later versions also offered photos, videos, and limited Internet searching. Image 3.6 is of my PalmPilot, which I STILL keep in my technology drawer! Why? Maybe one day I'll look through it to see the names in my life so many moons ago. It was a very cool device that I used faithfully until I got my first cell phone.

Image 3.7

This photo by Unknown Author is licensed under CC BY-SA-NC

THE BLACKBERRY – 1999 TO 2016

And how about the **BlackBerry**! I loved my BlackBerry. It was the first of the handheld devices that had both a screen and a keyboard. While the screen may have been small compared to today's standards, back then it was exciting. And it was so easy to type on. But it could not hold up to the clarity and ease of use of the iPhone. Many people held onto their BlackBerries until 2022, when support for them was discontinued.

Chapter 4

And Then the World Changed...

Table of Contents

The iPhone Arrives in 2007

Image 4.2

This photo by Unknown Author is licensed under CC BY-SA-NC

In June 2007, the world was introduced to the first smartphone—the iPhone 1, developed by Apple. Apple developers based its design on Apple's iPod, so it combined the idea of a cell phone with the screen and look of the iPod. It introduced touch controls (tapping, pinching, swiping) along with revolutionary technology allowing Internet communications such as email, searching the web, and a GPS.

The iPhone changed the nature of personal communication. For the first time, we could search the Internet (using Safari) while we were out and about. The look and feel of it were much the same as searching on a computer. It was revolutionary!

Image 4.3

This photo by Unknown Author is licensed under CC BY-SA-NC

In the first year, iPhone sales topped six million, and in the first three years, some 30 million iPhones were sold around the world! Clearly Apple was onto something!

Androids Hit the Market in 2008

Believe it or not, Androids predated the iPhone, with development dating back to 2003, before we knew the term "smartphone" or could fathom what it might be.

After Google acquired Android, Inc. in 2005, they brought the first Android phone to market in 2008. It worked with Google Maps, YouTube, and a very early incarnation of Chrome to access the Internet. Apple just beat them to the finish line.

This photo by Unknown Author is licensed under CC BY-SA-NC

Since then, the Android *operating system* has overrun all competition with just over 70% of the global market compared to Apple's nearly 28%. In the United States though, it's a bit different. As of January 2025 Android's share of the market is a bit over 42% versus Apple's nearly 58% hold on us Americans. It's interesting to note that Samsung has a 23.27% market share. It is clear that iPhones and Androids dominate the global and U.S. markets.

What exactly are the differences between Androids and Apples?

It has to do with the way the phones are built, specifically, their operating systems (OS). I know many of you are like, "Operating what?" In the simplest terms, the operating system is what makes the device work. I like to say the difference between the operating systems (OS) of iPhone and Android is akin to the differences between internal combustion engines and an electric engines. The internal *operating systems* are different, and the dashboards are different, but at the end of the day, they do the same thing.

With smartphones, regardless of their OS, they all make calls, send text messages, have Internet access, and can do almost anything, depending on what apps you use.

The iPhone OS is designed in a *closed-source* environment. This means that iPhones are developed and manufactured by Apple engineers ONLY, and no one else can play in Apple's garden. Apple phones are designed to work seamlessly within the Apple ecosystem. Apple iPhone users may be more likely to have an Apple Watch, Mac computer, and iPad. They sync together, so it's easy to switch from phone to computer to tablet and have the same information for email, contacts, and calendar on all the devices.

Image 4.4

This photo by Unknown Author is licensed under CC BY-SA-NC

Android phones, on the other hand, are open-source and as such are made by many different manufacturers because the code is public. Anyone can develop an Android phone. (Image 4.4) As a result, you can buy Android phones from Samsung, Motorola, Google, HTC, and others around the world that make Android phones. Android users can switch from phone to PC seamlessly if the user has a Google account. That makes for easy access to email, calendar, contacts, and more.

Why Choose One Operating System Over the Other?

Image 4.5

Image 4.6

Often, choosing which phone/operating system to get is a matter of personal taste, or it's the one your friend has or the one your kids have. The best part about having the same operating system as friends and family is for the chance to turn a phone call into a video call. That's because video calls using your phone number only work within the same operating system. If you're talking on your Samsung and your friend has an iPhone, you won't be able to show your friend the new hobby you just started. In this sense, Apple and Android are like Macy's and Gimbels. They didn't share so nicely, and Apple and Android don't either, especially on this point. I will discuss more about Apple and **Android texting on** **page 229**.

I loved my Android, but I got an iPhone because that is what my kids had, and I wanted to FaceTime with them. I love it when I'm talking with my son, and suddenly the screen changes and it's him FaceTiming me so I can see what cute things my granddaughters (or sometimes the grand dog or grand cats) are doing. Here you see David and I having a quick FaceTime conversation.

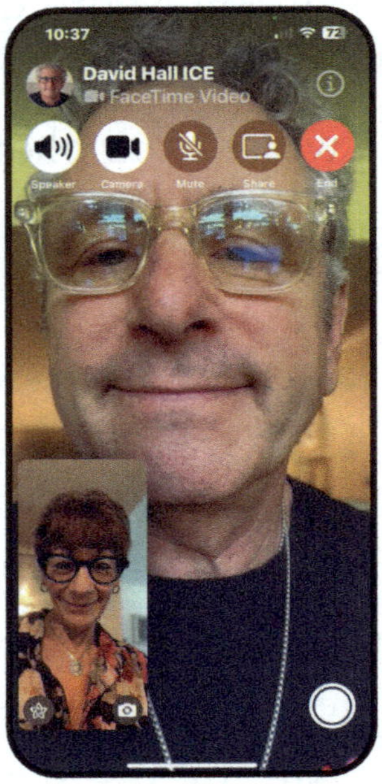

Image 4.7

Some manufacturers of newer Androids are integrating Google Meet into their phone app. Once a simple set-up is complete, you will be able to video chat with fellow Androidians.

An advantage of Androids is that they offer lower-end phones for people on budgets. While lacking certain bells and whistles, these phones function just fine as telephones and for texting and Internet access.

Another difference between the two platforms is that Apple supports its phones better. Most iPhones get operating system updates for up to five years and security updates for six years, and often longer than that. Android phone support varies according to manufacturer. To know for sure regarding your specific device, check online using the make and model combined with "How long is this supported?"

Having said this, iPhones will receive more frequent updates and bug fixes in any given year, which effectively makes it safer; plus, more frequent security updates offer a longer lifespan for the device.

A Word About Tablets, i.e. iPads

Image 4.8

This photo by Unknown Author is licensed under CC BY-SA-NC

Before I go any further, let's discuss tablets versus smartphones. A tablet is the generic term for these larger-than-handheld-smaller-than-a-laptop computers like iPads and Samsung Galaxy pads. Specifically, according to Wikipedia, a tablet is "a mobile device with a touchscreen display, a mobile operating system and a rechargeable battery."

There are just two differences. Tablets are MUCH LARGER than phones, and the standard telephone app is not available on any tablet. Your tablet cannot make a call to your friend using the same app as from a smartphone. That's not to say you can't make calls. You just have to use a third-party app like Facebook Messenger, WhatsApp, Instagram, Signal, or Telegraph.

Otherwise, Apple tablets look and operate EXACTLY the same as the iPhone, and Samsung Galaxy tablets look EXACTLY the same as Samsung Galaxy phones. Tablets made by other companies will look different from your phone. Does that matter? Only if it matters to you. If you get a great deal on a tablet and are comfortable using it, by all means get it.

Please keep in mind that Android is an open-source operating system, meaning any developer can create Android phones, and there are many companies that produce them. They look similar but not exactly the same, so if you have an HTC phone and a Samsung tablet, there will be differences.

Staying in the same operating system with your devices does make it easier to move from phone to tablet. If all of this is a bit overwhelming, then iPhone users should stick with iPads, and Android users may want to stay with Android tablets.

Should I Get a New Phone?

The newest features include AI capabilities like Apple Intelligence, which works on the latest iPhone 16s and last year's iPhone 15 Pro and Pro-Max, as well as on some iPads (M1 - 4 iPad Pro, M1 & 2 iPad Air) and Macs (a variety of models; check online for information on your model) released in the last four years. Should you upgrade?

Some of the newer phones are larger, so that may be of interest to you. Others have ridiculously good cameras, but if you're not a photographer, it may be meaningless. Apple offers support on its phones for at least five years and some models for seven to eight years.

With Androids, it's a bit different according to Androidauthority.com. Google owns the Android system and is responsible for issuing updates. Typically, Pixel phones get them first, as that brand is owned by Google. Other manufacturers have to modify code (i.e., translate) in order to accept the updates and so it takes longer for them to get updates to the consumer.

The Pixel phones are supported for seven years assuming you have a Pixel 8 or newer. Earlier phones are supported for just three to five years, depending on the model.

Motorola phones are supported for just two years, with an occasional exception of five years, model dependent.

Samsung is the largest of the Android manufacturers worldwide and offers six years of updates. The new Galaxy S25 will receive seven years of support.

Batteries in all smartphones are easily replaceable and not very expensive. It is certainly much less expensive to replace a battery than to get a new phone, and a new battery will give your phone a boost.

The bottom line on getting a new phone is that it's personal and up to you. Objectively, you can keep your phone if the hardware continues to accept the new operating systems. Once the operating system is out of date (because the hardware doesn't have the power to perform all the new features of the newer operating system), it is time for a new (or newer) phone. And once security updates have ended, it's absolutely time for a new phone.

In late 2024, Apple introduced iOS 18, its newest and most advanced operating system. While the update was available for all iPhones (other than very old phones that some seniors keep, like the 6s, 7 or 8), most of the newest features only work with the 15 Pro and ProMax and the 16 series phones.

If being able to send an emoji  at the tap of a button is something you must have, you may want to invest in a new phone. If you want Siri to integrate with ChatGPT, you may want to buy a new phone. But if you don't really care, save your money and continue using the phone you have.

For those of you who can't keep track of what phones are out there, here is something that may help you.

Androids: Samsung has its Galaxy series A and S, which have many versions, including the Galaxy Z Fold and the flagship model, S25.

iPhones: XS, XR, 11, 13, 14, 15, and 16 and the newest 16e (replacing the old SE model)

Chapter 5

The Phone Is Not a Phone: Smartphone Basics

Table of Contents

Image 5.1

This photo by Unknown Author is licensed under CC BY-SA-NC

Let's face it. The phone is not a phone. It is a sophisticated, handheld computer capable of doing so much more than making a call. Did you know that Steven Spielberg filmed part of *West Side Story* using his iPhone video camera? It's true. Look it up! And did you know that the little phone you keep in your pocket or purse has more computing power than the computers that were used to send the first astronauts into space?

You hold in your hand a complicated piece of equipment designed to appeal to people ages four to forty. They take to it like a fish to water. We seniors take to it like a fish on a dock, thrashing around to catch a breath!

But now, I hope you are feeling a bit more confident and ready to dive in and learn how to use it. I invite you to find a comfortable place with your phone (or tablet) and this book. Take a few deep breaths and tell yourself, **"I can do this!"**

Android and iPhone Basic Features

This chapter is about learning the basic features of the phones, things like touchscreens, storage, memory, battery, notifications, voice assistants (like Siri and Google Assistant), and security (i.e., face recognition or fingerprint sensors). Many of these features can be customized to your preferences. In this chapter, you will learn the very basics of on and off to the more detailed knowledge of how to adjust the display and sounds to your needs. You will find a lot more information on using the phone app in Chapter 12.

Ready to start? Here we go.

But first…let's talk about the **home button.** That is the virtual circle (on older or less expensive Androids) or a physical button you press to take you to the home (first) page of the device. It also acts as a GO BACK button. If there is no home button, then a simple swipe up is exactly the same.

NOW LET'S START AT THE BEGINNING...ON/OFF VS. POWER DOWN

Androids and iPhones

Let's talk about the difference between turning the phone on and off versus powering down the device. I'll explain…

Image 5.2

This photo by Unknown Author is licensed under CC BY-SA-NC

When the phone is on, but the screen is black, we say the phone is "off." What we really mean is that the screen is turned off, but the phone is still on.

The analogy is your TV. We don't unplug the TV to turn it off. We turn the screen off when we are finished watching by pressing the power button. Similarly, when you're ready to watch again, you press the power button on the remote, and the screen lights up almost immediately. That's because the power to the TV is still on. It's plugged in. To stop the power completely, you must unplug the television.

Image 5.3

It's similar with smartphones. Pressing the power button (on the side, top, or back) on any phone will turn the screen off, but the phone is still on. There is still power to it. That's why you can still get calls, texts, and emails even if the screen is dark.

But there is no plug. A note here—there is a plug for charging. But because there is a battery, unplugging does not turn the phone off. It only stops the charging. Well then, how do we "unplug" a smartphone?

To do the equivalent of unplugging an electrical device, you have to **POWER DOWN** your smartphone.

Android Powering Down

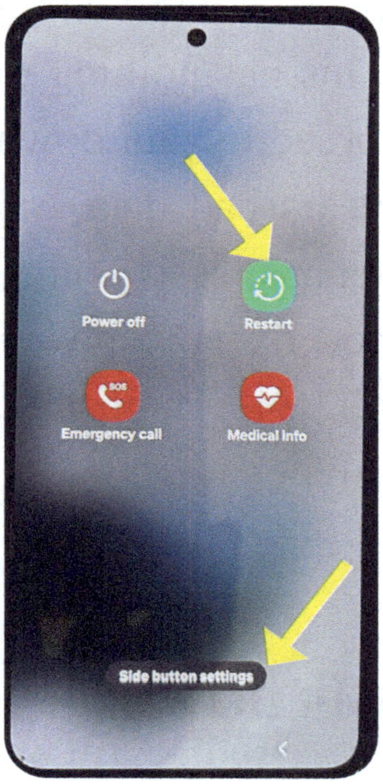

Image 5.4

To power down an Android phone, simply ***press and hold (and hold) the power button only,*** which may be on the side, at the top, or in the back, depending on the make and model of your phone. This will work on most Androids, but if not, it's best to do a quick search on the Internet. Put in the make and model of your phone with the words, "How do I power off?"

Once the power button is pressed and held, the screen changes, and it will look similar to Image 5.4. Again, different manufacturers have different dashboards, so it might look a little bit different.

Image 5.4 shows a Samsung power off screen, which offers the opportunity to **restart** the phone (which means the phone turns off and then immediately on again).

There is also a link to change the side button settings. Perhaps you want to use the side button as a quick access to your camera when you quickly press twice in succession and your camera will open.

On this Samsung, there is also a medical information icon. This may or may not appear on your Android device depending on its make and model. Please note that this screen may appear different on a different manufacturer's device.

It's good to power down or restart your device daily (if you use it a lot or every few days if you are a casual user for calls and texting only). Doing this is called rebooting your phone. This has nothing to do with footwear. When you reboot, the phone is forced to shut down all programs running in the background, which clears bad data and frees up memory. It also resets all the wireless antennas, so if you're having a problem connecting to the Internet, a good fix is to power down or restart the phone. Likely the connection will be reestablished. Rebooting your device will also make it run a bit faster.

POWERING DOWN AN iPHONE

PRESS AND HOLD THE POWER AND VOLUME DOWN BUTTON

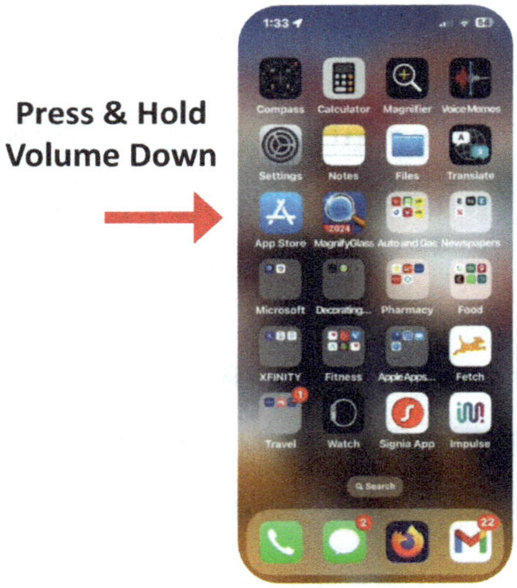

Image 5.5

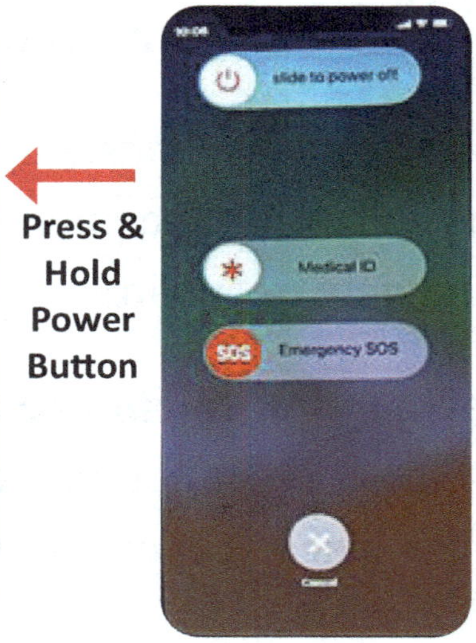

Image 5.6

Simultaneously **PRESS AND HOLD the POWER** button on the right (as the phone is facing you) and the **VOLUME DOWN** button on left. The screen will change, and you will see four choices. To activate any of them, gently slide your finger from left to right.

A few interesting things about the iPhone power off screen:

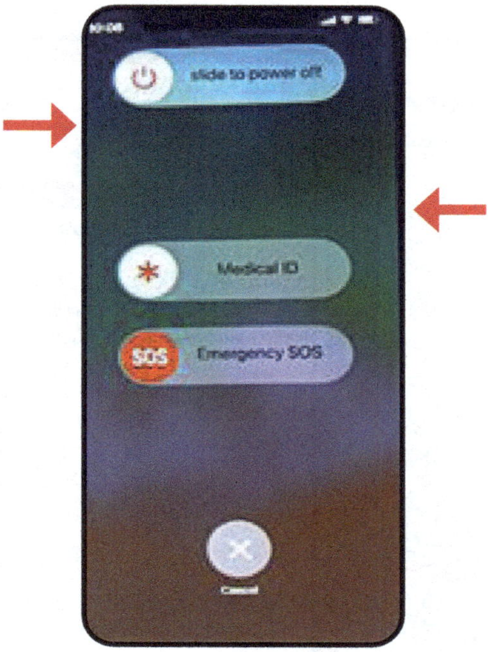

Image 5.7

If you continue to hold the **power** and **volume up** buttons, a countdown will begin. If you do not let go, you'll hear a siren. If you do not let go, the phone will call 911. This is great to know.

However, if you are just trying to power down your phone, make sure you let go of the buttons before the siren sounds!

The middle bar says Medical ID. This is for the heaven-forbid situations when a medical team is on the scene and wants to know your medical history. If you have put information into the iPhone Health app, this is what the emergency workers will see. If you have major allergies or conditions, this is a good thing to fill out. The Health app has a red heart on a white background. I encourage you to take a few minutes and fill out the information just in case.

Another option is the third box, which says **SOS** in bright red. If you need 911, simply **slide the Emergency SOS to the right, and the phone will call 911.**

If you got to this screen by mistake, no problem. Just tap on the **X** in the circle at the bottom of the screen, and you will be returned to the regular phone screen. Please note that you will have to enter your device passcode for security reasons.

ANDROID ANSWERING THE PHONE

There is a very simple rule when answering a phone.

GREEN IS GO. RED IS STOP. Tap or Slide to get or reject call.

Let's say you're doing something on your phone and a call comes in. It looks like Image 5.9. The rule applies. Red is reject (end call) and green is go (answer call).

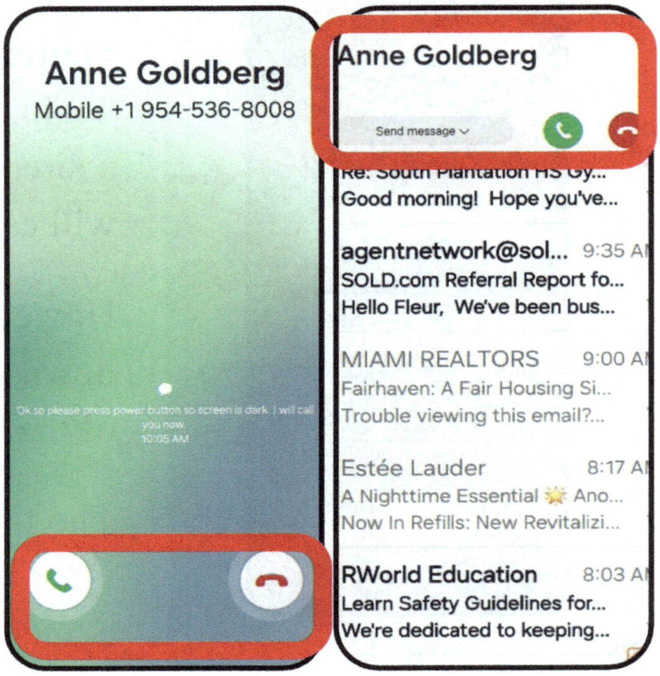

Image 5.8 Image 5.9

If you are on the phone and another call comes in, the screen may look a different way. Always know, red is reject the call and green is get the call.

iPHONE ANSWERING THE PHONE

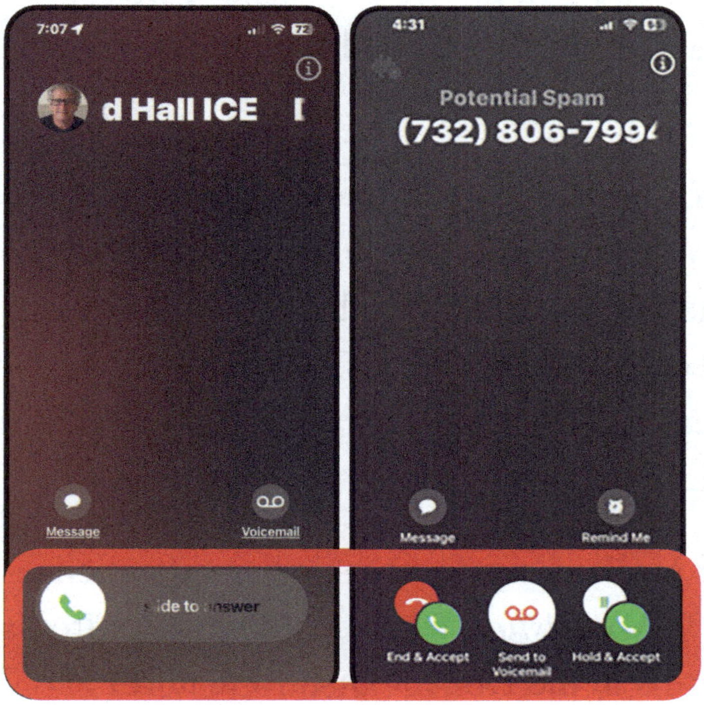

Image 5.10 Image 5.11

This photo by Unknown Author is licensed under CC BY-SA-NC

Just as in Android phones, **green equals ANSWER** the call and **red equals REJECT** the call**.** If the phone is locked and a call comes in, the screen will look like Image 5.10. To answer, simply gently move the green handset along the path to the right.

If the phone is unlocked and a call comes in, the screen looks like Image 5.11. There are three options here. Answer and put the existing call on **hold**, send the caller to voicemail and answer and **end** the existing call. You get to choose.

VOLUME CONTROLS AND SILENCING YOUR PHONE

When someone says, “Turn your phone off,” likely they are referring to the volume and not the actual phone. Yes, it’s a bit confusing, but context is everything. If you’re at the theater, you’ll be asked to turn your phone off, or sometimes, they’re savvy enough to ask that you *silence the phone*. That just means turning the volume off so a ringing phone or text tone doesn't disturb anyone. It's true that when you put your phone in silent mode, it won't ring, but if you have alarms or timers set, they will still sound a surprisingly loud tone at the selected time.

Some people will turn airplane mode on when they want to silence their phones. What's the difference between turning the ringer off and airplane mode? If you put the phone in airplane mode, the antennas are turned off, so no calls, texts, or emails can reach you. Silencing the phone means calls, texts and emails come in but sound notifications are muted.

Please remember that neither airplane mode nor silent mode silences alarms. It's the same with the *Do Not Disturb* feature (although Androids have the ability to turn off alarms in the Do Not Disturb feature).

If you require absolute silence from your phone, whether iPhone or Android, either ensure there are no alarms or timers **OR** *power it off.* (Just remember to power it back on when you're done!)

Volume Controls for Androids and iPhones

Volume controls on both Androids and iPhones are the same. When looking at the device, you will see two buttons on the LEFT edge of most smartphones. Image 5.12 shows one version of Android side

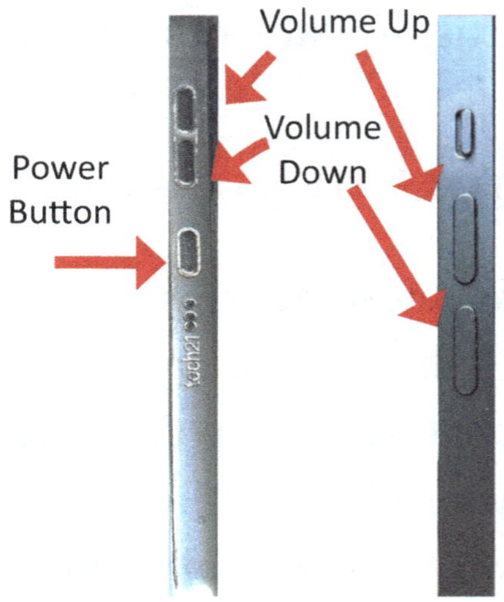

Android Image 5.12

iPhone Image 5.13

buttons. This is a Samsung. Other manufacturers have power buttons on the back or top.

On any device the top button is always VOLUME UP, and the bottom button is always VOLUME DOWN. Just press and hold for the volume to change in either direction. You can also do a series of presses, two, three, or four, etc., if you want the volume to significantly change. Image 5.13 shows the iPhone volume buttons.

Silencing Your Android

Image 5.14

To silence the ringer, **press the Volume Down button. As you press the volume key, a visual will open on the screen, and you will see the bar go down as you lower the volume.** (Image 5.14) If you want to confirm that the phone is silenced, you can tap on the three tiny dots at the top of the volume bar. (See yellow arrow in Image 5.14.)

When you tap on those three dots, the screen again changes, and you will see a **media** box open. (Image 5.15) There is information here. From the top of the box, I see the word "media," and to its right, I see the symbol for settings.  (Image 5.15)

Image 5.15

Tap on the settings icon. The screen will change. You are now in the phone settings having to do with sounds. (Image 5.16)

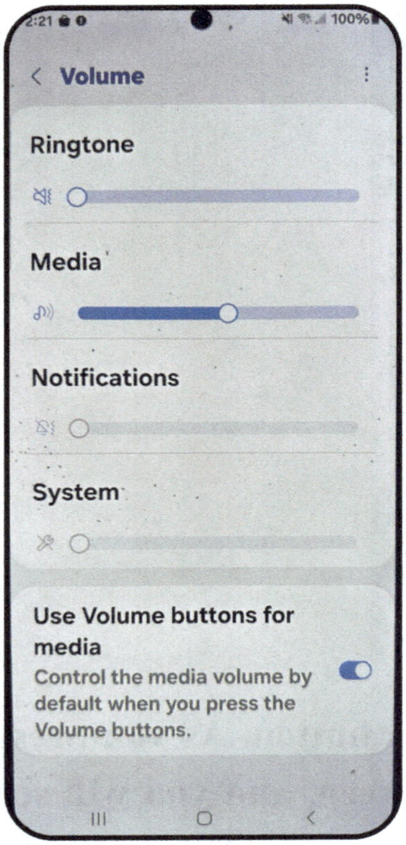

Image 5.16

This particular screen shows you the sound levels for your ringtone, media (i.e., music, podcasts), notifications, and system sounds. System sounds are the text, keyboard, and other sounds controlled by the operating system. If you tap on any of these, you will hear how soft or loud each sound is. SIMPLY SLIDE your finger to raise or lower the volume. You will see the line change from light blue/gray to a medium blue as volume goes up.

If you look at the top left of the screen, you will see a tiny back arrow < . Tap on that back arrow and the screen will change. (Image

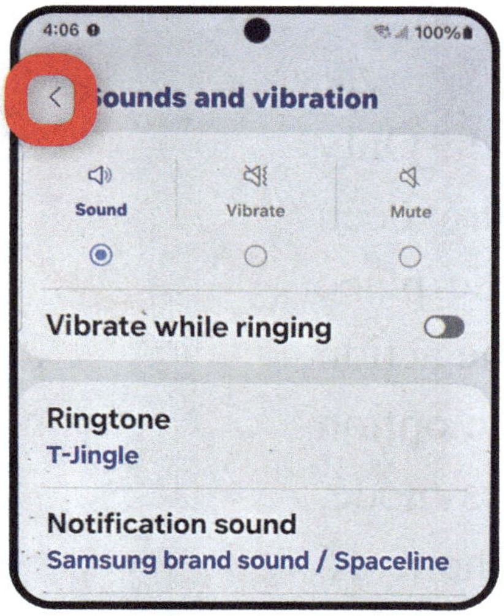

Image 5.17

5.17) This is where you get to **customize the sounds** on your phone. Want to change your ringtone? This is where you do it.

Read each option and tap on everything. Be curious! Now that you know you can always GO BACK by tapping on the **<.** Feel free to tap on everything and see what happens.

Of course, if this is too much for you, simply tap the home button or swipe up, and you'll be returned to the safety of the home screen. (Please refer to Chapter 7, the Home Page, for details on the home button.)

Within that media box are four symbols at the bottom. From left to right, you will see a wrench for system settings, a bell for notifications, and a loudspeaker for the ringer and call volume. (Image 5.18)

Image 5.18

Source: Material Design Icons

Silencing Your iPhone

iPhones are a little different. If you want to quickly SILENCE your phone, there's a tiny toggle switch right above the volume controls on the left side (as you face the screen).

This configuration has been on iPhones forever. Only beginning with the iPhone 15 has this feature been modified to an *action button*. It is in the same place and a bit easier to use. The default setting for the action button is to silence the phone, but you have the option of having it launch the camera, flashlight, focus mode, or voice memo, among other apps. On the iPhone 16 that button can be changed to be a shutter button for the camera. This is a programmable switch as well.

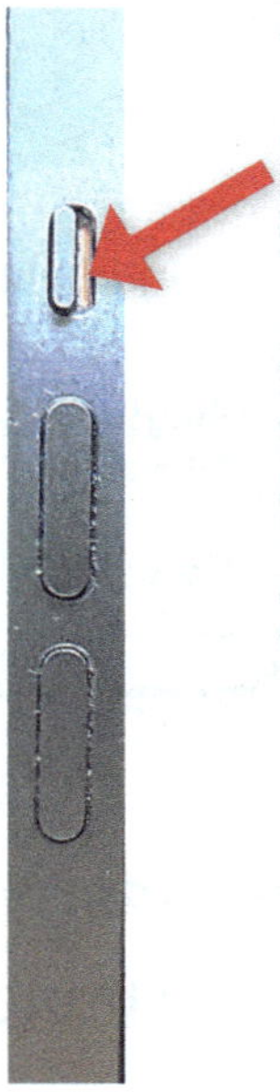

Image 5.19

When you move the switch to mute (Image 5.19), you will see a small announcement at the very top of the screen saying **SILENT MODE ON,** showing a **red bell** with a line through it. (Red = stop.)

When toggled on again, the screen will show **SILENT MODE OFF,** and the bell will be gray. To turn off silent mode, switch it back toward the front of the phone, and the red in the switch will go away.

The thing I've noticed with the toggle and seniors is that it can be tricky to move. **Helpful hint: Use your fingernail** to move the switch toward the back of the phone to turn silent mode ON. If your nails are too short, you can use the point of a pen to slide the switch more easily.

Remember to turn your volume on again. (If you don't, your kids and friends will go nuts wondering why you're not answering their calls and texts!)

iPhone Hack to Quickly Silence Unwanted Calls

PRESS AND RELEASE THE POWER BUTTON TWO TIMES CONSECUTIVELY WITHOUT LIFTING YOUR FINGER

On an iPhone, if you want the phone to stop ringing, you can **PRESS AND RELEASE the POWER BUTTON ONE TIME**, and the call is silenced. The call will show on your screen and quietly continue to ring until it goes to voicemail. The caller has no idea you silenced the call.

If you would like to stop the ringing and immediately send the call to voicemail, simply **PRESS THE POWER BUTTON TWO TIMES IN SUCCESSION.**

Note: Do not lift your finger off the button between presses as the phone will read that as two single presses—a different gesture. Remember, keep your finger on the button and **PRESS TWO TIMES QUICKLY.**

This can take practice for some people. Don't be discouraged if you can't get it at first. Just remember to keep your finger on the button while you quickly (in succession) press twice.

Now the call has gone to voicemail, and you no longer see it on your screen.

Learn To Read Android & iPhone Screens

For the past eleven years, I have noticed an unusual and confounding pattern in the majority of my students (whose average age is eighty-five). It seems that most seniors lose the ability to understand common words in their own language. I'll illustrate.

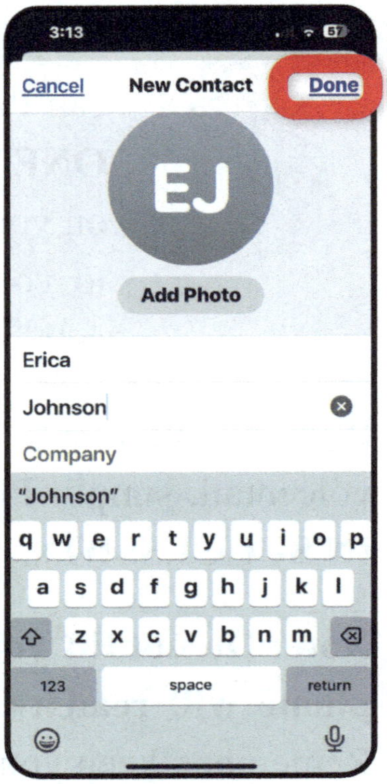

Image 5.20

I was working with this lovely eighty-something woman who was quite sharp. She played bridge; she played the piano. She had a vibrant social life. Now she was learning the phone and at this moment was working on how to add a contact. After inputting all the correct information, she looked puzzled. I noticed her hesitancy and asked her about it. She said she was done filling out the contact information but couldn't figure out what to do next.

I asked her to look carefully at the screen for any clues, and she went right past the word **DONE** in the upper-right corner of the screen. (Image 5.20) I pointed out the word and asked her to read it. She said, "Done." I asked what the word meant, and she said, "Done means finished." I asked her if she had finished filling out the contact. She said she had.

I asked, "So what do you tap?" And she looked at me like a deer in headlights and timidly answered, "I don't know." When I suggested that the word DONE on the screen and the one just spoken were one and the same, she lit up…and laughed at herself.

So let me be clear. The fact that the words are on a mini-computer screen does not change their meaning. Done equals finished equals done. Cancel means the same on the phone as it does in conversation. It means you don't want to do whatever it was you were doing anymore. You want out. Don't save it. *Just get me back to before.* That's when you tap CANCEL. Cancel equals done.

This is only one example. It seems to be a trend among my students. Why? Because the phone presents as a foreign object and elicits such fear that some people's brains just kind of dull out, and even everyday words lose their meaning when they are out of context of a conversation.

Now that you are aware of this phenomenon, try to notice when it's happening. If you feel tense with a level of overwhelm, take a breath, move around, and maybe even get up and walk away for a minute or two. Then come back with a clear head and the determination to figure this out. I literally tell myself, "Anne, the answer is on the page. You just do not see it. Look again. It's there!" Be curious. Challenge yourself to figure it out. It's good for your brain.

ANDROID & iPHONE HELPFUL HINTS WHEN READING THE SCREEN

Since we've been talking about contacts (i.e., address book), let's assume you you want to save a new contact.

Once you finish typing in (entering) the contact information, ask yourself if there is anything else to add. If you're done, look at the screen.

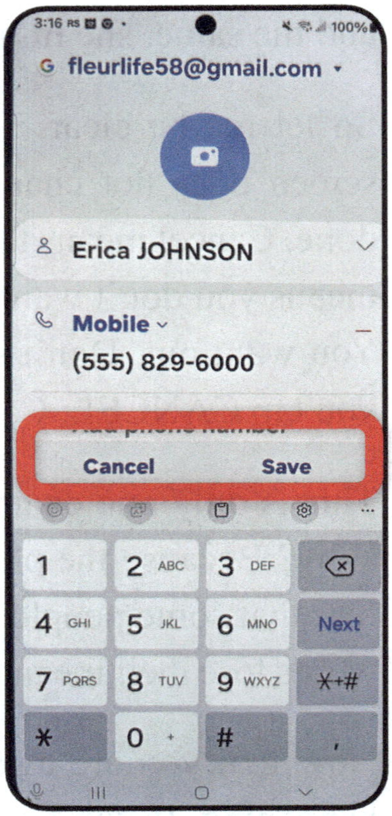

Image 5.21

If you want to save it, it's because you are done. Therefore,* Save *and* Done *mean the same thing.

Android gives you two choices: CANCEL and SAVE. (Image 5.21) What's the difference? Choose **Save** if you don't want to fill out the contact information again, because **choosing Cancel ends the action and erases whatever you did**, thus requiring you to begin again!

DOTS AND LINES ON ANDROIDS & iPHONES

Smartphone screens are small. They are way smaller than computer screens, yet they contain an enormous amount of information. How did the developers get all that information on the tiny screen? The answer is that they put dots and dashes on the pages. Wherever you see a series of three dots or three lines, that is your clue that there is more information hidden. In Images 5.22 & 5.23, you are looking at the Gmail App on an Android phone. (It's the same on iPhones.)

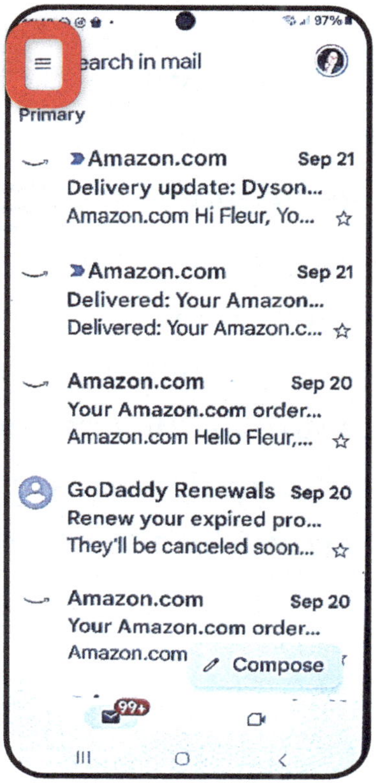

Image 5.22

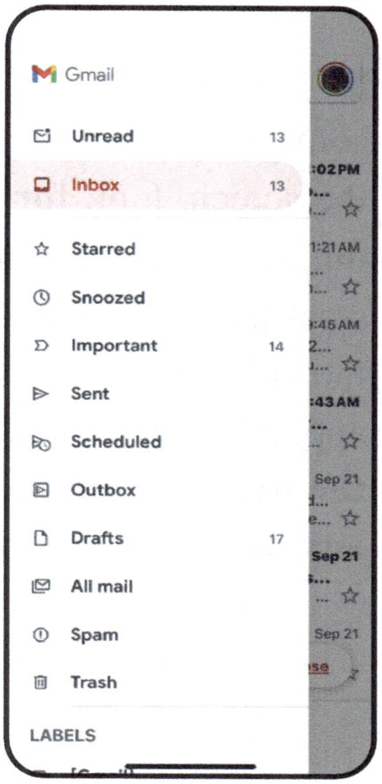

Image 5.23

Notice the three lines in the top left corner of Image 5.22. It is the first thing you see if you read the screen from the top left corner. These lines are always tappable. When you tap on them in Gmail as shown in Image 5.22, the screen changes (Image 5.23), and you get a whole lot more information about your email account.

That means there is always information hiding there. It’s a menu of more options available in that particular application/program/software.

So, when you are looking for something and you don’t see it on the screen, **look for dots or lines on any phone.** This is part of smartphone technology and how the developers were able to put massive amounts of information in an app, using lines, dots, or arrows. **In summary, a key piece in solving the puzzle of finding information on any smartphone is to tap on any dashes, dots, and arrows you see on the screen.**

Chapter 6

Gestures: The Key to Mastering Smartphones

Table of Contents

Arguably, learning gestures is one of the most important things you can do. Why? Because gestures (or how you touch the phone) is the language your phone speaks, and in order to effectively communicate with it, you have to learn the language.

All smartphones rely on touch as communication. That's why their screens are called TOUCHSCREENS. Touch is the "language" so the device will do what you want. Much like lovers, the way you touch the phone determines the reaction you get! You may think you are tapping, but perhaps, in reality, you are tapping and holding for just a millisecond too long. That's a different gesture and will result in something unexpected showing up on your screen. And if you tap and really hold, well, that's a whole other gesture. Swiping with one finger or two are different gestures.

If you don't know the difference between the gestures, you will touch your phone, expecting to see a particular screen, but because the gesture was incorrect, something unexpected happens, and a different screen appears. And when something unexpected appears on the screen, you become confused.

REMEMBER

A TAP OPENS THE APP!

Tapping

Remember this little ditty… **TAP to Open an APP**. When you want to open any app, just TAP! Tapping is the main way we tell the device to open whatever is on the screen. Tap, tap, open the app.

At a class recently, I was asked to describe the gesture of tapping. The art of tapping correctly can sometimes be tricky. I recommend you pretend that the screen is like a hot iron, and you want to tap really fast so as not to get burned. That's a tap! **When you TAP, keep it light and use the fleshy part of your finger (or a stylus at the end of a pen) to lightly but definitely touch the surface of the phone.**

Pressing

Pressing is sometimes called **holding** or "I thought I tapped it!" However, when a tap is held a micro-second too long, it's no longer a tap. It's a different command. It's a **PRESS** or a **TAP AND HOLD**. When surprises like this happen, and it flusters you…go home! By now you should know how to swipe, tap, or press the home button to get back to the comfort of the home page.

> The actions of swiping, pinching, tapping, pressing are common to all touchscreen devices.

Pinching

Sometimes what you see on the screen is too small, and you want to enlarge it. You can **pinch** the screen by drawing two fingers from the middle of the screen toward the outer edges as in Image 6.1. This gesture will enlarge the screen and is universal to all smartphones regardless of make and manufacturer. To reduce the size, place your fingers farther apart on the screen and pinch in to shrink whatever you're looking at—but sadly, it does not work in all apps. It works when it works. It always works in picture apps and is a great way to edit photos.

Image 6.1

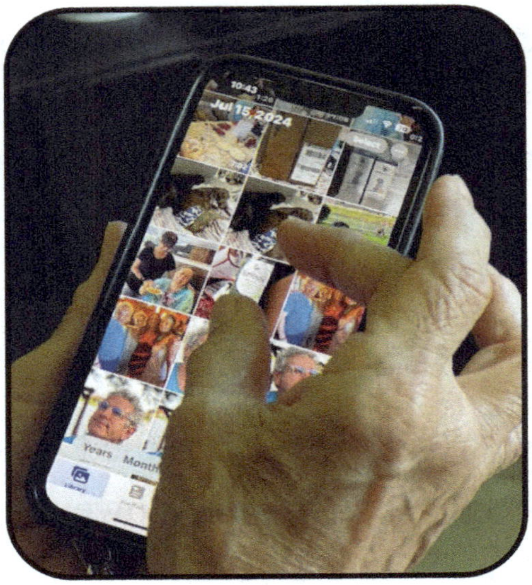

Image 6.2

Note: In the Android photo gallery, using this action will slightly enlarge the photos, whereas in the Apple photos app, the pictures will enlarge more.

Crazy Sensitive Phone Screens

One last thing about surprises on your phone. **The phone screens are very sensitive**. I swear sometimes I breathe on my screen and an app suddenly opens. Knowing this helps. If you happen to pick up your phone and the screen changes, it's because something brushed past it, likely part of your finger or hand (or your clothes, or the corner of a couch!). Or, you mean to open one app, but your finger moves and suddenly you tap on a different app. **There is no need to get nervous.** Just swipe up, tap or press and release the home button, and your screen will become familiar again.

Android Button Functions

On phones with physical buttons, the number of times you press them matters. For any Android, a single press and release of the home button brings the home screen into view. But, depending on the number of presses, there are different results.

> **Helpful Hint:**
> Screen changes unexpectedly? GO HOME by swiping up or tapping/pressing the home button.

When you PRESS and HOLD the power button, the screen changes and you have options like *power off*, *restart*, or *emergency mode*. Tap *power off* to turn the phone off. To turn the phone back on, you have to press and hold the power button again. From this screen you can also restart your phone, which means the phone will shut down and turn on again without you having to do anything. It's good to restart your phone every few days to keep it working properly.

If you tap the power button FIVE TIMES FAST, it will contact emergency services. If your device isn't programmed for this, go to:

SETTINGS > SAFETY & EMERGENCY > TAP EMERGENCY SOS > TOGGLE CALL EMERGENCY SERVICES ON. YOU CAN ALSO ENABLE "SHARE LOCATION WITH EMERGENCY CONTACTS."

You can also change the power button actions.

GO TO SETTINGS > SYSTEM (OR ADVANCED FEATURES) > GESTURES (OR SIDE KEY IN SAMSUNG)

Tap double press and choose what you want to do with it. Options are to:

- Open the camera app
- Open any specific app
- Turn off the screen

Android Long Tap & Shortcut Screen

When you tap on the phone icon to make a call, you expect it to open, and most of the time, it does. However, sometimes your finger lingers a millisecond too long, and your gesture is no longer a TAP. It has become a **LONG TAP,** and the result will be different. This is not necessarily a bad thing, as long as, when it happens, you don't freak out. Most smartphone-using seniors I know become very upset when the screen delivers a surprise. And it's the unexpected that sends most seniors into a panic. Now, instead of panicking, realize that if the screen changes to something unfamiliar, there is nothing wrong with the phone, or with you. It's simply that you did not communicate properly due to an incorrect gesture.

In Image 6.3, you see what happens on a Samsung when the phone app is long tapped. The screen changed. What is it? It's a **shortcut screen**. The options are to see your *Missed calls*, to *Search*, or to *Create contact* with two additional options in the darker area at the bottom.

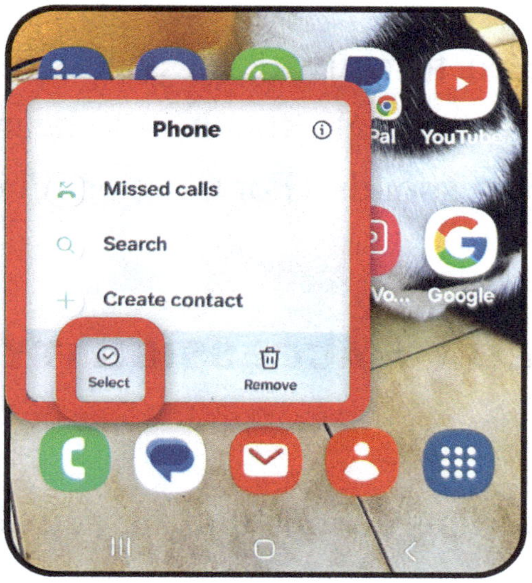

Image 6.3

Image 6.4

By tapping on ***Select,*** the top of the screen changes. (Image 6.4) In this location you can disable or delete the app. You can also put it in a folder on your screen. Do you see a little garbage pail with the word *Remove* under it? It's in the middle on the top. To its left is Disable and to its right is Create Folder. **Delete unwanted apps** by dragging them to the trash. More about that later when I teach you how to declutter your phone.

iPhone Button Functions

Of course, pressing the power button on your iPhone turns the screen on and off. Did you know you can also summon Siri by pressing and holding the power button?

And if you press the power button FIVE TIMES FAST, you will be connected to emergency services.

The side/power button can also be used to activate an accessibility shortcut (customizing your phone for visual, touch, or hearing disabilities) to change the way the button responds. (For more on iPhone accessibility settings, visit Chapter 9.)

OPEN SETTINGS > ACCESSIBILITY > ACCESSIBILITY SHORTCUT

Here you will be able to choose from various actions that are activated by triple-clicking the side/power button.

iPhone Long Tap & Shortcut Screen

A long tap on an iPhone delivers a different-looking shortcut screen. At the very top, IN RED, is the Remove app. This is an easy way to delete an app on an iPhone. This shortcut also offers the opportunity to:

- Edit Home Screen
- View Most Recent Voicemail

Image 6.5

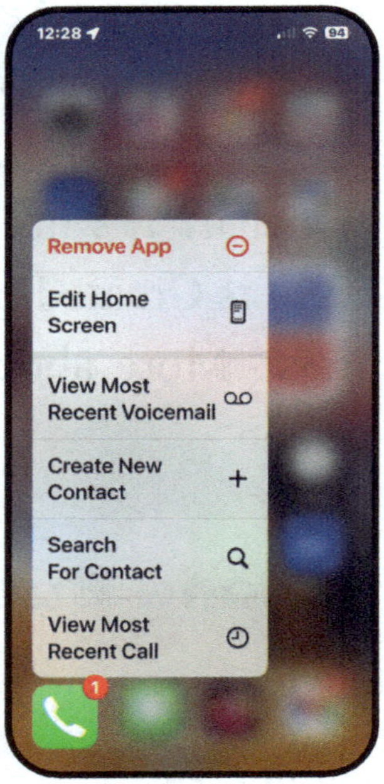

Image 6.6

- Create New Contact
- Search for a Contact
- View Most Recent Call

In summary, almost every app on your device has a shortcut screen that comes up when you perform a long tap. Practice this. Tap, Long Tap, Tap, Long Tap. Do it over and over until you are clear and comfortable as to what distinguishes these two gestures. Practicing gestures is a great way to curb surprises on your phone.

Chapter 7

Android & iPhone Home Page

Table of Contents

ANDROID AND iPHONE HOME SCREEN

The home screen is where you'll land after you put in your PIN, scan your fingerprint, or scan your face to unlock your phone. (And, yes, you NEED security on your phone. More about that later.) The home screen looks different from device to device.

In these images, you see an Android home screen in Image 7.1 and my personal iPhone home page in Image 7.2. They look a little bit different, don't they? Remember, we have two different operating systems, and the shape and size of the icons are slightly different from each other. One is more square and the other more rounded. Plus, the same apps do not appear on both phones. Smartphones are highly customizable, and you get to choose which apps you want and where you want them (on which screen, alone or in a folder).

Image 7.1

Image 7.2

Helpful Hint: When swiping up or down, make sure that your fingertip starts at the edge of the phone's case and very lightly (no pressing) slide your finger up.

Check out chapter 8 to learn how to move apps around.

ANDROID & iPHONE – THE DOCK

The dock is at the very bottom of the screen. On Androids, it's under the page dots (Image 7.3), and on iPhones, it appears with a colored background. (Image 7.4) This bottom area of the phone allows you to literally dock, or pin, a select group of apps that are always visible at the bottom of every page on the device—with one exception: You will not see the dock in the App Library or Drawer.

Image 7.3

Image 7.4

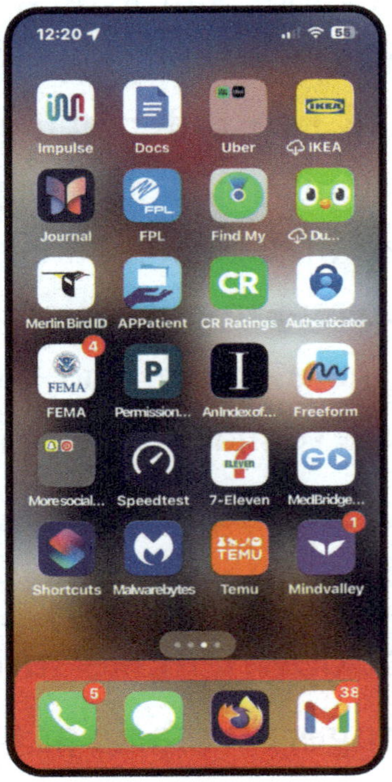

Image 7.5

What to keep in the dock?

This is where you place the apps you use most often and you can change them whenever you want. Absolutely the telephone app belongs here. If you text, then your messaging app should be here too. After that, it's up to you. I am always going on the Internet, so I have that in my dock. My husband is ALWAYS posting on Facebook, so he keeps that in his dock. A friend of mine has the electronic door controls to her apartment building in the dock. Easy peasy to find them every time.

You get to choose. What are your most commonly used apps? If you have an Android, there is space for five apps, but one of them is ALL APPS and is permanently in the dock. The other four spaces are for your most often used apps.

If you have an iPhone, a total of four apps can be placed there. As you can see from Image 7.5 (my phone), in the dock I keep the phone, messages, Internet, and email apps. Those are the ones I use most frequently.

How do I get my apps into the dock?

It's the same process as deleting apps, covered in Chapter 8.

ANDROID HOME SCREEN

In the Android world, the way you access the home screen can vary by manufacturer and model. There is always a power button on your phone that you press, just like the power button on your TV remote. Older Androids have a virtual home button, which means it's just a picture. (Image 7.6) Tapping it is just like pressing a physical button.

Image 7.6

If you are in your email and want to return to the home screen, tap or press on the virtual button or, on newer phones, swipe up from the very bottom on phones with no buttons. So, wherever you are on your phone, in any app you have opened, you can always get back to the home page by swiping up or tapping the home button.

ANDROID WHAT PAGE ARE YOU ON?

It's good to know how many pages of apps you have. How you know the page you're on is indicated at the bottom of the screen with a series of small circles. There are as many circles as there are pages. See Images 7.7 and 7.8. Look at the dots. It's hard to see here, but one of those dots on both screens is brighter and whiter than the others. This denotes the page you are on. In this Android, there are seven pages, seven dots, and the screen shown is the first screen of the seven. (Image 7.7) Each of those pages has an average of twenty apps for a total of 140 apps on this phone. That's 140 different programs that are installed on this little handheld computer. How many apps do you actually use?

Image 7.7

Image 7.8

iPHONE HOME SCREEN

To get to the home screen on an iPhone with no button, swipe up from the bottom. (Note: Swiping up is akin to "GO BACK." Sometimes you have to keep swiping up until you see the home page.)

There is another cool feature on the iPhone home page, and it's a search bar. (See Image 7.9.) It's at the bottom of the page. Tap on it and the screen changes (Image 7.10), and the search bar becomes larger. At the top of the screen, you'll see commonly used apps. Once you start typing in the search bar, the device looks for matches. I typed the letters **SE,** and the system showed me **SE**ttings and Word **SE**arch. (Image 7.11) This is a great way to find apps on your iPhone.

Image 7.9

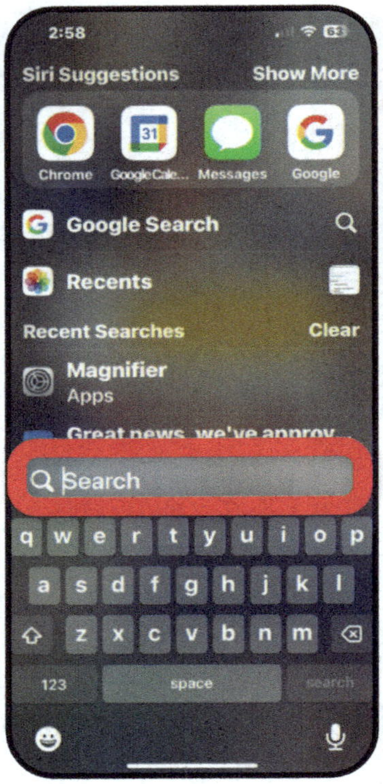

Image 7.10

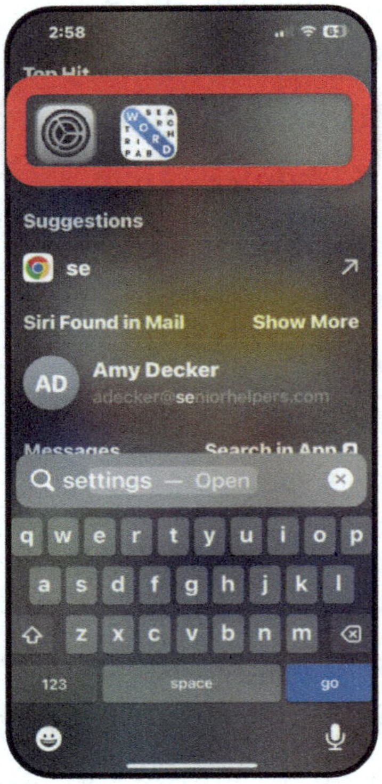

Image 7.11

iPHONE WHAT PAGE ARE YOU ON?

Did you know you can tell the number of pages of apps you have by the number of dots at the bottom of the page? Look at Image 7.12 and find the search bar. Tap on it and it will change. (Image 7.13) Notice the arrow pointing to a series of dots. The dot that is whiter/brighter (or somehow stands out as different from the others (but maybe not so much in this picture!) is telling you what page (or screen) you are on.

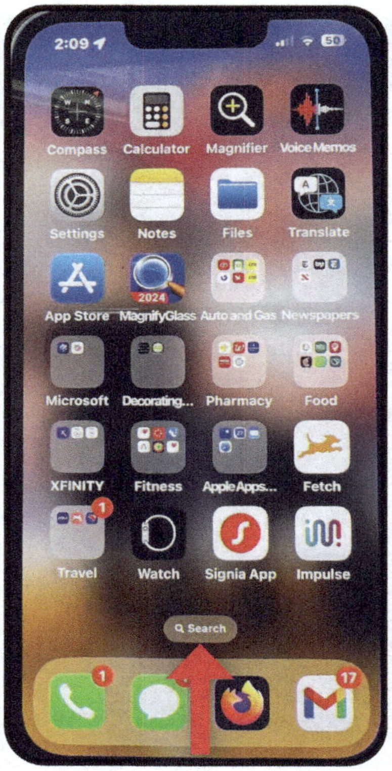

Image 7.12

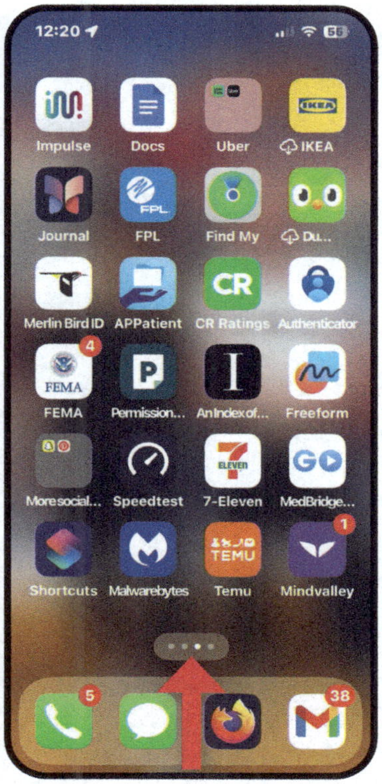

Image 7.13

Chapter 8

Android & iPhone Decluttering Your Phone –Moving and Deleting Apps

Table of Contents

Smartphones are not made for you and me. They are made for your kids, your grandkids, and maybe even your great-grandkids. But not us. The phones come bloated with all kinds of programs (bloatware) that you will never, ever use. So how do you get rid of them? It's simple—you declutter!

Much like when you declutter your home, decluttering your phone means less stress because things are now organized, and you know where to find them. There are fewer screens to deal with because you've gotten rid of all the apps you don't use or want.

I am a professional organizer, so I organize my phone carefully and put similar apps together in folders. I have folders for Entertainment, Games, Finance & Insurance, Business, Pharmacies, and more. I don't want a lot of pages. With folders, when I want to be entertained, all my choices are in one Entertainment folder. I don't have to go searching to find Netflix, YouTube, Amazon Music, or Xfinity Stream on different pages.

Androids Deleting and Moving Apps

DELETING APPS: FIND APP > HOLD APP ICON > POPUP MENU > TAP UNINSTALL OR GARBAGE PAIL OR

REMOVE

You are not going to believe how easy it is to remove or relocate any app.

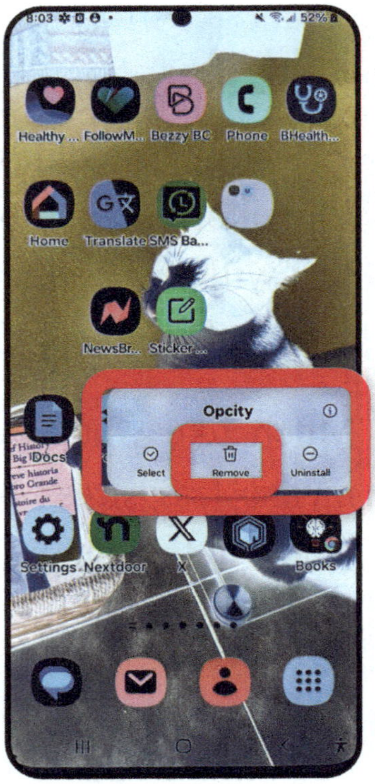

Image 8.1

To delete (i.e., uninstall) an app, **PRESS & HOLD** on the app **UNTIL THE SCREEN CHANGES** and a **white box appears**. TAP REMOVE (the trash can) and the app will disappear. Note: On some Androids the top of the screen changes, and you will have to drag (slide) the app to UNINSTALL (which removes it completely from the device) or to a garbage pail.

Keep in mind that not all Androids ask you to confirm your deletion, so be sure you want to delete the app. Of course, **if you do delete an app in error, you can go to the Play Store and redownload it.** So, no harm, no foul.

Now that you see how easy it is to delete apps on your Android, you can declutter your phone and get rid of apps you don't want and will never use.

Android Making Folders

Making folders is really easy, but you have to learn how to slide apps around. This requires properly touching the phone.

1. Choose two apps you want to be in the same folder. (Image 8.2)
2. PRESS AND HOLD until the app starts wiggling.
3. Now SLIDE the app right over the other app and voila! You have a folder with two apps in it.

Image 8.2

Image 8.3

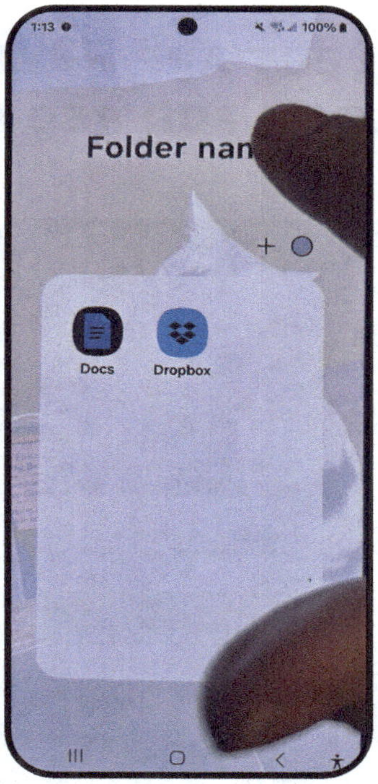

Image 8.4

If you want to add more apps to the folder, repeat. Press and hold on the next app and slide it on top of the folder. Now there are three apps in the folder.

You can change the name of the folder by just tapping. A blank space will appear, and you can name that folder whatever you want.

You will see these steps clearly in Images 8.2, 8.3, and 8.4.

iPhones Deleting and Moving Apps

SELECT APP > PRESS AND HOLD > SCREEN CHANGES > LOOK FOR RED DELETE.

Image 8.5

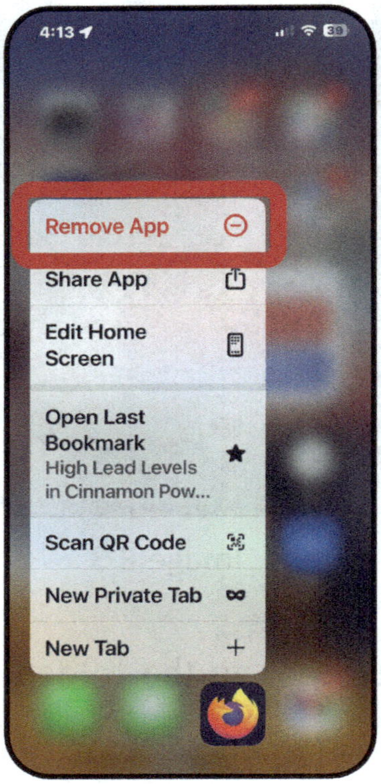

Image 8.6

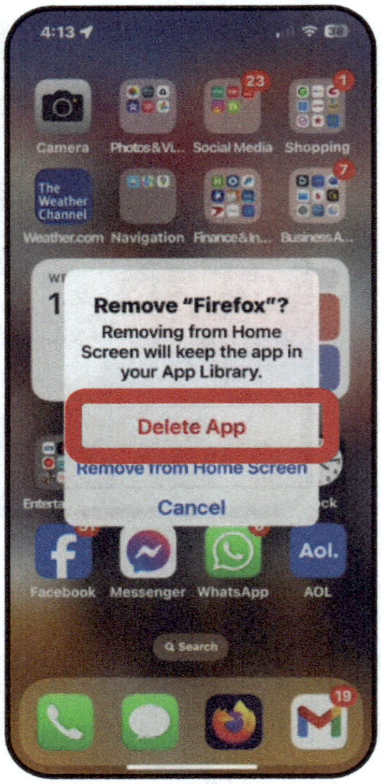

Image 8.7

The process is pretty much the same as it is on Androids. Select the app you want to delete. TAP AND HOLD. A box will open. Don't get nervous. This is good. This screen is a shortcut screen that pops up when you TAP & HOLD on the APP (which is different from pressing, which will elicit a different response). If you TAP & HOLD on any app, you will get shortcuts specific to that app. (Image 8.6)

Read the box that opened. The very first thing you will see—in RED—is Remove App. Tap on it. The screen will change, and you will be asked to confirm the action. Do you want to completely erase the app from your phone? Tap **DELETE APP**. If you want to keep the app, but don't want to see it, tap **Remove from Home Screen.** Likely you will have to confirm deletion at least one more time, likely two times. That's good. You won't delete anything by mistake. **And always remember, there are no mistakes because any app deleted can be reinstalled from the App Store.**

iPHONE DELETING MULTIPLE APPS AT A TIME

There is another way to delete iPhone apps. If you PRESS and HOLD, suddenly all the apps will begin to wiggle, and a small dash (a minus sign) will appear at the top left of each app. (Image 8.8) Simply tap on the minus sign of the app you don't want (see top left corner of the icon), and you will be prompted to delete it. You will go through the same confirmation of the delete multiple times.

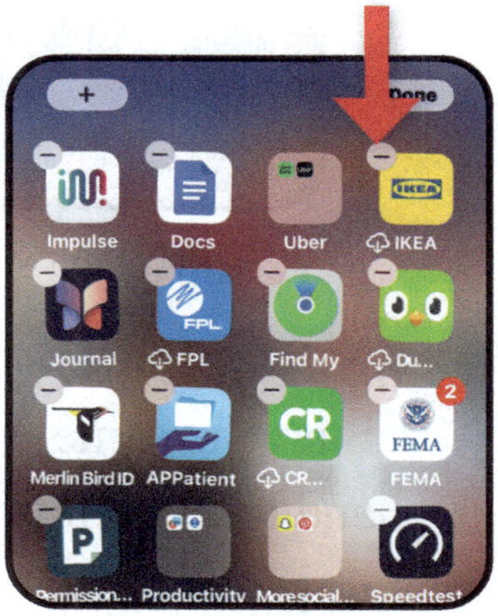

Image 8.8

iPHONE MAKING FOLDERS

I am an organized person. And I'm impatient. Put the two together and I am someone who wants to organize my phone in categories so I can find apps faster. The solution? Folders! If you'll notice in the third image below, I have a LOT of folders. In fact, I have nine folders with a total of ninety-seven apps I can easily find on my home page.

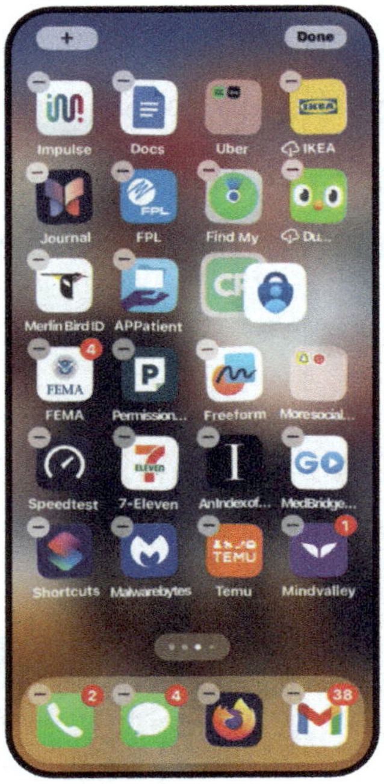

Image 8.9

Image 8.10

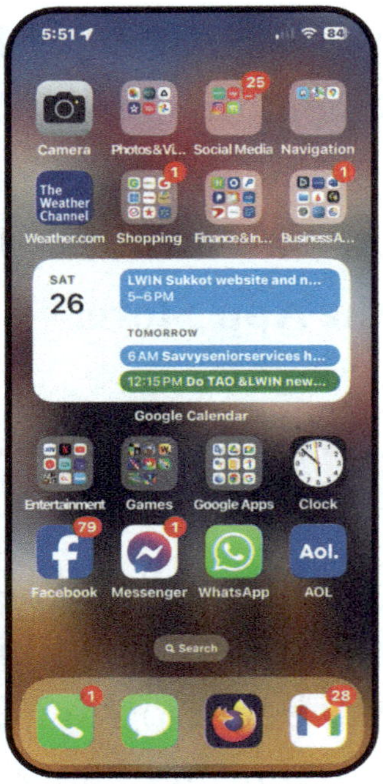

Image 8.11

1. Start the same way you would if you want to move an app. Press and hold until you see the apps begin to wiggle.
2. Release your finger and they will keep wiggling. That's good. That means they are now movable and deletable.

3. You can swipe and switch from one screen to another. It is a little tricky to get those little suckers to move from one page to the next, so it takes some getting used to. If you want to move an app to a screen that's a left swipe, kind of push the icon against the left edge of the screen. Keep trying. You need to master this if the apps you want in one folder are on different pages. I know you can do it.
4. To merge the apps into a new folder, move one app over the other, and all of a sudden the screen will change, and you will see two apps in the folder.
5. Tap where it says "folder name" and type in the new name. When you are done, TAP DONE!

The Android & iPhone App Switchers

This is, arguably, one of the most convenient features of smartphones. Why? Let's say you're about to join a Zoom call, and you tapped on the hyperlink (aka the blue, underlined Internet address) in an email. Now you are being asked for the password, but you didn't write it down. How do you get back to the email with the passcode? You open the App Switcher and switch between the two apps easily.

ANDROID APP SWITCHER

Newer Androids like the Samsung S25 do not have virtual buttons. To access the App Switcher, swipe halfway up the screen and make a right turn with your finger, the same as iPhones. For all other Androids that do not have virtual buttons tap on the three parallel lines at the very bottom of the screen. It's where the virtual home button and go back arrow are. See Image 8.12. Some models show it on the left, some on the right. Any open apps will appear, looking like they're floating in the middle of the screen. (Image 8.13) Some Androids will stack the open apps vertically, some horizontally. Simply slide the app either left/ right or up to close the app. (Image 8.14) You can also choose to close all open apps by tapping on the oval Close all. (Image 8.14) This will result in an incremental improvement in your battery life.

Image 8.12

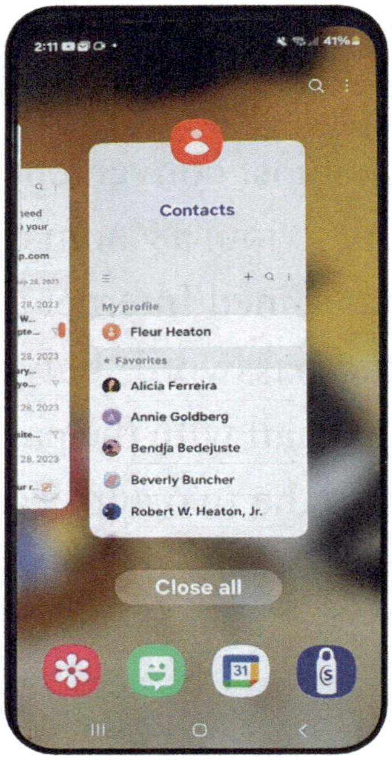

Image 8.13

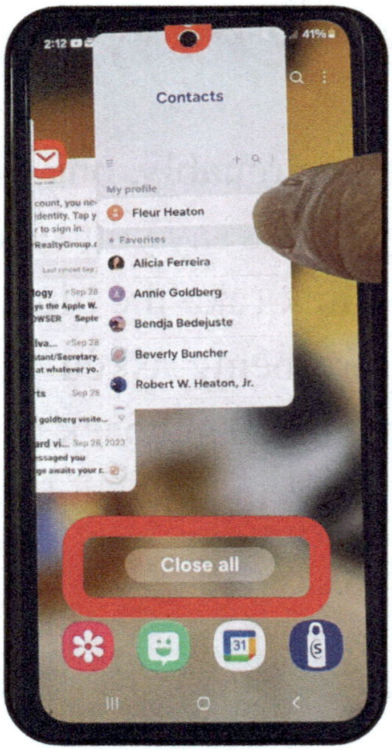

Image 8.14

TO CLOSE OPEN APPS, SWIPE THEM UP (OR SIDEWAYS) AND AWAY.

Please note that swiping up (or across) only closes the app. It does not delete the app; it puts it to sleep, so to speak. You can reopen it whenever you want.

> **Helpful Hint:** Practice opening and closing the App Switcher and moving through the apps.

Another use for the App Switcher. The name for this is appropriate because this is where you can also switch from one open app to another. For example, you open an email that contains a Zoom link and password you tap on the Zoom link and are prompted for the password. But you don't have the password; it's in the email. Since that email is still open, you use the App Switcher to find that email and look at the passcode. After writing down the password, do the reverse. Swipe up and find the App Switcher again. Slide the apps left or right until you see the Zoom page. TAP to open it. Now you can enter the password.

Easy peasy.

iPHONE APP SWITCHER

On iPhones you access the App Switcher with either one of two gestures. The first way is to swipe up from the very bottom, and when you get about halfway up, lift your finger. If you have trouble with this, there is another way that I find easier. Simply swipe up from the very bottom and turn right midway. (Image 8.16)

Image 8.15

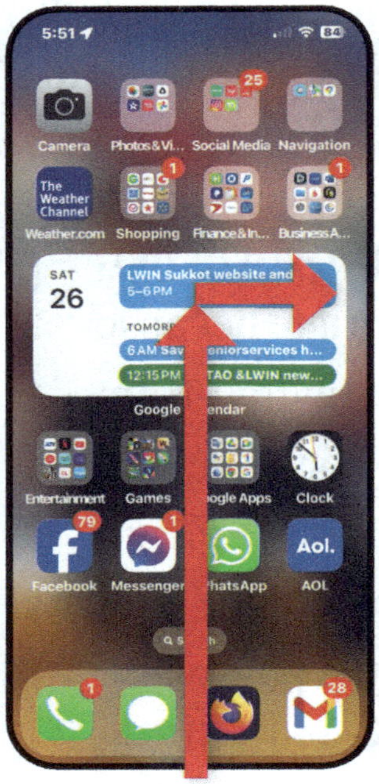

Image 8.16

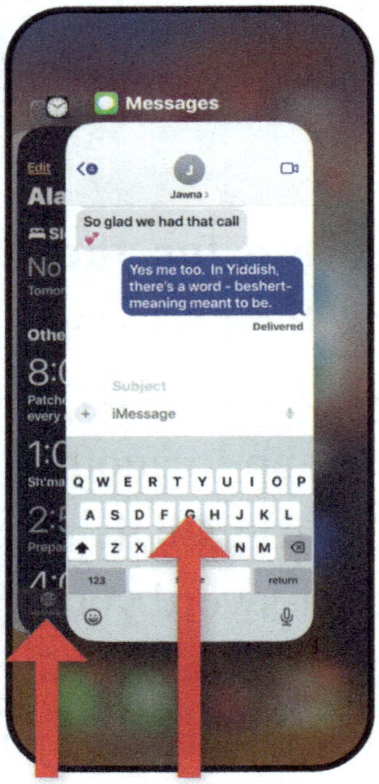

Image 8.17

Swipe through the open apps by sliding them right and left. Look at the pictures above. Text messages are sitting on top of the clock app. (Image 8.17) If you gently slide the text messages to the right, you will see the contents of the page below it. (Image 8.18) Going back to the Zoom example, tap on the email with the Zoom passcode to open that page. Write down or remember the passcode. Swipe up again to reopen the App Switcher and find the Zoom page. Tap on it to open it and enter the passcode. It's so easy.

Image 8.18

Open apps use the battery a bit more, so it's a good idea to swipe open apps to close them every day or so, especially if you open a variety of apps in the course of using the phone day to day.

Android & iPhone App Drawer/Library

There is one place on your device that shows all the apps, and that is called the App Drawer (Android) or App Library (iPhone).

Android App Drawer

Image 8.19

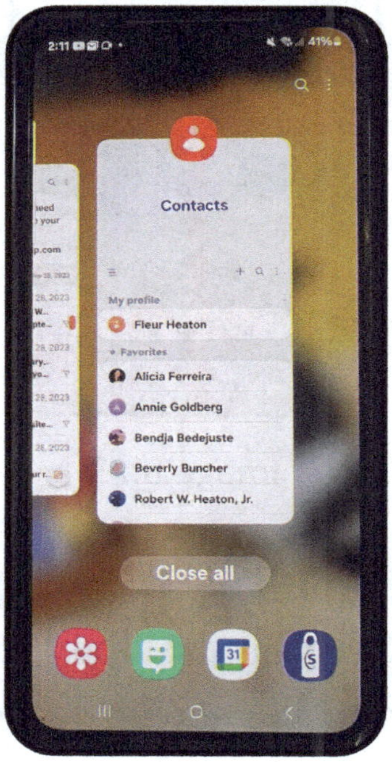

Image 8.20

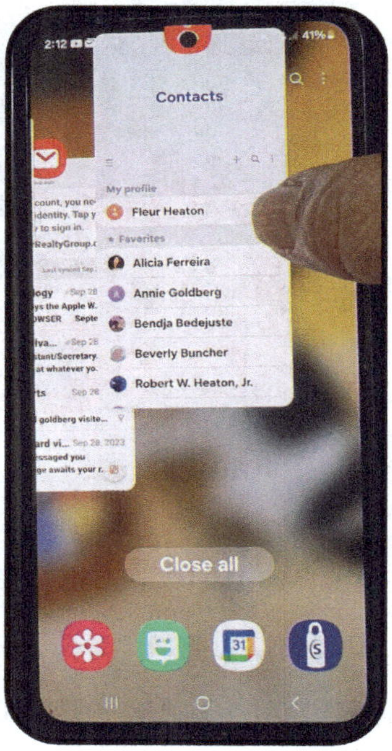

Image 8.21

Android App Tray or Drawer

Finding the App Tray or Drawer in most Androids is simple, but it also depends on the manufacturer and the model.

Look at the dock at the very bottom of the screen. **The first icon on the right has nine dots in it.** (Image 8.22) **A quick TAP on that, and you are whooshed to the App Drawer** (i.e., all apps). **(Image 8.24)**

Image 8.22

Image 8.23

Image 8.24

Another way to access the App Tray is to swipe up from the bottom of the screen. (Image 8.23) Start on the tippy top in the black area. You don't have to go very far up the screen to bring up the App Drawer. (Image 8.24) In some models, you had to swipe down from the top to open the App Drawer.

Once you're in the App Drawer, you will find the apps are alphabetized. There is also a SEARCH bar (Image 8.24). so you don't have to swipe to find what you want. Just start typing the name of the app, and you will see it appear. Alternatively, you can swipe left to see the many pages of apps listed.

iPhone App Library—Swipe Left

How many apps do you have on your phone? I have a lot—well over 300! Many people have more than that. It's astonishing really when you think about it.

How do you keep track of them? It can be annoying to search around for a particular app.

Image 8.25

Image 8.26

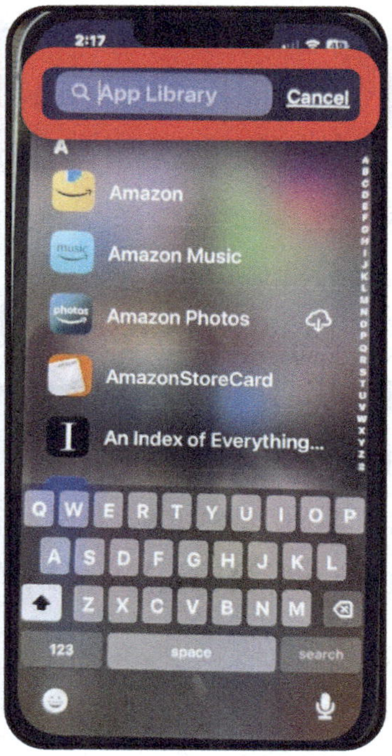

Image 8.27

Here's the solution. Simply **swipe left until you can't swipe any more**. (Image 8.25) You have now arrived at the **App Library** on an iPhone. (Image 8.26) Don't ask me about the logic of the folders you'll find in the App Library. It's Apple's organization. But it doesn't matter because there is a search bar at the top of the page. (Image 8.27) Other names are the App Drawer or App Tray.

How do I know it's a search bar? Because there's the *search* icon alongside the words "App Library." It literally tells you that you can search the App Library (by tapping in the bar area). It has the Universal symbol for search, which looks like a magnifying glass, doesn't it? (Images 8.26 & 27) How did Sherlock Holmes search for clues? He used a magnifying glass. Thus, the universally accepted icon for "search" is a magnifying glass. I've seen phones in Spanish, French, and Hebrew, and I could always find the search bar because it had that magnifying glass. This search symbol is found on every search bar in every app I've seen.

Once you tap in the search bar, the screen will change, and you will see an alphabetical listing of every app on your phone. You can either type the app you want in the search bar or tap on the far right of the screen on the first letter of the app to find it alphabetically. Of course you can also use **SCROLL DOWN**.

Chapter 9

Android & iPhone Settings

TABLE OF CONTENTS

Android & iPhone Display Settings

You all know what settings are. You have used them on ovens, washers, dryers, dishwashers, and even toasters since the sixties. Settings are your way of telling the machine what you want it to do, such as a delicate wash in cold water, with low heat drying. That's a setting. Are you vacuuming on carpet or hard floors? That's a setting. And if you have any of the newer HE washers and dryers, you have seen an insane selection of choices about how you want your clothes washed.

Smartphones have settings too. A lot of them. For the purpose of this book, I am going to discuss four settings:

- Display
- Sound
- Notifications
- Accessibility

ANDROID DISPLAY & BRIGHTNESS SETTINGS

SETTINGS > DISPLAY

Tap on settings. Scroll down to Display. (It's close to the top.) **TAP on DISPLAY.** (Image 9.1) The screen will change. (Image 9.2)

Tap on light vs. dark. Which do you prefer? Adjust the brightness. Just slide the circle to the left to make it darker and to the right to make the screen brighter. In this image you see that **adaptive brightness** is toggled on, which means the phone will adapt to the environment and brighten and darken according to the light around you.

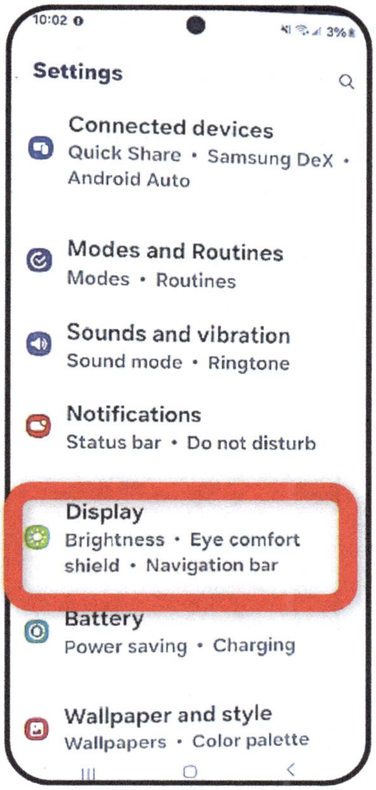

Image 9.1

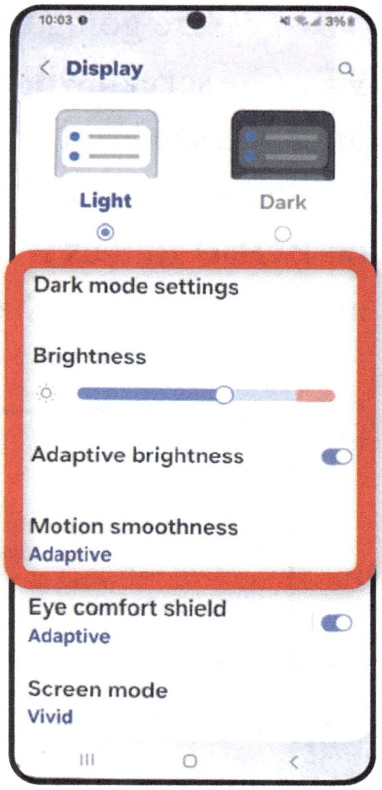

Image 9.2

Smartphones offer many ways to customize the screen, especially regarding text size and readability. The choices are the same between the two operating systems, with just some minor differences in how things are done. Here you will find how to customize the screen so you can see it better.

ANDROID FONTS

SETTINGS > DISPLAY > SCROLL TO FONT SIZE AND STYLE

Next, we are going to look at the font settings. **Tap on Display.** (Image 9.3) **The screen will change. KEEP SCROLLING** beyond Brightness until you see **Font size and style.** Tap on it. (Image 9.4) The screen will change again (Image 9.6), and you will have the opportunity to toggle on **BOLD** font as well as increase or decrease the size of the font. Tap and slide and see what happens.

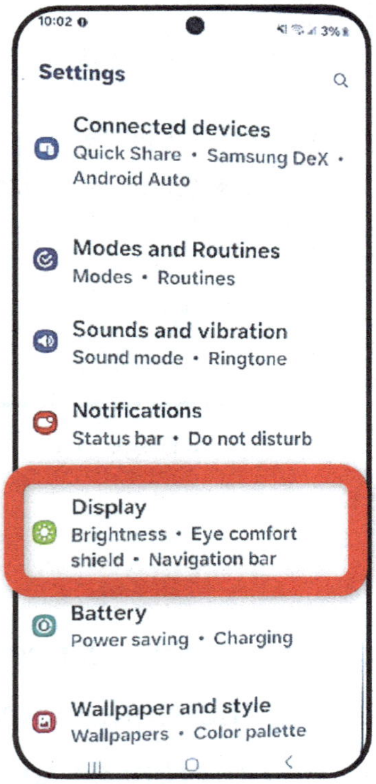

Image 9.3

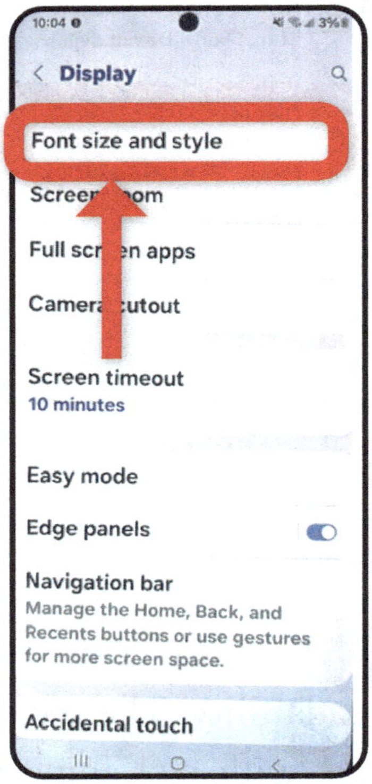

Image 9.4

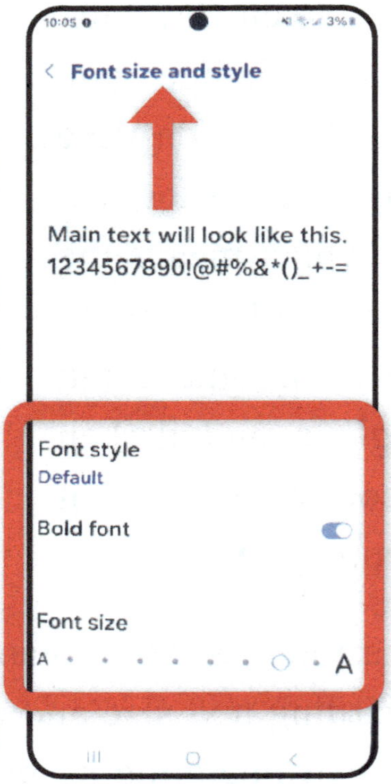

Image 9.5

Make the font **BOLD** for easier reading and use the slider at the bottom, where it says Font size, and adjust the size of the font until you are comfortable. For those of you with more severe vision issues, there are more font adjustments available in Accessibility. You will see that later on in this chapter.

When you're done, just **TAP ON THE BACK ARROW** at the top left of the page to go back to the previous page. (red arrow Image 9.5) Or, if you are done with the whole thing, GO HOME by swiping up or tapping on the home button.

ANDROID SCREEN TIMEOUT

ANDROID SCREEN TIMEOUT
SETTINGS > DISPLAY > SCREEN TIMEOUT

One of the biggest annoyances is when the screen on your phone darkens and you have to put your password in again. This feature is called **Screen Timeout** in Androids and can be set from thirty seconds to ten minutes. (Images 9.6 & 7) That means the screen will stay on for the chosen amount of time. By choosing ten minutes, there will be a small lessening of battery life because the screen uses a lot of battery power. That is a small price to pay for not having to constantly input your password because the screen went black.

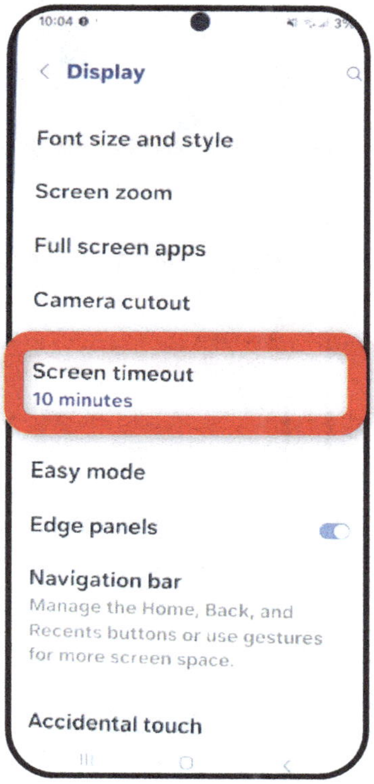

Image 9.6

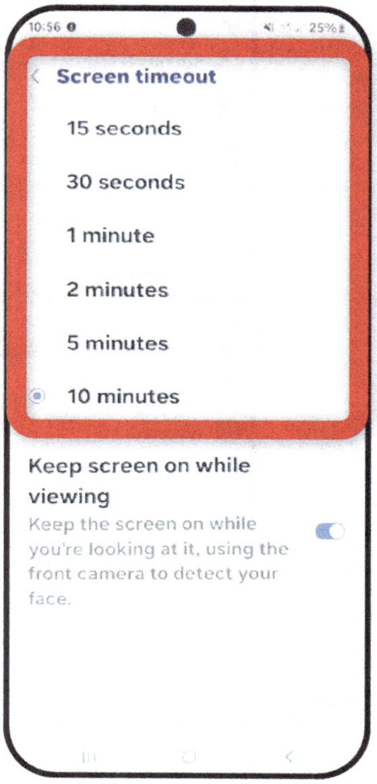

Image 9.7

iPHONE DISPLAY SETTINGS

SETTINGS > DISPLAY & BRIGHTNESS

Images 9.8 and 9.9 illustrate how to make your iPhone brighter or darker. Go to **Display and Brightness** (Image 9.8) and play with light and dark screens to determine which you prefer.

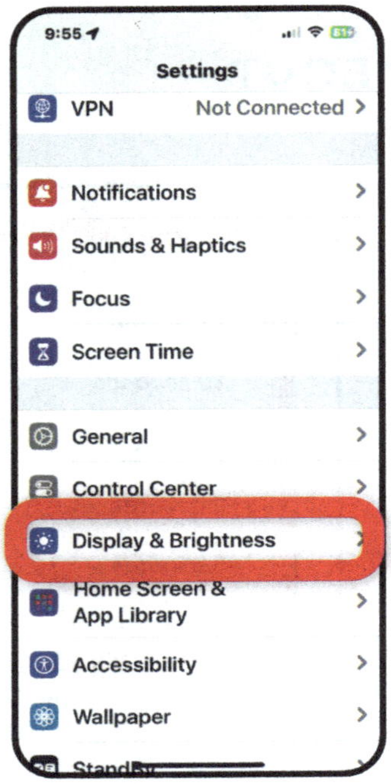

Image 9.8

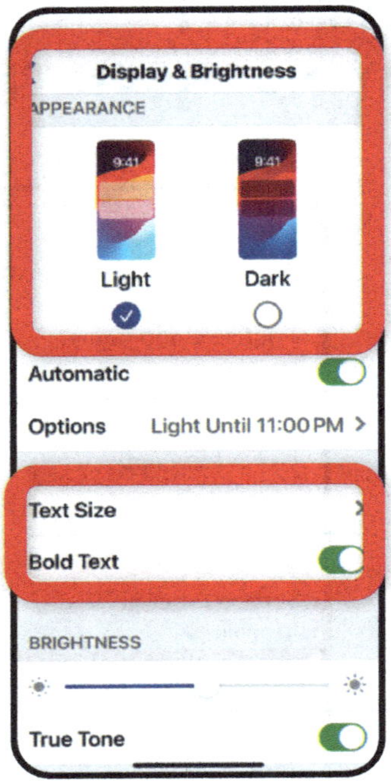

Image 9.9

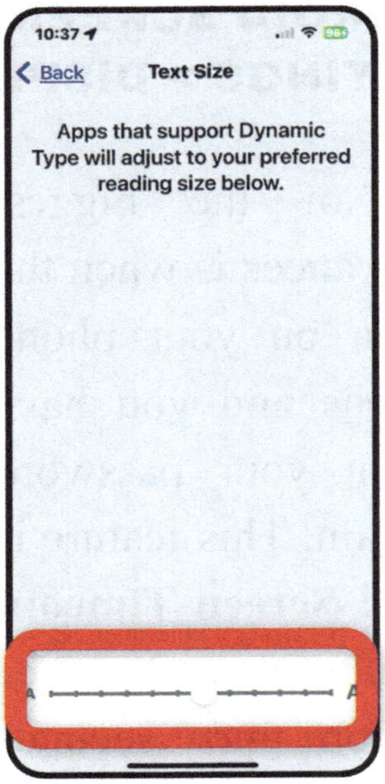

Image 9.10

iPhone Text (Font) Size

If you look a teeny bit farther down, you'll see **Text Size.** (Image 9.9) To make the font larger, **TAP TEXT SIZE**. (You always know there is more to a setting when you see the right-facing arrow.) The screen will change, and you are able to move the slider to larger or smaller fonts. Note that this will only apply to certain apps on the phone. (Image 9.10)

It's always good to toggle to **BOLD** as the increased contrast makes seeing what's on the phone much easier.

iPHONE AUTO-LOCK

SETTINGS > DISPLAY & BRIGHTNESS > AUTO-LOCK

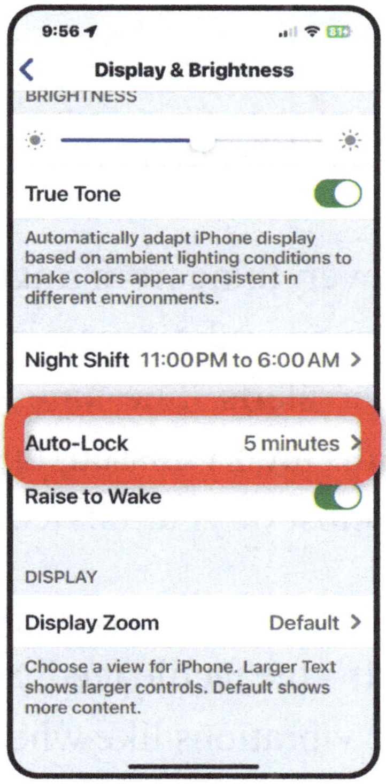

Image 9.11

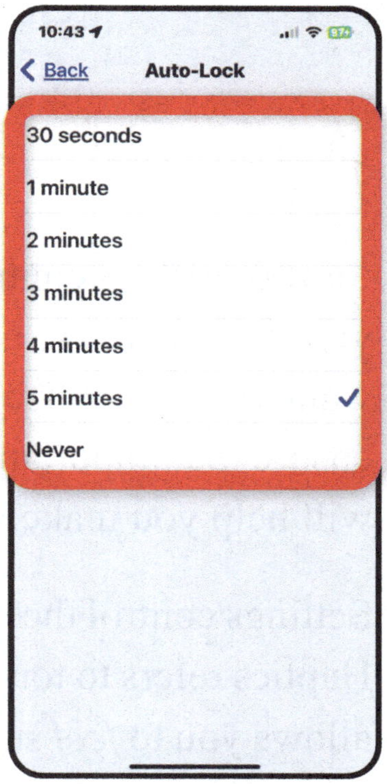

Image 9.12

One of the biggest annoyances is when the screen on your phone darkens, and you have to put your password in again. This feature is called **Auto-Lock** and can be set from thirty seconds to ten minutes. That means the screen will stay on for the chosen amount of time. (See Images 9.11, 12.) By choosing five minutes, there will be a small lessening of battery life because the screen uses a lot of battery power. That is a small price to pay for not having to constantly input your password because the screen went black.

My phone is set to five minutes. I do set it to *Never* if I am doing something and do not want the phone to shut itself off. Typically, once done, I will reset to five minutes.

In Summary

I've only shown you a few of the display settings available to you. I encourage you to explore on your own. Tap on them all! Then use the < to go back. Tap on another setting. Use the < to go back. Get used to that. Explore and go back. Maybe even change a setting or two. Relax and enjoy the control you are beginning to master over your device.

Android & iPhone Sound Settings

Sound settings control everything from ringtone volume to silent mode, vibration patterns, and even audio accessibility options. Whether you want to personalize your alerts, fine-tune your music experience, or ensure that important calls aren't missed, understanding sound settings will help you make the most of your device.

Settings control the specific **sounds and haptics.** What? Haptics? Huh? Haptics refers to touch. It's the tactile feedback the device produces that allows you to *feel* subtle vibrations like when you type on the keyboard or toggle something on or off. Let's explore how to adjust, customize, and optimize your iPhone's sound experience.

ANDROID SOUND SETTINGS

SETTINGS > SOUNDS

There are many sound settings from ringtone sounds to notification sounds, to system volume and phone ring volume, to vibrate or not to vibrate… These are some of the choices you have regarding the noises your phone makes. Think of it like adjusting the volume and ring style on your old telephone…but more.

Smartphones are highly customizable. This is a good thing. You can change the ringtone for calls and notification sounds by tapping on **Notification sound**. Make sure the sound you choose is loud enough that you hear it!

ANDROID SETTINGS > SOUNDS AND VIBRATION > NOTIFICATION SOUNDS

Androids have one *system notification sound*, so you cannot distinguish between text messages, WhatsApp, or voicemail, or any other app. These sounds are all the same. When you tap on Notification sound, you will see a large selection of ringtones. (Images 9.14 and 9.15) Listen to them and choose

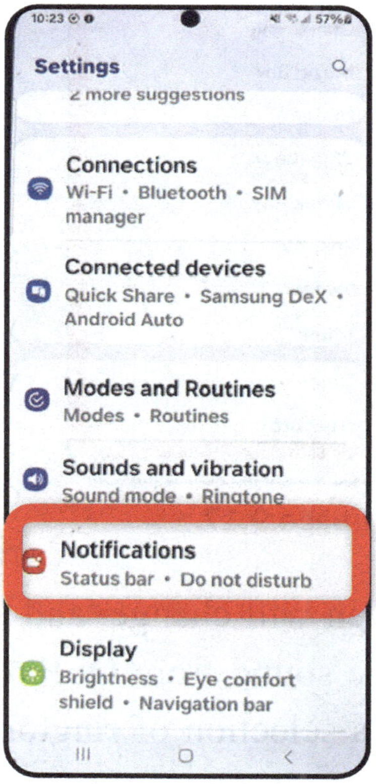

Image 9.13

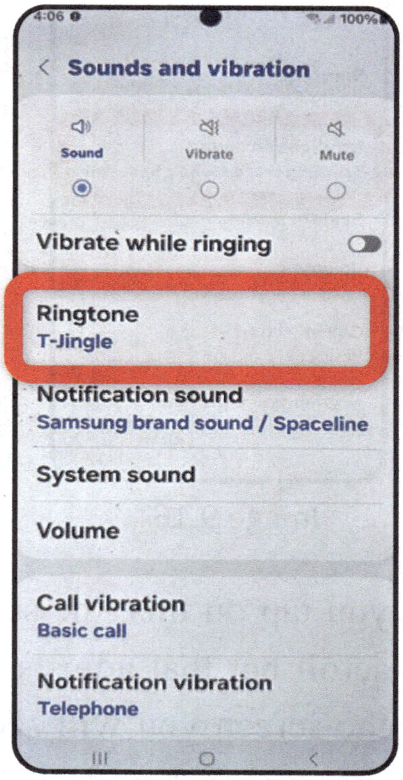

Image 9.14

one that is loud enough to hear. Now you will know that particular sound is some kind of notification. Notice that you can select to have sound and/or vibration or mute all sounds from this screen.

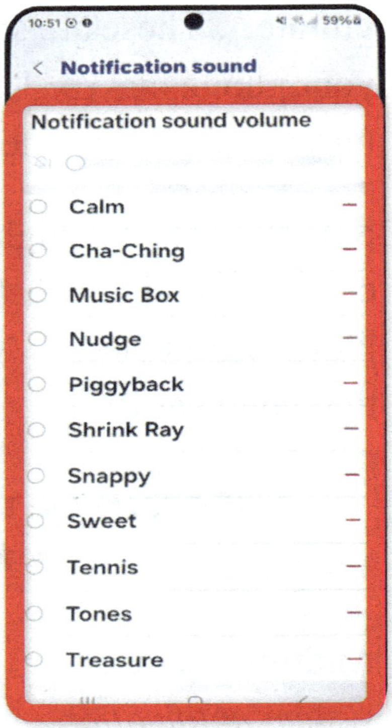

Image 9.15

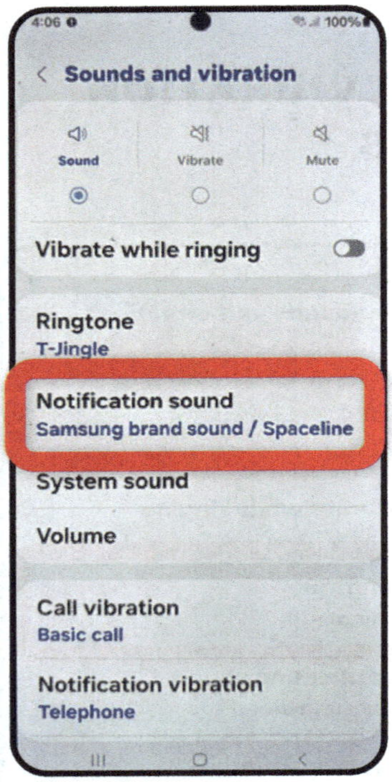

Image 9.16

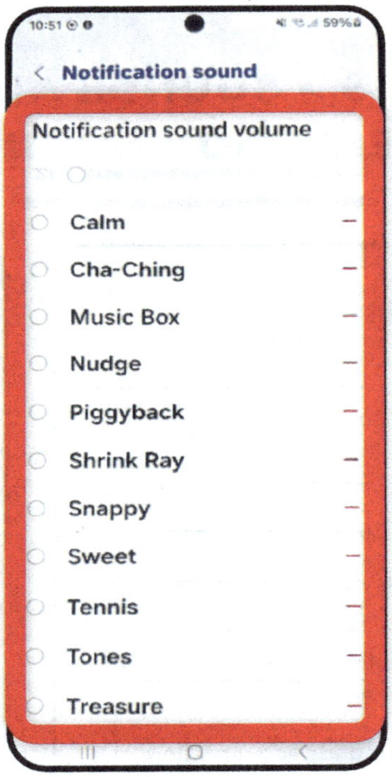

Image 9.17

Moving down the page, you will see **Sounds and vibration**. (Image 9.16) This is the sound your device makes when you receive a phone call. When you tap on this, the screen will change, and you will see a horizontal scroll bar that adjusts the sound from OFF to loudest. Looking down the screen you will see a selection of ringtones. (Image 9.17) Tap on any one of them to listen to it. Once you've made your selection, you can tap on the back arrow at the top left of the screen to go back to the main *Sounds and vibration* screen. Once again, make sure the sound you pick is loud enough that you will hear it.

ANDROID SETTINGS > SOUNDS AND VIBRATION > SYSTEM SOUND

In the pictures below you will see the *System sounds & vibration* settings page. Tap on *Sounds and vibration.* (Image 9.18) The screen will change (Image 9.19) and you will see an overview of the sound settings available. (Image 9.20)

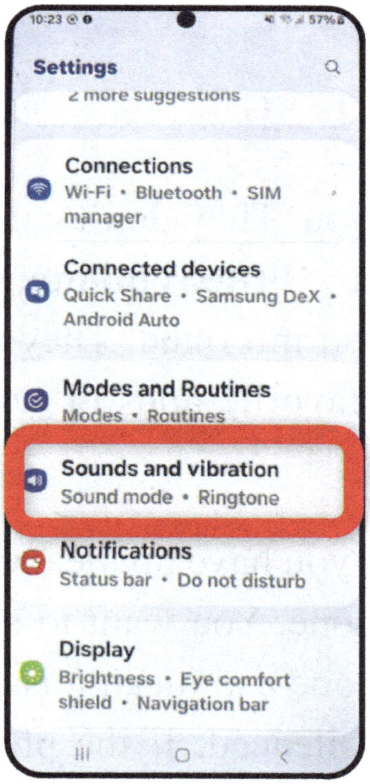

Image 9.18

Image 9.19

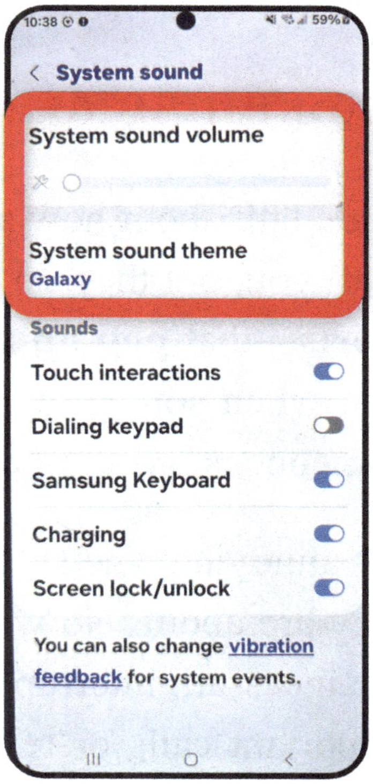

Image 9.20

In the system sound settings, you'll see the horizontal scroll bar for adjusting the sound (Image 9.20), plus you can choose what actions will be confirmed with an audible tone or sound. You can set it so that when you type, the keyboard will make a sound. You can choose to hear a sound when you connect your phone to a charger, or a sound when you lock or unlock your screen. You can choose to hear a sound as you *dial* (i.e., press) a phone number on the keypad. Once done with these settings, you can once again tap on the back arrow to go back to the *Sounds and vibration* page, or you can tap on the home button to leave these settings completely.

ANDROID/iPHONE NOTIFICATION SETTINGS

Let's talk about how apps stay in contact with you. They don't call or mail you, but they do bing, bong, and badge you…**little reminders—alerts**—that **pop up on your screen** to keep you informed. They tell you when something happens in one of your favorite apps or when someone is trying to reach you.

It's annoying when the phone makes noises, and you have no idea what they are about. No wonder you silence your phone. You want to stop the incessant interruptions. But silencing the phone can mean missing important calls or texts because everything is silenced. If the phone didn't ring, how would you know someone was calling you? The phone ringing is a sound notification. You can customize or turn these sounds off if they become overwhelming.

On the positive side, notifications can keep you on track. Voicemail notifications are critical. After all, it's our old answering machine, except it no longer takes up space. I absolutely rely on badges to know when I've got a new voicemail or text. Often, it's the only way I know that something new came in. Notifications can be extremely useful when you give permission to only certain apps like text messages, WhatsApp, and Facebook Messenger.

Every app wants you to allow them to send notifications. They hope to hook you in and engage more. Maybe you want that, maybe you don't. You get to choose. Just know that new phones have many apps that, by default, are set to send sounds, banners, and/or badges.

Sounds

The ringtones and bells that alert us to calls, texts, emails, and more are highly customizable. You can have unique ringtones for your spouse, kids, and friends or one tone for everyone. Make sure to pick a tone that is loud so you can hear it. Some of the ringtones are soft, even at high volume.

Banners

A banner is a quick message that appears at the top of the screen for a few seconds, then disappears. You can tap on it to open the app or swipe it away if you're not interested. Banners can be very distracting when you are reading or playing a game. But there may be some apps that you want to alert you due to their content.

Badges

The red circle with numbers is called a badge. It's a visual clue that stays until you open it up. Badges help me to know I've missed some calls or there are voice or text messages waiting for me. I don't always hear the phone, or it's silenced because I'm with a client. Those badges are good reminders for me to check what's going on.

ANDROID NOTIFICATIONS

Android Lock Screen Notifications

Even when your phone is locked, notifications can still show up on the screen so you can glance at them without unlocking the phone.

To access the **Notification Summary** screen on Androids, **use one finger to Swipe Down from the top of the page**. (Image 9.21) If you want more information on any of the notifications, just **TAP** and it will open to the specific information.

If you want to clear all the notifications, look for **CLEAR** near the bottom of the screen on the right and TAP on it. All the notifications will disappear.

Image 9.21

SETTINGS > SOUNDS > NOTIFICATIONS

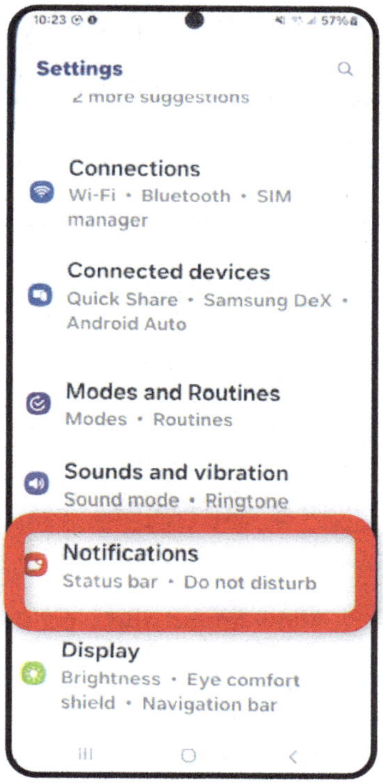

Image 9.22

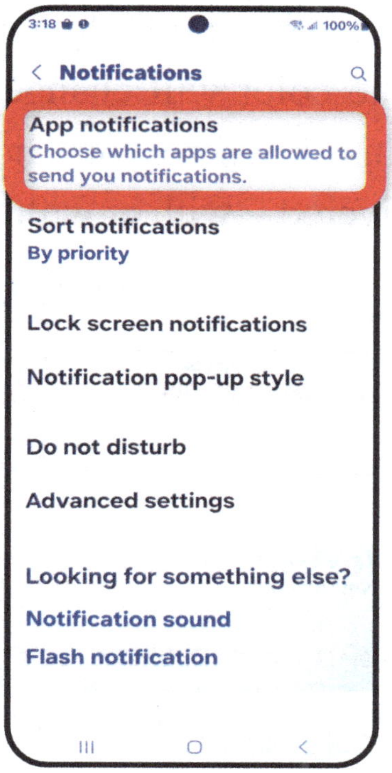

Image 9.23

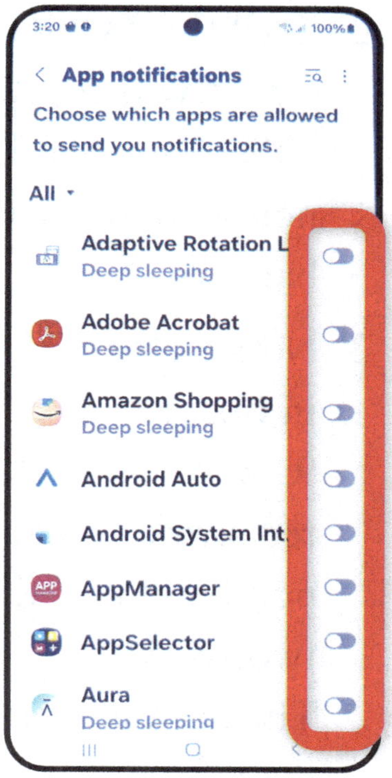

Image 9.24

1. Open Android **settings** and look for **notifications.** (Image 9.22) TAP on it. The screen will change. (Image 9.23)
2. Tap on **App notifications**, as shown in Image 9.23. The screen will change. (Image 9.24)
3. Now you see all the apps listed along with a toggle indicating their notification status (i.e., on or off). Scroll down until you find Facebook.

Notice on Image 9.25 that all the notifications are turned off, except for Facebook. If I want to change this, here are the steps:

1. Tap on Facebook. (Image 9.25) The screen will change. (Image 9.26)
2. **TAP the TOGGLE** to turn it off. (Image 9.26) If it's off and you tap, it will move, the color will change. and you've switched it either on or off. This is where you choose how individual app notifications are delivered—with or without sound, with or without banners.
3. Notice also in Image 9.26 the red arrow pointing to two boxes. The one on the left says **Lock screen allowed** and the other says **Badge allowed**. Tap to allow or disallow. (Remember, a badge is the red circle with a number in it.) You can have a badge and no banners. You can have only banners or only sounds. I typically choose badges and banners, with sounds only for apps I really need.

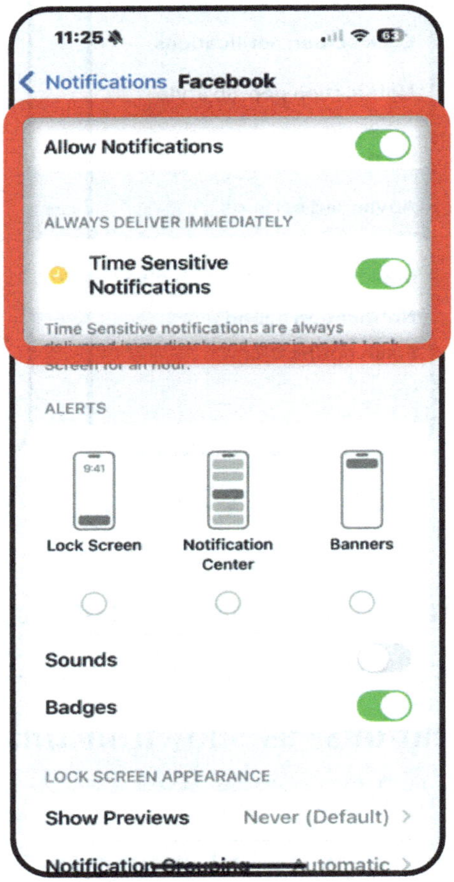

Image 9.25

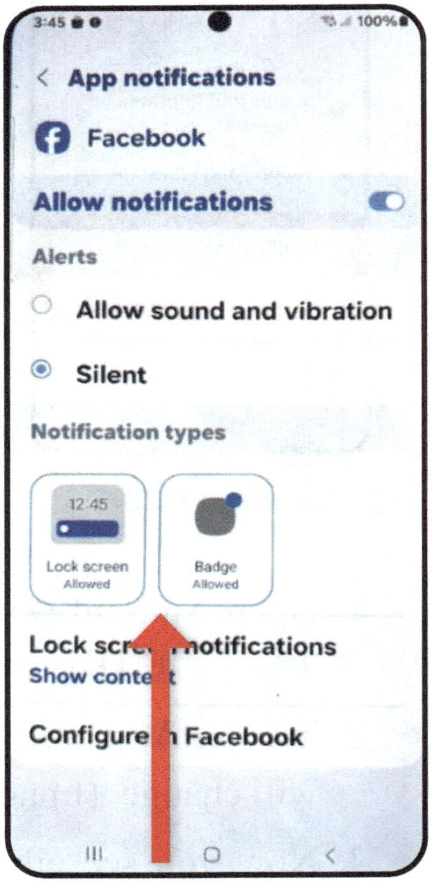

Image 9.26

Go through every app and decide which ones get to notify you about recent activity and the ways in which they are allowed to do it—sounds, badges, or banners. For example, I allow phone, voicemail, messages (texts), Messenger, and WhatsApp to notify me with sounds. I have badges on ten apps out of more than three hundred. I simply do not need to be interrupted. If I want to know about any recent activity, I can go to the app and look for myself. One of the nice things about these devices is that they are so customizable. The point is that you get to choose.

Once you're done, you can **tap the back arrow** at the very top left of the screen. This will return you to the app notifications screen (Image 9.26), where you can choose a different app to modify. (See Image 9.24)

Image 9.26a

Of course, if you've had enough, you can swipe up or tap the home button and be done.

On the main notification screen (accessed by swiping down from the top of the screen), you can clear all the notifications. Look for **CLEAR** near the bottom of the screen on the right (Image 9.26a) Tap on it and all notifications will be dismissed.

iPhone Notifications

iPhone Lockscreen notifications

SETTINGS > NOTIFICATIONS

Even when your phone is locked, notifications can still show up on the screen so you can glance at them without unlocking the phone.

To access the **Notification Summary** screen on your iPhone, **use one finger to Swipe Down from the very top of the page**. (Image 9.27) If you want more information on any of the notifications, just **TAP** and it will open to the specific details. **SWIPE LEFT** to delete individual notifications or tap on the **X** at the top right. The **X** will change to the word **CLEAR**. (Image 9.28) Tap on it to delete all current notifications.

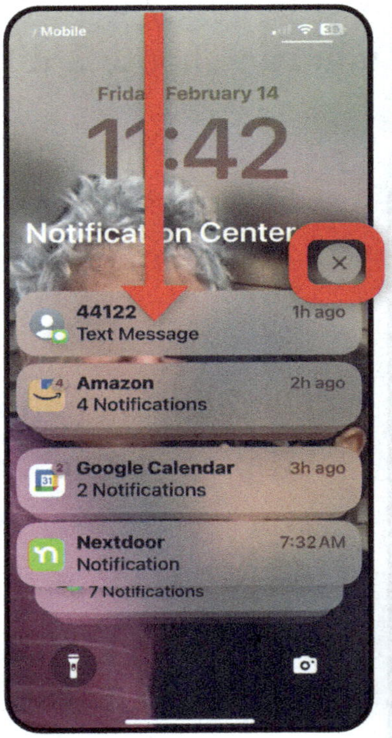

Image 9.27

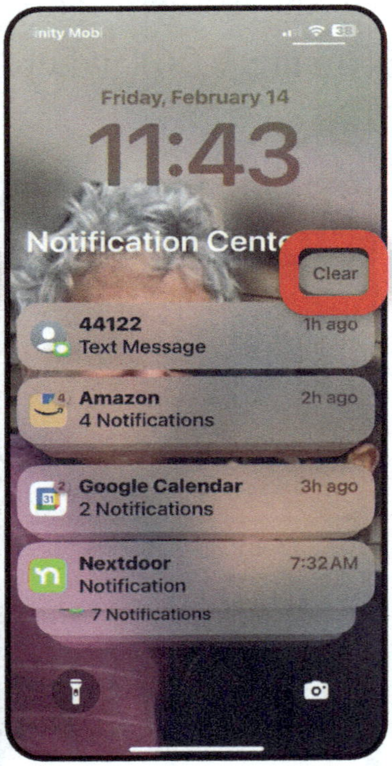

Image 9.28

iPHONE NOTIFICATIONS SETTINGS ARE EASY TO FIND AND CUSTOMIZE.

Open settings and tap on Notifications. The screen will change, and you will see a variety of choices. (Image 9.30) Look at my choices. I like my notifications stacked. You might want a different view. Click and see how it looks. You can always go back and make a different choice by going to Settings > Notifications.

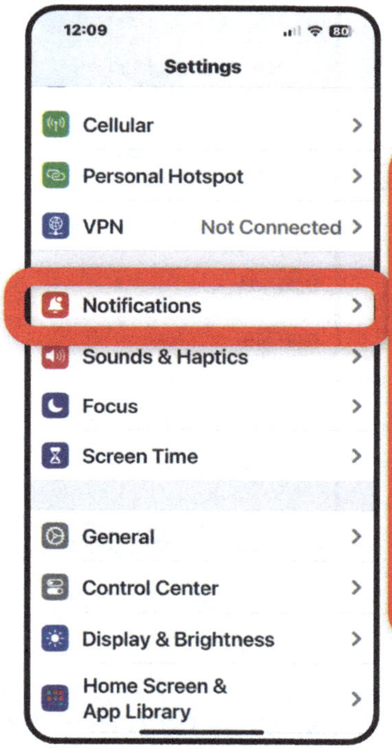

Image 9.29

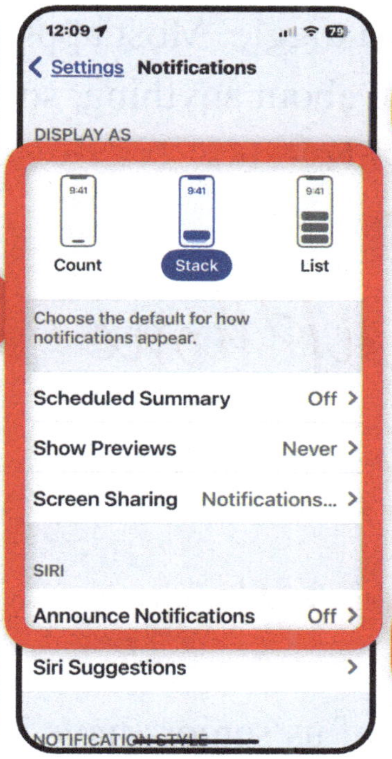

Image 9.30

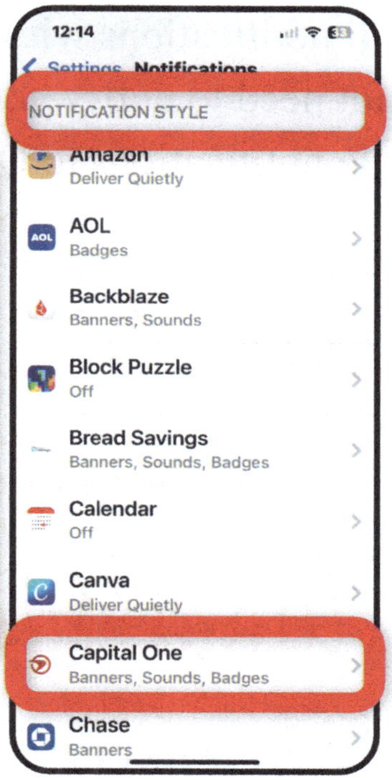

Image 9.31

In order to adjust the notification settings for all of your apps, keep scrolling down to **Notification Styles** (Image 9.31) (It's a pale gray, so look for it.) I don't like too many interruptions on my phone, so I only allow a few apps to notify me. Some have a banner and/or a sound and/or a badge. I mostly choose only badges so, at a glance, I can see if there is anything new that requires my attention.

In the case of Capital One bank above, you will see that I have selected a temporary banner (slides on and off the screen at the top), badges, but no sounds. In Image 9.32, you can see that there is an option to turn off all notifications with a toggle. Most apps do not need to notify you about anything, so toggle notifications to OFF.

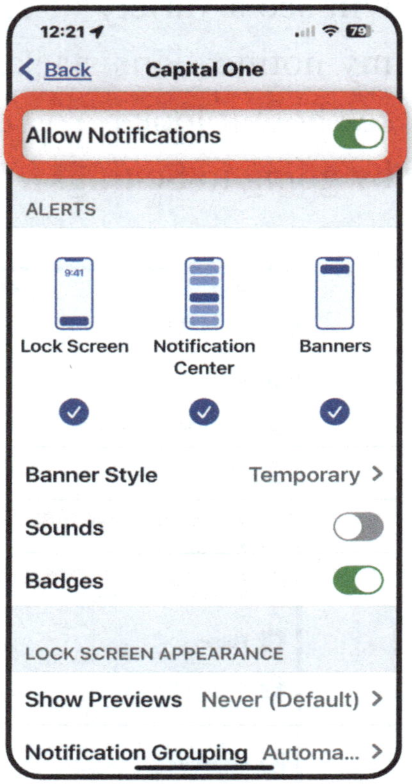

Image 9.32

Android & iPhone Accessibility Settings Overview

The reality is that many of us seniors have issues with hearing, vision, and tremors. Each of these can make using a smartphone more difficult. The manufacturers are well aware of this and allow you to make changes to your phone that make it much more user-friendly. These are called **Accessibility settings**, making the phone more accessible to people with disabilities. Both Android and iPhone operating systems offer accessibility settings.

In this chapter, I have selected a few of the most commonly needed accessibility settings To detail each and every setting would be a book on its own. But there is a shortcut to finding every single setting. Use your voice! "OK Google or Hey Siri, Open Vision Enhancements settings" or "Hey Siri or OK Google, open hearing aid support " This will get you quickly to the page so you can toggle on or off the settings you prefer

ANDROID ACCESSIBILITY SETTINGS

SETTINGS > ACCESSIBILITY

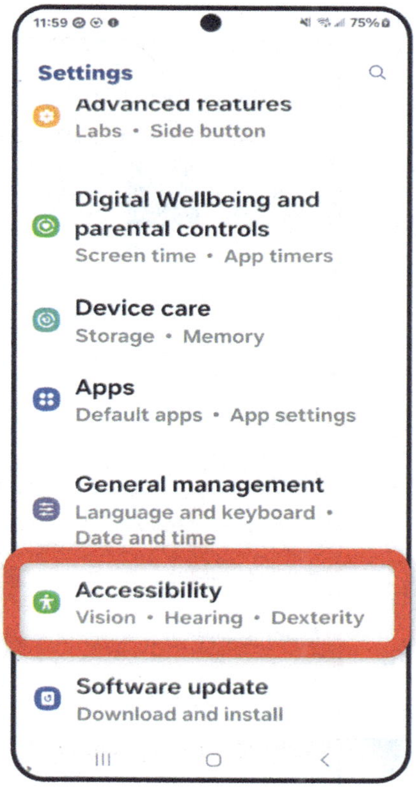

Image 9.33

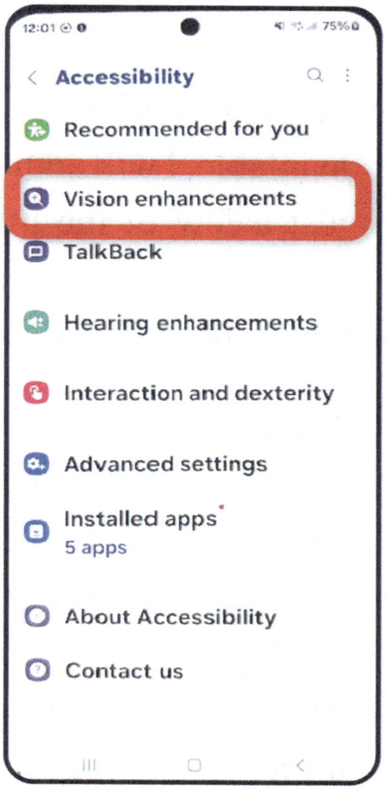

Image 9.34

Once you get to Accessibility (Image 9.33) you will need to scroll down. Once there, tap on it and the screen will change (Image 9.34) Now you will see all the Accessibility options. Scroll through the whole page in order to see all the choices. I am going to highlight some of the more useful features.

Android Vision Enhancements

SETTINGS > ACCESSIBILITY > VISION ENHANCEMENTS

There are many ways to adjust an Android to address your specific vision requirements. From increasing contrast to magnification, font adjustments, spoken assistance (the phone reads the screen to you), there are myriad adjustments to make.

Due to the sheer number of adjustments available, I will address just a few of the most important here. Let's start with contrast.

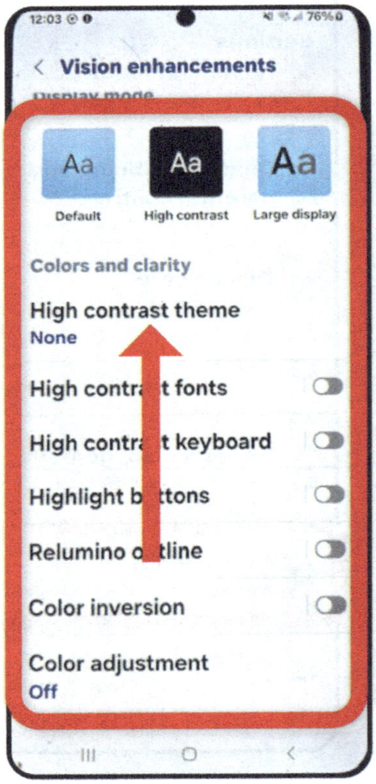

Image 9.35

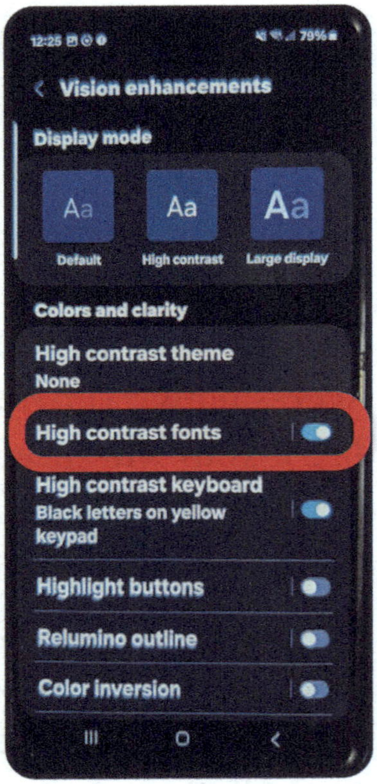

Image 9.36

Notice that when you choose a high-contrast screen, the result is a dark background with white lettering, much easier for some people to read. (Image 9.36) Notice that the toggle for high-contrast fonts has been turned on. If you want to revert to the standard contrast screen, simply toggle off that button.

Android Magnification

SETTINGS > ACCESSIBILITY > VISION ENHANCEMENTS > MAGNIFICATION

This feature is like a magnifying glass, allowing you to zoom in on objects and text using the device camera. Magnification turns screen zoom on or off.

While zoomed in you can: Pinch to adjust or swipe with two fingers to scroll. When you tap on magnification, the screen will change (Images 9.37, 38), and you will have options as to how you want this to work. If you want to install the magnification shortcut, toggle that switch on, and the screen will change. You will see four options as to how to turn this feature on while using the phone. Your options are:

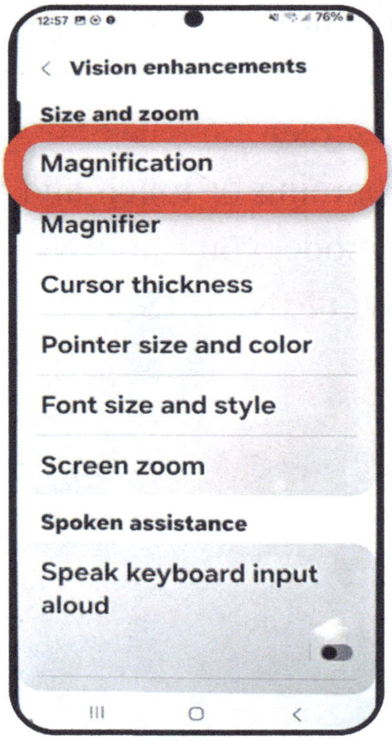

Image 9.37

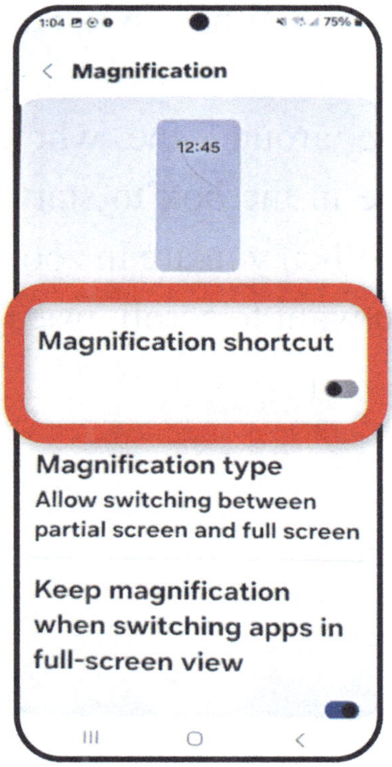

Image 9.38

1. Tap the Accessibility button with the image of a little person. (Image 9.39)
2. Press the side and volume up buttons.
3. Press and hold volume up and down buttons for three seconds.
4. Triple-tap the screen.

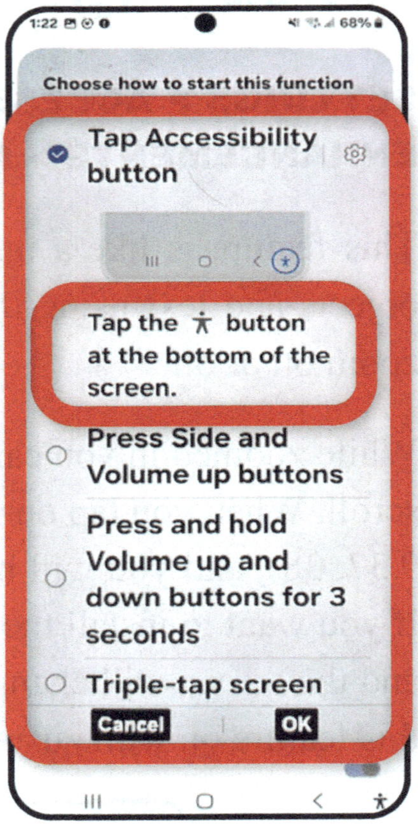

Image 9.39

You can choose any of these ways to access magnification. I think it's easiest to tap the Accessibility button. The screen will change, and you will see an icon that looks like a little man. If you made changes and want to keep them, tap OK. If you're there just to look and not make any changes, tap cancel to exit. When in magnification mode, you'll see either a zoomed-in area or an outline around the whole screen. Tap anywhere in the box to start zooming or touch and hold to zoom temporarily. When you are in zoom mode, you can PINCH to adjust the image. If you want to scroll, use TWO FINGERS.

ANDROID MAGNIFIER

SETTINGS > ACCESSIBILITY > VISION ENHANCEMENTS > MAGNIFIER

The Magnifier is a tool that opens the camera and allows real-time ability to adjust brightness and contrast and even apply color filters, making it easier to see details. **Tapping on the little magnifier man** (Image 9.41 and 9.43) **creates a screen change.** Now you are asked to use the **Magnifier** or **Magnification.**

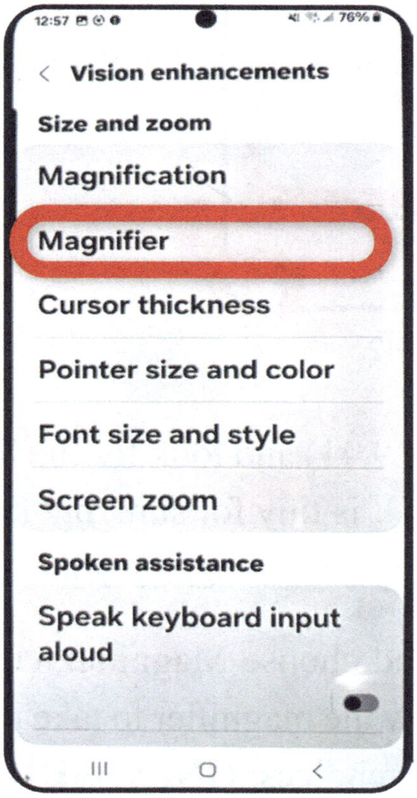

Image 9.40

Image 9.41

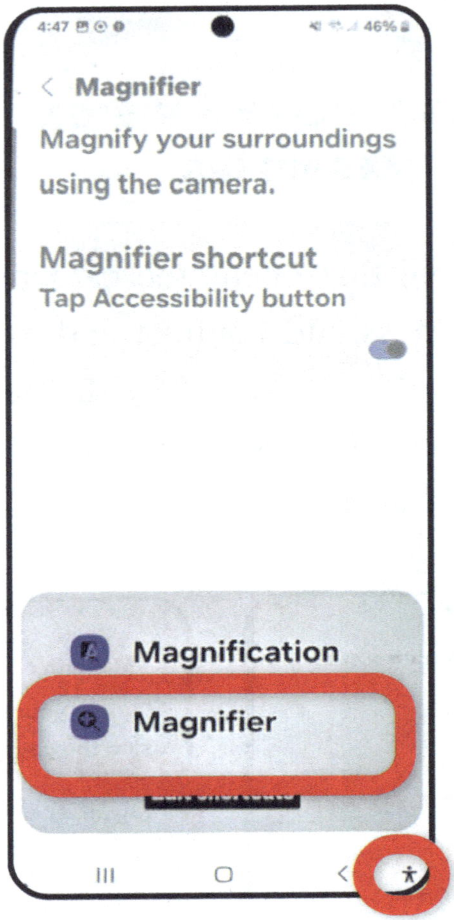

Image 9.42

TAP the magnifier shortcut (Image 9.41) and look for the little person at the very lower right of the screen. It is tiny for sure, but knowing it's there will be very helpful when you want to magnify your screen.

Tap the person at the lower right, and choose Magnifier. (Image 9.42) You will be asked if you want to allow the magnifier to take pictures and record video, and you are given three choices: **ONLY WHILE USING THE APP, ONLY THIS TIME, and DON'T ALLOW**. Typically, I allow *only while using the app.* That is my default response for all app permissions.

Within the Magnifier is a zoom feature. (See Image 9.44.) To make what you're looking at larger, just slide your finger to the right on the line provided.

You can take a picture and magnify it much larger.

Image 9.43

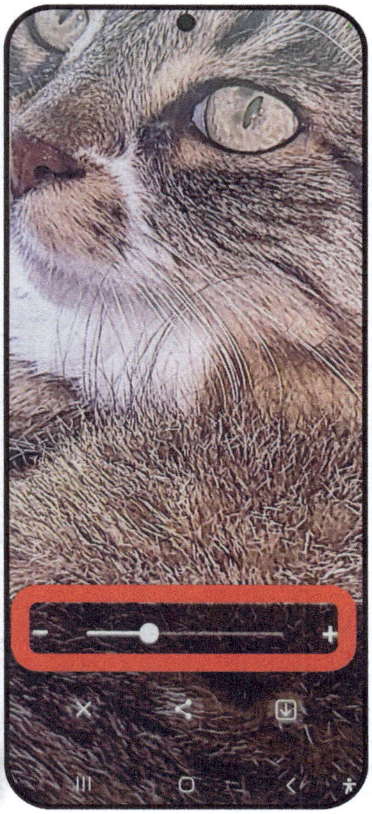

Image 9.44

You will see in these next images what the Magnifier can do. Here is a photo of our cat, Fibonacci, enjoying a sunny window (Image 9.43) and a close-up of her in Image 9.44. Use the Magnifier slide to reduce or enlarge the image. You will be able to make it quite a bit larger, making text and photo details much easier to read/see.

ANDROID HEARING ENHANCEMENTS

SETTINGS > ACCESSIBILITY > HEARING ENHANCEMENTS

Depending upon your hearing loss, you may want to enable transcriptions, live captions, or hearing aid support on your phone.

ANDROID LIVE TRANSCRIBE

SETTINGS > ACCESSIBILITY > HEARING ENHANCEMENTS > LIVE TRANSCRIBE

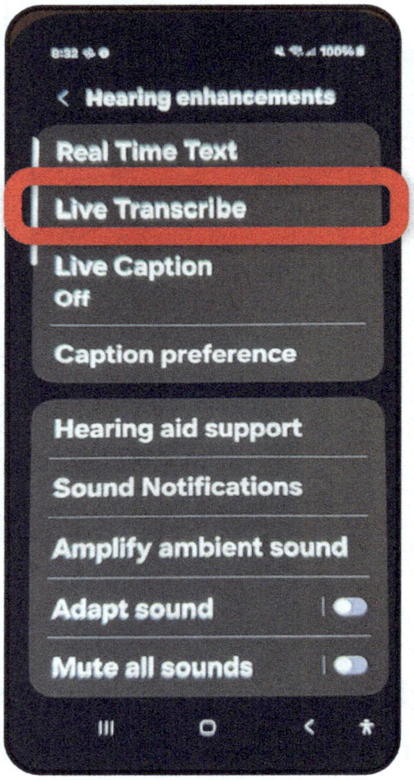

Image 9.45

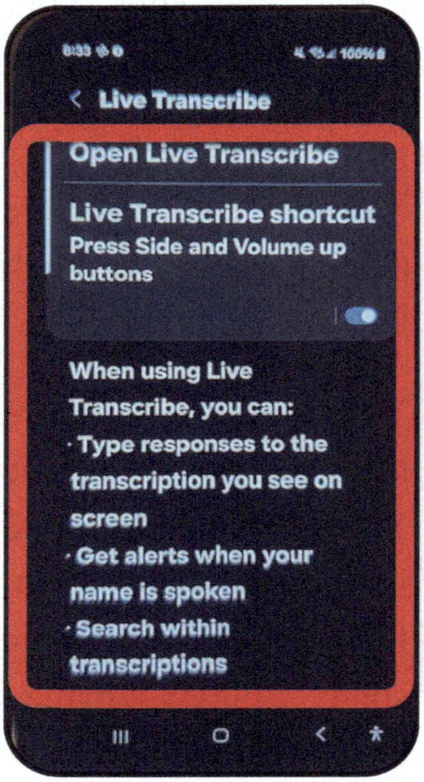

Image 9.46

Live Transcribe is like having a helper who writes down what people are saying in real time. When someone speaks, their words appear on the screen, just like on the TV when you have captioning turned on. It comes on most Androids, but if your device doesn't have it, you can download it from the Google Play Store.

It's easy to use. Once the app is opened, it will start converting speech into text.

SETTINGS > ACCESSIBILITY > HEARING ENHANCEMENTS > LIVE CAPTION

Just like on TV you can have real-time captioning (i.e., subtitles) for videos and audio playing on your phone.

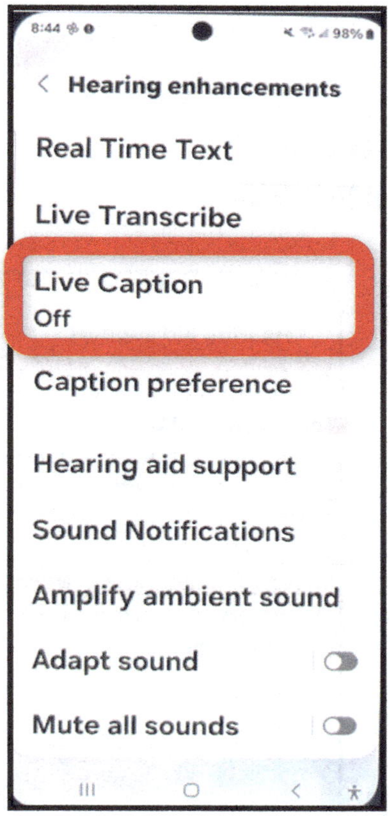

Image 9.47

Image 9.48

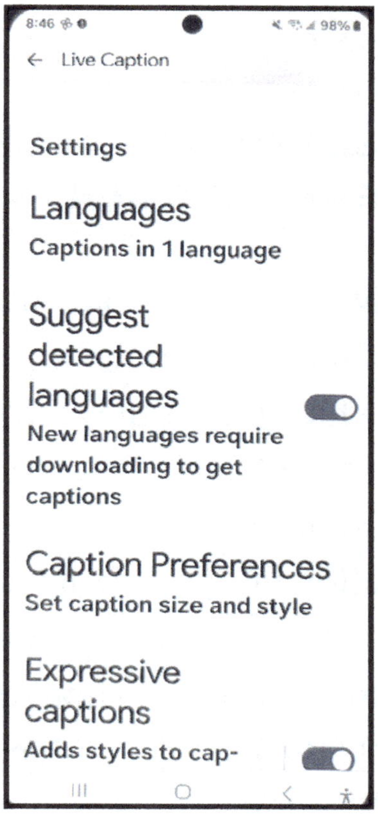

Image 9.49

How to Use Live Caption

Open settings and search for Hearing Enhancements (Image 9.47), then Live Caption.Follow the prompts and toggle it on. (Image 9.48) There will be many settings you can adjust. Just scroll down the page to view the choices.

Once toggled on, Live Caption will automatically appear when your phone plays a sound. So now, when you watch a video, listen to a podcast, or get a call, your phone will show subtitles automatically.

To turn it off, press **VOLUME BUTTON and tap the Live Caption icon** within the volume bar.

ANDROID HEARING AID SUPPORT

SETTINGS > ACCESSIBILITY > HEARING ENHANCEMENTS > HEARING AID SUPPORT

Many hearing aids are Bluetooth compatible, which means they have an antenna that can connect to your phone, allowing you to make some basic adjustments to the volume. (Images 9.50 & 51) Many hearing aids also come with their own app that allows you to make adjustments to its products.

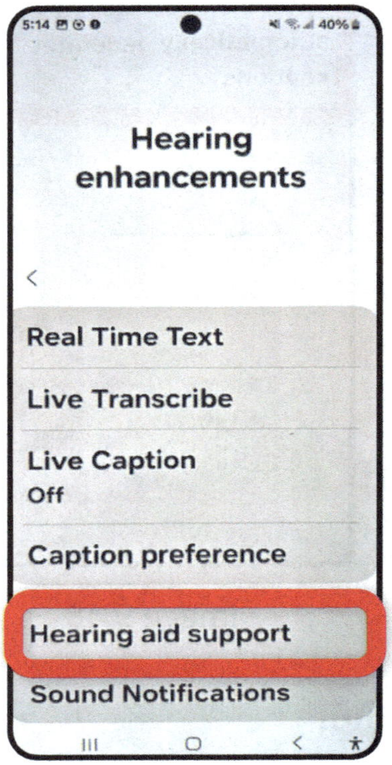

Image 9.50

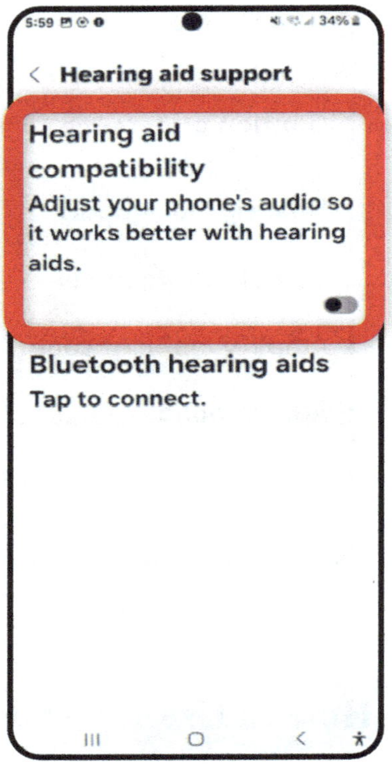

Image 9.51

When you get your hearing aids, the audiologist will help you connect them to your phone and show you how to work your particular brand with the phone.

ANDROID SOUND NOTIFICATION

SETTINGS > ACCESSIBILITY > HEARING ENHANCEMENTS > SOUND

Sound notifications help you know when certain sounds are made, such as a baby crying (for all of us babysitting grandparents) or the doorbell, sirens, alarm clocks, and the like.

To activate it, tap the toggle to on and the screen will change. (Image 9.52) Now you can decide how to access this feature.

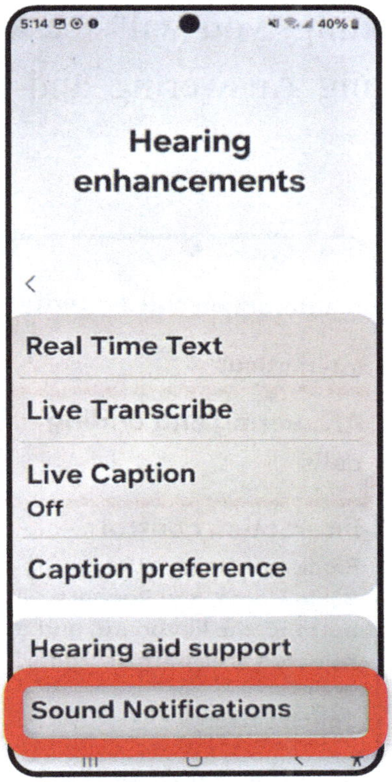

Image 9.52

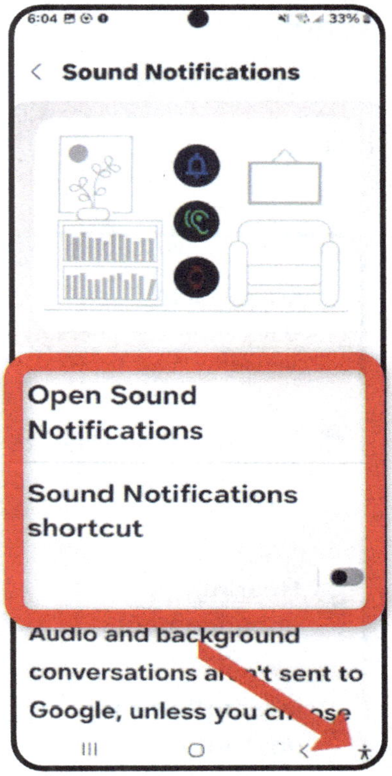

Image 9.53

Here's how it works. When the phone hears one of your selected sounds, it will send you a notification. (Image 9.53) It could be a vibration, a visual alert, or a message on the screen. Once again, you get to choose how to activate this feature. I like the idea of using the little man at the bottom as access to these various settings. Ultimately, it's a visual clue and easier to remember!

ANDROID INTERACTION AND DEXTERITY SETTINGS

SETTINGS > ACCESSIBILITY > INTERACTION AND DEXTERITY

When you open this setting, you will see a LOT of choices. In this section I will be detailing Answering and Ending Calls and Touch Settings.

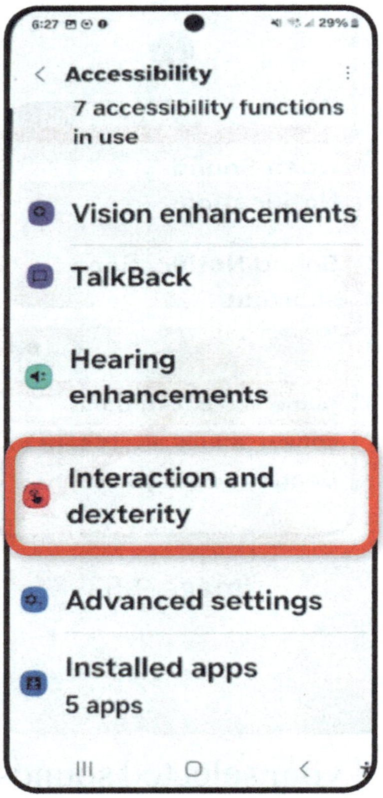

Image 9.54

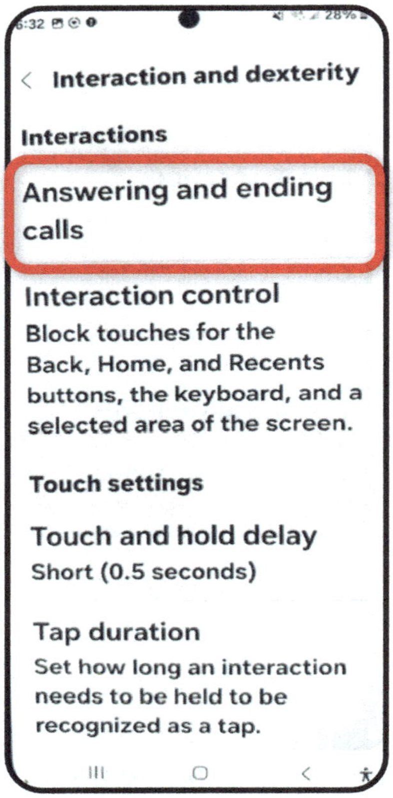

Image 9.55

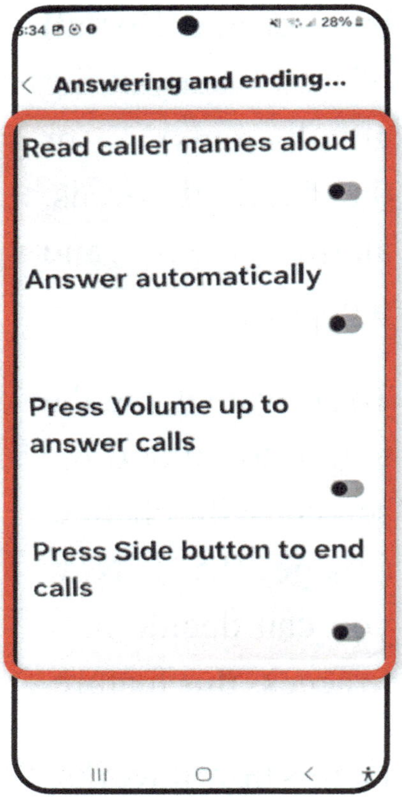

Image 9.56

ANDROID ANSWERING AND ENDING CALLS

You will notice that you have several options here. In Image 9.56 you see that you can have the caller's name read aloud as the phone rings. You can have the phone answer automatically. You can press the VOLUME UP button to answer calls, and/or you can press the side button to end calls. As you toggle each option on, the screen will change slightly, and you'll be able to read exactly what is next.

If you want privacy about who's calling you, you can set the phone to announce calls via Bluetooth, which means through your hearing aids.

If you toggle Answer Automatically, you will be given a choice as to how long the phone will ring before it's answered.

These settings are pretty straightforward. I don't think you'll have a problem figuring them out.

ANDROID TOUCH SETTINGS

Android Touch Settings: Settings > Accessibility > Interaction and dexterity > Touch settings

This is the section to pay attention to if you have any kind of tremor that causes you to have trouble communicating by tapping on the phone. Touch settings allow you to customize the sensitivity of the screen.

ANDROID TOUCH AND HOLD DELAY

SETTINGS > INTERACTION AND DEXTERITY > TOUCH AND HOLD DELAY

Touch and hold delay refers to how sensitive the device is to touch. If you have trouble tapping quickly, you can set the phone to recognize a slightly longer tap, up to four seconds.

This is a very important setting for people with tremors. It tells the device how long a tap needs to be held to be recognized as a tap. You have choices from very short to a custom setting.

Tap on **Touch and hold delay** (Image 9.57) and the screen will change. Now you can see the options. (Image 9.58) You may need to play with this a bit to find the setting that works best for your particular level of dexterity.

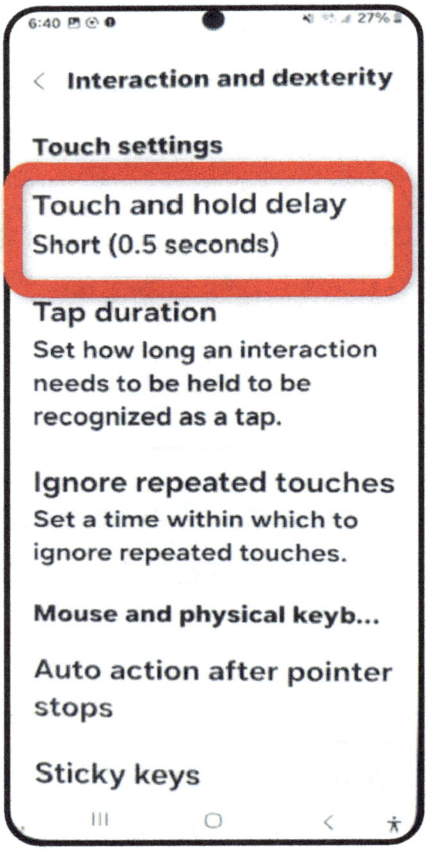

Image 9.57

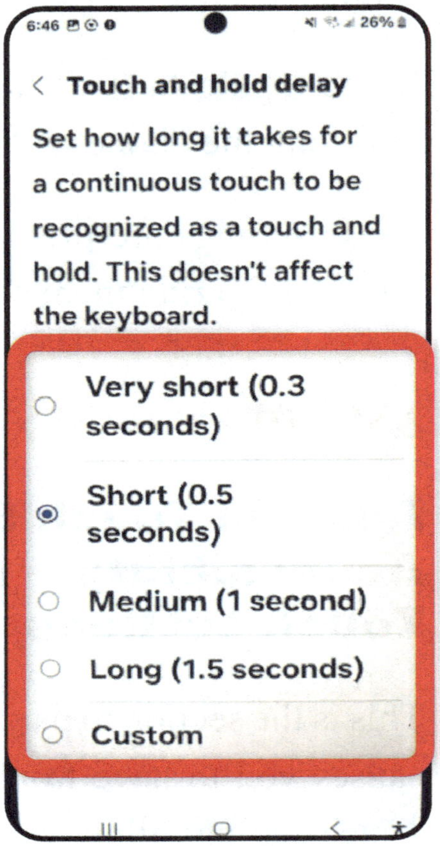

Image 9.58

If your phone seems to **react too fast,** and you are consistently accidentally **triggering different gestures**, adjusting the **Tap Duration** to be longer can make using your phone easier.

ANDROID TAP DURATION

SETTINGS > ACCESSIBILITY > INTERACTION AND DEXTERITY > TAP DURATION

When you **tap** on your Android phone's screen, the phone responds based on **how long** you keep your finger on it. This is called **Tap Duration**—and it affects what happens when you touch different things on your phone. (See Images 9.59 & 60) These are related to gestures as covered in Chapter 6.

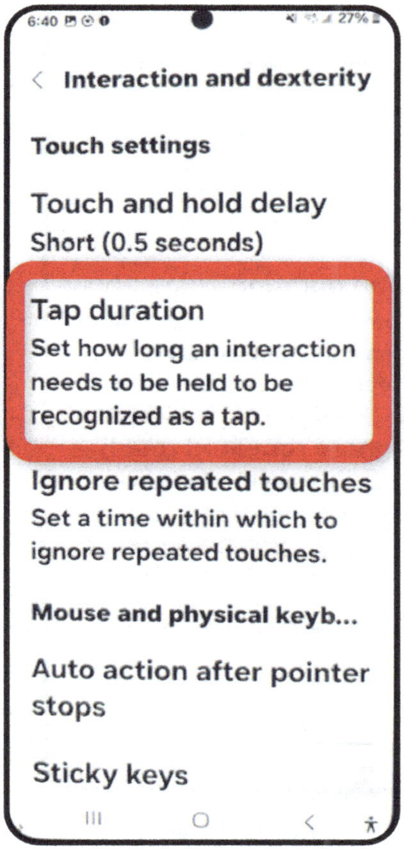

Image 9.59

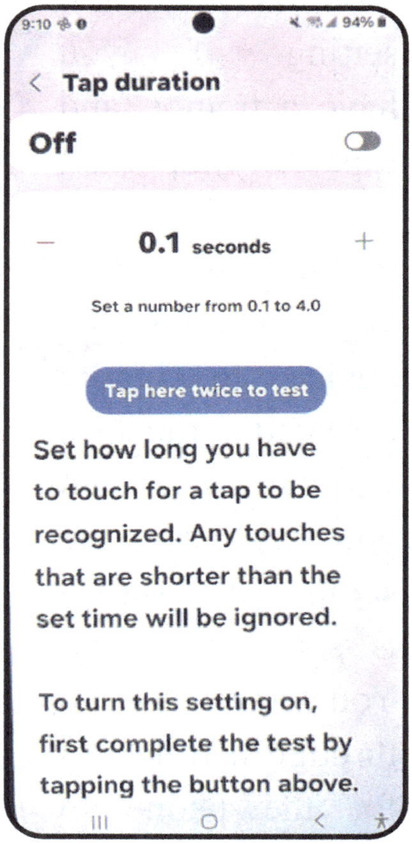

Image 9.60

If tapping is difficult, you can **change** the phone's settings so it **waits longer** before deciding if a tap was short or long. This is **Custom Tap Duration.**

Ignore Repeated Touches

SETTINGS > ACCESSIBILITY > INTERACTION AND DEXTERITY > IGNORE REPEATED TOUCHES

This is the best setting if you have a tremor, and especially important if you suffer with Parkinson's. Here you can set the device to ignore repeated touches. Just tap on it and you will see the settings. The screen is self-explanatory. You have to go through a little test for the phone to accommodate itself to you. Read the screen. I promise you will understand. The device will "read" how long you touch when you tap and will adjust itself to you. Just follow the prompts.

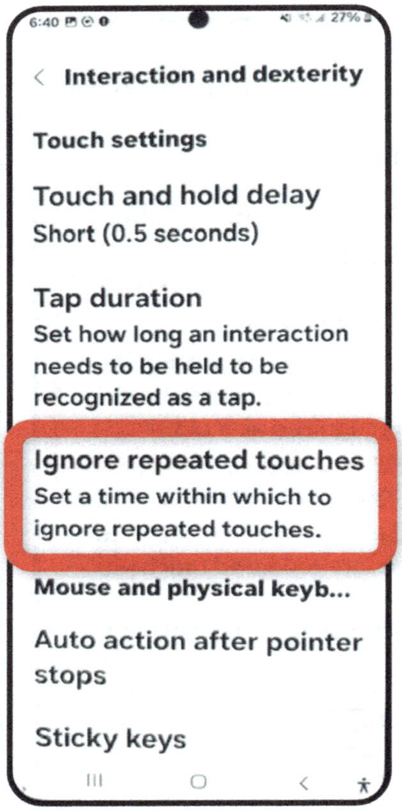

Image 9.61

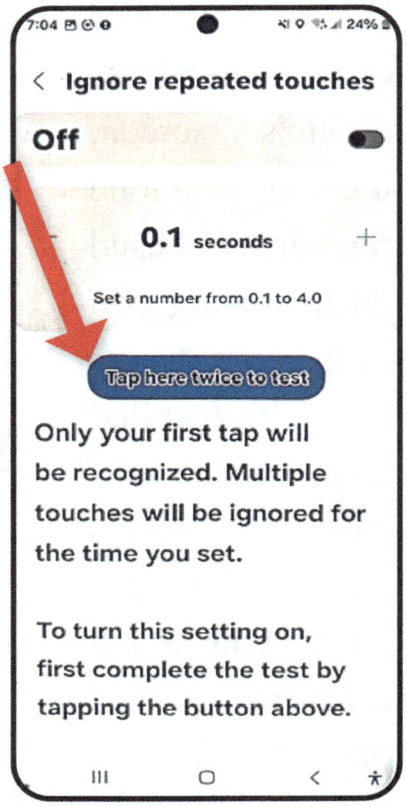

Image 9.62

There are more settings here to explore, but if I put them all in one book, it would be too heavy to pick up! Here I am showing you what I believe are the most important. But please explore all the settings in Accessibility. You will have a much better experience using the phone if you program it to accommodate your needs.

ANDROID QUICK SETTINGS SHORT SCREEN

ONE-FINGER PULL DOWN FROM THE CENTER

When you swipe down with ONE FINGER, you will see a **short screen**, which has some quick access settings at the very top of the page. (Image 9.63) There are just six round circles that are a shortcut to certain features, so this is an abbreviated, quick access with just six settings allowed.

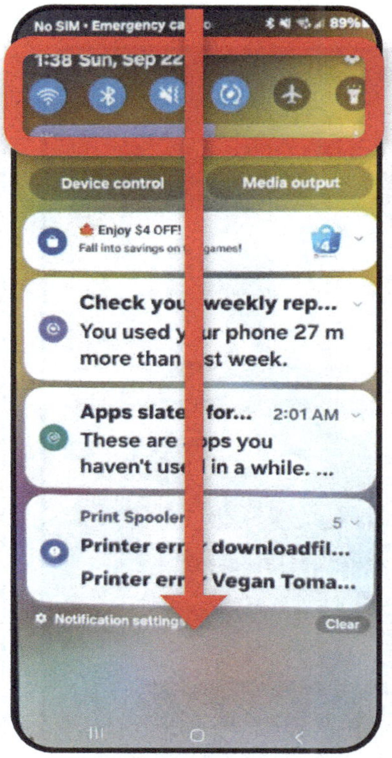

Image 9.63

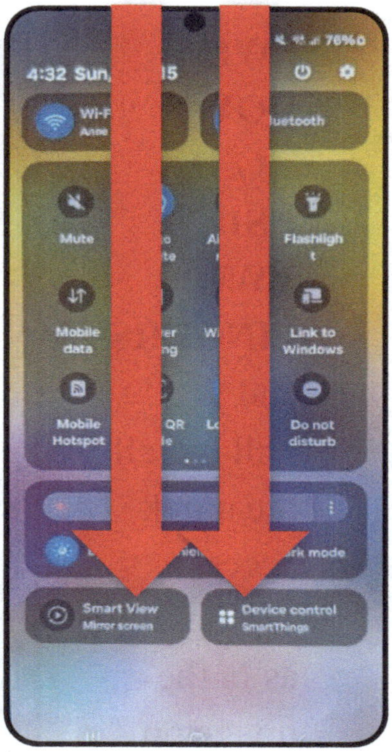

Image 9.64

TWO FINGERS to SWIPE DOWN from the CENTER of the screen from any app

Pulling down with two fingers from the top on Androids will open the full quick settings box. Whether on Android or Apple, quick access or control center allows you to customize the order and content of your quick access options. (Image 9.64)

EDIT Android Quick Access Settings:

SWIPE DOWN WITH ONE FINGER from the top. The screen changes and looks like the image on the left above.

1. **SWIPE DOWN AGAIN USING TWO FINGERS** and you will see all the quick access settings, as in the image on the right above.

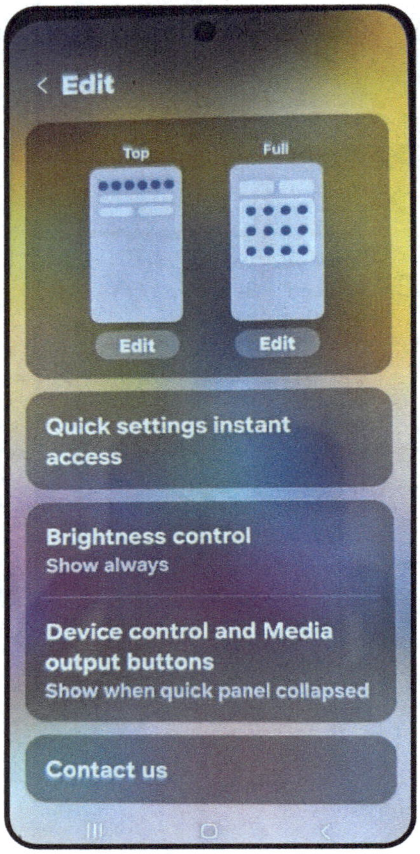

Image 9.65

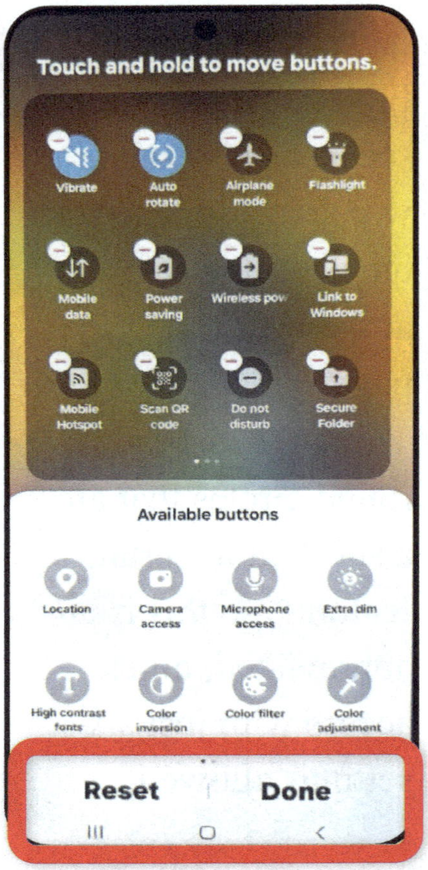

Image 9.66

2. **TAP ON THE "EDIT" BUTTON**—Typically it's a pencil.
3. **CHOOSE WHICH SCREEN TO EDIT** (Image 9.65) and the screen will change.

Notice that there are circles in the top area. Tap on the tiny **red minus sign** (Image 9.66) at the top left of each of these circles to remove that app from either quick access screen. (On some Androids, you can drag the apps out of the top.)

Now, please look at the bottom half of the screen. These are apps you can **add** to quick access. All you have to do is **TAP ON THE APP** you want, and it will be added to quick access.

There are more things you can control in this area. Tap. Play. See what happens.

You can also **change the order of the apps in quick access. TOUCH AND HOLD THE CIRCLE.** It will "free up" from its location, and you can move it around. Sometimes it's tricky to move the icons but keep at it. It takes practice, especially on iPhones. Remember, anything you turn on can be turned off and vice versa.

When you are finished, look at the bottom of the page on Image 9.66 and you will see **RESET** and **DONE.** If you **DON'T WANT TO SAVE** your changes, **TAP RESET**. If you **WANT TO SAVE** your changes**, TAP DONE**.

iPhone Accessibility

iPHONE ACCESSIBILITY: SETTINGS > ACCESSIBILITY

Apple offers users a vast number of modifications to make the phone easier to use when you have hearing, vision, or touch accommodations. Let's get right into it.

IPHONE DISPLAY & TEXT

SETTINGS > ACCESSIBILITY > DISPLAY & TEXT SIZE

You were able to make certain changes to display and text in the regular Display settings. (See iPhone Display & Brightness earlier in this chapter under Display settings.) But if those settings are not quite enough for you, Accessibility settings allow you to make additional accommodations. (Image 9.68 & 69))

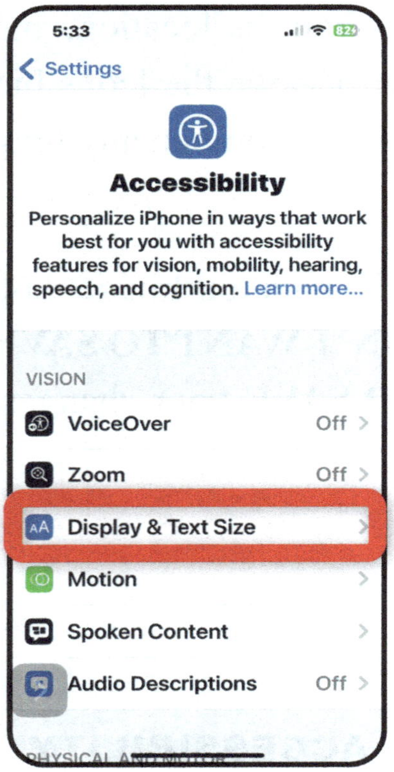

Image 9.67

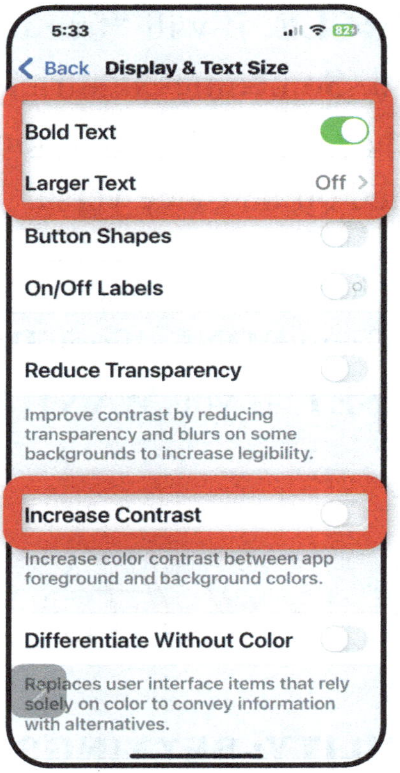

Image 9.68

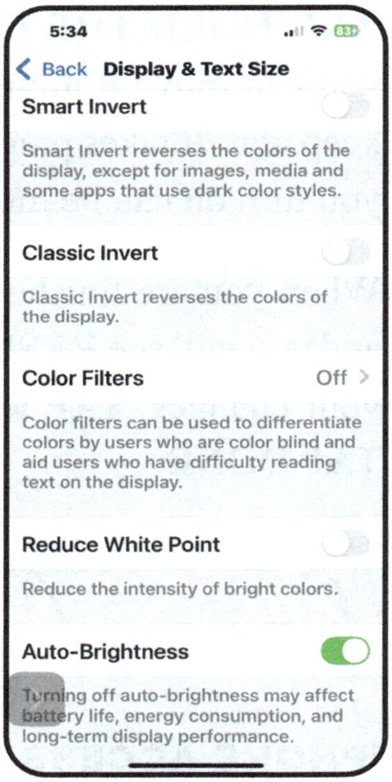

Image 9.69

Look at all the options there are. From **Bold** text to LARGER text to increased contrast (Image 9.68), there are many ways to make your phone easier to see. In the interest of brevity, I am not going to go through each of these settings. I recommend that you toggle settings on and off to see how they affect the display.

There are many settings in Display and Text under Accessibility. I am only covering some of the ones I think make a difference for people without severe hearing or sight deprivation.

Go through each of the settings under vision. Be sure to make your text BOLD by toggling that on. Tap on larger text and you will be amazed at how you will understand your phone so much better!

APPLE VISION ACCOMMODATIONS

SETTINGS > ACCESSIBILITY > VOICEOVER

VoiceOver allows you to use your iPhone even if you can't see the screen. When you turn VoiceOver on, your phone will describe what's happening on the screen, like what app you're touching, what buttons are available, or what text is displayed, allowing you to control your phone without needing to see it.

VoiceOver gives audible descriptions of what's on your screen, from battery level to who's calling, to which app your finger lands on.

You can adjust the speaking rate and pitch to suit your needs.

It's easy to set up. Simply toggle on the VoiceOver button (Images 9.70, 71) and the phone will begin to speak with you. Tap OK.

Scroll through the page as there are lots of related settings to VoiceOver. Tap and try them out. You can always go back and turn off what you turned on! **Keep in mind that using VoiceOver changes the gestures.**

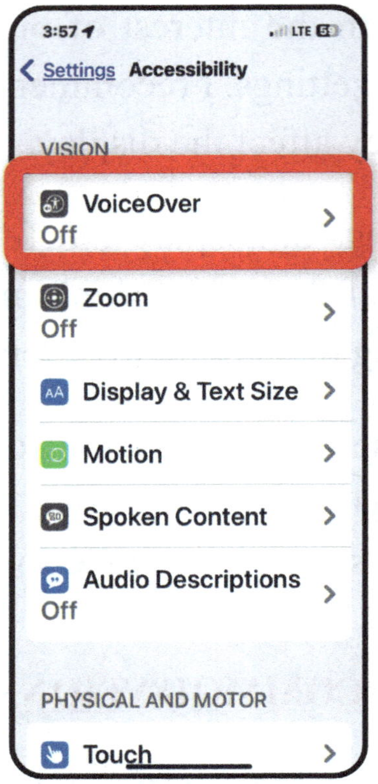

Image 9.70

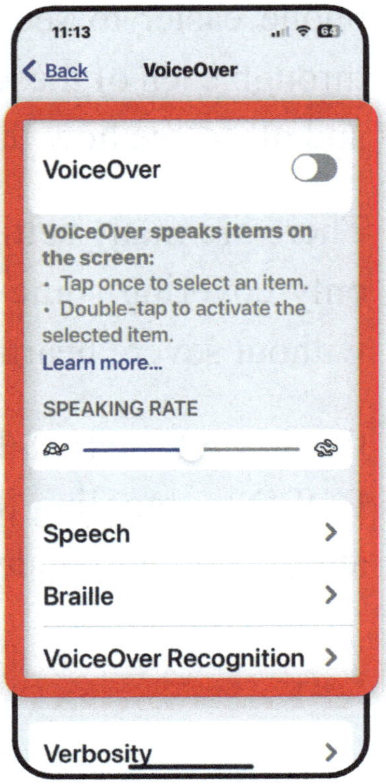

Image 9.71

IPHONE VOICEOVER GESTURES

These gestures are specific to when you are in VoiceOver.

1. **Single Tap** – VoiceOver will speak out loud about what you're touching. It doesn't select the item, just tells you what it is.
2. **Double Tap** – VoiceOver tells you what the item is. You can double-tap anywhere on the screen to select or activate it, like opening an app or pressing a button.
3. **Swipe Left or Right with One Finger** – Moves you between items on the screen, like scrolling through icons, text, or buttons. As you swipe, VoiceOver will read each item aloud.

4. **Swipe Up or Down with One Finger** – Changes the setting or option for whatever you've selected. For example, if you're on a menu, swiping up or down might adjust the volume, change a setting, or scroll through a list.
5. **Two-Finger Swipe Up** – Scrolls to the top of a list or page.
6. **Two-Finger Swipe Down** – Makes VoiceOver read the entire screen, starting from where you are.
7. **Two-Finger Double Tap** – A handy gesture! It starts or stops an action, like playing or pausing music, answering or hanging up a phone call, or stopping a video.
8. **Three-Finger Swipe Left or Right** – Moves between pages on your home screen or scrolls left and right.
9. **Three-Finger Swipe Up or Down** – Scrolls through pages or lists, like a long webpage or your photo library.
10. **Three-Finger Double Tap** – Turns speech on or off so VoiceOver will stop reading aloud.
11. **Four-Finger Tap (Top or Bottom of Screen)** – Tapping with four fingers at the top of the screen selects the first item on the screen. Tapping with four fingers at the bottom selects the last item.

Turn VoiceOver on or off

To turn VoiceOver on or off, use any of the following methods:

- Say, "Hey Siri, turn on VoiceOver" or "Hey Siri, turn off VoiceOver."
- Triple-click the side button (on an iPhone with Face ID).
- Triple-click the home button (on an iPhone with a home button).

iPHONE SPOKEN CONTENT: SETTINGS > ACCESSIBILITY > SPOKEN CONTENT

Spoken Content (Imge 9.72) works two ways. The first is SPEAK SELECTION (Image 9.73), which provides a *Speak button* when you select text. The device *will read specific selections of text*. Toggle it to ON.

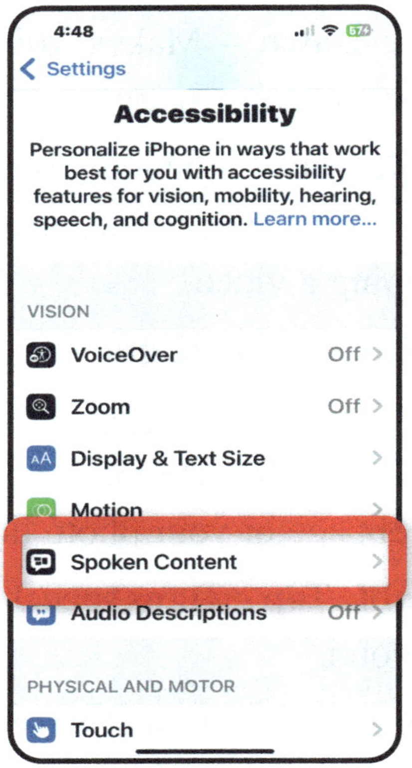

Image 9.72

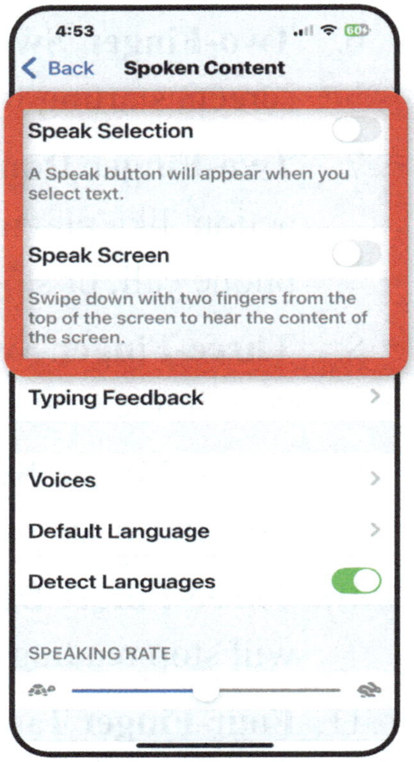

Image 9.73

If you want the whole page to be spoken, SWIPE DOWN WITH TWO FINGERS FROM THE TOP OF THE SCREEN and you will hear the whole screen.

But what if you only want a little bit of text read to you? Find the text you want to hear out loud. It gets a teeny bit tricky here. When you press and hold any text, a small selection turns blue, and there are blue circles at the top left and bottom right. (Image 9.74) You can drag these circles with your finger or stylus to select a larger area. (Image 9.75)

At the same time the blue highlight appears, you will also see a box above. (Image 9.74) Notice the arrow on the right. Tap on it and you get different options. In Image 9.74, you can see **COPY** and **SEARCH WITH GOOGLE**. Tap on the arrow and you will see **GOOGLE TRANSLATE.** (Image 9.75) (This is wonderful if you want to translate the text into a different language.) Image 9.76 shows **LOOK UP** and **SPEAK**. (The former will open the Internet and provide description/ definition.) **TAP SPEAK.** Make sure your volume is up so you can hear the selection.

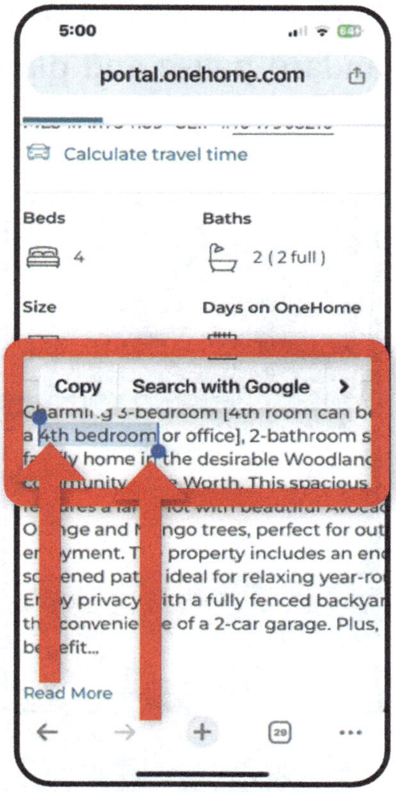

Image 9.74

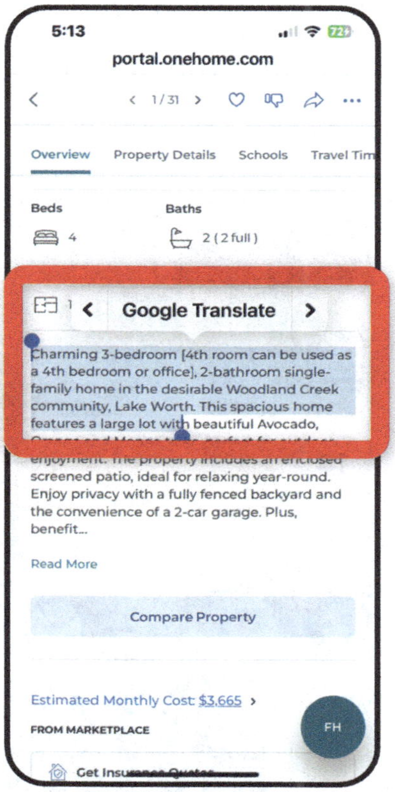

Image 9.75

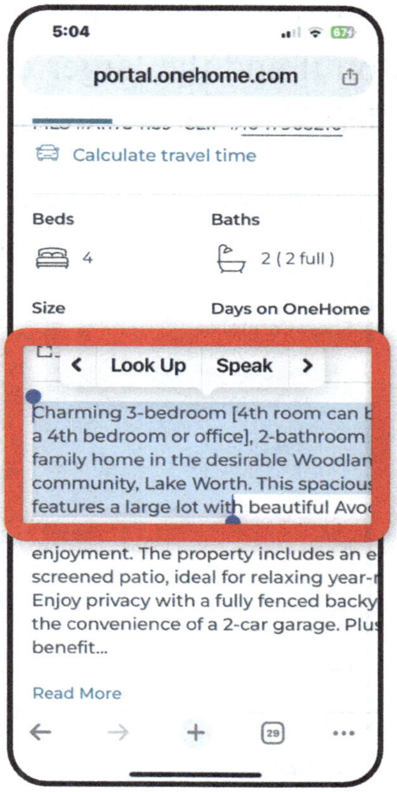

Image 9.76

iPhone Speech Controller

SETTINGS > ACCESSIBILITY > SPOKEN CONTENT > SPEECH CONTROLLER

Tap the **SPEECH CONTROLLER** (Image 9.77) and the screen will change. (Image 9.78) When you enable the Speech Controller, a small black box will open. Tap on it. It will prompt you the way a tape recorder used to, with an arrow for play and parallel lines for pause. Looking at Image 9.78, you will see a small black box with a forward-facing arrow on the bottom left. This box can be moved anywhere on the screen. Tap on it and the larger control box appears with standard pause and play icons, as shown in Image 9.79.

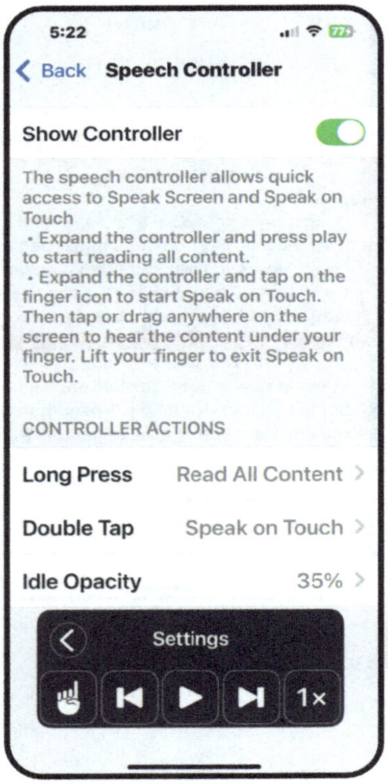

Image 9.77

Image 9.78

Image 9.79

Once you toggle your choices on, you will see slightly different options for each. READ THE SCREEN. The information you need is there. Tap and look at all the settings. You don't have to make changes. It's up to you.

iPhone Magnifier

SETTINGS > GENERAL > ACCESSIBILITY > MAGNIFIER > TOGGLE IT ON

After you've followed the above prompts, activate the magnifier by a **TRIPLE PRESS of the HOME BUTTON**.

TIP: When you are double- or triple-pressing the home or power button, it is important to **keep your finger on the button and press successively**. If you lift your finger, the taps will not be successive, and you will see something unexpected.

iPhone Zoom

SETTINGS > ACCESSIBILITY > ZOOM

The Zoom feature is like a magnifying glass. If you have trouble reading small text or seeing images, use Zoom to enlarge any part of the screen.

iPhone Zoom Gestures

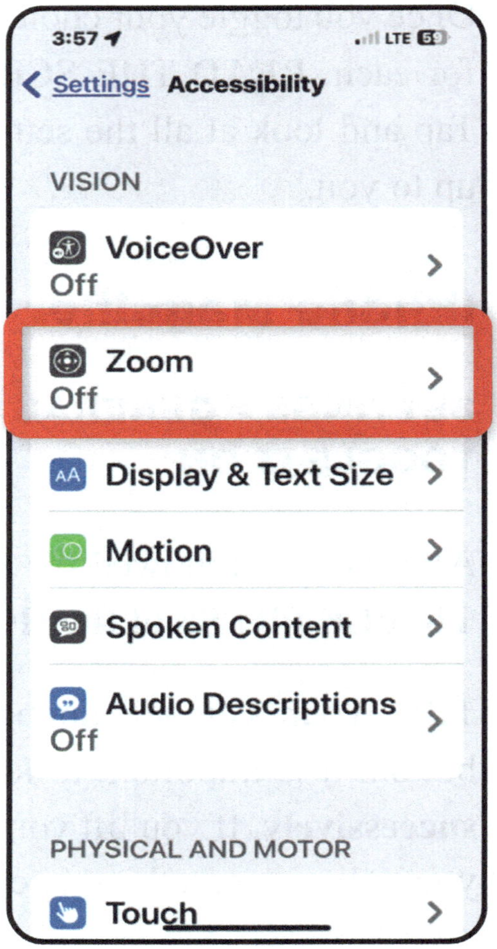

Image 9.80

After enabling Zoom by toggling it on (Image 9.81), you will see a box open, and the text within it will be larger than the rest of the page. (Image 9.82) To move the text left to right or up or down, **USE THREE FINGERS AND SLIDE** them across the page. **Don't lift your fingers**; just slide them easily.

DOUBLE TAP WITH THREE FINGERS to open or close the Zoom feature. Zoom will automatically zoom out when you are typing so you can see the whole keyboard, then zoom back in to what you're typing when you're done.

If you use an iPhone with a pointer device, you can *Adjust Size of pointer with Zoom:* Allow the pointer to scale with zoom.

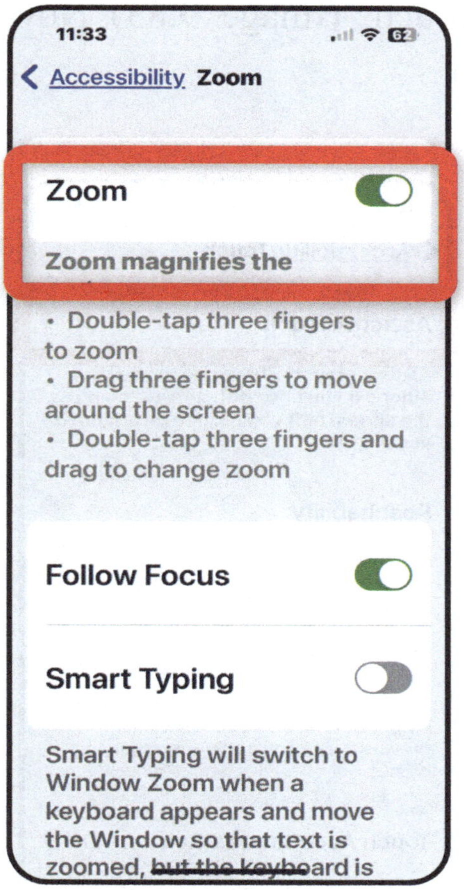

Image 9.81

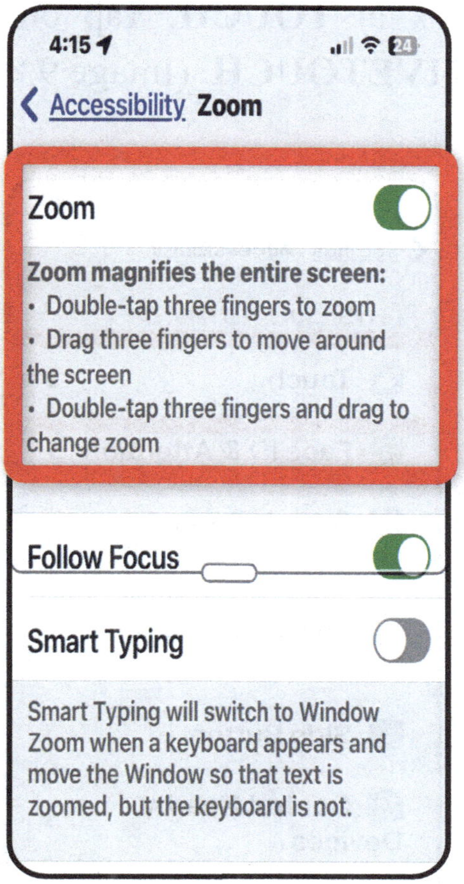

Image 9.82

iPHONE PHYSICAL AND MOTOR

iPHONE PHYSICAL AND MOTOR ACCESSIBILITY: SETTINGS > ACCESSIBILITY > SCROLL TO PHYSICAL AND MOTOR

This is where you can tweak the device to help you with gestures, i.e., touch. If you have any kind of tremor, this is the part of settings you want to pay attention to.

Let's look at **TOUCH.** Tap on Touch. (Image 9.83) Now tap on **ASSISTIVETOUCH.** (Image 9.84)

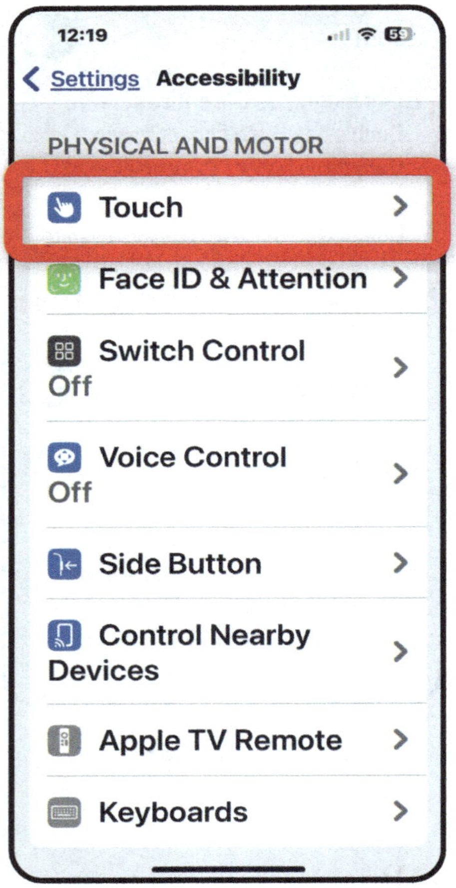

Image 9.83

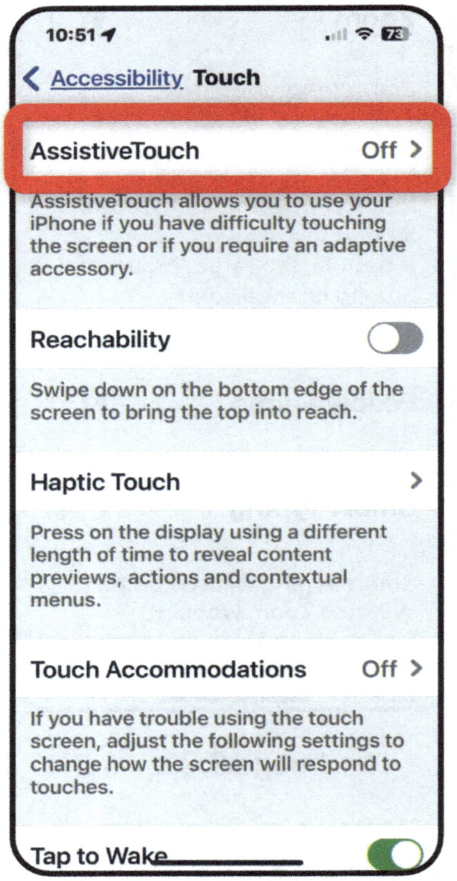

Image 9.84

You will see a small circle appear on the screen. **TAP the CIRCLE.** See Image 9.85

You will enjoy this feature if it is hard for you to press physical buttons. AssistiveTouch allows you to tap to:

- Turn volume up or down
- Lock your screen
- Turn your phone off
- Take screenshots
- Adjust brightness

If your hands shake, the button will stay steady, and you can adjust it as well for an easier target to hit.

iPhone Assistive Touch

SETTINGS > ACCESSIBILITY > TOUCH > ASSISTIVETOUCH > IDLE OPACITY > USE SLIDER

Use the slider to adjust how opaque the circle is, i.e., darker and easier to see. You will be able to rest your finger on this circle without accidentally activating anything. If multiple finger gestures are difficult, you can substitute simple taps for pinching, swiping, etc. All gestures become single touch.

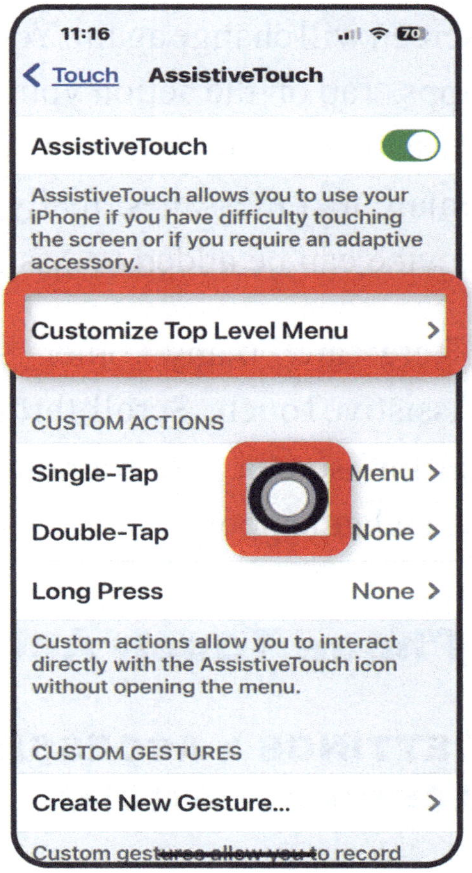

Image 9.85

iPhone Add and Customize AssistiveTouch

SETTINGS > ACCESSIBILITY > TOUCH > ASSISTIVETOUCH > CUSTOMIZE TOP LEVEL MENU

Turn on AssistiveTouch by tapping the toggle. **Tap on Customize Top Level Menu.** (Image 9.85) The screen will change. Now you will see a box with squares (Image 9.86). Notice the plus and minus signs toward the bottom left of that box.

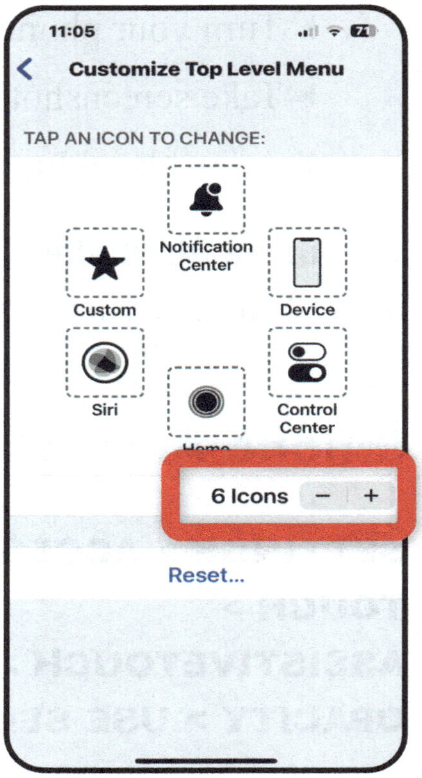

Image 9.86

Tap on the "+" sign. (Image 9.86) The screen will change again. You will see a list of apps. Tap on the action you want to use with AssistiveTouch. You can add the camera, email, text messages; really, any app on the device can be added to AssistiveTouch.

There are many other settings within AssistiveTouch. Scroll through the settings on this screen. I encourage you to tap and see what happens.

iPhone Touch Accommodations

SETTINGS > ACCESSIBILITY > TOUCH > TOUCH ACCOMMODATIONS

This is one of the best settings if you have a tremor. Tap on Touch Accommodation. (Image 9.87) It will toggle on and the screen will change. (Image 9.88) Now you have the opportunity to make changes to how the phone responds to your touch. You can change the hold duration. You can tell it to IGNORE REPEAT TAPS or to recognize either the first or the final tap, according to your needs.

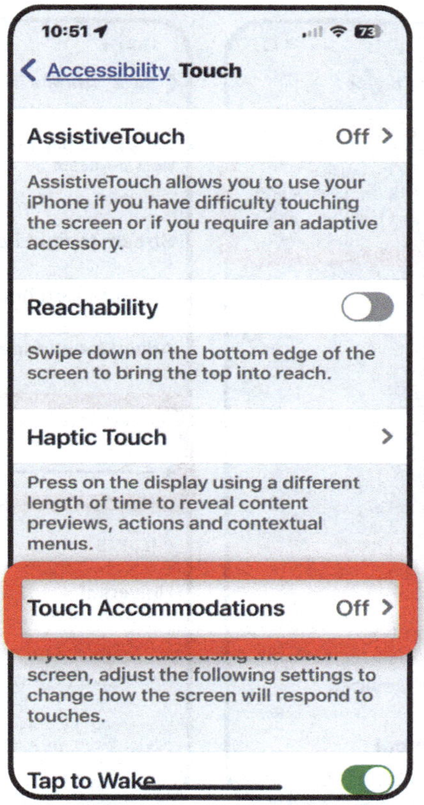

Image 9.87

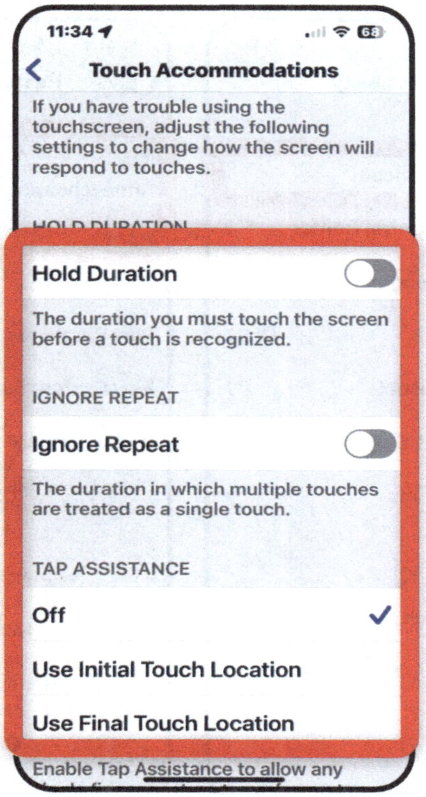

Image 9.88

iPHONE HEARING: SETTINGS > ACCESSIBILITY > HEARING

Many hearing aids are Bluetooth enabled, which means they will connect and communicate with your phone, whether it's an iPhone or Android. Tap on Hearing Devices. (Image 9.89) You will see your hearing aids listed. (Image 9.90) These are separate controls from the app associated with your devices, i.e., Signia, Jabra, Widex, etc. By sliding the Microphone level (Image 9.91), you may find your hearing aids get louder. It's just another way to help you get the most from your hearing aids.

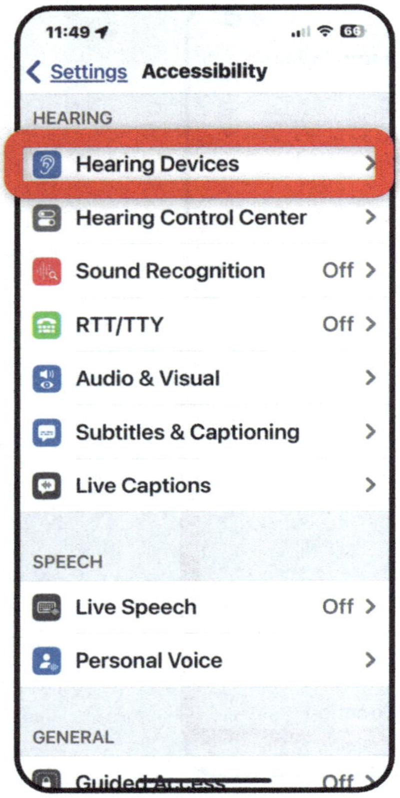

Image 9.89

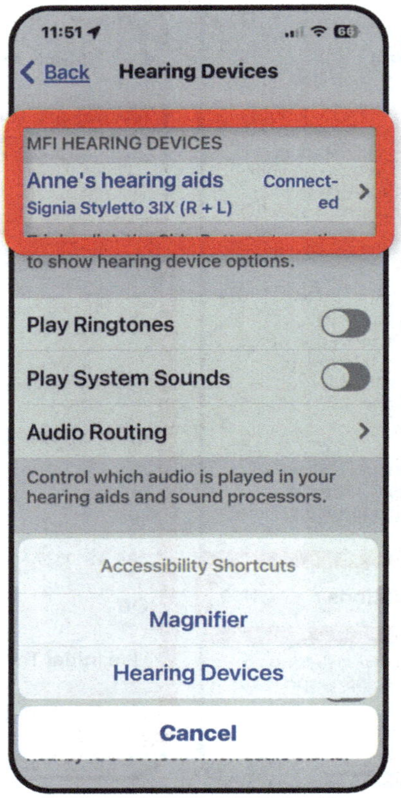

Image 9.90

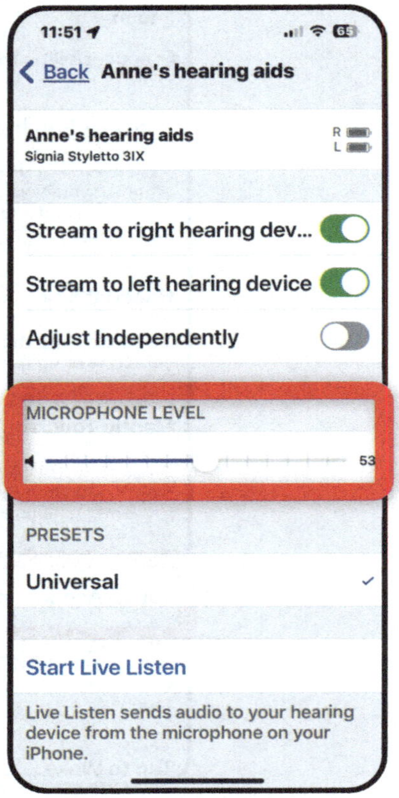

Image 9.91

iPhone Accessibility Shortcut

SETTINGS > ACCESSIBILITY > SCROLL TO ACCESSIBILITY SHORTCUT

Sometimes you need to access accessibility settings quickly. There is a way to do that by configuring the power button to respond to a triple click. Open settings and go to Accessibility Shortcut. (Image 9.92) You have to scroll a lot to get to it near the bottom of that screen. Tap on it and the screen changes. See Image 9.93. Now you can choose what shortcuts you want to see when you TRIPLE CLICK THE POWER BUTTON. Practice the triple click. Do not lift your finger between clicks as the phone will understand that as a single click. Leaving your finger on the power button, quickly CLICK-CLICK-CLICK. You will know you did it correctly because the screen will change.

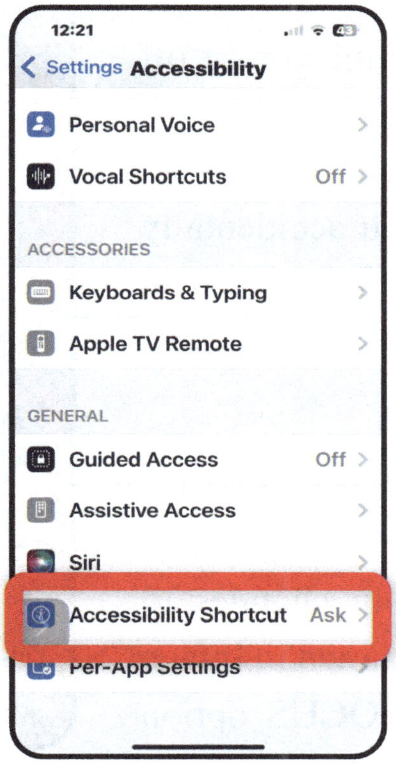

Image 9.92

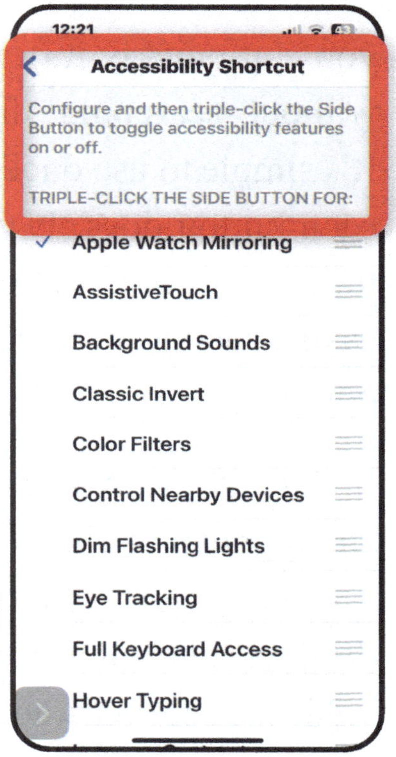

Image 9.93

iPHONE CONTROL CENTER

SWIPE STRAIGHT DOWN FROM THE TOP RIGHT CORNER FROM ANY APP.

The **Control Center** (or Control Panel) is another type of shortcut menu that gives you easy access to important features. It's like a dashboard where you can quickly turn things on or off without searching through settings. It's simple to use once you know what each button does. If you accidentally turn something on or off, you can easily change it back by tapping the button again.

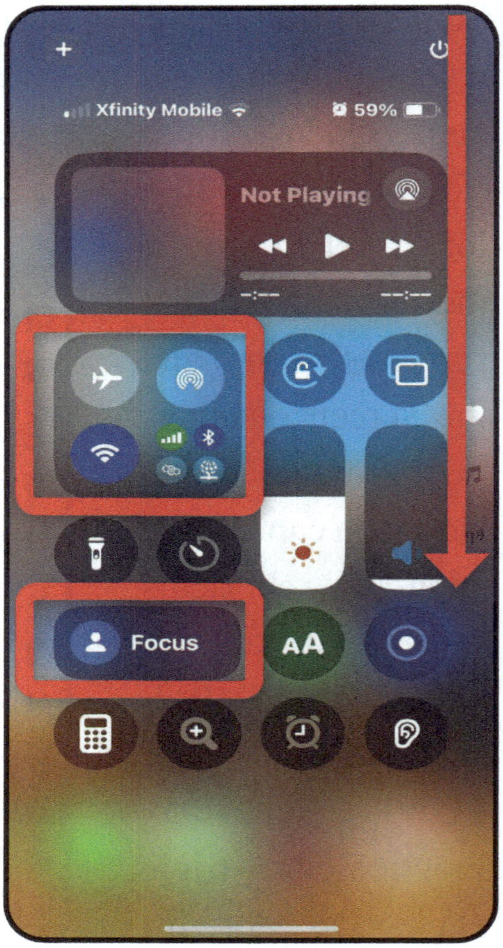

Image 9.94

In late 2024, Apple issued iOS 18, an upgrade in the iPhone operating system. This resulted in changes to the Control Center, as shown in Image 9.94. Notice that the FOCUS option has moved down the screen. Also notice that you must tap on the box with airplane mode, Wi-Fi, Bluetooth, and other antennas in order to access those settings.

It's easy to access. Place your pointer finger at the very top right and **swipe down gently** (Image 9.94). If you don't get it right away, keep practicing.

Here are the main buttons and features you'll usually see:

Wi-Fi – This button lets you **turn Wi-Fi on or off**. When Wi-Fi is on, your phone connects to the Internet without using cellular data.

Bluetooth – This is for connecting your phone to **wireless devices**, like headphones, hearing aids, or speakers.

Airplane Mode – Looks like an airplane. **Turns off all wireless connections**, like Wi-Fi, Bluetooth, and cellular data. Use this on flights or when you don't want to be disturbed.

Flashlight – A quick way to **turn on your phone's flashlight**. It's absolutely wonderful to always have a flashlight available to read the menu in a dimly lit restaurant or to use as a night light to guide you safely to the bathroom in the middle of the night.

Brightness – A slider that lets you **adjust how bright or dim the screen** is. Move it up for brighter, down for dimmer.

Volume – Some control panels let you **adjust the volume** from here. You can raise or lower it without using the buttons on the side of the phone.

Screen Rotation – This allows you to choose whether you want your phone to display only vertically, or both horizontally and vertically. For some seniors, it's good to lock the screen so it does not rotate. For others, I highly recommend that they allow their phones to rotate because the keyboard for typing emails and texts is quite a bit larger when you hold the phone horizontally as opposed to vertically. Also, if you want to watch any videos on your phone, they look much better (and larger) horizontally.

Cellular Data (Mobile Data) – **Turns your mobile Internet on or off**. If you're not using Wi-Fi, this lets you connect to the Internet through your phone plan.

Battery Saver (Low Power Mode) – Helps save battery by **reducing background activity** and dimming the screen (which is the largest user of battery power on your device).

iPhone FOCUS & DO NOT DISTURB

How Is Focus Different from Do Not Disturb?

Focus is a more advanced version of **Do Not Disturb**, where you can customize who and what can reach you during specific times or activities. It's a great feature to reduce distractions while you're busy (lectures, classes, playing cards, volunteering) or resting (there's nothing wrong with a nice nap). Fundamentally, Focus and Do Not Disturb do mostly the same things.

If you have an iPad or Mac laptop or desktop, Focus works across all your devices in the same way at the same time. It's automatic. You can set certain Focus modes to turn on automatically, like when you start driving, at bedtime, or during pickleball.

SWIPE DOWN TO OPEN CONTROL CENTER > TAP FOCUS > TAP 3 DOTS INSIDE DO NOT DISTURB > DO NOT DISTURB SETTINGS

This setting allows you to **silence your phone** so it won't ring or beep for calls or notifications. You'll still get them, but your phone won't make noise; hence you will not be disturbed. It is set for a *specific amount of time and turns itself back on when done*. For example, you have a one-hour class and do not want to be disturbed. Set it for one hour. Done!

Tap on Do Not Disturb if you want a different setting than the standard. Tap on the three dots within the Do Not Disturb box. (Image 9.95) Image 9.96 shows how you can choose exceptions by tapping on settings inside the box.

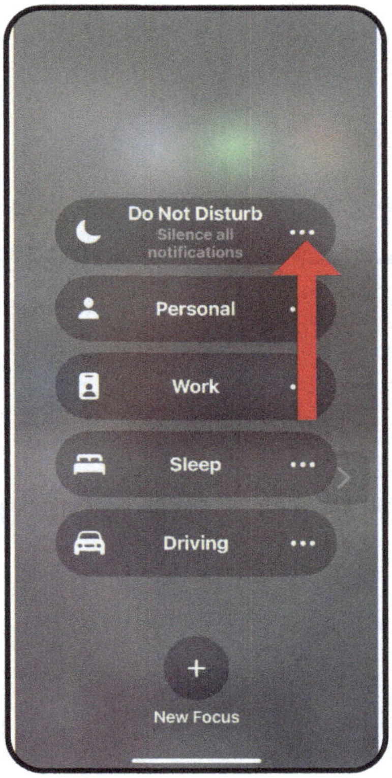

Image 9.95

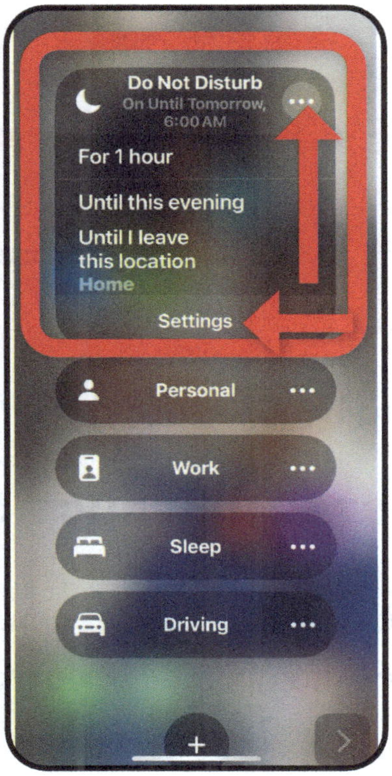

Image 9.96

(Image 9.96) Since my phone is silent from 10:00 P.M. until 6:00 A.M., I set exceptions for my children and David so they can get through to me 24/7.

Notice that you can set Do Not Disturb for sleep, driving, work, or some personal time. (Image 9.96)

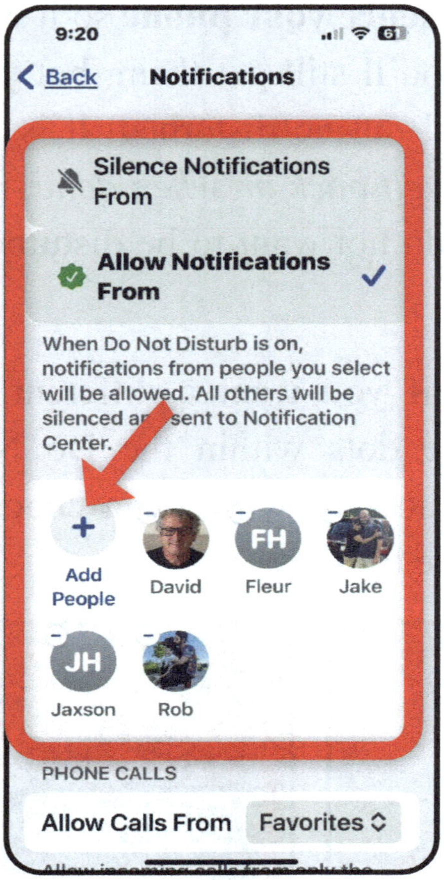

Image 9.97

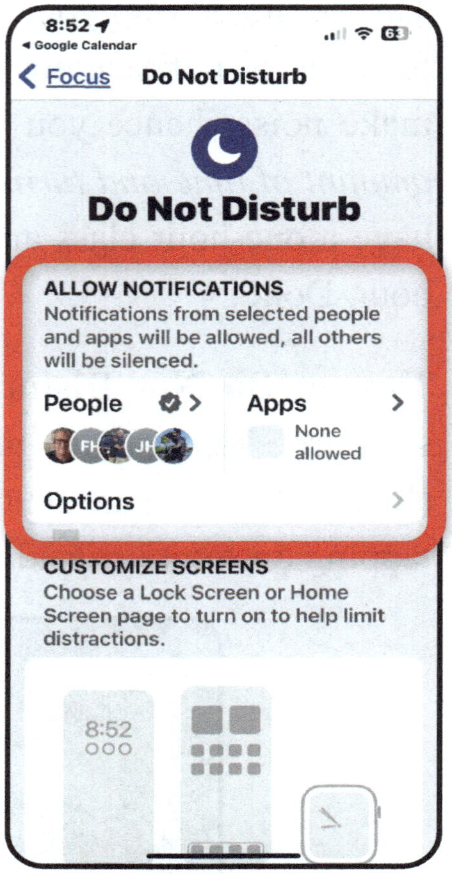

Image 9.98

In Image 9.97 you will see a circle with a blue "+" sign that says, ADD PEOPLE. Tap on it to add your exceptions to Do Not Disturb.

STEP-BY-STEP INSTRUCTIONS FOR DO NOT DISTURB

1. To access Focus on an iPhone, swipe down along the right side of the screen to open the **Control Center**. (See Image 9.99)
2. About halfway down on the left is a box called **FOCUS.** Tap on it. The screen will change, and four long ovals appear, each with a particular setting.
3. Tap on the three dots of Do Not Disturb and the screen will change.

Now you are on the main Do Not Disturb settings screen. Read the screen. This is where you allow notifications from important people. Tap the forward-facing arrow > where it says **People,** and the screen will change.

4. Now you can add people whose calls will get through no matter what.

I encourage you to tap on everything on this screen and see what happens. You can always use the back arrow to return to the previous screen or go home.

Control Center iPhone – Adding & Removing Apps

It is SO EASY to personalize the control center in your iPhone. Open the Control Panel (Image 9.99) Now press and hold anywhere in the control panel and the screen will change to gray and each circle will have a red circle with a minus sign. Tapping on it will remove the item from the Control Center.

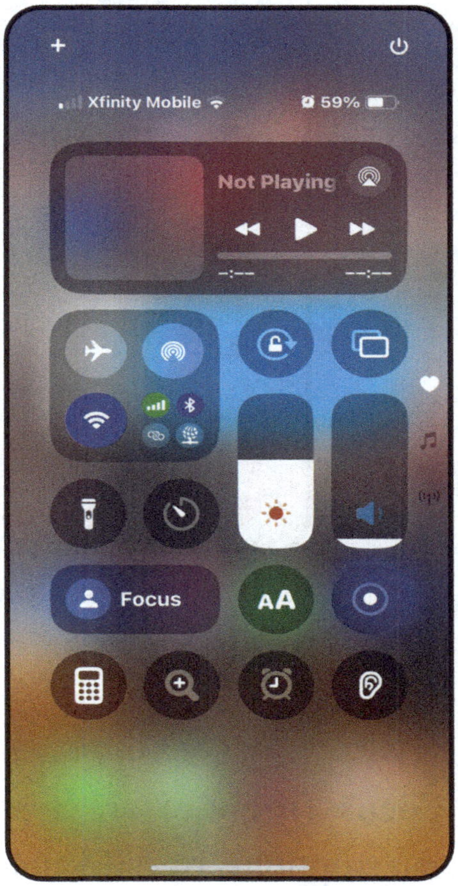

Image 9.99

Adding Apps to the Control Center

Scroll down the page and at the bottom you will see **Add a Control**. (Image 9.100) Sadly, in this photo, the words are a bit hard to read, but it should be better on your device). To add an app simply tap **Add a Control**. The screen will change to Image 9.101. Now you can add controls easily. Scroll down the page for the full selection of apps to add. Easy peasy!

Image 9.100

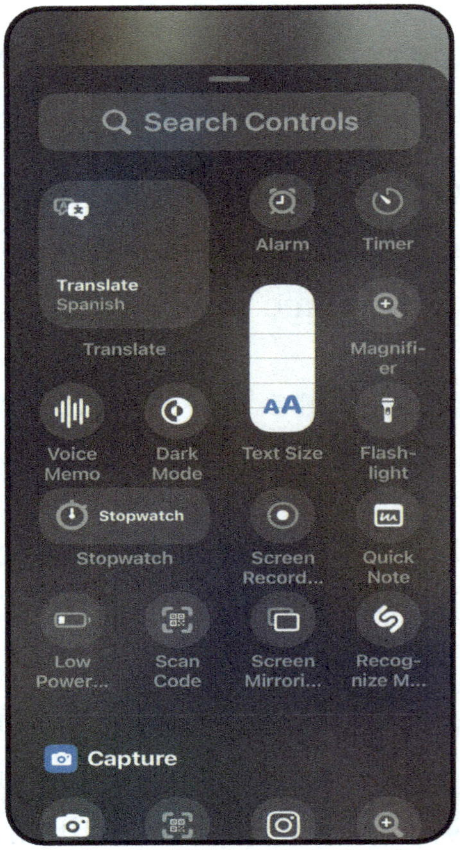

Image 9.101

iPhone Focus

Focus (iPhone) are features on smartphones that help you avoid interruptions by silencing your phone when you don't want to be disturbed. **This is the absolute BEST WAY to quiet your phone for a period of time without having to turn it off.** The danger of turning it off or putting it on silent or airplane mode is that you will forget to switch off those settings. That will cause your kids to go ballistic when they call and call, and you don't answer because your device is silenced and you don't know you're missing calls and texts.

With Do Not Disturb, though, all sounds will come back on once the set time passes. So, if you're going to the movies, you can set it for two hours. Movie done—phone back on. You don't have to remember to turn your phone on, and your kids are happy.

Just remember that all notifications are turned off during Do Not Disturb EXCEPT (there's always an exception to the rule!) your alarms will still sound, so be aware that if you're in the movies or at a lecture, you'll want to have your device near so you can silence the alarm ASAP. **Calls and messages still come through**—you just won't hear them until you check your recent calls, voicemail, and/or texts.

Taking a Screenshot

Depending on the phone make and model, there are options for a screenshot. If these tips don't work for your device, go on the Internet and search using the make and model of your phone and the word SCREENSHOT, and you will get instructions.

The simplest way to take a screenshot is to use Siri or OK Google and say, "Siri (OK Google) take a screenshot" and that's that! There are other ways as well that I detail below. Keep in mind that, even if you use a voice command to take the shot, you still have to do something with that photo. Read on.

ANDROID SCREENSHOT

Simultaneously press the **POWER and VOLUME DOWN** buttons for one to two seconds. **Squeeze and release both buttons equally at the same time. Quickly PRESS AND RELEASE.** (If this does not work for your Android, go to the Internet and search for the make and model of your phone plus 'screenshot' and you will get directions for your device.) You can also use a palm swipe (Settings > Advanced Features > Motions and Gestures > Turn on Palm Swipe to Capture.

Once the screenshot is taken, the screen will flicker slightly and then **a small image will appear at the bottom left in a larger rectangle.** (Image 9.102) You tap on the next icon in that box to crop/edit your image. The third is a # and you tap here to add a *tag* (an identifier for online use). The fourth image looks like a "V" with little circles at the three points. Tapping this

Image 9.102

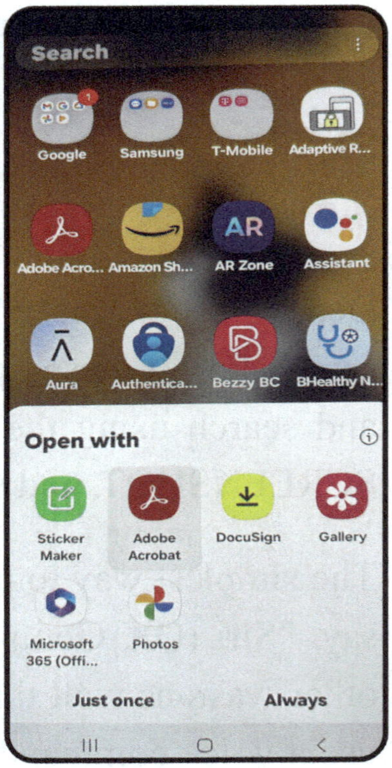

Image 9.103

allows you to share the image via email, text, Facebook, etc. (Image 9.103)

Screenshots are automatically saved in your Gallery. Once the screenshot is taken, you can go to the Gallery where you will find the image. Here you can edit and/or share the photo.

iPHONE SCREENSHOTS

Screenshots are easy to do. The trick is to **simultaneously press and release the power button on the right and the Volume UP button on the left to capture a photo of your screen**. (Image 9.104) This is not a press and hold gesture. **Squeeze and release both buttons equally at the same time. Quickly PRESS AND RELEASE.** Once you've taken the screenshot, you will see a small photo appear at the bottom left of the screen.

Image 9.104

(Image 9.105) Tap on that little picture, and it will fill the screen. Now you have the opportunity to crop out unwanted edges of the photo. Simply drag the small white lines to where you want them. (See Image 9.106.)

Image 9.105

Image 9.106

Next you will be prompted to share it, delete it, or save it. (Image 9.107) Tap on everything and see what happens. If the screen changes, scroll right and left and up and down to see all the options.

It took me a few tries before I was able to do the gesture correctly. I noticed that I had to make sure I applied even pressure to both buttons simultaneously. Try not to press too hard nor too lightly. It's kind of a Goldilocks thing! Don't get discouraged if you end up turning off the phone or changing the volume at first. Try again. **Be patient with yourself and with your phone.**

Image 9.107

Chapter 10

Essential Apps Step by Step

Table of Contents

This chapter teaches all the things the apps you use most often can do. Because of the depth of each chapter, this book will only cover:

- The Phone
- Messages (including texts, Facebook Messenger, & WhatsApp)
- Email—Gmail and Apple Mail
- GPS—Apple and Waze (Waze is owned by Google)
- Clock

I invite you to reawaken your curiosity as you go through these apps. **TAP ON EVERYTHING**. **Look for dots, lines, and arrows pointing in either direction and anything that is blue.** Remember, the screens are tiny, so not all the information can be displayed all at once. There is not enough room, so there are economies of space. The developers hide lots of actions behind these symbols, usually found in the corners of the screen, but not always. So, get curious and TAP away!

What If I Get Confused?

Uh-oh, the screen changed and now you're confused. Remember, you have two options. The first I recommend is to USE THE BACK ARROW TO GO BACK to the page before. This way you can start over. Of course, you can always SWIPE UP OR PRESS THE BUTTON and go home. There is nothing to be worried about. Get up, get a drink. Take a few deep breaths and come back to try again.

If you decide to change a setting, I suggest that you write down what you changed and where you find it in settings. Use the format I use:

Settings > fill in every place you tap. That way if it turns out to be something you don't want, you can easily backtrack and undo what you did.

Phone Apps

This particular software, this app, is what allows you to use the handheld computer as a telephone. Arguably, it's the single most important app on the phone, isn't it? After all, without it, it's no longer a telephone in the traditional sense of the word, where people are identified with a unique series of ten or more numbers that are associated with being able to speak or text directly with them.

To start out, let's revisit our 1970s home. Somewhere, typically in the kitchen, was the telephone, answering machine, pad and paper, a calendar, an address book and the yellow and white pages, nearby. That was a lot of equipment in one place. Now most of that equipment is in the telephone app. It contains the phone, address book (now called Contacts), and your answering machine (now called Voicemail), and the old Caller ID (where we scrolled to see what calls we missed) has been replaced by Recents (i.e., recent calls). The phone app is a one-stop shot on iPhones. With older Androids, there's a third-party app to use for the Answering Machine/Voicemail. Newer phones have it integrated with Google Meet.

First, I ask you to look at Image 10.1 and notice the very bottom of the screen. The writing is tiny. It's made for young eyes. In that micro type you will discover five different icons representing three features offered by this app. They are the Keypad, Recents and Contacts. Let's go deeper.

ANDROID PHONE APP

Android Keypad

The keypad is familiar. Use it like any other keypad. A few things to know.

Androids may have a green or blue phone icon. It has a picture of an old-fashioned phone handset on it, so you can identify it.

Image 10.1

Image 10.2

Notice the video camera to the right of the call icon? Tapping that will start your video camera and will connect seamlessly to any Android phone. It's a nice reason for families to have the same operating system for everyone.

Tapping on the three dots at the top right of the keyboard opens more options, giving you the chance to view your speed dial numbers. (Image 10.2)

By tapping on "OPEN TO KEYPAD," your phone app will always open to the keypad. Tap on it to enable. Once enabled, the dropdown menu changes and now says "OPEN TO LAST VIEWED," which means if the last thing you did on the app was to look at Contacts, that's what you will see the next time you open the app. For some seniors, it may be useful to always open to the keypad to avoid confusion.

You can access your voicemail here and, again, Call Settings.

Android Video Calling

When you want to video chat with a fellow Androidian, simply tap the video camera on the keypad instead of the phone icon. (Image 10.3)

Image 10.3

If you're on the phone with someone with an iPhone, you will have to use a third-party app to make that call. Apps to use are WhatsApp or Facebook Messenger. There are other apps that allow this, but I think for seniors it's better to stick with platforms with which you have some familiarity, like Facebook and WhatsApp. My experience is that about 85 percent of seniors use one or the other of these apps. Learn more about WhatsApp and Facebook Messenger on page 243.

Android Making and Ending Calls

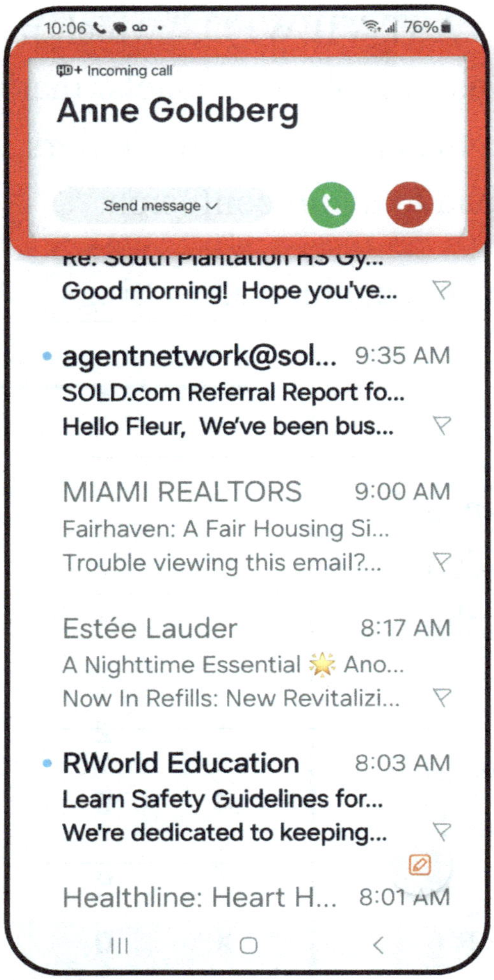

Image 10.4

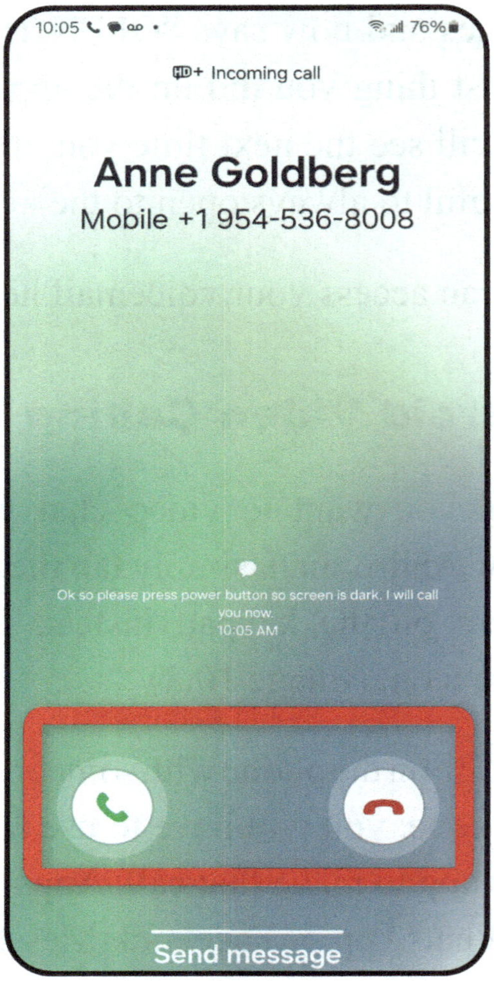

Image 10.4a

Images 10.4 and 10.4a show the screens when a call comes i.e., you will have the opportunity to answer or reject the call.

As discussed in Chapter 5, to answer the call, tap, swipe, or slide on the green button. To decline a call, either do nothing or tap on the red (decline call) button.

Green = Go and Red = No

If you do not know who the caller is, tap red and deny the call. Why do I recommend this? So that you are not answering the phone sounding confused, poised to be a victim! Let the call go to voicemail. If it was an important call, call them back. If no message is left, it was not an important call. If it was spam, you can now block the caller—which we will cover later in this chapter.

Image 10.4 shows how an incoming call looks when received while the phone is in use. Image 10.4a shows how the incoming call looks when the screen is dark (i.e., the phone is off). In both cases you see red and green circles to tap or ignore.

Android Recents

ANDROID RECENTS: OPEN PHONE APP > TAP ON RECENTS AT BOTTOM OF SCREEN > SCREEN CHANGES > RECENT CALLS

So you missed a call or two (or twelve), and you're curious about who it was. That's when you visit **RECENTS** (i.e., Caller ID) on your phone app.

Tap on the three dots at the top right of the screen. (Image 10.5) The screen will change, and you will find your speed dial numbers, voicemail, and settings. (Image 10.6)

Image 10.5

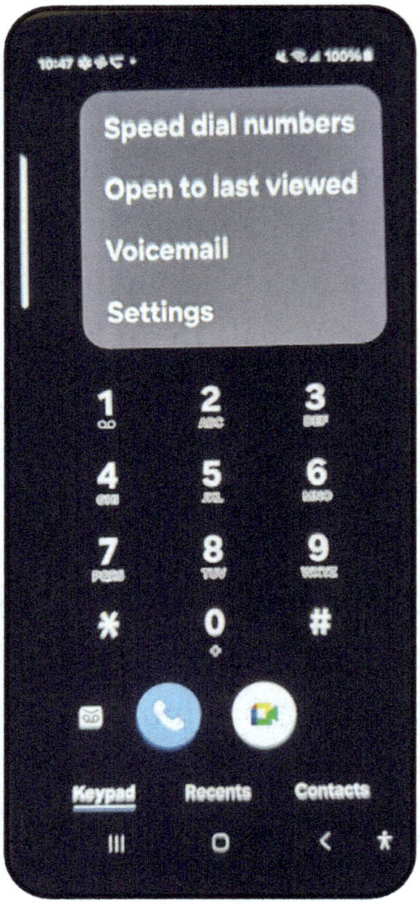

Image 10.6

Now, tap on Recents at the bottom of the page as shown in Image 10.7. The screen will change. You know that's the screen you're on because the word "Recents" at the bottom of the page will be darker than the other words that are there.

Tapping on the three lines in Image 10.7 (with the little "golf tee") opens a page where you can view calls by category: All calls, Missed calls, Rejected calls, Outgoing and incoming calls. Tap everything and see what happens. (Image 10.8)

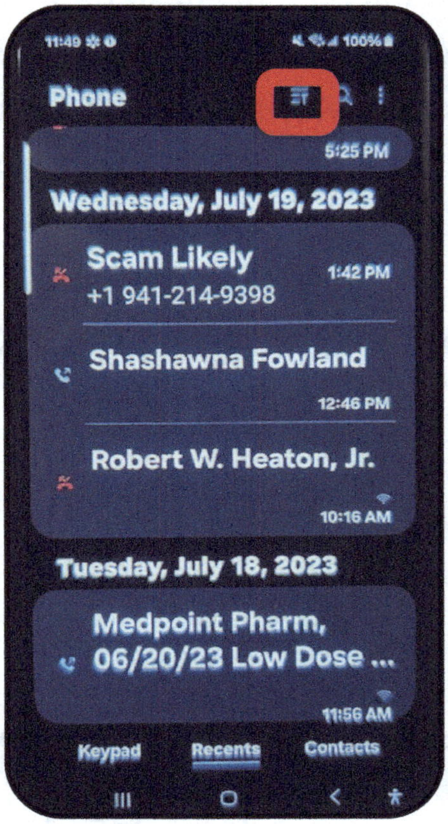

Image 10.7

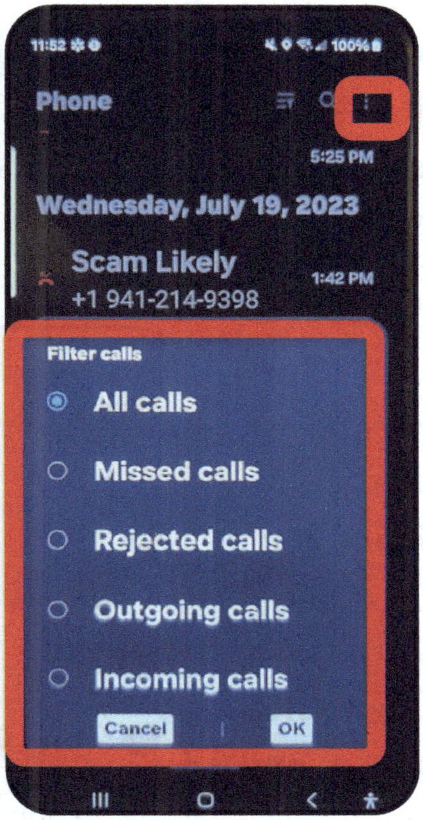

Image 10.8

The last option on this screen is to tap on the three dots at the top right. If you care about seeing your blocked calls, this is where you can find them. If you tap **HIDE blocked calls**, Total call time, View and edit tags and Settings. FYI, when you tap HIDE blocked calls, it changes and becomes **SHOW blocked calls** which means you can undo the action easily.

I can't imagine why you'd care about total call time or view and edit tags unless you use the phone for work and have to monitor your time. Settings is another way to get to the device's phone settings.

Android Contacts

We used to call this an address book. But now it's Contacts. Huh? The way I see it is that there are twelve characters in the words "address book" and only seven in "Contacts." In designing the screens, developers had to consider the economies of space and use the least amount of space possible. Answering Machine became Voicemail. Address book became Contacts. My theories, of course, but I think they make sense!

Now, back to contacts. Have you ever noticed that there are **three icons** at the top right of the screen? There's a **plus sign, the search icon, and three dots**.

- The PLUS SIGN is to add a new contact. (Image 10.9)
- The three vertical dots allow you to manage your Contacts.

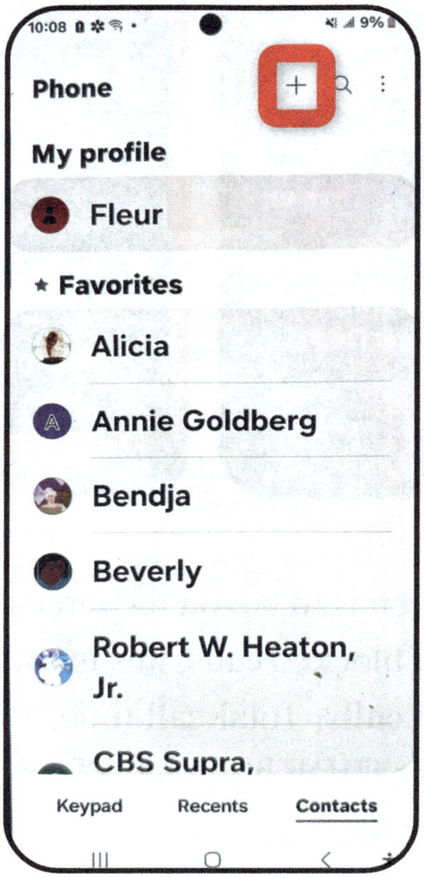

Image 10.9

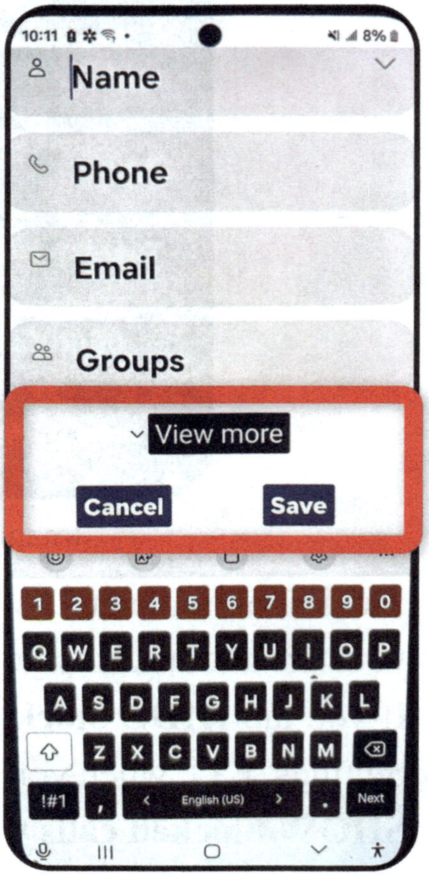

Image 10.10

Android Add a Contact

When you want to add a new contact, tap on the “+” sign at the top right of the screen. (Image 10.9) The screen will change, and you can fill in the information. (Image 10.10) **TAP VIEW MORE** to see more fields. NOTICE at the bottom of the screen, there are two words. **CANCEL. SAVE**. They mean what they say. If you want to keep the added contact, tap Save. You don’t want to keep the added contact, tap Cancel. Once you click Save, the screen will change, and you will see the added contact.

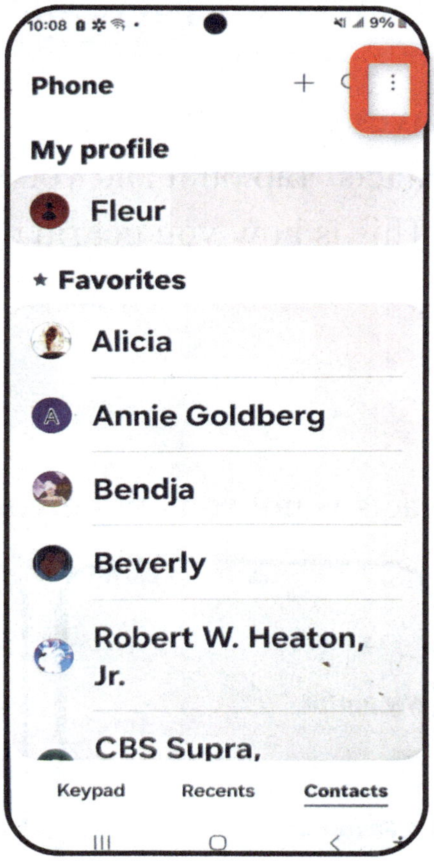

Image 10.11

Image 10.12

Android Contacts Editing

Tap on the three dots at the top right of the screen (Image 10.11) and read the box that opens. (Image 10.12) From here you can:

- **Edit** the contact
- **Reorder Favorites** allows you to put your favorite favorites at the top of the list.
- **Manage Contacts** gives you a few options you may want to use when organizing contacts. Tap on it and you will have the chance to **Merge contacts.** This is how you get rid of duplicates.
- **Trash**
- **Contact Settings**
- **Settings**
- Move and Sync contacts is not something you need to deal with.

Android Contacts – Editing a Specific Contact

- Open Contacts.

Tap lightly on the contact to edit. (Image 10.13) It will darken (Image 10.14), and options will appear right under the contact in small circles. From left to right you will see:

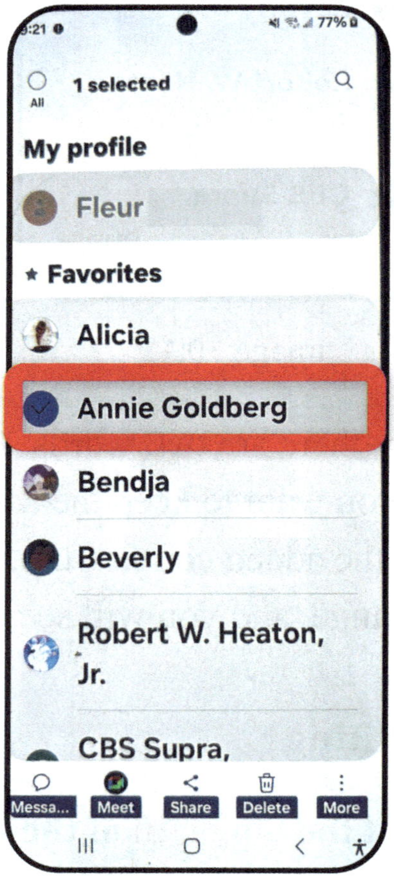

Image 10.13

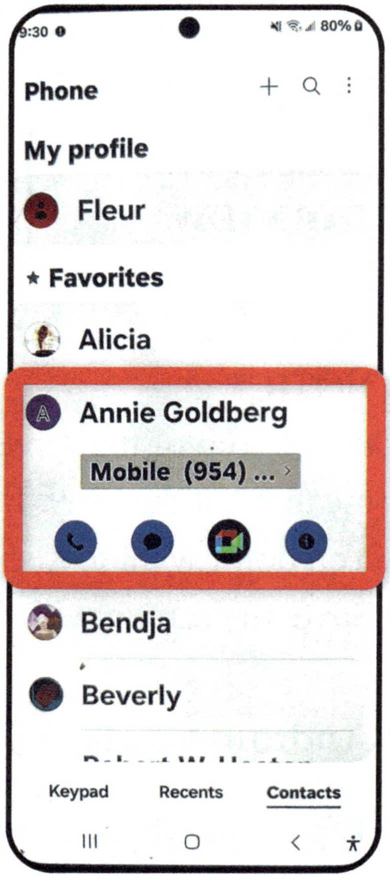

Image 10.14

- Call the Contact
- Text the Contact
- Video Chat with the Contact
- Information (tapping here opens the whole contact page for this person)

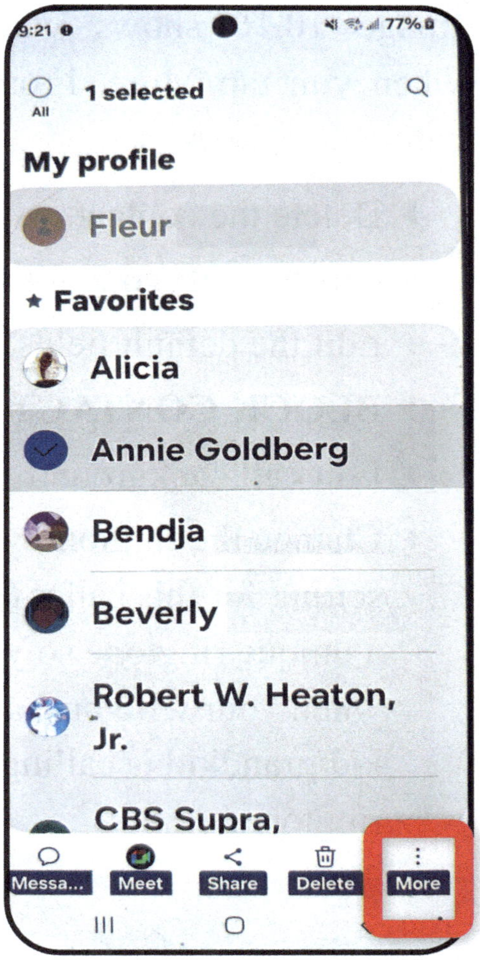

Image 10.15

Please keep in mind that Android phones and how they operate can be different from manufacturer to manufacturer and model to model.

Now let's take another approach. **Tap and HOLD** on the name **for a millisecond** and the screen will change. (Image 10.15) At the very bottom of the screen, you will see choices. From these icons you can:

- Send a text **Message.**
- Open **Google Meet.**
- **Share** the contact
- **Delete** the contact.
- **More** is where you can add or remove the contact to Favorites. This is also where you can block a caller.

Image 10.16 shows what happens when you tap More. From here you can:

- Delete the contact.
- Create a QR code for the contact.
- Edit the default fields.
- **BLOCK CONTACT.**
- Edit call background.
- Change the ringtone/vibration setting for this caller (creating a unique ringtone so you know when your wife/husband/lover/kid/grandkid is calling just by the ringtone.

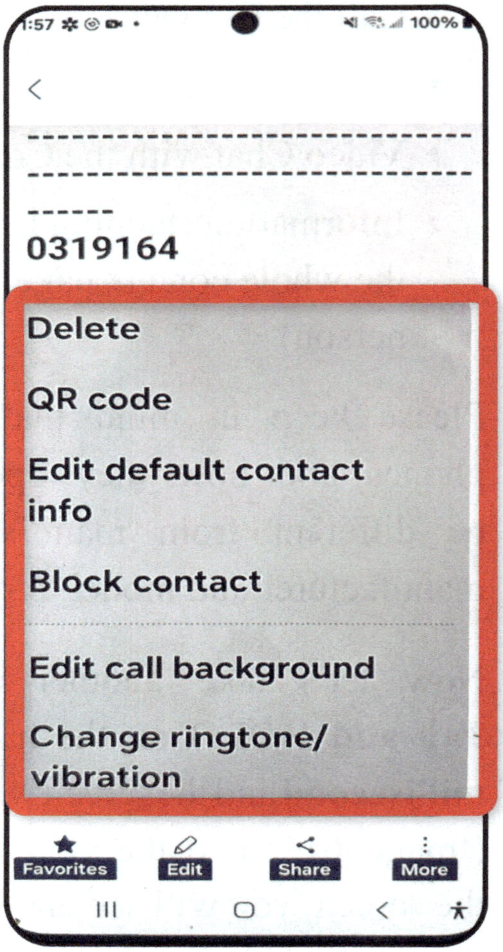

Image 10.16

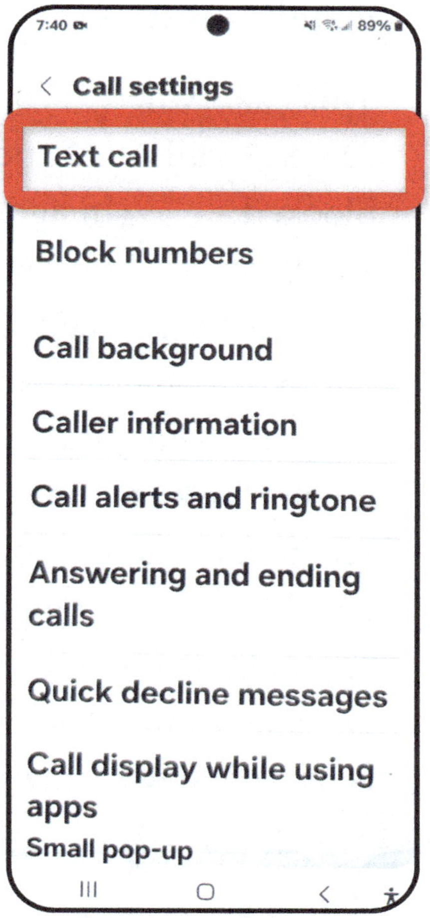

Image 10.17

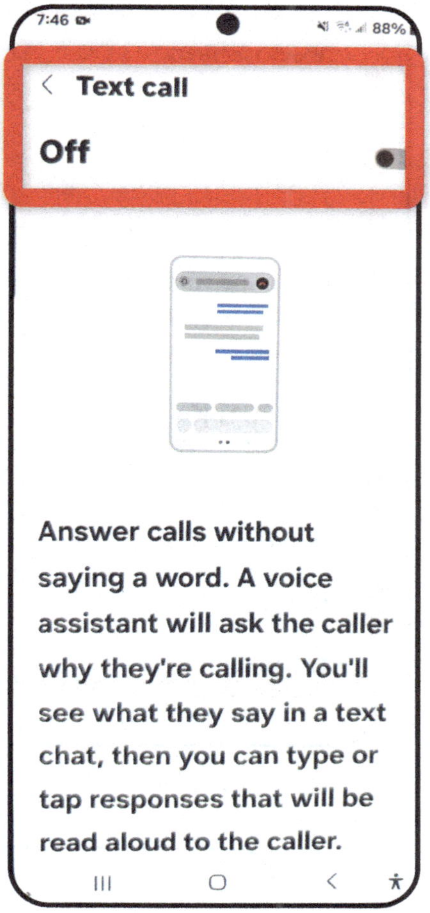

Image 10.18

Text Call allows you to answer calls without saying a word! Read the screen and you will know exactly what this does. (Images 10.17 & 18)

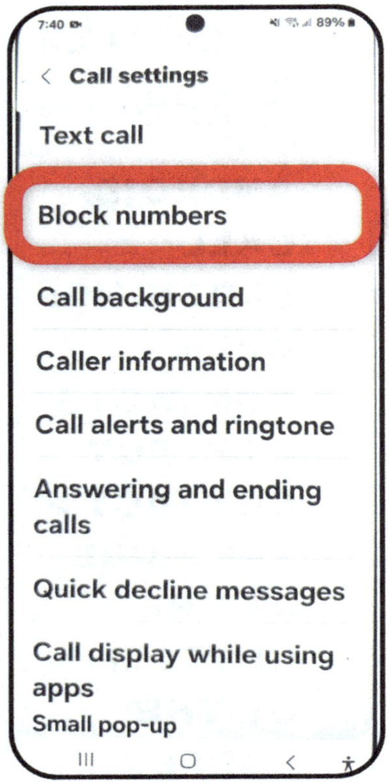

Image 10.19

Image 10.20

Block Numbers

This is where you can see calls that are blocked. (Images 10.19 & 20) You can also manually add a number to block. For seniors who are at greater risk of being scammed, here you can choose to block any unknown number. Of course, the danger is if you have a new doctor who is not yet in your contacts, the call will be blocked. So be judicious turning this on.

Call Background is where you can choose a picture or video that will appear when you make or receive calls. (Images 10.21 & 22)

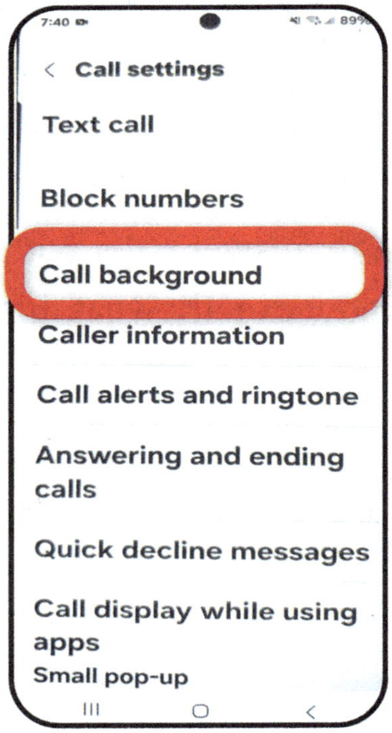

Image 10.21

Image 10.22

Simply TAP on the very bottom of the screen in the area that says **Background,** and it will open your Gallery. Select a picture, follow the prompts, and your callers will see a nice photo of you or something you love.

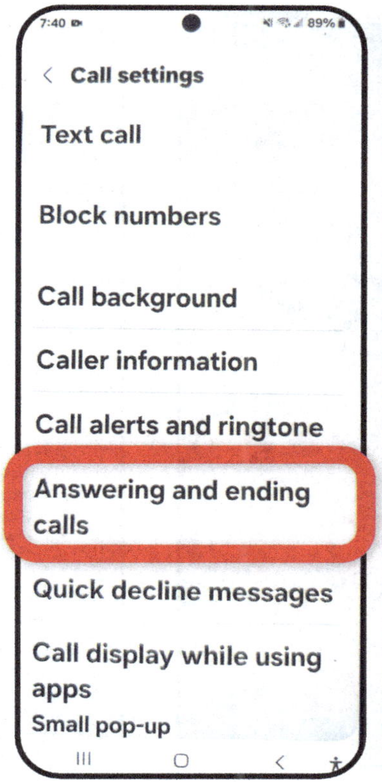

Image 10.23

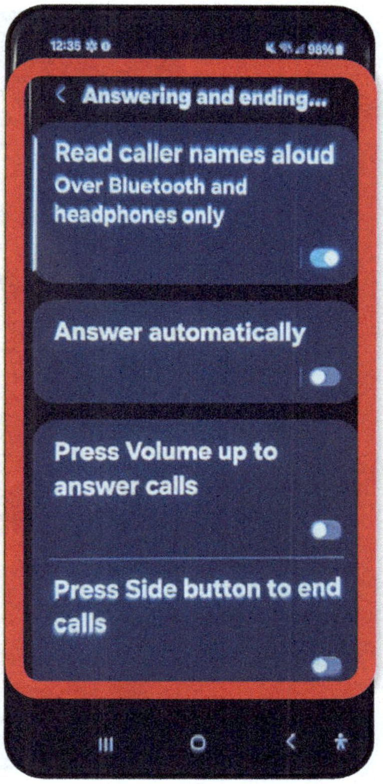

Image 10.24

- **Caller Information** shows details about the caller, including recent conversations.
- **Call alerts and ringtone** allow you to decide when the phone makes noise when a call ends, connects, and more.

Answering and Ending Calls (Images 10.23 & 24) is an important feature if you're visually impaired as the phone can read the caller's name through your hearing aids. Look at the choices here. Tap and see if you like the change. Go back and tap again to return to the way it was.

Android Visual Voicemail

Back in the day when we had landlines with voicemail, you had to dial press a number or series of numbers in order to hear your voicemails.

Image 10.25

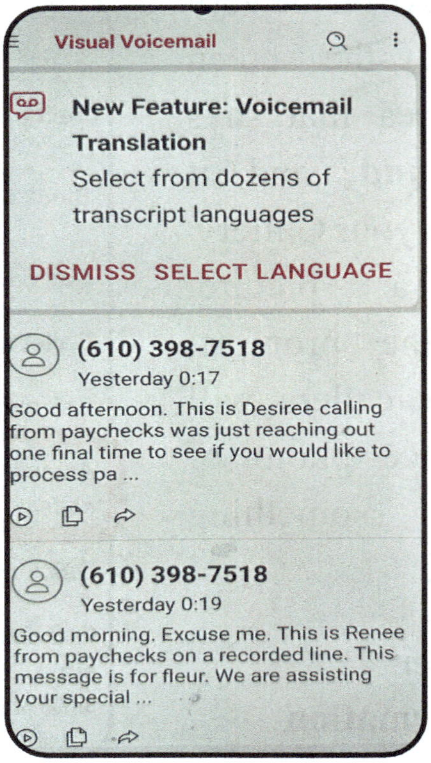

Image 10.26

In the world of smartphones, there's Visual Voicemail, which allows you to read your messages right from your phone. (Images 10.25 & 26)

In older Androids, visual voicemail is a separate app from the phone. This app allows you to listen to any message without having to listen to them all. That is a vast improvement over the old way. As soon as you open the app, you will see a list of all the voicemails you've received. You'll see the caller's name or number and the time. Just tap on any message to listen to it or simply read it. You can save or delete. To delete, select the voicemail you want gone or just press and hold. Look for a trash can icon or the word DELETE, usually at the bottom of the screen. You may be asked to confirm the delete. That's a good thing as you can't delete a message by accident.

Each carrier (Verizon, T-Mobile, AT&T, Xfinity Mobile, etc.) has its own version of visual voicemail. It's not feasible here to describe how each works, but below is a general overview that will help you sort it out. Visual voicemail may require a small monthly fee from the carrier. Note that some Android phones do have visual voicemail built into the phone app. It is highly variable according to manufacturer, model, and carrier.

Visual Voicemail Basics

Open the app and tap play. You know how to do that because every tape deck you've had since the seventies has had a **forward-facing arrow** as the symbol for PLAY. In this case, it's the first of the symbols you see in this image. You will want to hear the message if the text translation is gibberish and/or you don't see well.

Image 10.27

IPHONE PHONE APP

iPhone Keyboard Explained

Notice in Images 10.27 that the keyboard has not changed since 1968, when touch-tone phones appeared. Now it's a virtual keypad, i.e. pictures of buttons but no actual buttons.

Looking at the iPhone, you will notice that the icon at the bottom that denotes the keyboard is **blue**, telling you the name of the screen you're on.

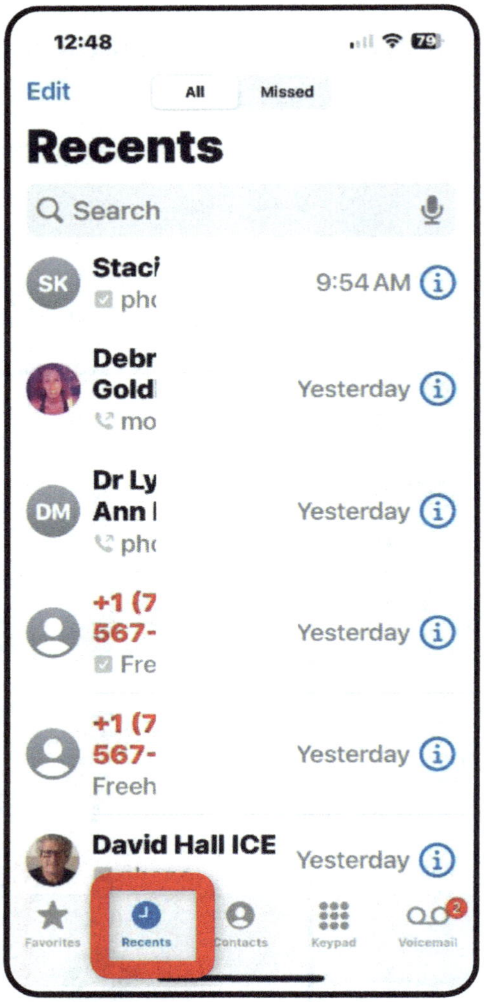

Image 10.28

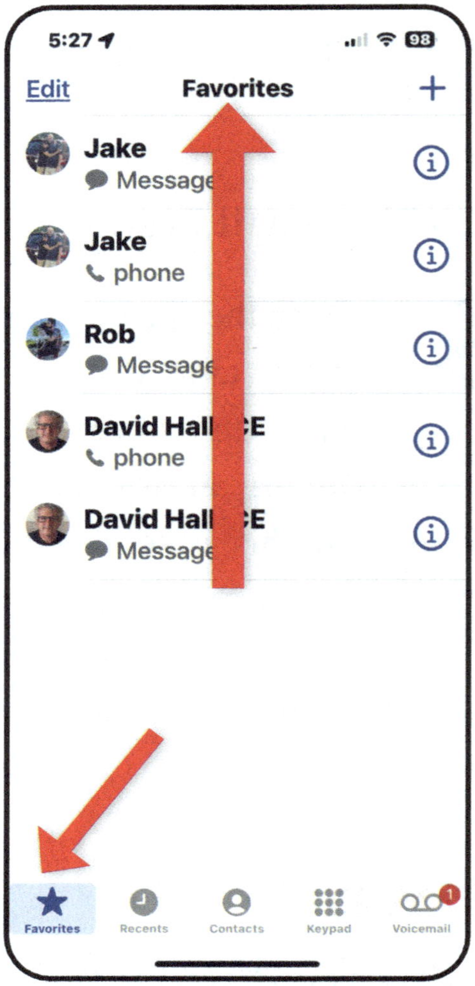

Image 10.29

TAP on **RECENTS** and the screen will change, and the **RECENTS** icon on the bottom will be blue. Try it. (Image 10.28)

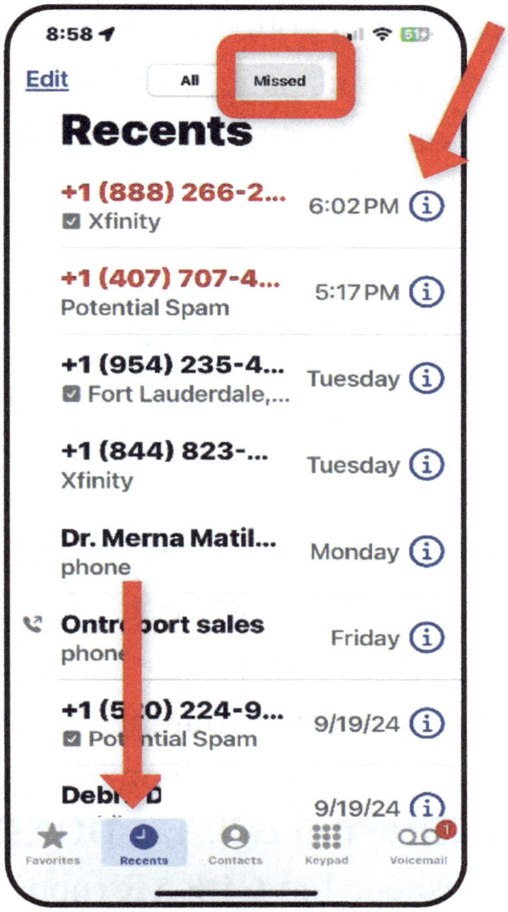

Image 10.30

On the iPhone, the first icon on the very bottom left of the screen, denoted by a star, is **FAVORITES**. (Image 10.29) Tap on it and the screen will change. The little star icon at the bottom will now be blue, and at the top of the page, you will see the word "Favorites," big and bold. It's where you create a shortcut to text or call someone. This used to be called speed dial back in the day.

The second icon is **RECENTS**, with an icon that looks like a clock. (Image 10.30) This is a list of recent activity on your phone. Do you remember how on early portable phones we could review the missed calls by pressing on a particular button and scrolling through missed calls? Well, this is the same thing, only this one distinguishes between calls you missed and calls you either made or received. The names in red are calls you missed or didn't want to answer. Numbers/names in black indicate an outgoing call or an incoming call that you made or answered.

ⓘ Some callers may not leave a message. If you want more information who called, tap on the circle with the "i" in it. The screen will change. You will see when exactly they called and how long the call lasted. If the caller is in your Contacts, then tapping on the "i" will bring you to that person's contact (i.e., page in your address book) with all their information. If you scroll down on this page, you will see BLOCK CALLER in red. This is where you stop that number from reaching you again.

If you want to see only the calls you missed, look at the very top of the screen. You will see two boxes next to each other. On the left it says **ALL,** and the one on the right says **MISSED**. Tap on Missed and all those calls will be listed (Image 10.30).

Tapping on Edit allows you to delete calls from Recents. Why do this? There is a small benefit regarding storage space, but it's not a huge benefit. Some people like to delete everything, and some like to keep everything. There is no wrong way…UNLESS you are running out of device storage. Then you may want to consider deleting. Tap on the red circle with the minus sign in it. That will delete that call. Tap **DONE** (upper left side of screen) when you are finished. Tap **CLEAR** (upper right side of screen) if you want to delete all the callers.

In the middle, you will see the **CONTACTS** icon, aka your address book. You don't need a dedicated contacts app, as your contacts can always be found right in the telephone app.

The icon that is second from the right is the **KEYPAD**. We all know what that is. It's how we dial a number manually. It's the same keypad that the first push-button phones had.

And finally, the icon on the right is your **VOICEMAIL.** We used to call this function an answering machine, but "voicemail" has fewer letters, so it fits better into the small screen. Not only can you listen to your voicemail on the iPhone app, but you can also read a copy of the message. Note that this feature does not always work perfectly. A bad connection or a thick accent may show up as nonsensical gibberish. But you can always listen to the person's message to know exactly what they said.

iPhone – Making and Ending Calls

Remember, **GREEN means GO** and **RED means STOP!** If you see a green thing to tap or swipe, you are answering the call. If you touch or swipe the red thing, then you are ending the call.

Image 10.31

In Image 10.31 you see a call coming in while I'm on the phone. There are three options. From left to right: End & Accept, Send to Voicemail and Hold & Accept. Tap the center circle and the call will go right to voicemail. Tap End & Accept and the current call is ended and you are routed to the incoming call. Tapping on the circle on the right puts the existing call on hold while you talk to the incoming caller. When you hang up on the second call, you will be returned to the first caller.

Remember, you can also single tap the power button to silence the call or double tap the power button to send the call directly to voicemail.

Image 10.32

Image 10.32 shows how it looks when a call comes in and the phone is not in use. This time the entire screen is taken up, and there is an obvious white circle with green handset. Slide to the right to answer. If you want to send it to voicemail, tap where it says Voicemail. And if you want to answer the call with a text message, tap Message for options.

If you can't answer the phone and want to send a text, perhaps saying, "I'll call you back," tap where it says message (Image 10.32 and the screen will change. There are standard messages from which you can choose. "I'll call you later" is always a good one. In the second image, I tapped on the banner, and it went full screen. From this screen, you can:

- Decline the call (Tap Red).
- Answer the call (Tap Green).
- Send it to voicemail.
- Send a text message.

The information is all on the screen.

Image 10.33

iPhone Video Chat, i.e., Facetime

Image 10.33 shows how the screen looks when you FaceTime someone who also has an iPhone. The screen is fairly self-explanatory. I initiated this call, and this screenshot of my phone shows me in the lower left corner and my beloved (whom I called). The small picture of me can be moved around or closed just by placing your finger on it and sliding it.

Near the top there are five circles. The first has an image of a speaker—tap to turn on speaker. The second is a video camera—that's video on/off. Believe it or not, you can FaceTime with or without video! Sometimes someone FaceTimes you and, well, let's just say that you are not looking your best. Nix the camera or hold the screen to the ceiling!

Ready to end the call? Tap on the red X. That will stop the FaceTime. You will still have to hang up the call by tapping the RED circle. The third icon in the center is the microphone—tap for on and tap for off (i.e., mute). The fourth circle is to share what's on your screen. Per Apple:

1. Start FaceTime.
2. Tap the Share Content circle.
3. Tap Share My Screen.

If you have an Android and your kids have iPhones, you cannot FaceTime with them. Keep in mind that the term *FaceTime* is Apple's trademarked term for video chatting. It's like *Q-Tips* is the trademarked term for cotton swabs. FaceTime only works between Apple devices. You can video chat between Android phones easily. Newer Androids have a video camera option in the phone app.

Image 10.34

In order to have a video call between an iPhone and an Android, meaning two different operating systems, you need to use a third-party app like Facebook, Messenger, WhatsApp, Telegram, or Signal. More on that in the chapter on messaging apps.

iPhone Conference Calling

If you want to have multiple people on a call, it is SO EASY to do. (Image 10.34) Make the first call. Once the call is connected, you will see the option to ADD CALLER. Tap on it. Your contacts will open. Choose the contact to add to the call and done! You can add four other people to the call, assuming your carrier (ATT, Verizon, etc) supports this.

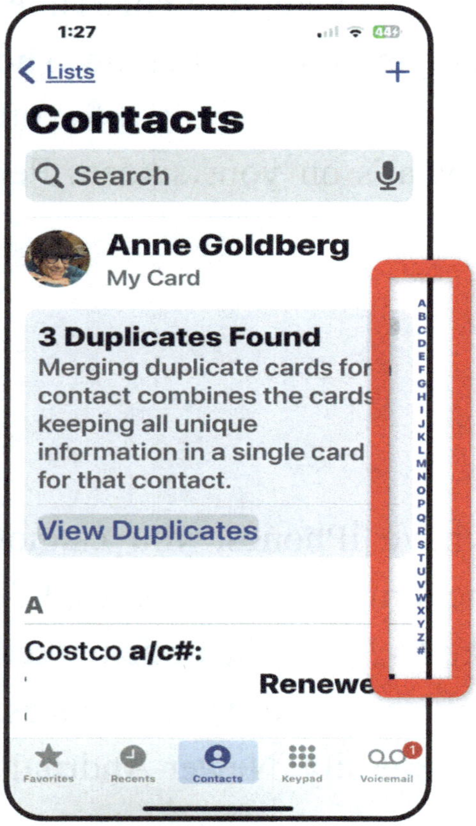

Image 10.35

iPhone Contacts

Contacts (i.e., address book) is an alphabetical listing of all your people.

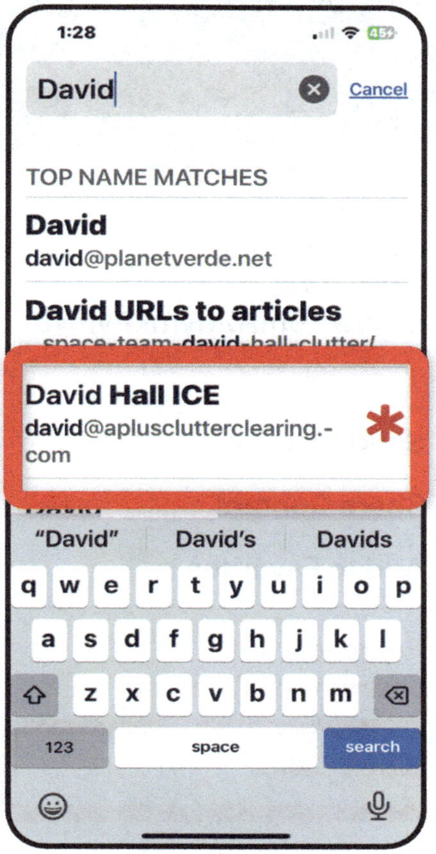

Image 10.36

When you open Contacts, you may (or may not) see a notice about duplicate entries. It's always good to allow the system to merge duplicates so all the information you need is in one place for any given contact. **Tap on View Duplicates and then Merge All or Ignore on the next page**. (Image 10.35)

When you want to search for a particular contact, you can tap on any letter in the alphabet or type the name in the search bar. (Image 10.36) As you type in the name, the system will give you suggestions as to whom you may be looking for. In this case, I'm looking for my beloved, David Hall. When his name comes up, you will notice the letters ICE next to it and a big red star. That means **IN CASE OF EMERGENCY**, this is the person to contact on my behalf.

When I tap on his name, the screen changes. (Image 10.37)

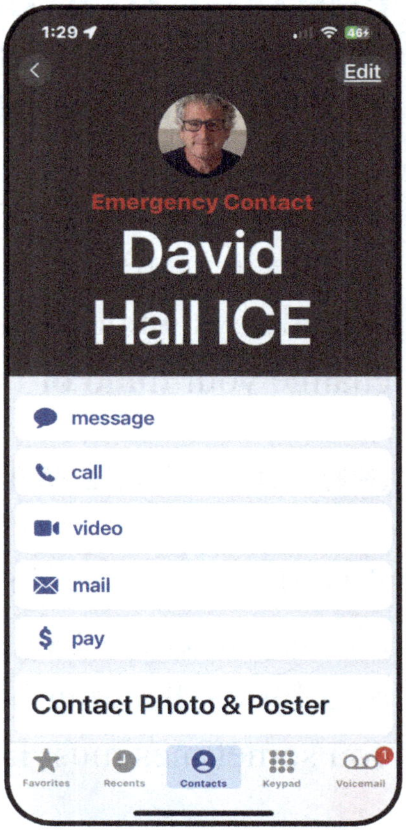

Image 10.37

At the top are quick actions. From here I can call, message, video (i.e., FaceTime), mail, or pay him. Scrolling down, you can see whatever contact information there is.

Keep scrolling all the way to the bottom, and you see **BLOCK Caller. (Image 10.38)** To be clear, when you want to block a caller in your Contacts:

iPHONE BLOCK CALLER: OPEN CONTACTS > SELECT CONTACT TO BLOCK > SCROLL TO THE BOTTOM > TAP BLOCK CALLER

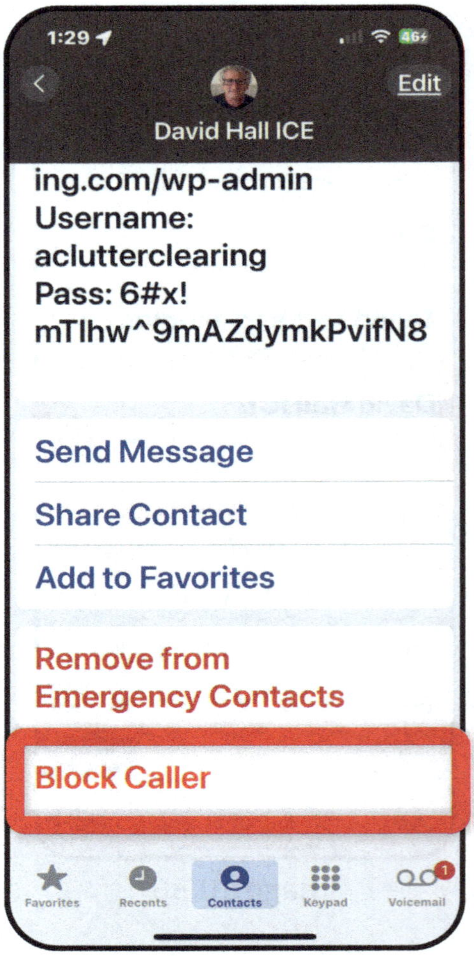

Image 10.38

Once you block a caller, this line will change to UNBLOCK Caller, so you can always undo this action if you change your mind or made a mistake.

iPHONE VOICEMAIL

Who doesn't love voicemail? It's so convenient, and with smartphones, it's easy to either listen to or read the message. Although, reading can be a bit challenging because the translation is not always spot-on, so you sometimes must listen to the message to get it right.

Accessing Voicemail

Tap on the Voicemail icon on the right side of the bottom of the screen. The screen will change and a list of your voicemails will appear. Tap on any name to read or listen to the message. (Image 10.39)

Image 10.40 shows the page offers a few options. Starting from the top left of the page, you'll see a back arrow and Voicemail. You know you can "go back" to the page before by tapping the back arrow. Below, we see is the name of the caller. Next to that is a box with an up arrow, indicating you can share this voicemail via text, email, Facebook, and more.

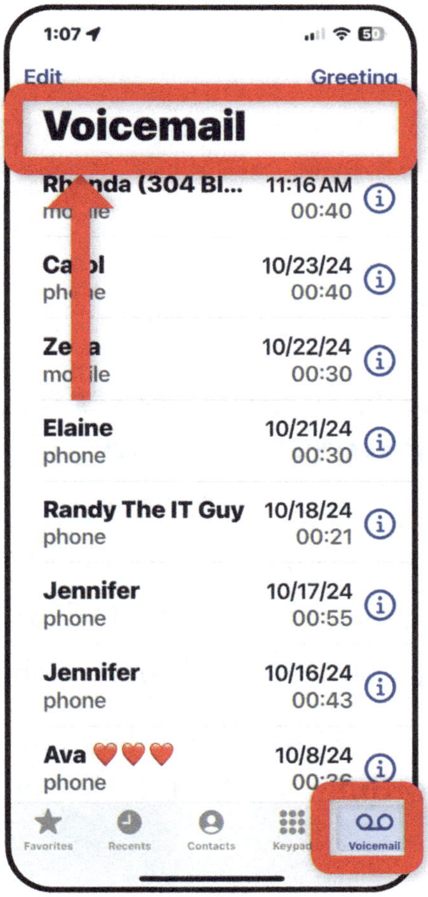

Image 10.39

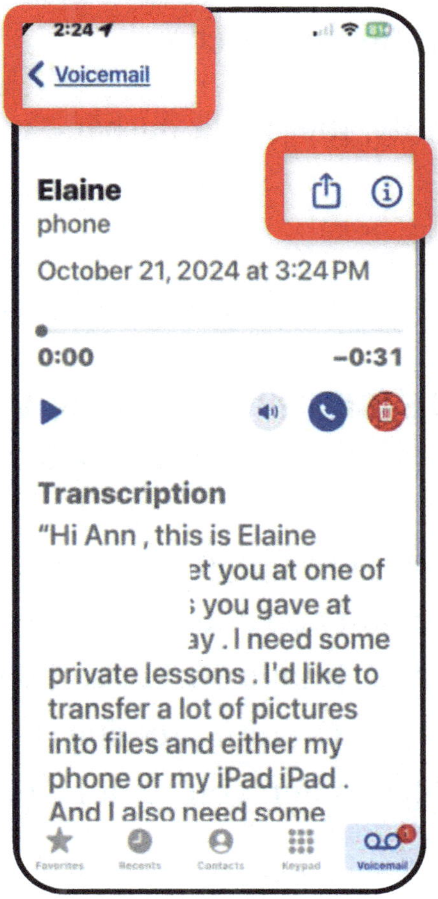

Image 10.40

Next to the Share icon is that little "i" in a circle. Remember, this means there's INFORMATION about the caller, and it is where you can block this caller.

As you move down the screen, you see a forward arrow, the symbol for PLAY. You know this symbol from the first tape decks in the seventies. Two parallel lines means PAUSE. These symbols are the same on tech today.

Moving along the line, you see a speaker. If you want to listen hands-free, tap the speaker.

Next to the speaker is a phone handset indicating that you can call this person from this screen.

And finally, there is a garbage pail. Done with the message? Throw it out.

iPhone Voicemail Record Greeting

iPHONE SETTING YOUR VOICEMAIL GREETING: VOICEMAIL > GREETING > CUSTOM > RECORD

Recording your outgoing message for your voicemail is easy. Open the voicemail app and tap on **Greeting**. (Image 10.41) The screen will change (Image 10.42) and you will have a choice of the **default** greeting or a **custom** greeting, i.e., a personal message from you. **Tap RECORD**. When you're done recording, tap **STOP**. When you're satisfied with your recording, remember to **TAP SAVE** at the top right.

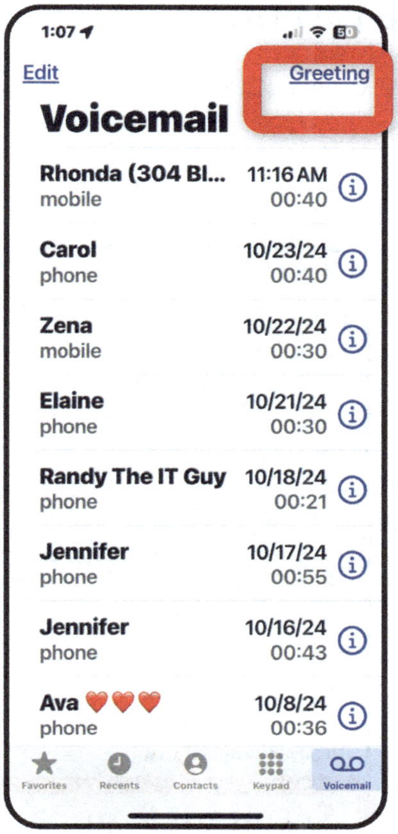

Image 10.41

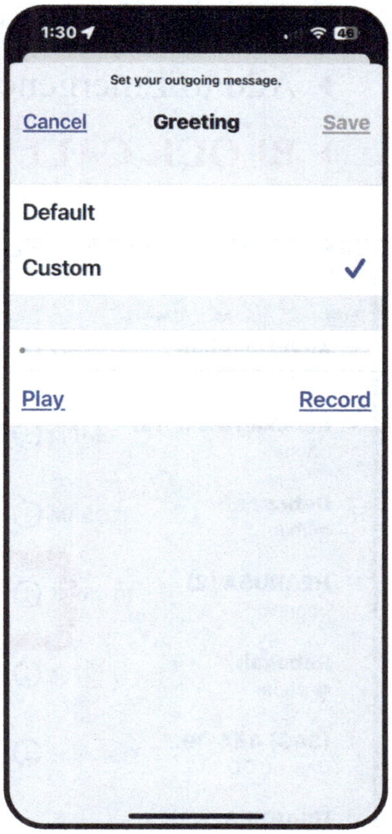

Image 10.42

iPhone Blocking Calls

When you look at your recent calls and voicemail screens, you will see an "i" in a circle. (Image 10.43) The "i" stands for INFORMATION. Tap on it, the screen changes, and you will see more information relating to that caller—whether or not this person is in your Contacts. (Image 10.44) This is what the phone knows about the caller. Let's see what this looks like.

In image 10.45, you will see recent call activity, the option to add a photo or poster to the Contact, and the telephone number. Scrolling up (so the page moves down), you will see additional options. You can:

- Send a message to the number.
- Share the Contact.

- Add the Contact to Favorites.
- Add to Emergency Contacts.
- **BLOCK CALLER.**

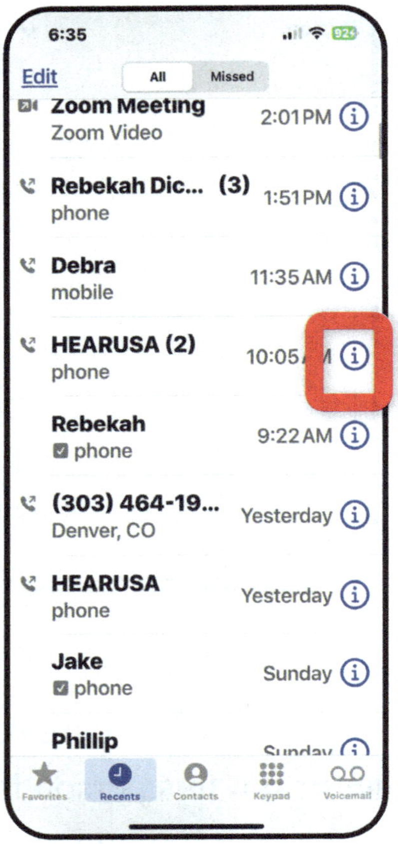

Image 10.43

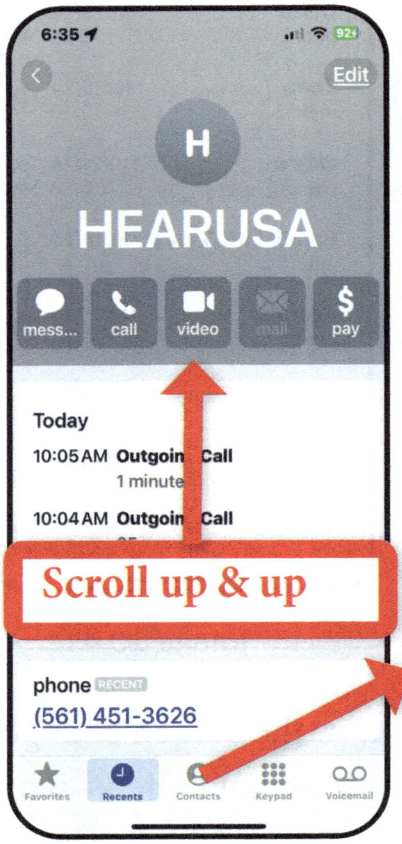

Image 10.44

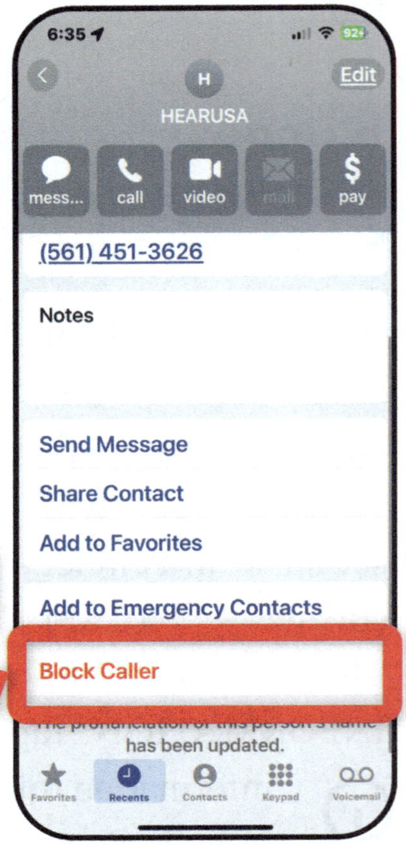

Image 10.45

Now you know how to block calls!

APPLE BLOCK CALLER: RECENTS > TAP ON THE I > SCROLL TO BLOCK CALLER

iPhone Block Calls from Voicemail

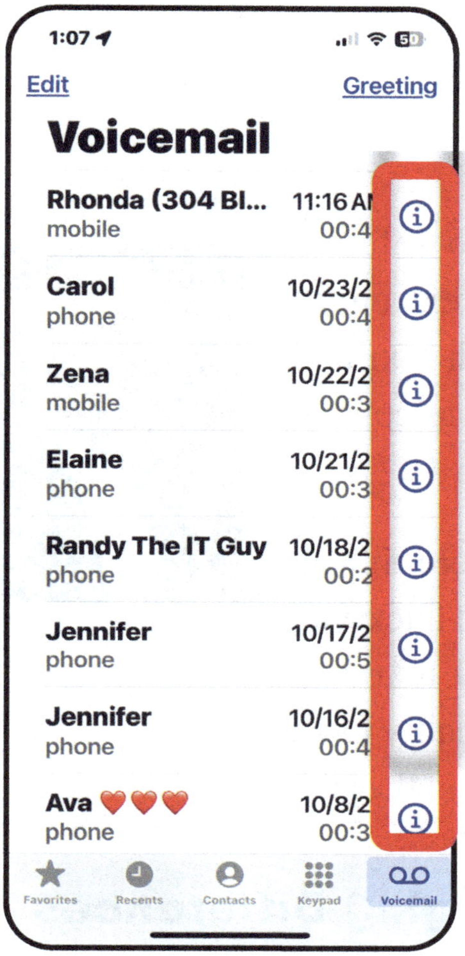

Image 10.46

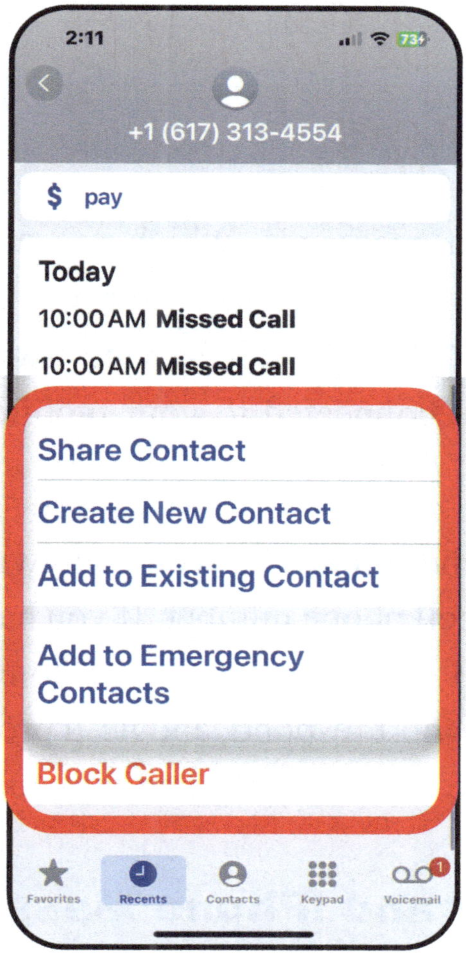

Image 10.47

You will see that little "i" in a circle in Voicemail as well. (Image 10.46) If there's a call you want to block or make as a new contact, simply tap on the caller and scroll down. You will see: Share Contact, Create New Contact, Add to Existing Contact, Add to Emergency Contacts, and **BLOCK CALLER.** (Image 10.47)

Messaging Apps (aka Text Messages)

Classic text messages, which are also referred to as SMS (Short Message Service—text only), and MMS (Multi-Media Service—with text and images) are connected to your mobile telephone number.

This Photo by Unknown Author is licensed under CC BY-SA-NC

You can send a text to anyone, anywhere, if you have their cell phone number. If you had Dick Van Dyke's cell phone number, you could text him. Likely, he won't respond, and he'll probably block you, but the capability to send that text is there!

Android and iPhone Messaging Differences

When you send a text from one iPhone to another iPhone, it is considered an iMessage and exists within Apple architecture. This means the data is technically end-to-end encrypted.

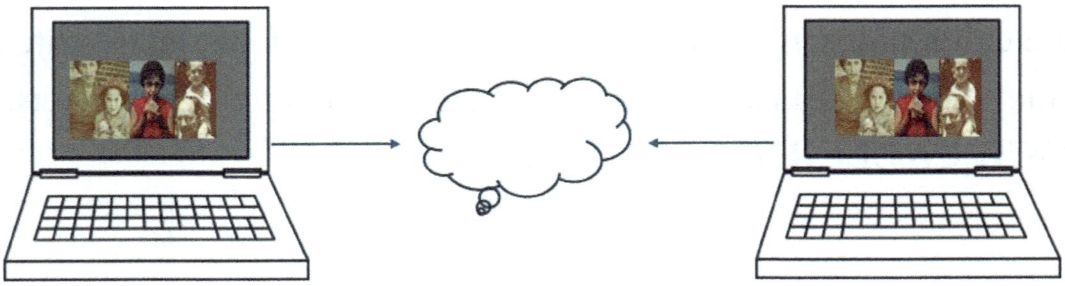

Wait, what? End-to-end encryption means there is a virtual lock (i.e., security) when sending and receiving these messages, promising 100 percent privacy and protection. Not even law enforcement can access those files. There is a caveat, though. *If you are BACKING UP YOUR TEXT MESSAGES IN YOUR iCLOUD, that is not end-to-end encrypted, and thus it can ultimately be accessed by law enforcement or hackers.* (Although, hacking into Apple systems is definitely not easy.)

There is a way to encrypt your iCloud, but doing that means if you lose that password, you are out of luck. Not even Apple can get access to the information in your cloud storage. Because of this, I am reluctant to teach this in the book. It is, however, available to those of you who want that extra level of protection. Simply search the Internet for "Advanced Data Protection for iCloud" and you will learn how to do this.

I'm not engaging in illegal activities, and there are no state secrets on my phone—I am good with the current iPhone security. I'm thinking that my average reader is not a drug dealer or involved in espionage, so perhaps this information is overkill. But I think it's important that you understand these distinctions as it helps to demystify the phone.

In an ever-increasing "big brother" society, it's good to know how to keep your conversations and activities as private as possible, even if you're not planning a heist.

When my dear friend Fleur texts me from her Android, her thought bubbles are gray and mine are green. (See Images 10.48) But when my beloved, David, texts me from his iPhone, his bubbles are gray, but mine are bright blue. (Image 10.49) Do different colors mean anything that I care about? Maybe a little.

Image 10.48

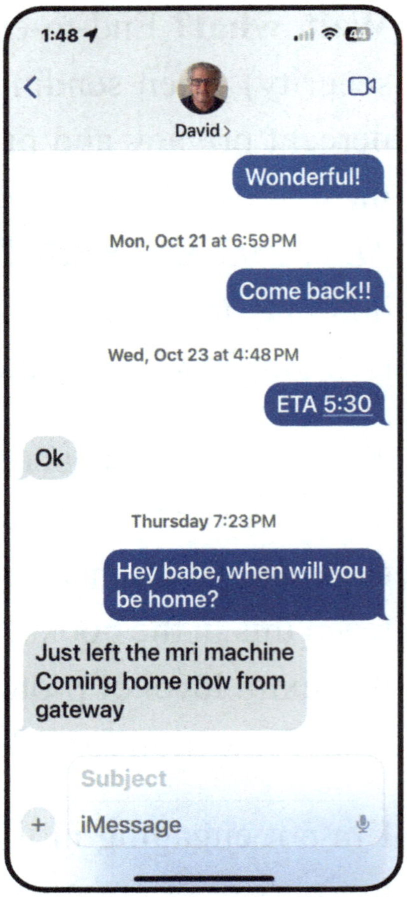

Image 10.49

Texting between Androids and iPhones is not straightforward. Messages take longer to be received, and pictures and videos are pixelated and don't look good.

Like the old Macy's and Gimbels, there's a rivalry between the two companies and, historically, they have not played well together.

However, with iOS 18, Apple will begin to use a different messaging technology called RCS. It's what Androids have been using for decades. With this update, texting between iPhones and Androids gets an update. What this means is that now you can see that your message has been delivered. Additionally, videos and pictures will be clear and sharp, group chat experiences will be better managed, and emojis work across platforms.

In order for it to work, iPhone users must enable RCS, once they have installed iOS 18. The downside to RCS is that these iPhone-to-Android messages are not end-to-end encrypted, so there are potential privacy issues. It's expected that the GSM Association, which is responsible for developing RCS standards, is working on that now.

If you still want to enable RCS on your phone, first you must verify that your carrier supports it. Follow these steps:

RCS: SETTINGS > GENERAL > ABOUT > CARRIER

If your carrier does support RCS, here are the steps to take to activate it on your iPhone:

ENABLE RCS TEXTING: iPHONE/ANDROID TEXT SETTING: SETTINGS > APPS > MESSAGES > SELECT RCS MESSAGING UNDER TEXT MESSAGING > TOGGLE IT ON.

If you follow these steps and RCS has not turned on, restart your phone.

The Traditional Text Message from Your Mobile Number

Text messaging has been around for close to thirty years. A text message is either an SMS or an MMS. Simply put, SMS texts are words only. MMS texts may contain pictures and/or videos with or without words.

We all know texting. It started on cell phones decades ago. Somehow, a text message implies a greater urgency to respond than an email. If I receive a text message with information, I feel I must respond fairly quickly, as opposed to receiving an email, which can wait a day or sometimes two!

Can I Text to a Landline?

No, you cannot text a landline. They are two different technologies. You can text to email, but the recipient receives an email from a phone number. Your message is sent via an attachment in plain text, with no images. It can be confusing if the recipient doesn't recognize your phone number.

G-Message

When you TAP on the APP to open it, you will see a list of your text messages. (Image 10.50) The only reason you won't see a list is if you are deleting everything that comes in. Open any existing text message and look at the very top right of the screen. (Image 10.51) You will see three icons, from left to right: Phone, Video Camera, three dots. (Image 10.51) You can call this person directly from the messages app by tapping on the handset. You can video call (assuming you're Android to Android) by tapping on the video camera.

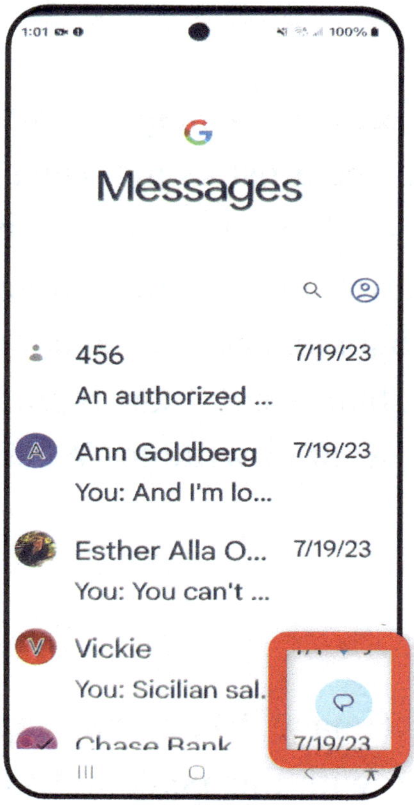

Image 10.50

Image 10.51

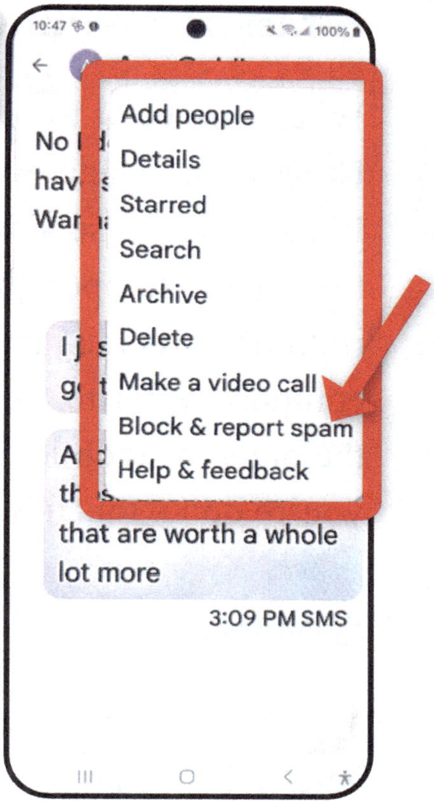

Image 10.52

Now tap on the three dots. The screen changes (Image 10.52) and you have options. From this screen you can **Delete** or **Block and report spam** for this particular message. There is more you can do. Just read the list.

A note regarding stopping legitimate (but unwanted) political and corporate text messages. Simply text back "STOP." There will be one final text confirming the unsubscribe. You won't hear from them again. Now, this doesn't work with bad guys. They don't follow rules. So just keep tapping on **Block and report spam,** as shown above.

G-Message Writing New Text

When you want to send a text, open the Messages app. (Image 10.50) Unless you delete every text you get, you will see a list of messages. If you want to send a message to one of the people in the list, tap on their name to open that thread of messages. If not, look at the bottom right of the screen and you will see a thought bubble, or a "+" sign, or compose or write. Tapping on this will open a blank text. Start typing the name or mobile number of the person you want to write to. When you're done, touch Send or the icon for it.

G-Message Creating Group Texts

You'll also notice that you can **Add people**. (Image 10.52) You tap here if you want to create a new group starting with this person. **TAP ADD PEOPLE**. A contact list appears with a circle in front of each name. Tap on however many names you want to be in this new group. Then **TAP NEXT**. Now you can give this group a new name. Maybe it's Pickleball Tuesday. Click **DONE** to complete the new messaging group.

There is another way to create a group text. Open a new text message by tapping on what looks like a blue voice bubble at the lower right side of the screen. The screen changes and the cursor defaults into the To: section. Type in the first name and select the correct person from the list that appears. Next type in another name and select that person from the list. You can do this time and again. Some group texts I've seen had twenty-seven people!

G-Messages Settings

To access various settings, tap on the circle as shown. I want to draw your attention to the very bottom of the image to **MESSAGES SETTINGS.** (Images 10.54 & 10.55)

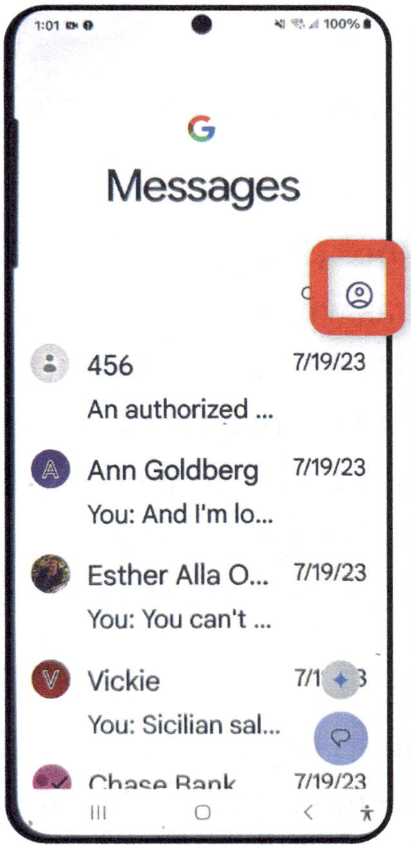

Image 10.53

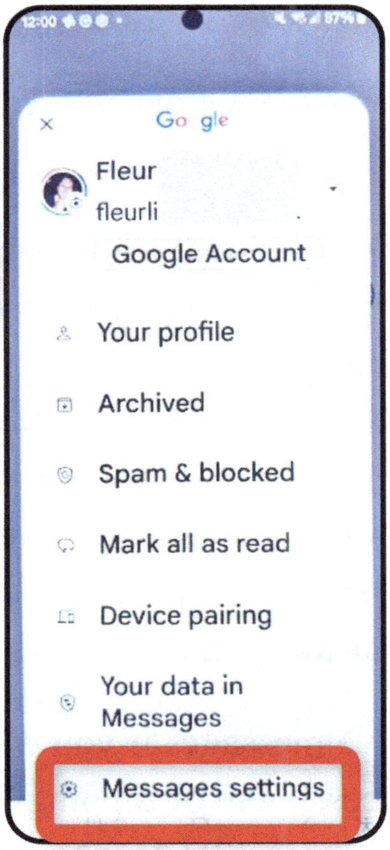

Image 10.54

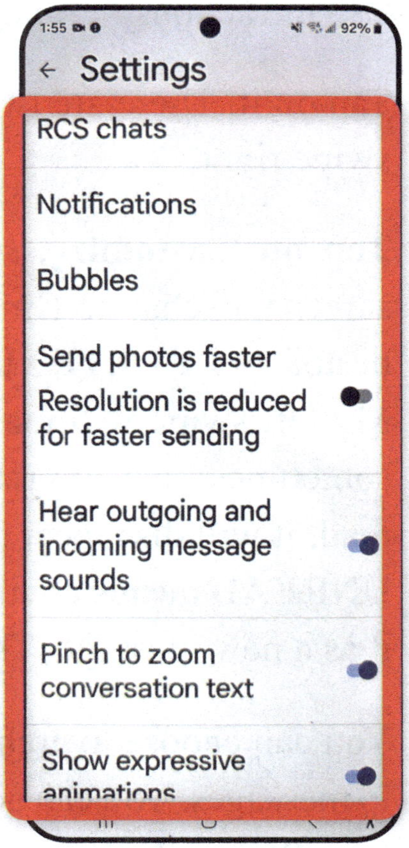

Image 10.55

RCS chats – tTap here to see if your device is compatible with the technology to make texting with iPhones more enjoyable.

Notifications – Turn them on or off for your messages.

Bubbles – Allows you to choose to make the message bubble movable around the screen. This feature depends on the make and model of your phone.

Swipe Actions

Scroll down further on settings and you will find a very useful setting, "Swipe actions." (Image 10.56)

Tap on it. There are two swipe actions you can control: swipe left and swipe right.

Tap on Customize, starting with right swipe. (Image 10.57) The screen will change. (Image 10.58) A pop-up opens with choices. I like to be able to **DELETE** a text by swiping right, so I have that checked here. My left swipe will mark a message as **UNREAD.** I like that because sometimes I have to remember to do something, and if that message is read, it will disappear as future messages come through. Marking it as **UNREAD** means it will stay bold, and my notification badge will show it as a new message. That way I don't lose it.

You can choose to archive messages if you want. They will not appear in messages. You can access them by tapping the three dots and tapping on **ARCHIVE.** It is just above **SPAM AND BLOCKED** texts.

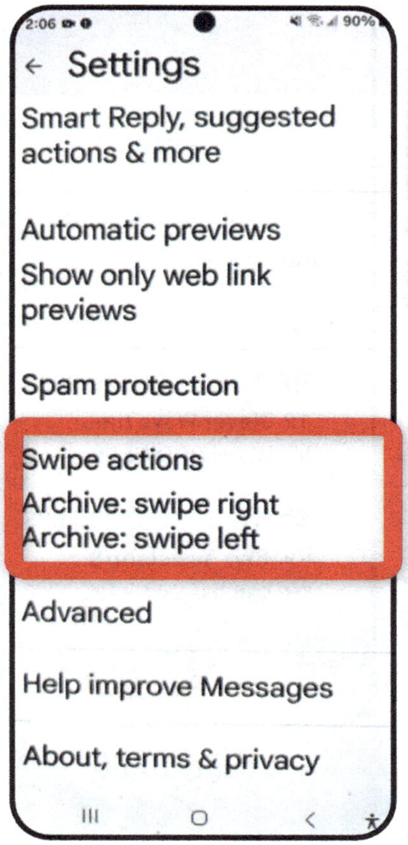

Image 10.56

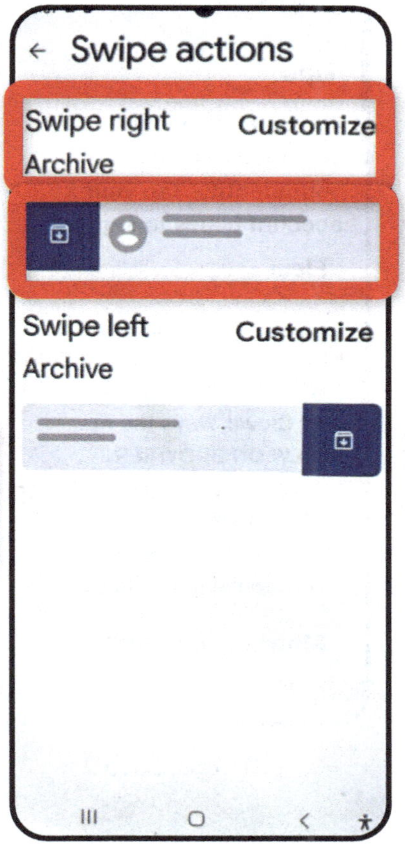

Image 10.57

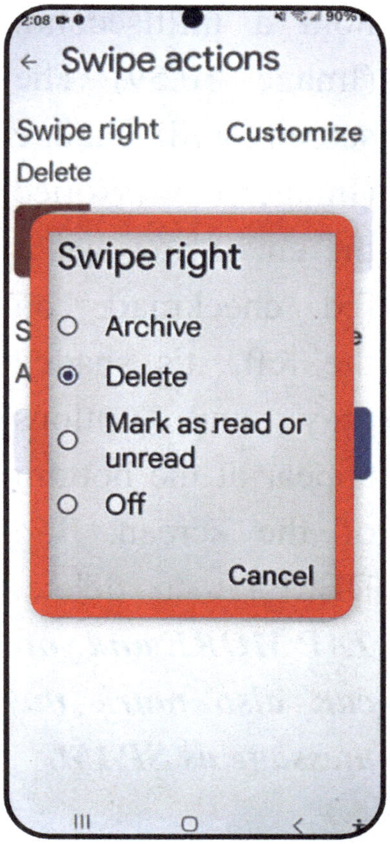

Image 10.58

Deleting Android Texts

CHOOSE MESSAGE TO DELETE > TOUCH AND HOLD > TAP DELETE AT SCREEN BOTTOM

If you want to delete the message, tap and hold a millisecond. (Image 10.59) The screen will change (Image 10.60) Notice the email now has a red checkmark on the left, it's shaded gray and options appear at the bottom of the screen. Tap DELETE to delete. ***TAP MORE and you can also mark the message as SPAM.***

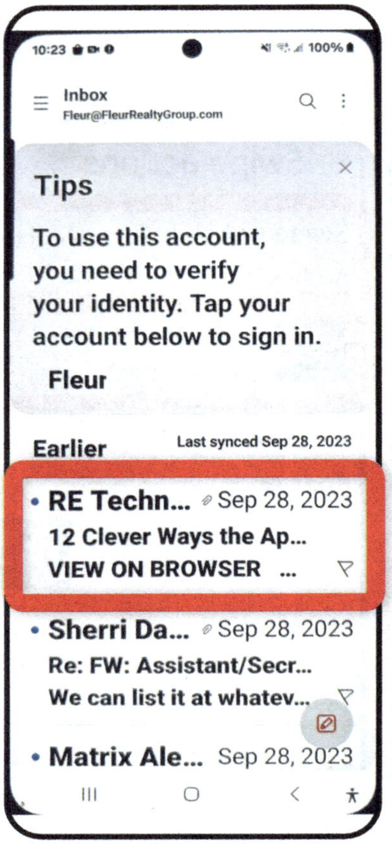

Image 10.59

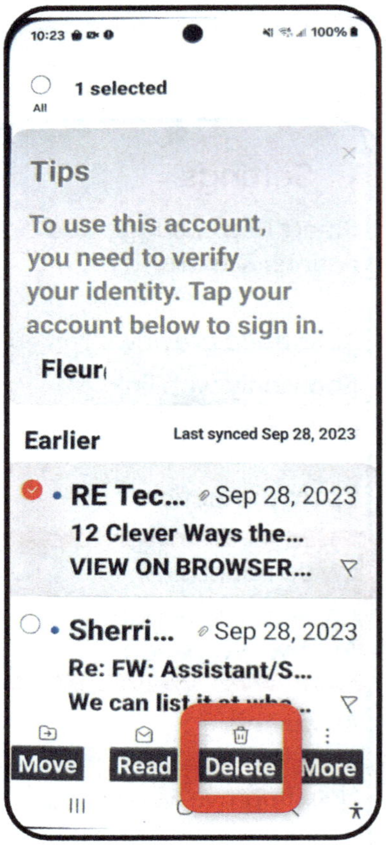

Image 10.60

iPhone iMessage

iMessage is the proprietary messaging app from Apple. Let's see it in action. Keep in mind it's easy to know if I'm texting someone with an iPhone because all the bubbles are blue. Any messages from an Androidian will have green bubbles. If you have enabled RCS on your iPhone, then your messages show up in green, and the Android messages are gray.

iMessage New Text

Open the app. To write a new text message, tap on the icon that looks like a pen on paper (i.e., writing) in the top right corner of the screen. (Image 10.61) The screen changes and a blank text opens along with the keyboard, ready for you to choose a recipient. (Image 12.62) As you start typing in a name, the system will automatically suggest possibilities. (Image 12.63) Either keep typing or choose from one of the suggested contacts.

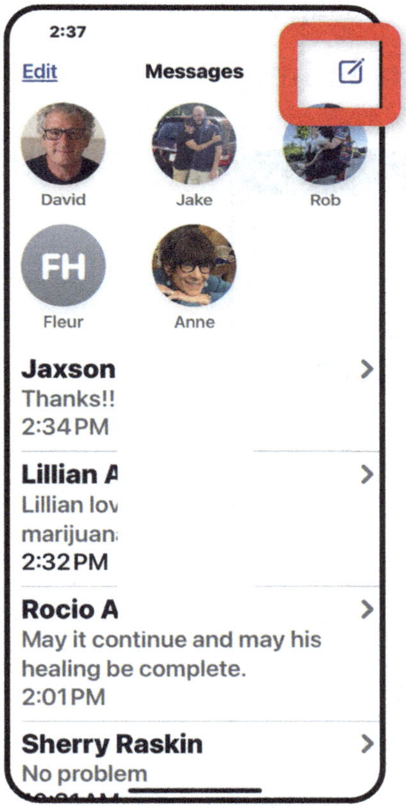

Image 10.61

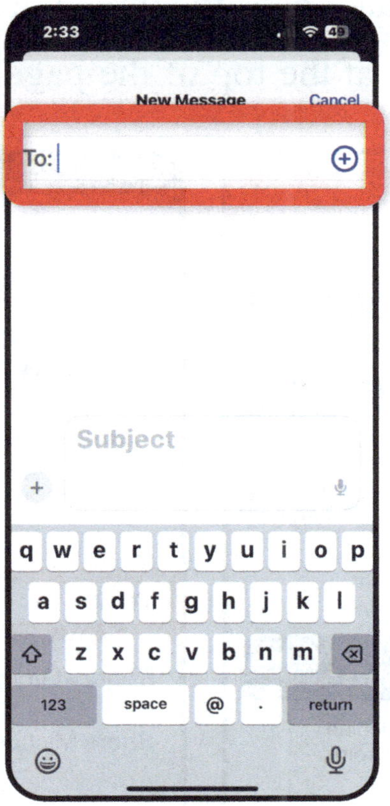

Image 10.62

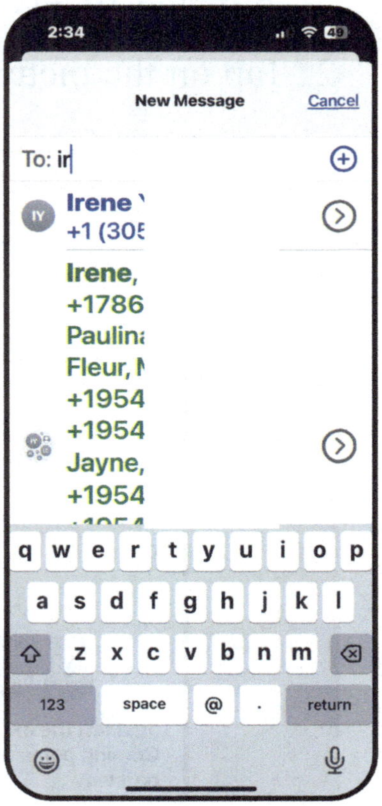

Image 10.63

If you want to send this text to more than one person, simply tap on the plus sign at the very top right as shown in Image 10.68. Tapping the plus sign will open contacts. Simply choose the contact to add. You can add lots of people to one text thread. Just know that everyone gets notified as each person responds to the text.

In the iMessage app you can access more information on that person by tapping on their photo at the top of the page. Here's how to do this:

1. Open the person's text thread. In this case, I chose David as shown in Image 10.64. That opens the thread of messages between us.
2. Tap on the picture at the top of the page as in Image 10.65 and a

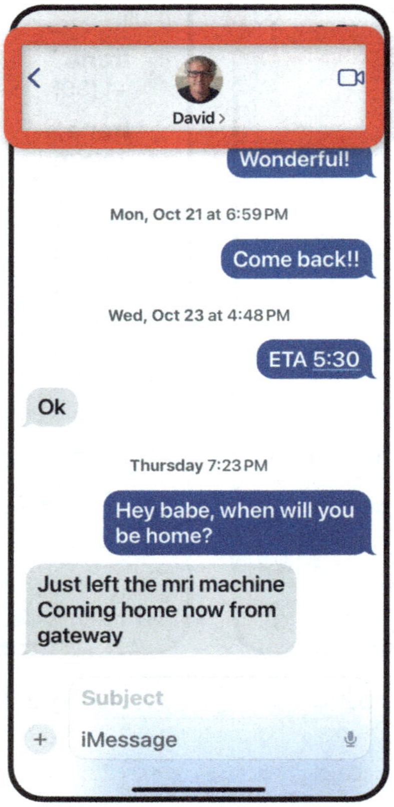

Image 10.64

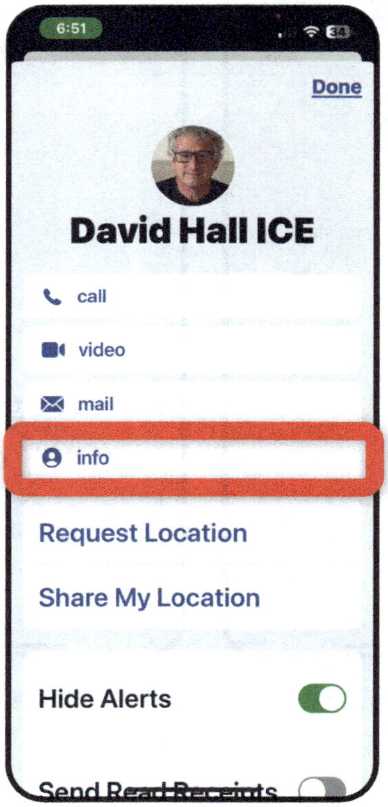

Image 10.65

new page opens from which I can call him via phone or FaceTime or email him. There is also **info**.

3. Tap on **info**, and his contact page opens shown in Image 10.66. From this place, I can scroll way down and **BLOCK** any further contact from him. I can also edit his contact from here, so if he got a new email address, I could add it. Tap **DONE** (upper right-hand corner) when finished.

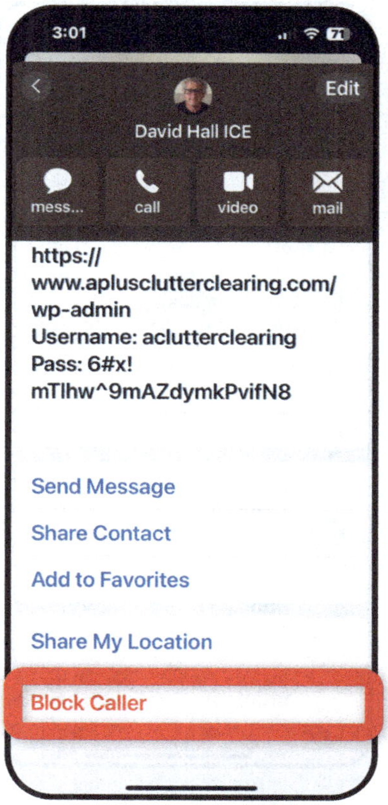

Image 10.66

Look again at Image 10.64. At the very top of the page on the right, you'll see a little video camera near his picture. Tap on that camera icon to FaceTime the person from the text screen. Again, you can only do this if the person has an iPhone, and you will know if they do by the color of the bubbles.

iPhone Pin Contacts

When you PIN any text message, it creates an easy access at the top of the screen to send and see messages from your favorite people. On my phone, I have David, my two sons, and my friend Fleur. So how do you pin a contact? It's easy. Just press and hold on the person's text

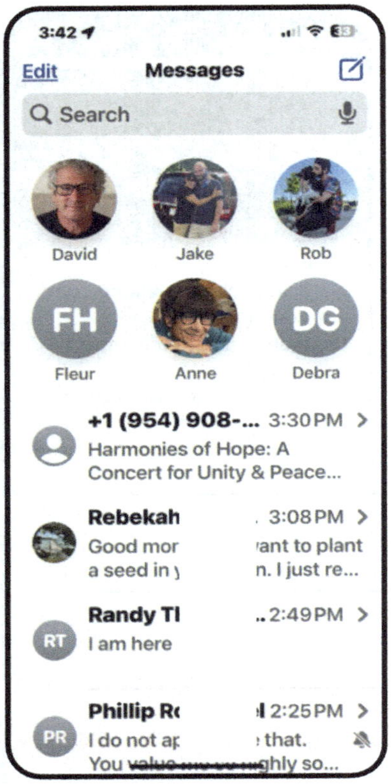

Image 10.67

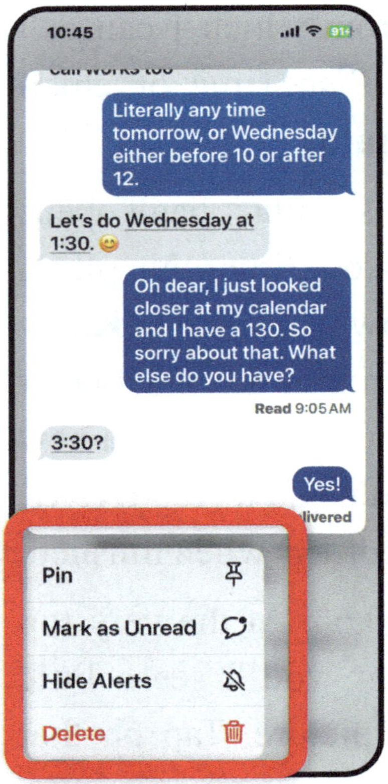

Image 10.68

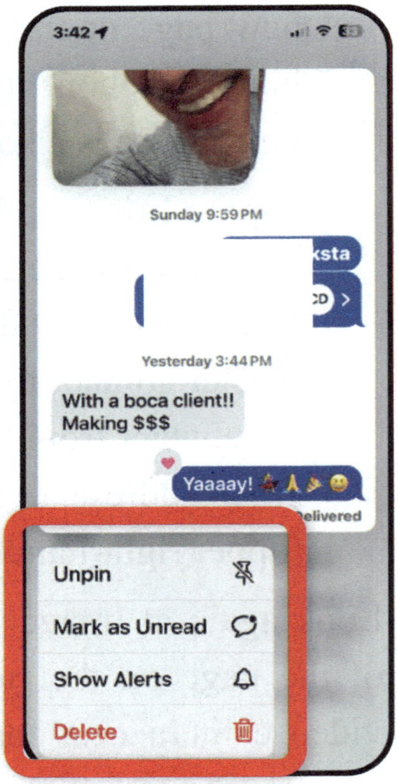

Image 10.69

message. (Image 10.67) The screen changes and a box opens, as in image 10.68. Here you will see the option to **PIN** with a picture of a pushpin. Tap on it and that's all there is.. If you decide you don't want to pin that contact, simply press and hold again until the screen changes and **TAP UNPIN**. (Image 10.69) Easy peasy!

You will also see some other options in image 10.68 & 10.69 such as MARK AS UNREAD. Why is this important? Let's say you read a text and have to do something related to that text. But more texts come in, and you forget about that text and what you were supposed to do! Marking that text as UNREAD means it will have a blue dot and be **bold.** It will catch your attention. It's a great memory aid. You can also **silence or turn on alerts** from that particular person. Finally, this is how you can **DELETE** the whole text thread if you no longer want it. I keep my messages. I've found that I refer to old messages from time to time.

iMessage Editing, Unsending, Deleting Messages

Image 10.70

iPhones offer the opportunity to edit a sent text message. This feature is wonderful when you realize the text contains a weird spelling error. There are a number of reasons why you might want to edit or unsend a recently sent text message. It's so simple to do. Just touch and hold the message to edit and the screen will change (Image 10.70)

You can't edit outside of the Apple architecture, so there's no undo or editing when texting to an Android. You have **two minutes** from sending the message to be able to **UNDO.** You have **fifteen minutes** to **edit** this message up to five times.

EDIT OR UNSEND IMESSAGES:
OPEN THE SPECIFIC MESSAGE >
TOUCH AND HOLD ON THE MESSAGE AND A POP-UP WILL APPEAR > TAP UNSEND OR EDIT.

Make the desired changes and tap the checkmark that appears. ✔ Or tap the **X** to discard changes and leave text as is. The message will be marked as "edited."

DELETING IMESSAGE

SELECT THE MESSAGE TO BE DELETED > TOUCH & HOLD > TAP DELETE

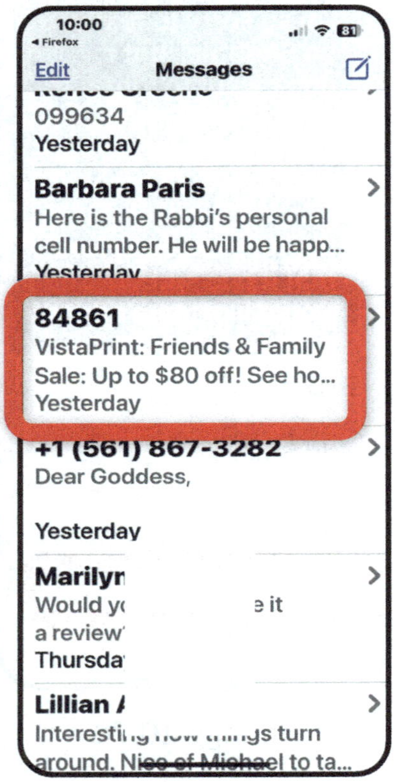

Image 10.71

Image 10.72

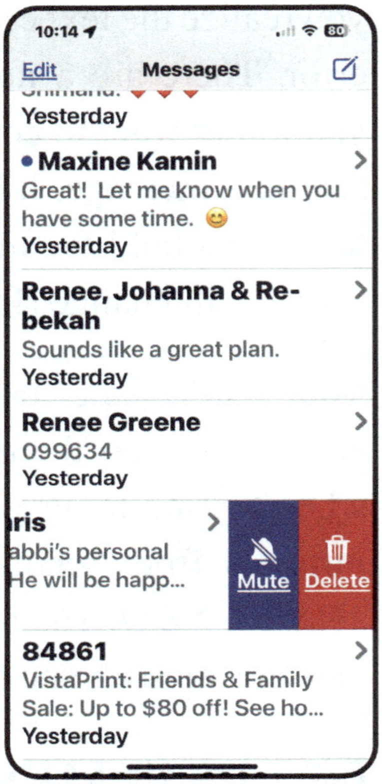

Image 10.73

You will be surprised how easy it is to delete any message. Just touch and hold the message to delete in messages. (Image 10.71) The screen will change. (Image 10.72) Here you can delete the messages from this sender.

Look at Image 10.73. You can also delete by sliding the entire message to the left and an option to delete the entire thread (i.e., all the messages from a particular person or group), here are the steps.

DELETING A TEXT THREAD: CHOOSE THE MESSAGE FROM THE MAIN PAGE. GENTLY SLIDE TO THE LEFT, BUT NOT ALL THE WAY. YOU CAN MUTE THE CONVERSATION OR DELETE FROM HERE.

Other Messaging Apps

WhatsApp, Facebook Messenger, Instagram, Signal, and Telegram are other apps that offer messaging services. Each is a separate company. If you want to send messages, you have to be signed into that app. For the purpose of this book, I am only going to focus on WhatsApp and Facebook Messenger.

Remember the days of expensive long-distance calls? With both of these apps, you can make audio calls or video calls to people anywhere in the world **for free** because these apps use the Internet to make connections, not your phone number.

If you have family in Switzerland and they use WhatsApp or are on Facebook, you can see each other and talk anytime you want. You just have to remember that calls from WhatsApp and Messenger are not identified with the caller's name or number. They come through with a weird variety of numbers that you may think is spam. It's best to make an appointment to talk so the receiving party understands it's an expected call.

WhatsApp

WhatsApp is owned by Meta (which owns Facebook too). It is a way of staying in touch with friends and family. WhatsApp is **free to use**. You can message, call, or video call from here to anyone, anywhere in the world for free. Before using it, make sure the person you want to communicate with uses WhatsApp. If they do not, this will be of little value. WhatsApp automatically detects contacts from your phone's address book who are also using WhatsApp.

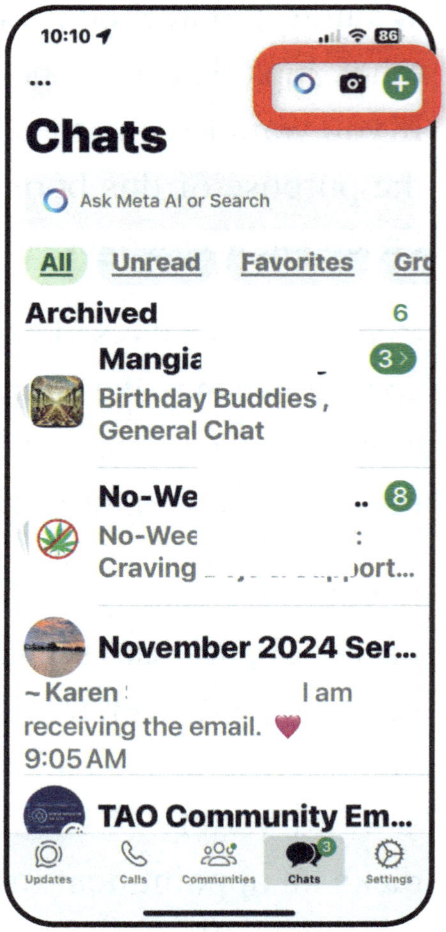

Image 10.74

Let's take a look at what's on the page here. Direct your attention to the top right of the screen in Image 10.74. **From left to right:** The first icon is Meta's AI "bot." (Remember, Meta owns WhatsApp.) It's like a virtual assistant and can search, have conversations with you, answer questions, and even create images to share. (Note: You have to have the most recent version of WhatsApp on your phone to use this. You can download the latest version from the App Store or Google Play Store.)

The second icon in Image 10.74 is the camera. You can take a new picture or attach an existing picture or video to a message. Notice you can do a selfie here too.

The third icon is a '+' sign. Tap on it and the screen changes. From here you can start a new chat, share, search, or choose default voice. If you scroll the page up, you will find your contacts on WhatsApp, making it easier to begin a new conversation.

When using WhatsApp or Messenger, it's important to keep the app on your front page and allow notifications so you know when new messages come in.

Here are a few significant differences between WhatsApp and traditional text messaging apps:

1. WhatsApp has to be downloaded and requires a good Wi-Fi connection.
2. Text messaging comes preinstalled on every phone.
3. WhatsApp is 100 percent encrypted and more secure than texting. Remember, although iPhone text messages are encrypted, that protection disappears if you are backing up to iCloud (which is not encrypted, unless you jump through hoops).
4. WhatsApp allows for group **voice *and* video calls,** which can be fantastic for families who don't want to bother with Zoom. There are no passwords or links to tap for a group call.
5. You can send large files via WhatsApp, so that folder of wedding pictures/videos can be uploaded and shared easily with loved ones.

Facebook Messenger

If you have a Facebook account, you can call or video chat with any of your "friends." This can be very convenient if you don't have someone's phone number, yet you want to have a conversation with them. It is free and also works internationally. So, if you have a cousin in France with whom you are friends on Facebook, you can video chat with them for free anytime. My cousin lives in London, and we communicate in this way. It is simply fantastic to be able to see him even though he is 4,000 miles away.

At the end of the day, Messenger is the message portion of Facebook. When you open the Messenger app, you will see the main message page. The circles at the top are not pins. They show up organically, based on Facebook posts of friends. Tap on any message to open and read all the conversations between you and that person.

I invite you to bring your attention to the top left of the page in Image 10.75. You will see three lines (with or without a red dot). Tap on the lines and the screen will change. In Image 10.76 you can see my name at the top. If I tap on my name, the screen will change, and I will be shown all the pages that I am associated with on Facebook. You may or may not care about this. It's good to tap and review your information.

Telegram & Signal Messaging Apps

These are other communication apps. Telegram is only fully encrypted if you create a "Secret Chat," whereas Signal is fully encrypted. Personally, I don't care. None of my friends use these apps, so I don't

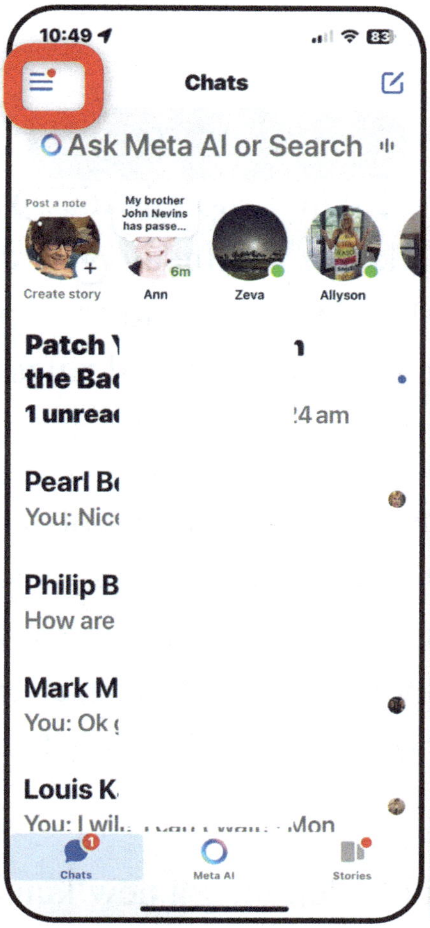

Image 10.75

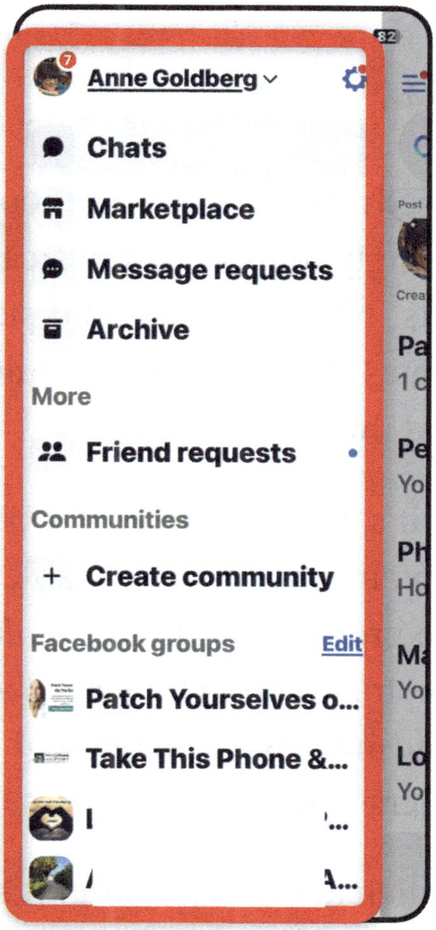

Image 10.76

either. They are of little value if your friends and family don't use them. I think Facebook Messenger and WhatsApp are better choices because that's where seniors are. Please don't think I'm dissing these apps. They don't fit into my life and how I do things, and I am not looking for yet another messaging app. Three are enough!

Email

As discussed much earlier in the book, email—short for electronic mail—is increasingly replacing physical letters, birthday and anniversary cards, gifts, bills, invoices, and statements, much to the horror of the United States Postal Service. While the USPS is not thrilled there are a lot of good things about email.

First off, it's fast and free. It's particularly convenient to have your email on your phone and/or tablet and/or laptop. Easy access. Many of you are probably thinking, *Yeah, Anne, easy for you but not for me.* I get that. It's alien. The screen looks like nothing has ever looked before, and now we're supposed to rely on this thing that we don't really understand.

It's only alien at the beginning. It's like learning a new language. It's a challenge to our brains-at first. That's why I'm here with you. I know you can do this. Now, let's get onto some learning.

Many companies have email apps. Gmail, Apple Mail, Yahoo, AOL, Hotwire, and Outlook are some of the most commonly known and used. They are all the same, and they are all different just the way dashboards are the same and different from one auto manufacturer to another.

For the purpose of brevity, I am only going to talk about Gmail and Apple Mail. If you use a different company, you can still benefit from reading these pages because there are similarities across the board.

They all do the same thing. They just put the commands in different places. Let's start with Gmail.

Gmail for Android and iPhones

Android's whole architecture is Google-based, and Gmail is part of your Google account. If you have an Android, you have a Google account and a Gmail address. It is the master account under which all your Google accounts live. If you have an iPhone, you may or may not have a Gmail address and the attendant Google account. You do have an **Apple ID** (soon to be your Apple Account).

Google Accounts have:

- Gmail
- Google Calendar
- Google Contacts
- Google Photos
- Google Drive (free cloud storage)
- Google Account
- Google Maps
- YouTube

I enjoy using Gmail. I think the interface (i.e., what you see on the screen) is clean and easy to navigate, especially on the small screen of a smartphone. I've had my Gmail address for more than twenty years. The reason is mostly that I have an iPhone and a PC, which means I cannot get the Apple Mail app on my PC. I *can* get Gmail on my iPhone.

Gmail Step by Step

First, let's take an overview. Notice there are emails that are darker. That means they are UNREAD. Either read them or trash them!

Now I'd like to bring your attention to the three lines at the top left of the first screen in image 10.77. Tap and the screen will change. Image 10.78 shows that you are now at the *dashboard* for your Gmail. Here you will find Sent mail, Drafts, Starred, Spam, Trash, and more. It's important to empty your Spam and Trash folders on a regular basis. Otherwise, all that data is just taking up room in your device storage. Be sure to check your Drafts folders for emails you began to write but

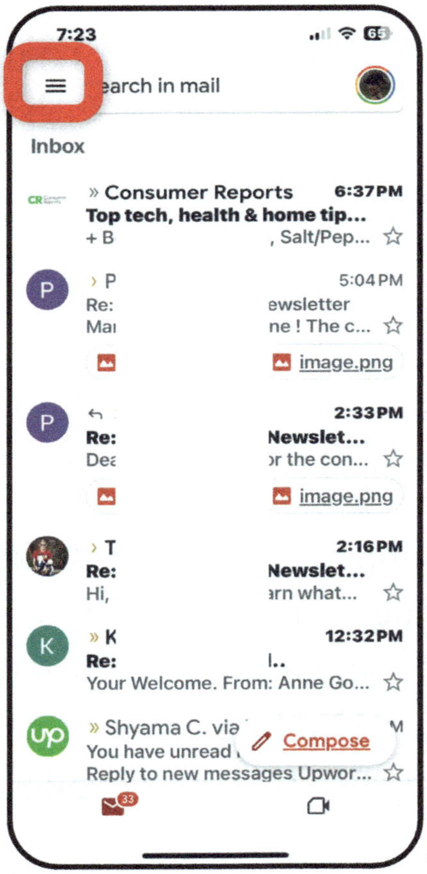

Image 10.77

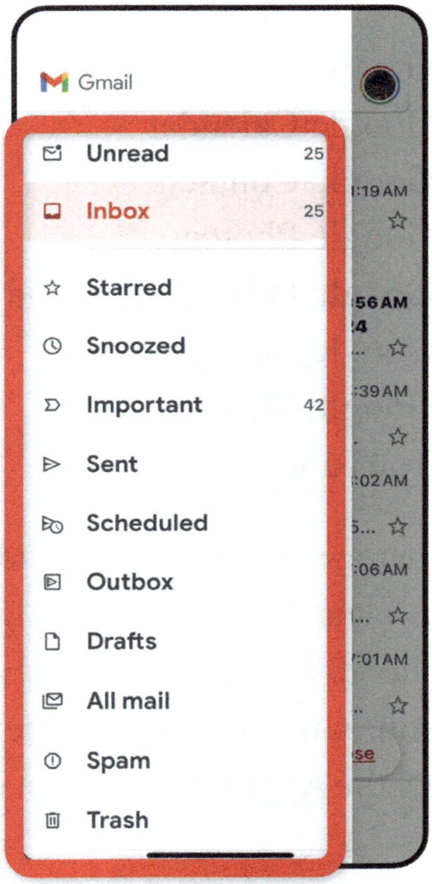

Image 10.78

never sent. These end up being saved in Drafts. Delete any that you will not send. Send any that you meant to send and forgot.

You Star an email when you want to designate it as important. Emails that are shown in **BOLD** are unread. UNBOLDED emails have been read.

Back at the Inbox in Image 10.79, gently pull down from the top of the page with one finger when in Gmail and a search bar appears at the top of the page. (Image 10.79) Let's say you're looking for a specific email, but it was from a while ago. You know who sent it, so you tap in the search bar and begin typing in their name or email address as shown in image 10.80. If you remember the subject, add that too. Gmail will find all the mail from that person with those words. It's easy

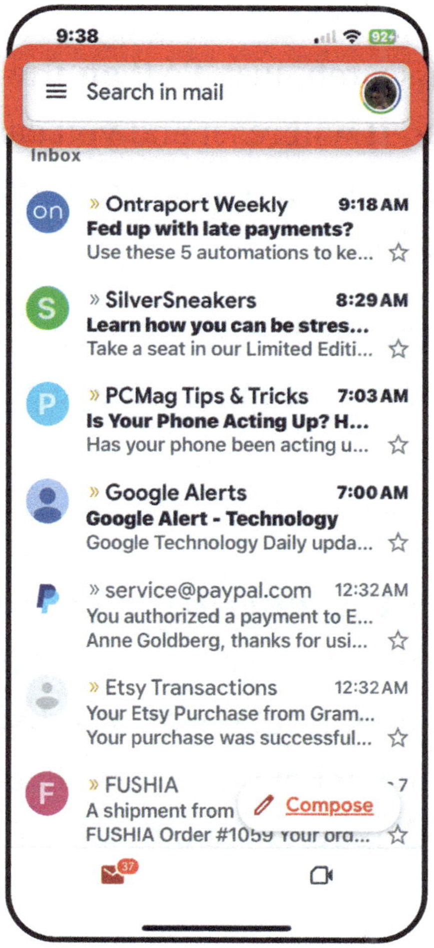

Image 10.79

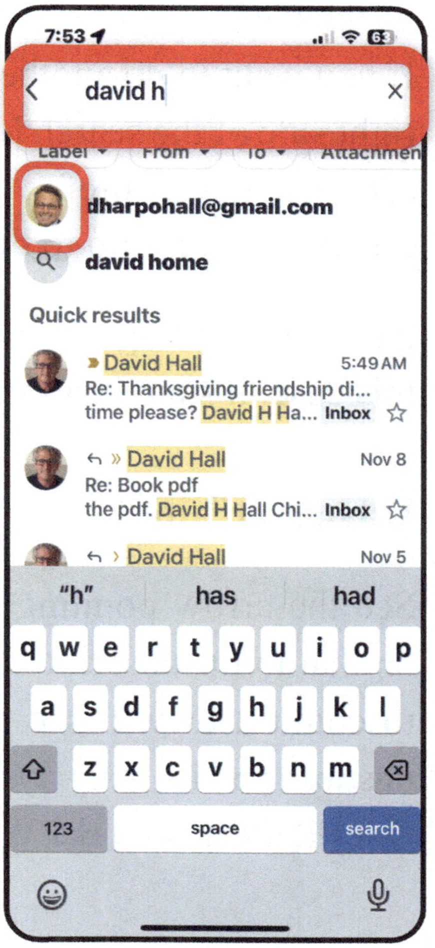

Image 10.80

to find what you need by searching.

Gmail Search

1. Tap on the search bar.
2. Start typing and AI predicts results, and I keep typing until I see the email address I want.
3. Notice the box that says **Quick Results** in image 10.86. Emails below that will all be from David. Now I just scan to find the one I want.

If you want to do another search, just **TAP on the X** all the way on the right side of the search bar. It will reset and you can look for something else. Or, if you prefer, tap on the back arrow on the left side of the search bar to return to the Inbox.

Next we're going to look at what happens when you open an email. In this case, it's an email from TechSmith. (Image 10.81)

Unsubscribing

See the arrow pointing to **Unsubscribe** in blue in image 10.82? Tap on that to unsubscribe from future newsletters. You'll likely either ask to confirm or will see a confirmation of unsubscribing. That link to unsubscribe isn't always there, but there is another way to unsubscribe. Does it always work? With reputable companies? Yes.

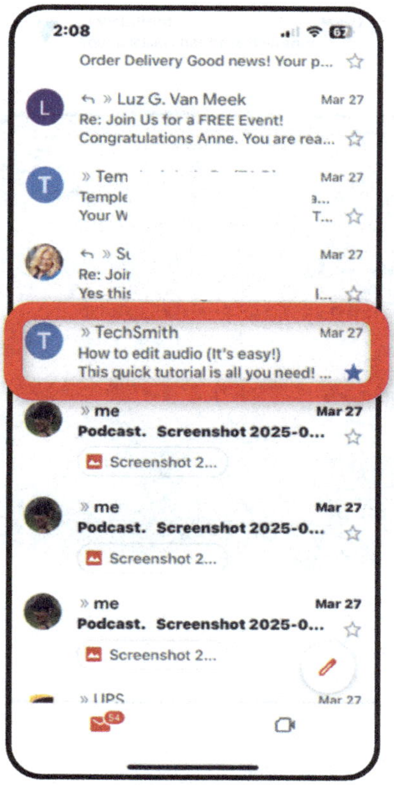

Image 10.81

Image 10.82

Image 10.83

If you don't see the blue unsubscribe at the top, scroll all the way to the bottom of the email. (Image 10.83) You may see a whole lot of language. Look carefully for **UNSUBSCRIBE** hidden in the language. It's typically quite small. (See Image 10.83) Sometimes it says **MANAGE SUBSCRIPTION,** and you unsubscribe there. If the screen changes, don't get nervous. Follow the prompts by reading the page that comes up.

Gmail – Reporting Spam & Blocking Senders

Do you see the three dots at the very top right of the page? (Image 10.84) Tap on them. The screen will change, and you will see a list of options. (Image 10.85) There are some nice features here to explore, but the most important one for you is **REPORT SPAM.** Tap on it and the email goes right to spam.

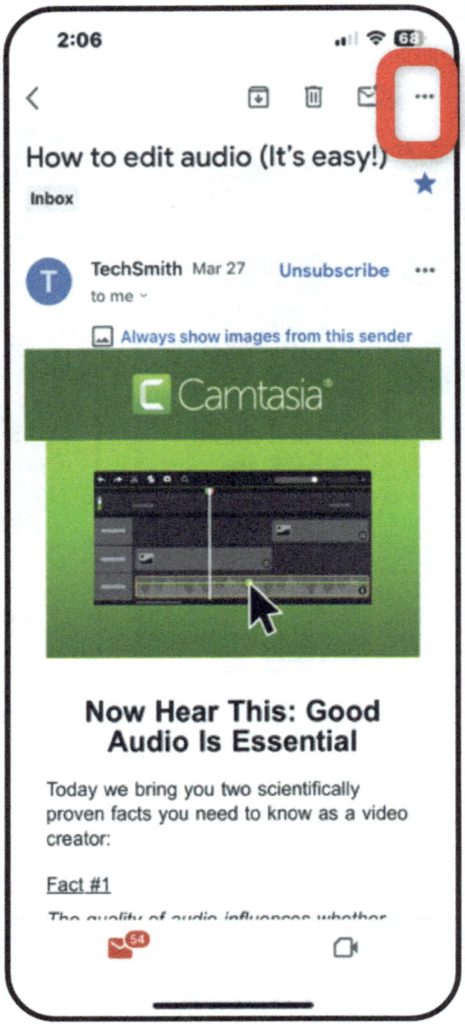

Image 10.84

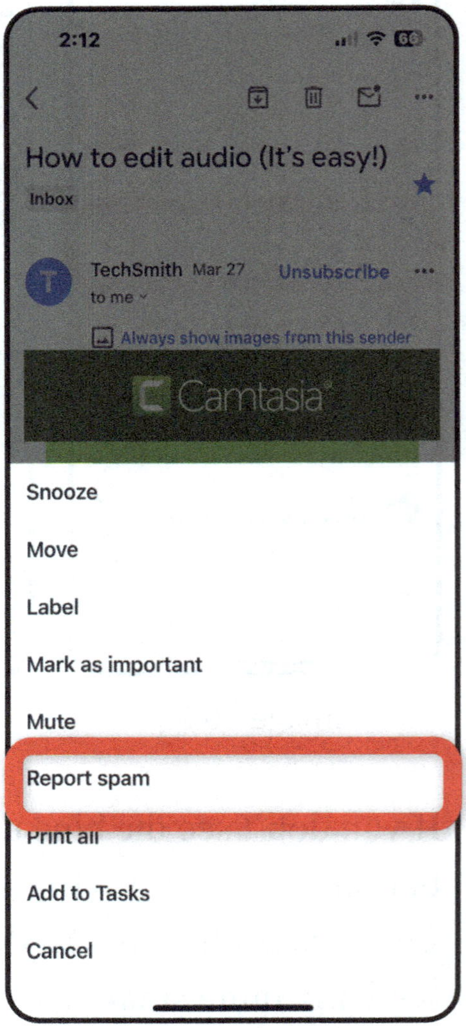

Image 10.85

Another way to unsubscribe is to look for the three dots on the same line as the sender. (Image 10.86) Sometimes you will see the word UNSUBSCRIBE here as well.

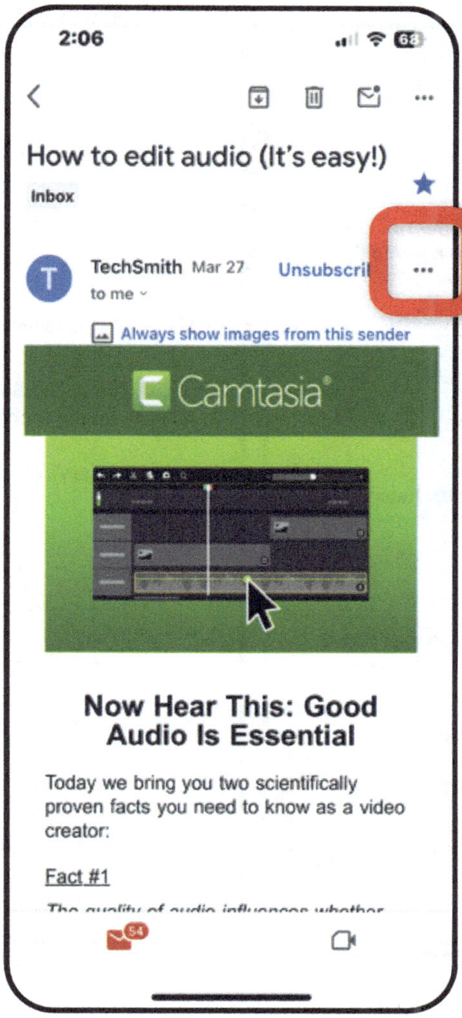

Image 10.86

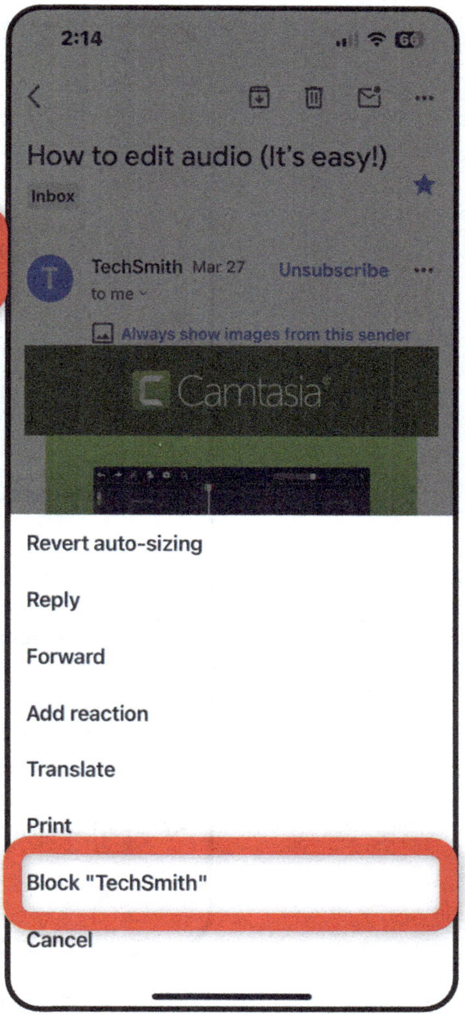

Image 10.87

Tap on the three dots, the screen will change, and a whole different set of options opens up. (Image 10.87) This screen offers the opportunity to **BLOCK** a specific email address from your mail. Upon blocking, Gmail will ask if you want to report spam. Say yes!

Notice in this area is how you can print that email, assuming you and a Wi-Fi printer are on the same Wi-Fi network. That would be the case if you were home.

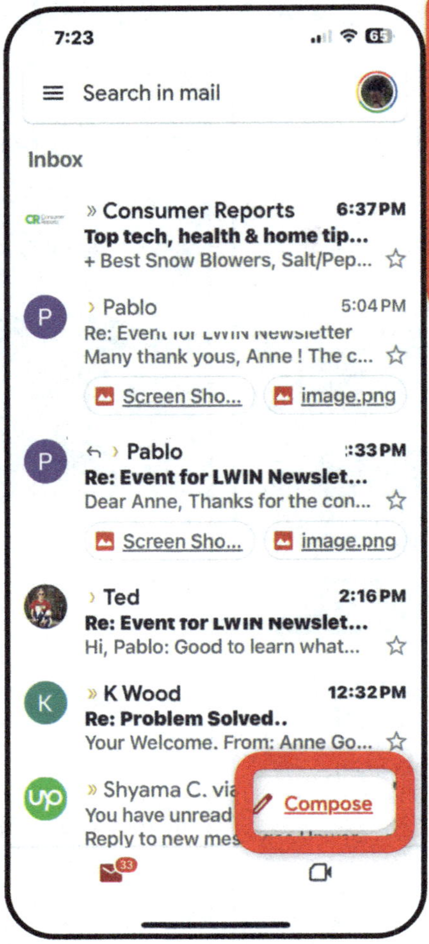

Image 10.88

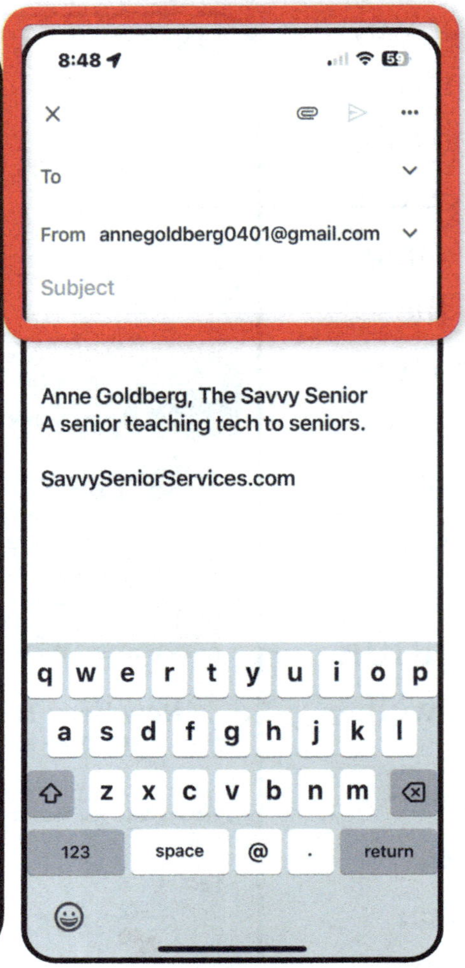

Image 10.89

Gmail – Compose New Email

Tap on **Compose** as shown in image 10.88**.** The screen changes and a blank email opens, with the keyboard ready. (Image 10.89)

Looking from the top left, I see the time and some little things on the right. Then just below, I see an **X**, what looks like a paper clip, a pale arrow, and **three dots**.

On the next line I see **To:** This is like the front of the envelope. It's where the address goes. Only now the address is not a street, city, and town; it's an email address or a name. (You can type just the name if that person is in your contacts and there is an associated email address.) You will notice that the pale arrow will darken as you provide an address.

From: This is like the upper-left corner of the envelope. It's the return address and will always be your email.

Subject: It's always good to write a subject. It's nice for the recipient and makes it easier to search for, if the need arises.

Once you've filled in these fields—i.e., you've addressed the envelope and created your subject—it's time to write the email. Just tap in the area under subject and type away.

It's always good to put something in the subject line to give your reader an idea of what's in the email. Plus, a good subject line makes it easy to search for emails later on. Once you've completed the top area, move your cursor to the body of the email, just below the subject, denoted here by an arrow. (Image 10.89)

After you have filled out the "TO" field, the little arrow at the top right, next to the paper clip, will darken. Once you've written your email, it's ready for you to tap on the arrow ➤ and send the email.

Emailing Multiple People

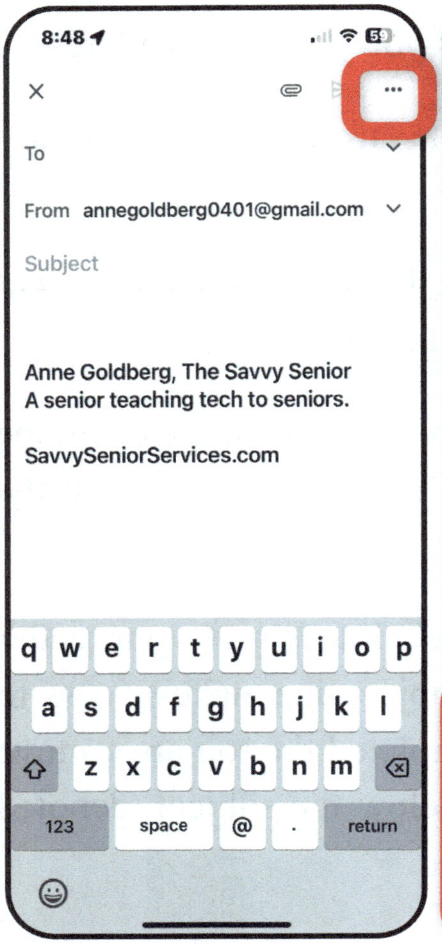

Image 10.90

Image 10.91

When you are filling out the "TO" section, TAP RETURN on the keyboard after each name. You can add as many names as you want. At the top right of a new email are three horizontal dots. (Image 10.90) Tap on the dots and the screen will change. You'll see the little box open (Image 10.91) with options to **Schedule** a particular time to send the email, the option for **Confidential Mode,** which allows you to set a password for the email. This is followed by **Discard** (i.e., throw it out) and **Cancel** (i.e., I don't want to do anything except exit this screen).

Gmail – Replying / Forwarding Email

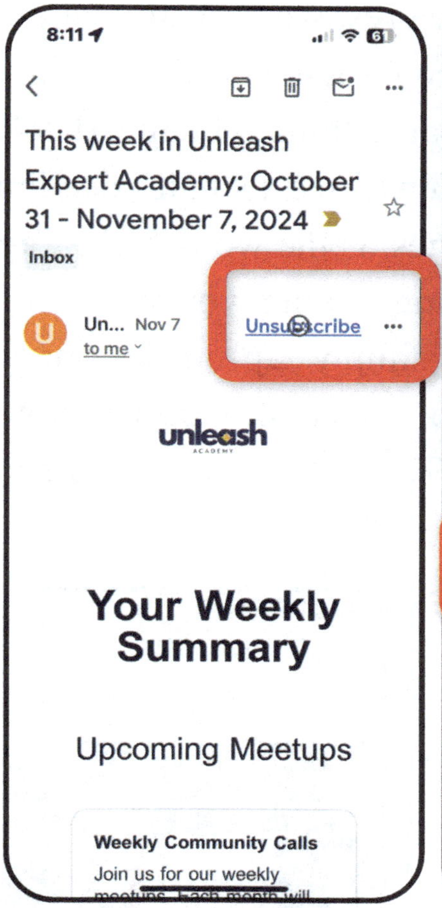

Image 10.92

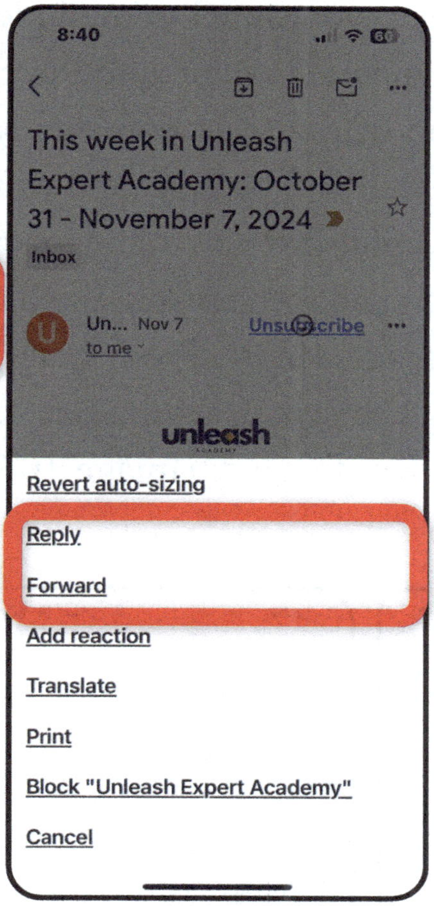

Image 10.93

When you want to reply to any Gmail, look again at the three dots to the right of Unsubscribe. (Image 10.92) Tap on them and the screen will change as in Image 10.93. This email was sent only to me. Therefore, there is an option to REPLY, but no option to REPLY ALL. Be careful when you REPLY ALL. Not everyone wants to know you're going to be late for the meeting. Maybe only the organizer cares. Tapping Reply means only the sender will get the response. Not everyone needs to know your response. Forward means sending it along to someone else.

Attaching a Picture to an Email

Back in the day when we wanted to mail pictures, we typically would use a paper clip to attach the photos to the cover letter. Well, the little paper clip at the top of the page does the same thing. (Image 10.94) Tap on it and the screen will change, and you will see a small selection of pictures. On the right, just above the images, is the word ALL. **Tap on All** (Image 10.95) and the screen will change so that you are seeing all your photos. (Image 10.96) From here, simply tap on the image you want to attach. The screen will revert to the email with the photo attached, ready for you to send. (Image 10.97) Just enter the name(s)

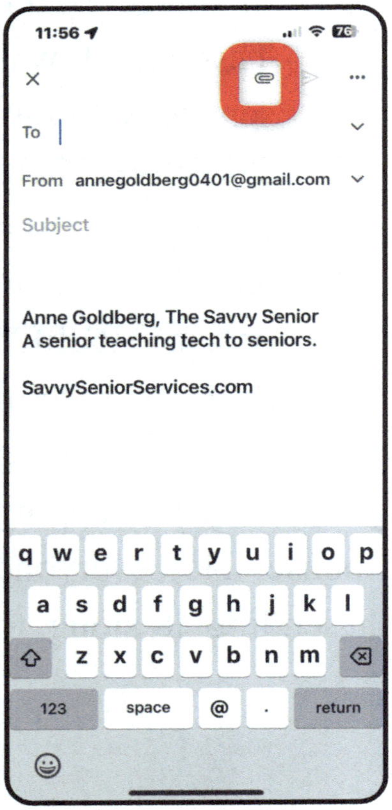

Image 10.94

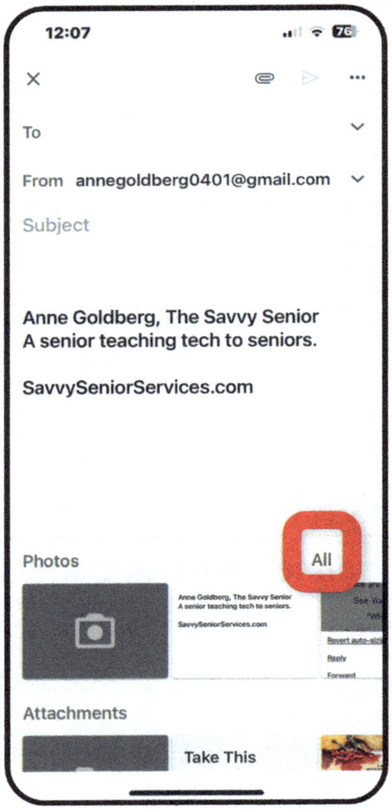

Image 10.95

Image 10.96

of recipients with a nice subject and then tap the arrow at the top right to send.

Finding Your Google Account

At the upper right of image 10.98 there's a circle. Tap on it. This is your Google Account access area. **Tap on Google Account** to view and make changes to privacy and security settings.

If you have more than one Gmail address, you can add them here by tapping on

ADD ANOTHER ACCOUNT. (Image 10.99) You can also see how much Google storage you are using. In this case, I'm using just 5 percent of my total storage. (also Image 10.99)

Image 10.97

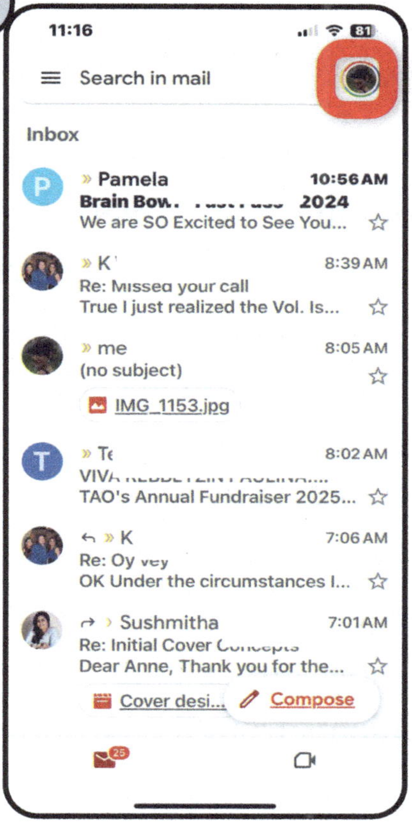

Image 10.98

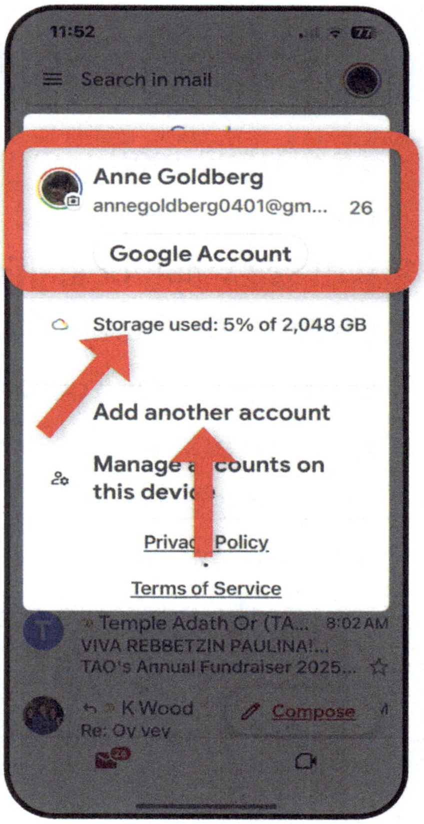

Image 10.99

Apple Mail

This is the default email app for Apple devices. A lot of people use this for their mail. This app can display many different email addresses, which can be added in settings. You will need the password for any email addresses you're adding, so make sure you have them.

Adding Email Accounts to Apple Mail

SETTINGS > SCROLL TO MAIL > ACCOUNTS > ADD ACCOUNT > FOLLOW PROMPTS

APPLE MAIL – WRITING NEW EMAIL

The Apple mail app is blue with a white envelope. Open the app and bring your eye to the bottom of the screen (Image 10.100) where you will see what looks like a pen on paper (i.e., writing). Tap on it and the screen will change. The cursor defaults to **To:,** which is where you will start typing the recipient's name. (Image 10.101) A list will populate. Keep typing until you see the person's name or their email address come up. (Image 10.102) TAP ON THE NAME. It's super easy. Emailing multiple people is just like emailing one person. You can either start typing the person's name to bring up their email address, or you can tap on the "+" sign on the same line. Doing that will open your contacts and you can choose recipients from there.

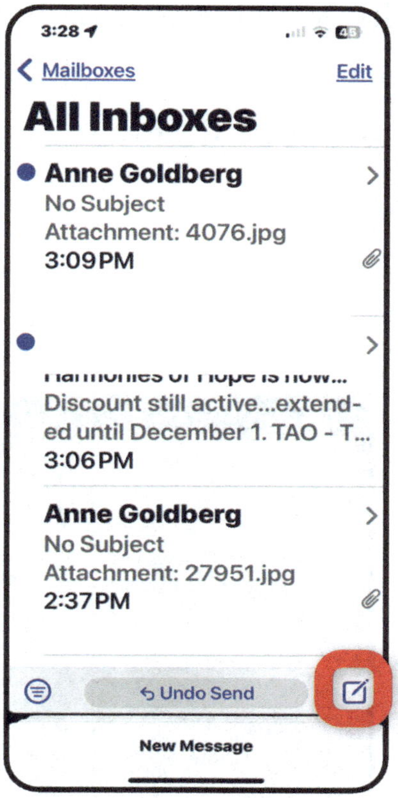

Image 10.100

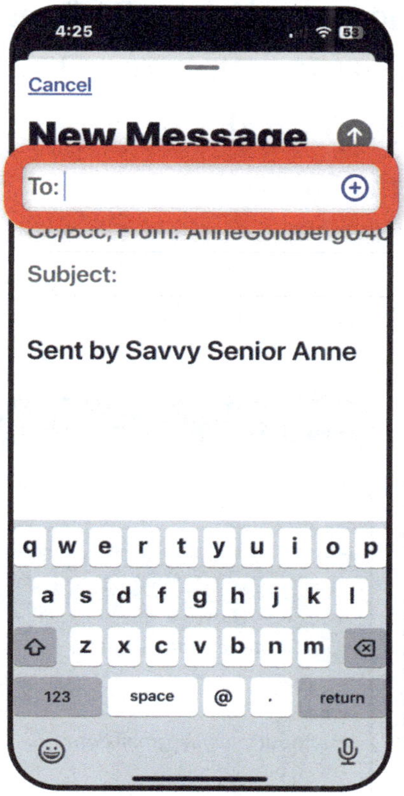

Image 10.101

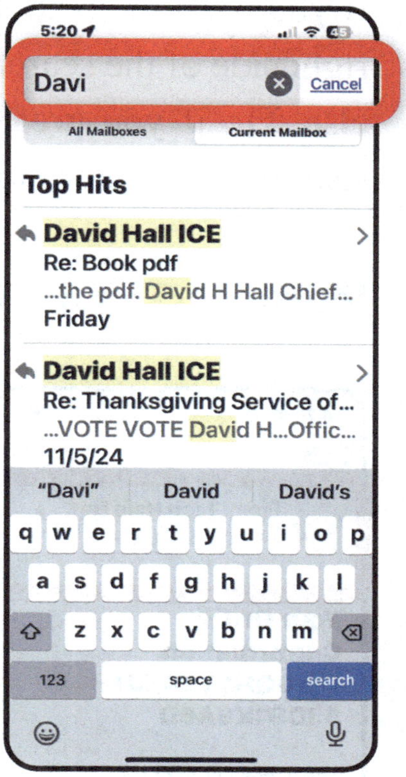

Image 10.103

Write your message in the white space below the subject line (always good to add a subject). Once done, tap on the arrow at the top right and your email is on its way.

Search for Apple Mail

Apple hides the search bar in its various locations. To find it, gently swipe down from the top and it will appear. (Image 10.102) Now you can enter a name or subject to find all emails from that sender or with that content. If you have multiple email addresses coming to Apple Mail, here you have the chance to search all emails (i.e., all mailboxes) or just the current email address (current mailbox).

If you want to do another search, just **TAP on the X** all the way on the right side of the search bar. It will reset and you can look for something else. Or, if you prefer, tap on the back arrow on the left side of the search bar to return to the Inbox.

Report Spam/Block Sender

Image 10.103a

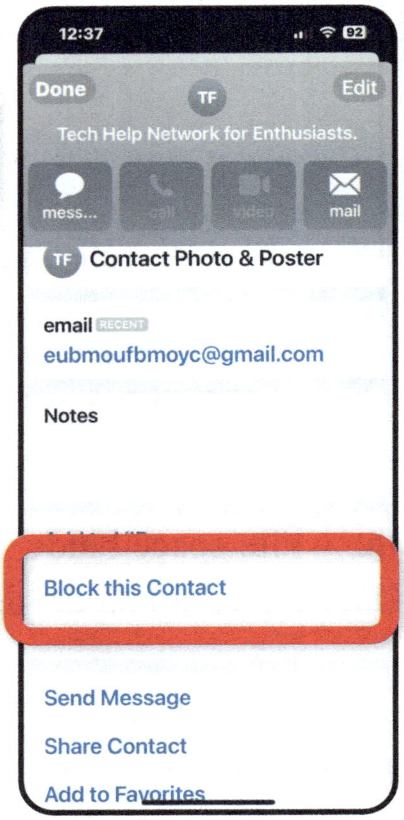

Image 10.104

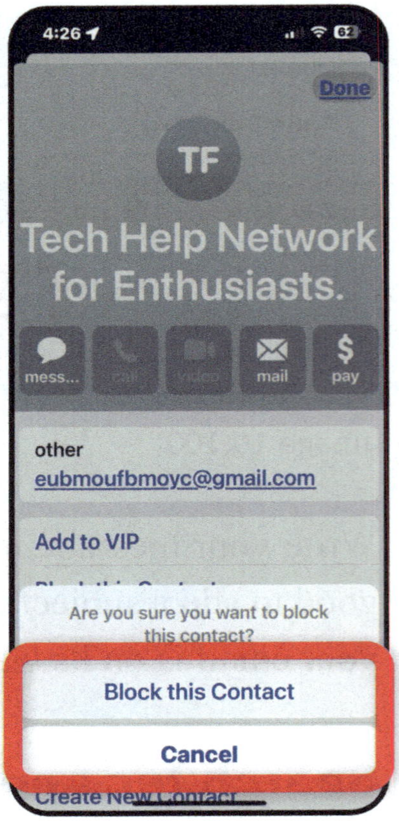

Image 10.105

Open the email in question. Tap on the address and it will turn blue. Look for the ***From:* and *To:*** sections in Image 10.103a. The screen will change. (Image 10.104) As you scroll down the page, you will see options to:

- **Add to VIP –** Contact is added as VIP. You can find the VIPs when you tap on the three lines at the top left of the page.
- **Block This Contact** – If you choose to block the contact, you will confirm or cancel when the screen changes. (Image 10.105)
- **Search Mail for Contact**
- **Send Message** – A new text message will open, addressed to sender.
- **Share Contact** – Will open the share screen (the box with an upward facing arrow) where you can save, text, email, etc.
- **Create New Contact** – A new contact page will open, ready to be saved.
- **Add to Existing Contact (not shown on this screen)**

Replying and Forwarding in Apple Mail

TAP ON THE BACK FACING ARROW at the bottom of the page. (Image 10.106) The screen will change, and you can choose what to do. (Image 10.107) SCROLL DOWN because there are a lot of things you can do from this page, including PRINT and BLOCK sender. (Image 10.108) It's super easy to reply, reply to all, and forward emails in Apple Mail.

Image 10.106

Image 10.107

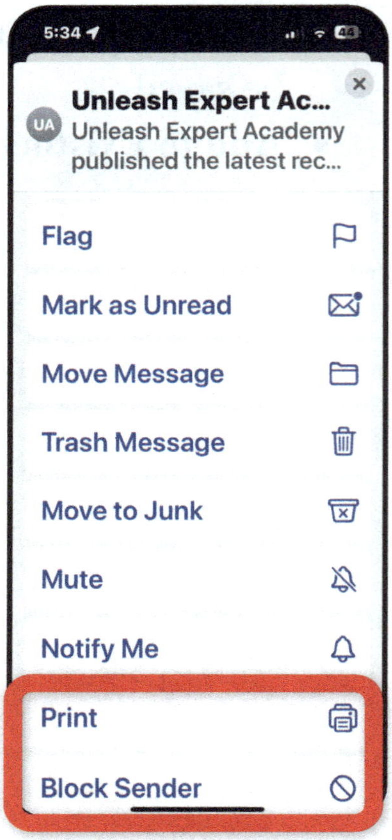

Image 10.108

Attaching Photos to Email

Begin a new email. (Image 10.109) If you don't see a gray area above the keyboard, tap the area just above the keyboard and it will appear. (Image 10.110) If you don't see the paper clip, then tap on the left facing arrow on the very right side of the gray area. Now you can see **Aa**, a **paper clip** and a **pencil in a circle** (edit.) (Image 10.111) Tap on the paper clip and the screen changes (Image 10.112) and now you have options to attach a photo you will take (the camera), attach a picture you've already taken (photo library), scan document, scan

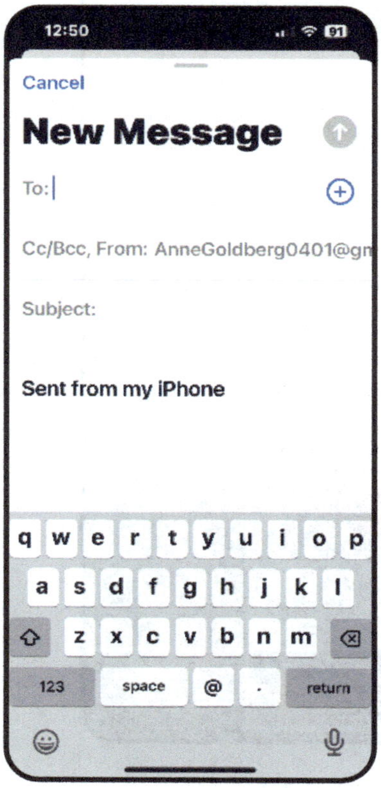

Image 10.109

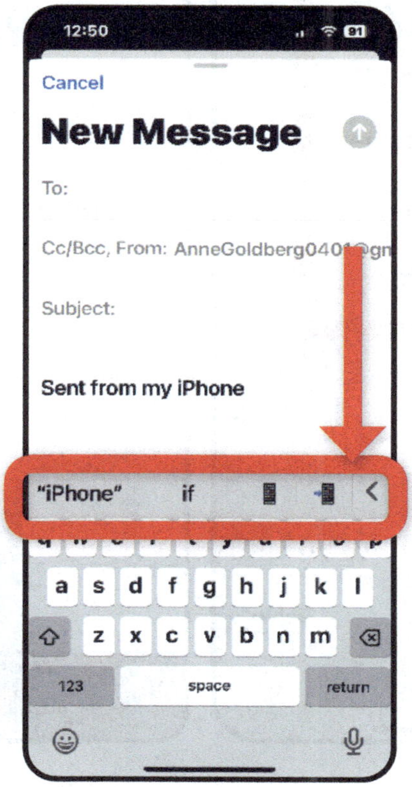

Image 10.110

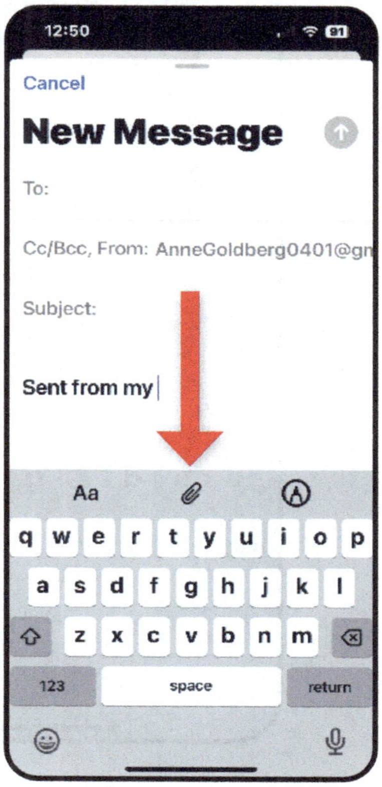

Image 10.111

text and attach file. These are all the thing you can attach to this email. Tap on what you want to attach and follow the prompts. If you tap on Photo Library, the screen changes (Image 10.113) and you can select the image from your photos.

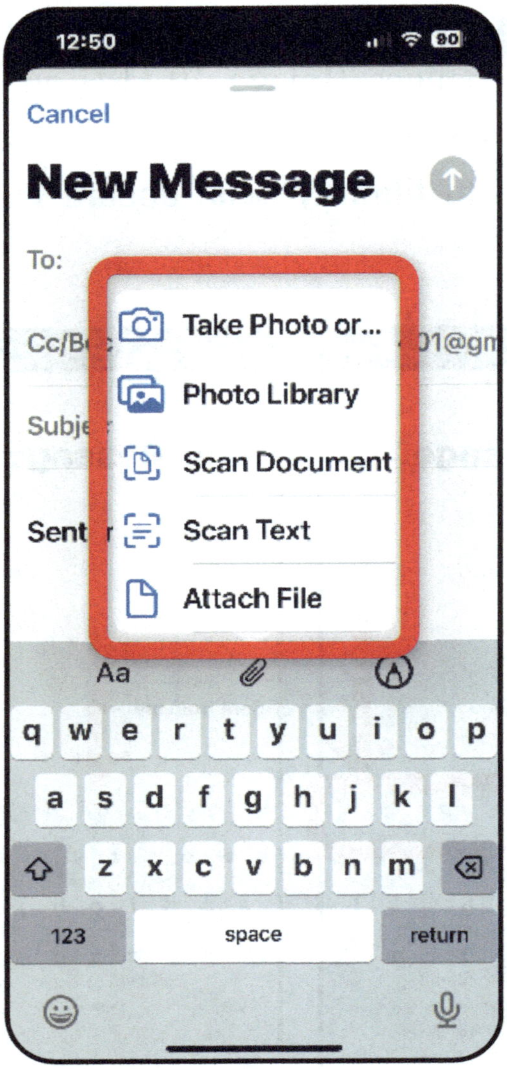

Image 10.112

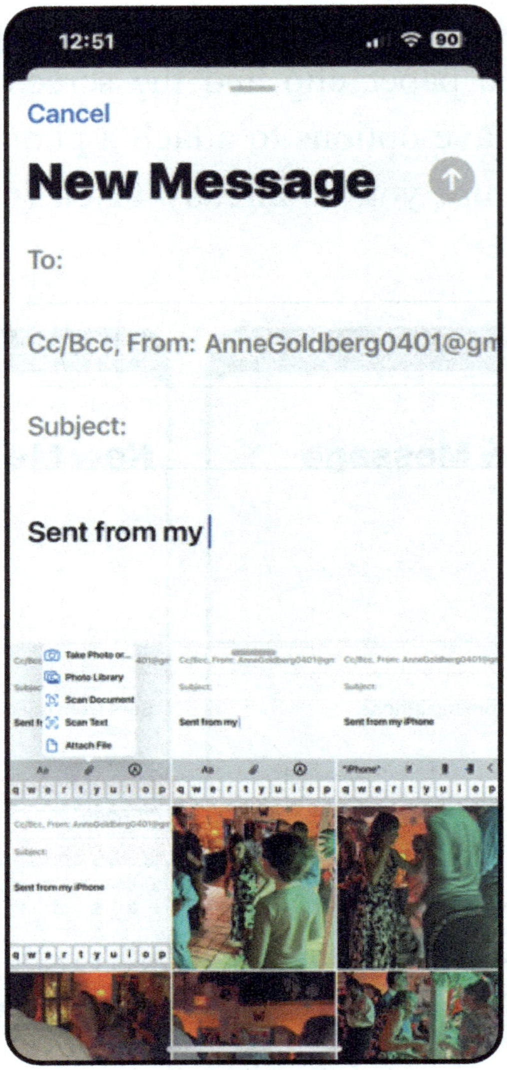

Image 10.113

Unsubscribing in Apple Mail

See the arrow pointing to Unsubscribe in blue? (Image 10.114) Tap on that to unsubscribe from future newsletters. You'll likely either be asked to confirm or see a confirmation of unsubscribing. Does it always work? With reputable companies? Yes. However, that link to unsubscribe isn't always there. But there is another way to unsubscribe.

Image 10.114

Image 10.115

If you don't see the blue unsubscribe, scroll all the way to the bottom of the email. (Image 10.115) You may see a whole lot of language. Look carefully for **UNSUBSCRIBE** hidden in the language. Sometimes it says "Manage Subscription," and you unsubscribe there. The screen will change. Don't get nervous.

Email Display Options in Apple Mail

Sometimes you just want to see your UNREAD emails. Well, there's a white circle with lines in it at the very bottom of the page on the left in image 10.116. This view is ALL mail. In Image 10.117 you'll see the circle is blue with lines. Now the view is only NEW (i.e., UNREAD) email.

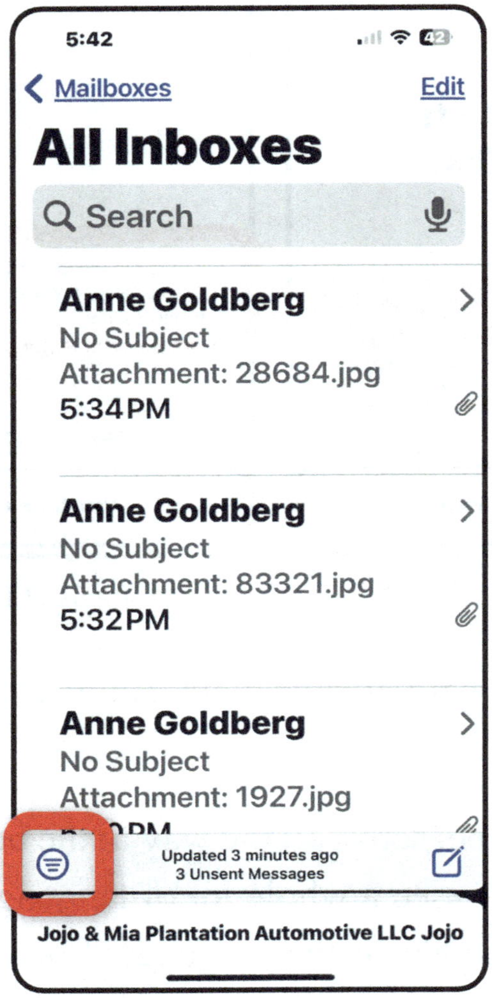

Image 10.116

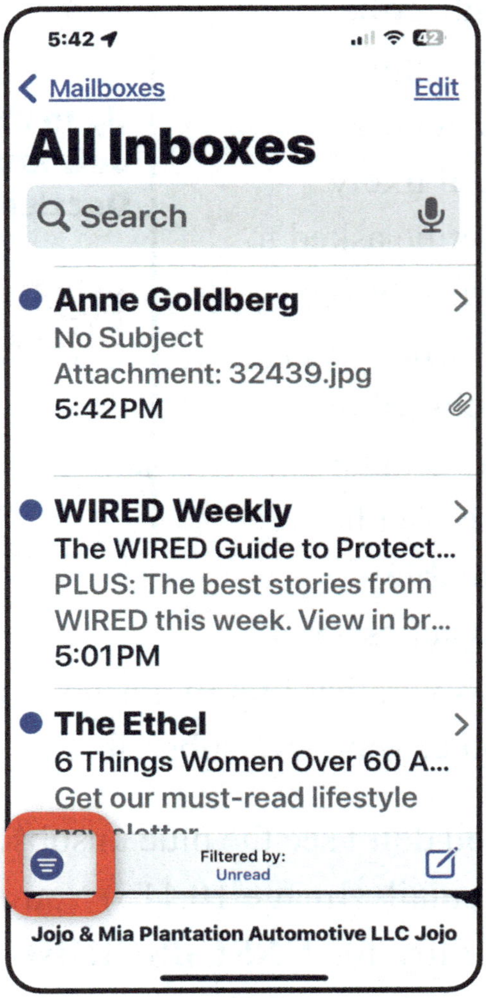

Image 10.117

GPS

Remember those AAA TripTik multi-page flip books with the route highlighted for long trips? Well, now there's a GPS on your phone—Google Maps, Waze, and Apple Maps—that will give you turn-by-turn instructions wherever you want to go. Looking back, I remember getting lost a lot more often before GPS came to be.

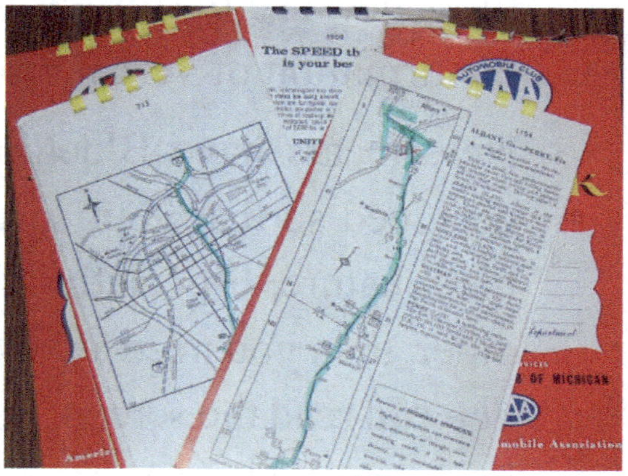

This Photo by Unknown Author is licensed under CC BY-SA-NC

In this chapter, we are going to explore Google Maps and Apple Maps. Waze is owned by Alphabet Inc, which also owns Google. It's great and works very similarly to the others.

Before we get into how to use Google or Apple Maps, it's good to know a few things first.

1. You can verbally instruct your device to take you to any specific address just by saying, "Hey Google (or "Hey Siri") take me to the nearest supermarket." You will hear the responses. When the voice assistant says the place you want, tell it yes. You will be asked if you want to call or get directions. It's that simple. From there you'll get specific directions.

2. Sometimes the voice assistant will tell you to turn about a half mile from the actual turn. Glance at the GPS and see just how far it is. Usually, you'll see .4 of a mile or so. I have made a few wrong turns because of this early prompt. Always refer to the screen for confirmation of verbal directions.
3. Newer cars have Bluetooth or Google or Apple Play. They are designed so that your screen will show on the car's screen. It's a nice feature, especially when it comes to the GPS. If your car is older, then you need a good phone holder so that, at a quick glance, you can read the screen. It should be placed near the steering wheel in a way that does not obstruct your view of the road. Amazon carries great car phone holders, and they are typically under $20.

Note: All GPS apps work exactly the same in Androids and iPhones.

I could write an entire book on all the things you can do with these GPS apps. Here I'll go over just the highlights I think you will appreciate.

Google Maps

SETTINGS > LOCATION > LOCATION SERVICES > LOCATION ACCURACY—TOGGLE ON

The first thing you want to do is make sure that Location Settings are turned on. **Settings > Location Services (Toggle on if off.)** The GPS will not work without this setting turned on.

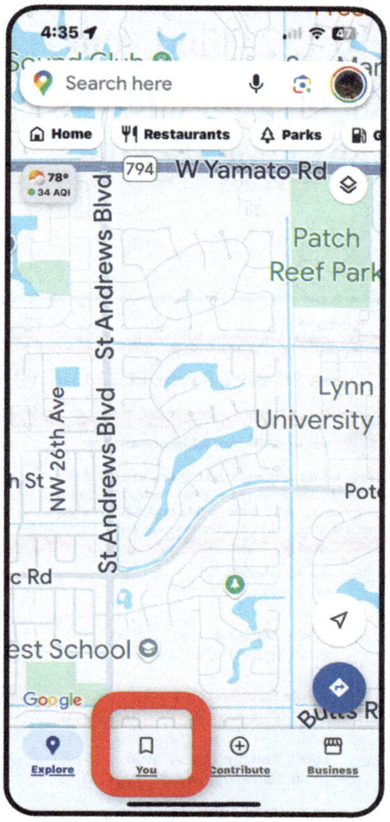

Image 10.118

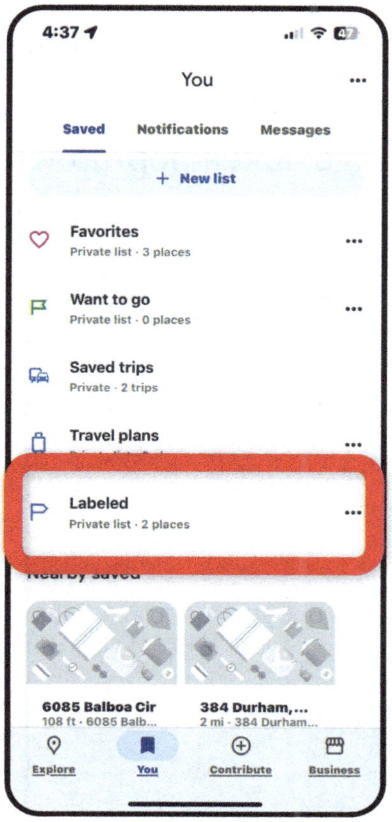

Image 10.119

Image 10.120

GOOGLE MAPS SETTING HOME ADDRESS

1. Tap on **You** at the bottom of the page. (Image 10.118)
2. Tap **Labeled.** (Image 10.119)
3. Tap **THREE DOTS** next to Home. The screen changes. (Image 10.120)

4. Tap **EDIT HOME.** (Image 10.121) The screen changes.
5. Type in your address in the top bar. (Image 10.122) Find your address in the auto-populated area below. Tap on your address. The screen will change, and a pop-up will notify you that the HOME ADDRESS HAS BEEN SAVED.

Getting Directions

Now that you have saved your home address, you can always say, “Hey Google” or “Hey Siri, take me home!” and you’ll be on your way.

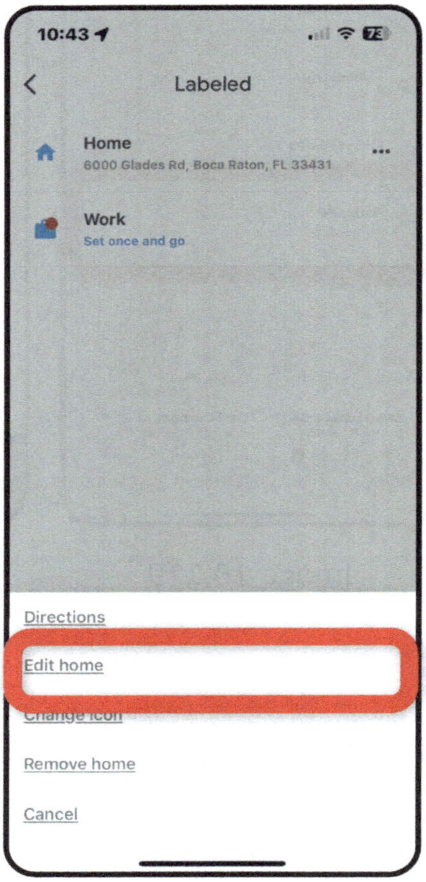

Image 10.121

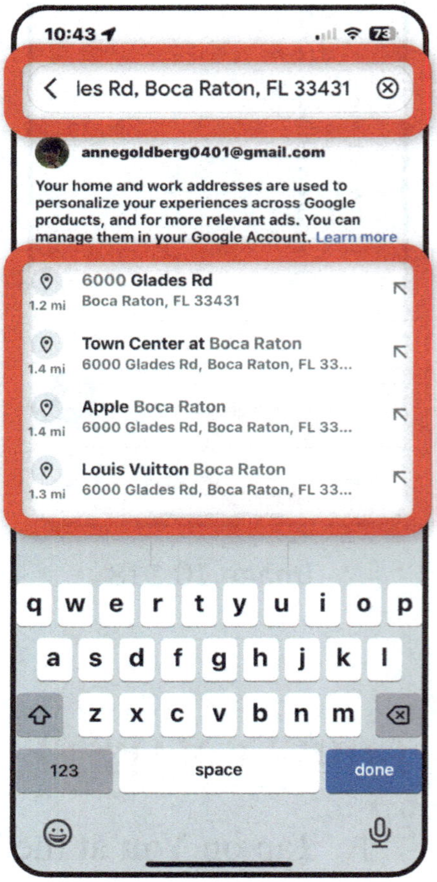

Image 10.122

Image 10.123 is the home screen for Google Maps. Just under the search bar you will see little ovals with suggestions. Want to go home? Tap Home. Want to find a restaurant near you? Tap Restaurants, and so on. Notice in the search bar there is a microphone. You do not need to type to tell Maps where to take you. You can tap on the microphone and speak the address. (See Image

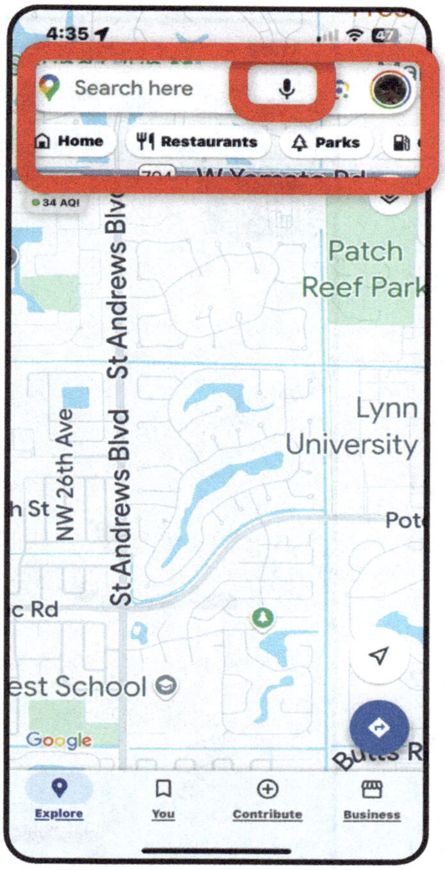

Image 10.123

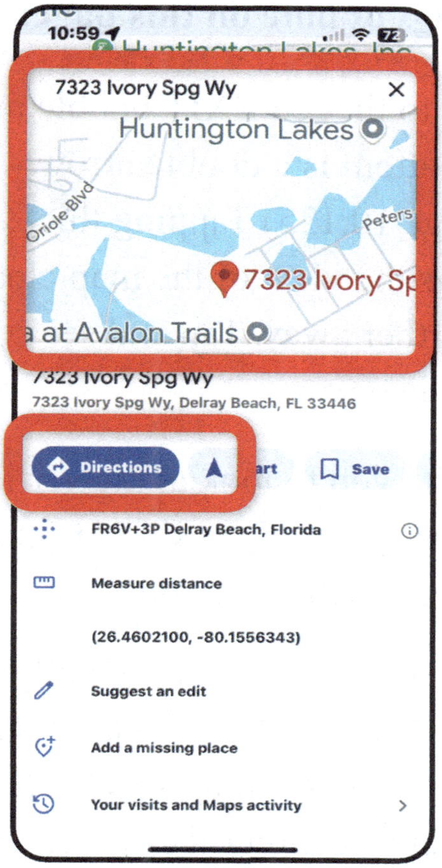

Image 10.124

10.123) You can also use Siri to direct the GPS. Of course, you can always type in the address or name of the place you want to go to directly into the search bar.

As you begin typing in the address, the app will predict what you want and suggest addresses. When you see the one you want, tap on it. The screen will change. TAP DIRECTIONS (Image 10.124) if you want to view the directions. TAP START if you want to begin the route. You'll notice you can SAVE frequently visited addresses. I invite you to explore all the options on the page.

A few things of note on this page:

- Next to the red EXIT bubble on the bottom is a double arrow. (Image 10.125) Tapping this brings the view of the map closer or further away. Tap and see what happens.

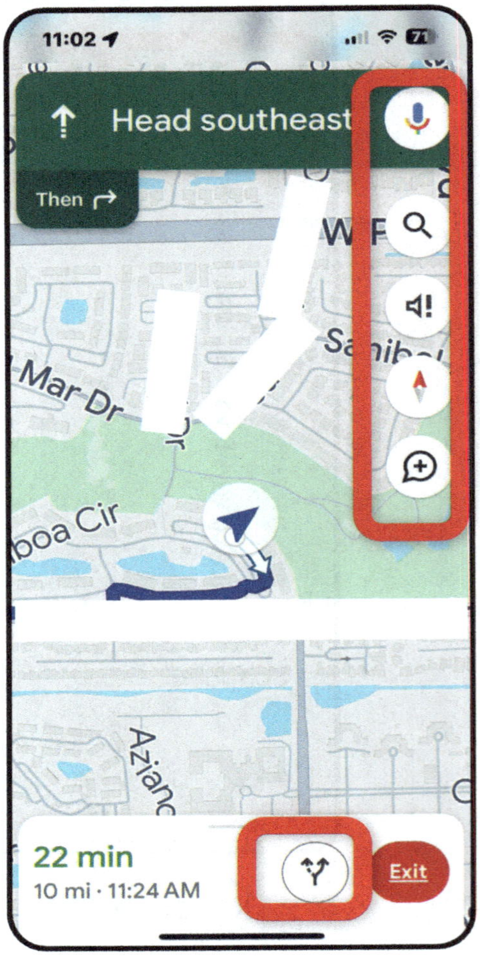

Image 10.125

Now I invite you to look at the vertical list of icons on the right side of image 10.125. Here's what they do:

- The first one is a magnifying glass, so you know this is what you tap if you want to search for something along the route, such as a gas station or restaurant. When you tap on it, the screen will change, and you will see options to add various types of stops along the way.
- The second one is a speaker. This is where you can turn the speaker on/off if you do/don't want to hear turn-by-turn instructions.
- The third one will reorient the map. Tap and see what happens.
- The fourth one is a plus sign in a bubble and is for reporting a crash, slowdown, lane closures, and more.

DROPPING PINS

This is a useful tool when you want to mark a specific location. Restaurants, a favorite store, hotels in foreign locations, or a favorite movie theater are reasons to drop pins. Your GPS will give you walking directions to the spot. It's a good thing to know about. It's also great when you are meeting friends, and someone has the wrong address. You can drop a pin at your location and SHARE it with your friend, who can now navigate right where you are!

1. **Open Google Maps.** The map that you see is your current location. (Image 10.126)
2. **Zoom in by PINCHING OUT** so you can set an exact location for your pin. (Image 10.127)

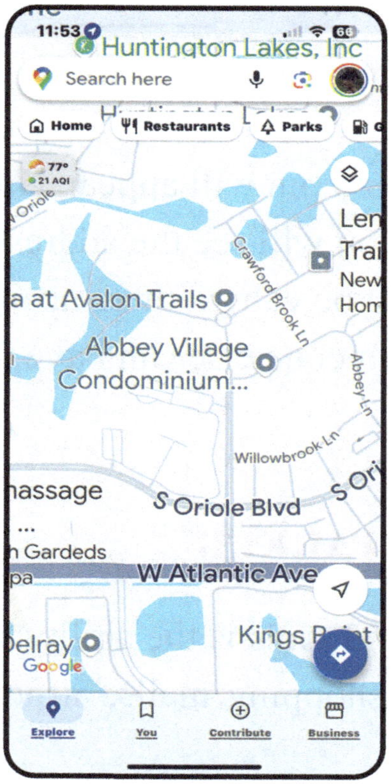

Image 10.126

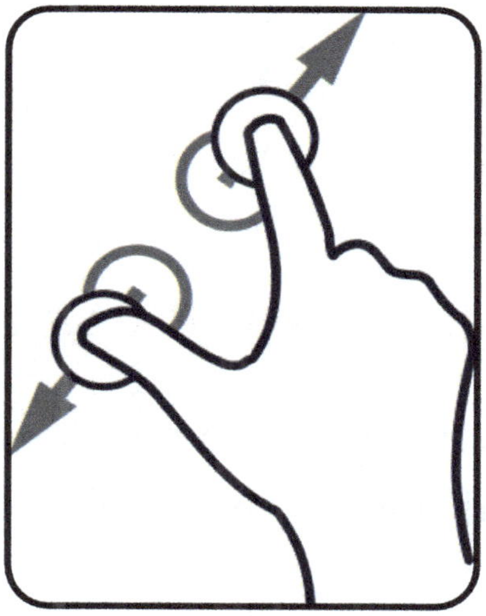

Image 10.127

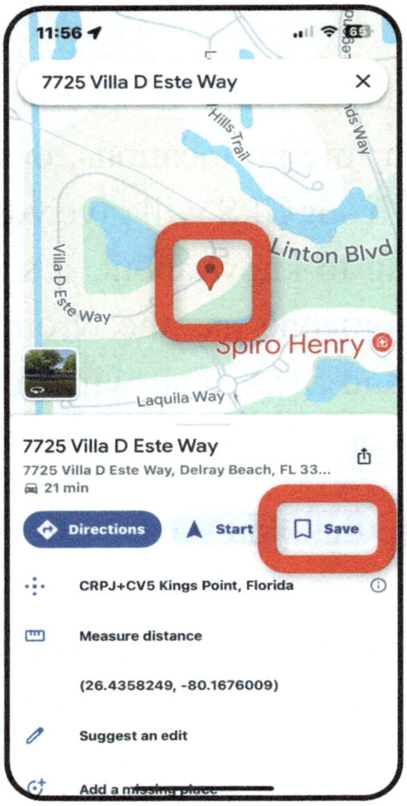

Image 10.128

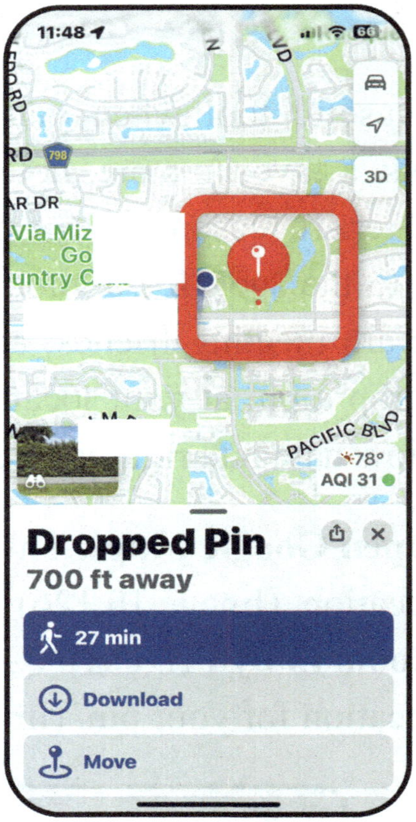

Image 10.129

3. **TAP ON THE SPOT**. A red pin will appear. (Image 10.128)
4. **TAP ON THE PIN** and you will see the address of that pin. You can **SAVE** the pin so you can go there again, and you can **SHARE** the pin so someone else can have the address. (Image 10.129)

SAVE WHERE YOUR CAR IS PARKED

Undoubtedly, one of the most useful tools is the ability to know where we parked our car, especially at shopping malls, airports, and travel destinations.

Per Google's own instructions, you must ensure that Location Services is turned on. **(Page 280)** as well as Bluetooth, connecting your device to the car.

Park the car and turn off the engine. When you disconnect from the car's Bluetooth, your iPhone will automatically mark the car's location. Open Apple Maps and look for a pin labeled "Parked Car". Tap it. Now, if the location is slightly off you can edit it, you can add notes (level 3 by the staircase) and/or add a photo (useful).

You can also manually save where you parked. Open Apple Maps and tap the blue dot that shows your current location. Tap "Mark My Location" and a pin will drop on the map. That's your car! You can tap the pin to edit the label and add notes.

Apple Maps

The same as Google Maps and somewhat different. Again, we are back to the difference in dashboards.

But before we go further, the first thing to do to insure the app will work properly is to **turn on Location Services in settings**.

Location Settings

SETTINGS > PRIVACY & SECURITY > LOCATION SERVICES—TOGGLE ON APPLE MAPS SET HOME ADDRESS

Another setting necessary to enable you to find your parked car:

System Services

SETTINGS > PRIVACY & SECURITY > LOCATION SERVICES > SCROLL TO THE BOTTOM > SYSTEM SERVICES

Unlike Google, Apple uses your contact (in Contacts) to find your home address. (Image 10.130) Make sure your information shows at the top of the Contacts page. (Image 10.131) Fill this out with your complete home address. Make sure you label it as HOME, not work. If you have to make other, tap on EDIT at the top right of the screen in contacts. (Image 10.131) Tap DONE when you're finished. Now, when you ask, "Siri, take me home!" you will get directions to home.

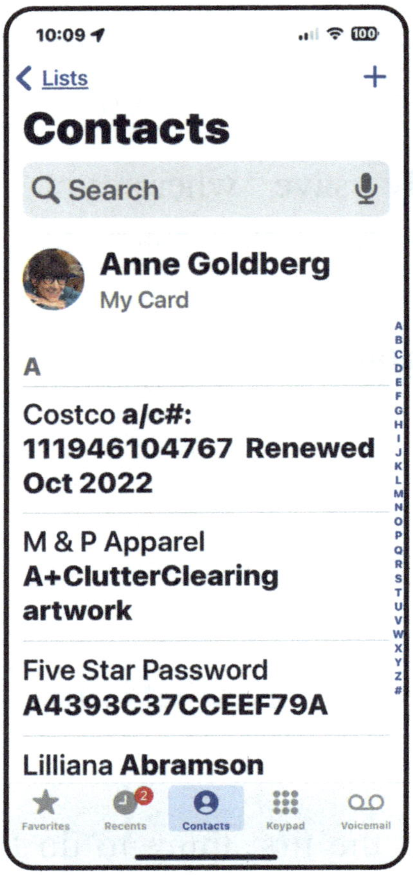

Image 10.130

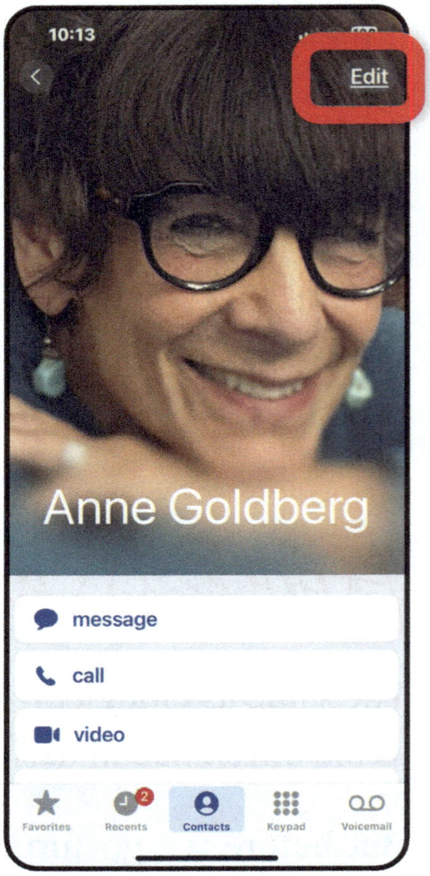

Image 10.131

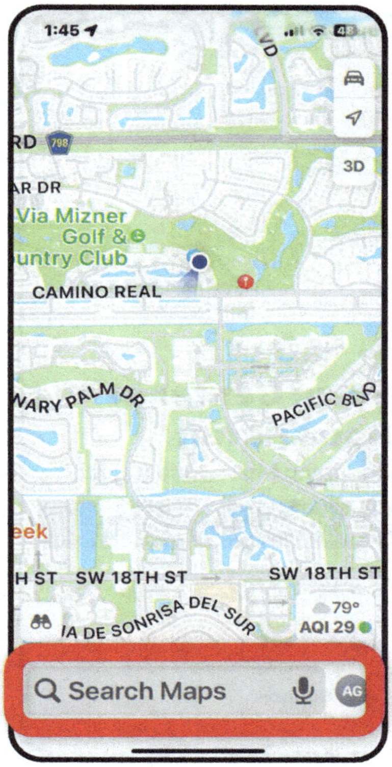

Image 10.132

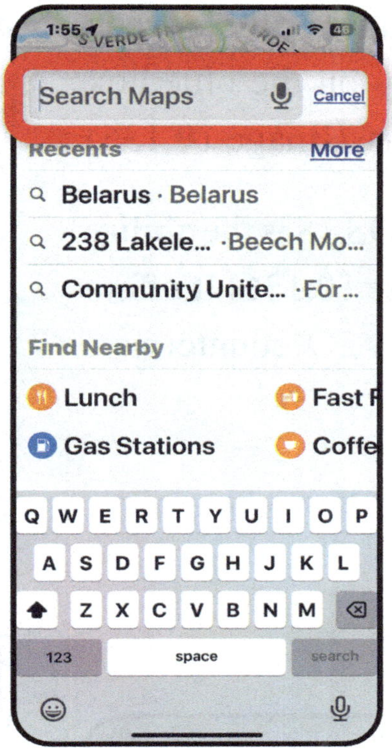

Image 10.133

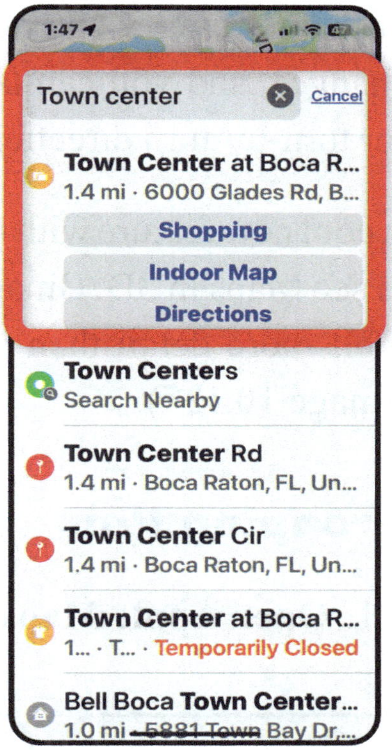

Image 10.134

Apple Maps Directions

Open Maps and you get to the main page. (Image 10.132) **Tap Search Maps** and the screen changes. (Image 10.133) Once you begin typing a name or address, autofill suggestions come up. In this case, Town Center Mall is my target. In Image 10.134, you will see the app has all kinds of information about the mall: shopping, indoor map, and directions.

Tap on Town Center again, the screen changes, and you can tap on the blue box for turn-by-turn directions. (Image 10.135)

A cool new feature with iOS 18 is the ability to see Maps in 3D. (Image 10.136) It offers a bit more detail than its 2D counterpart. (Image 10.137)

Dropping Pins

1. **Open Apple Maps**.

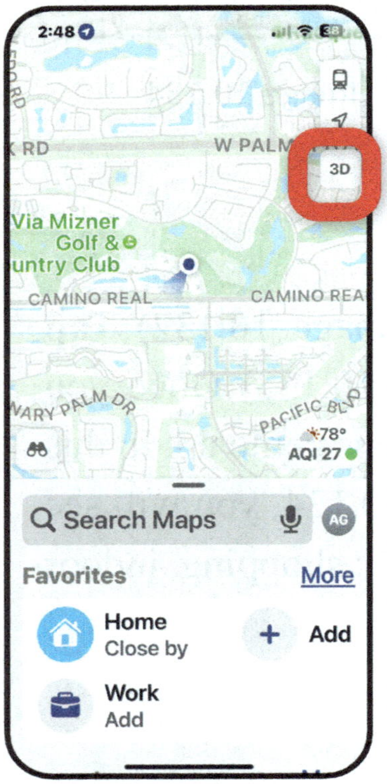

Image 10.136

Image 10.137

Image 10.135

2. Use your fingers to move around the map (using pinch in and pinch out).
3. Tap *Mark My Location*. A small red marker will appear. (Image 10.138) You can drag the pin if it's not exactly where you want it.

You can share the location by tapping on the box with the arrow (Image 10.138) The screen changes (Image 10.140) and you see: Directions, Remove the Marked Location, or Share Location via text or email. (Images 10.139 & 140)

The pin will stay until you remove it or close the app.

Finding Your Parked Car

OPEN SETTINGS > SCROLL ALL THE WAY DOWN TO MAPS > SCROLL TO THE BOTTOM TO SHOW PARKED LOCATION. MAKE SURE IT'S TOGGLED ON.

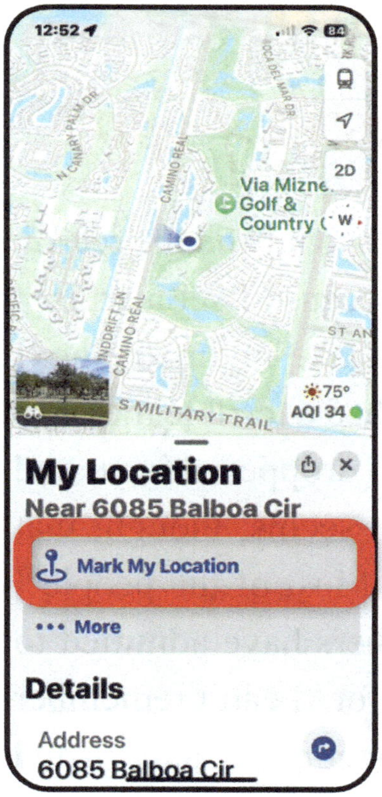

Image 10.138

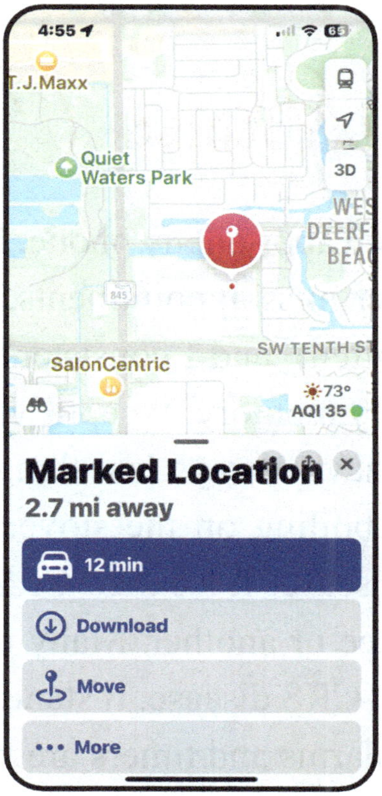

Image 10.139

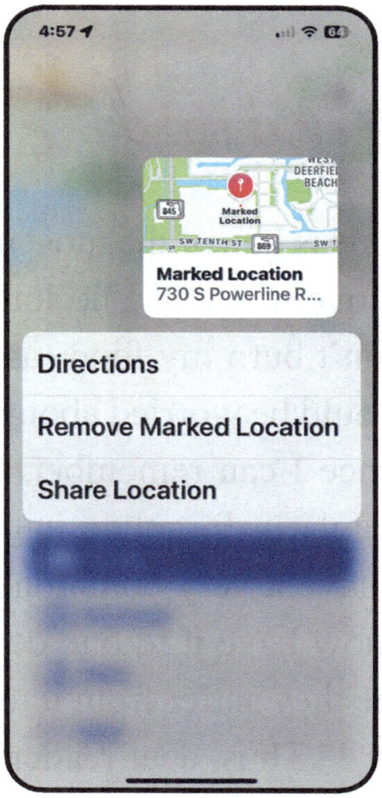

Image 10.140

There are two ways to find your parked car. First, when you arrive at your location, drop a pin to mark where you parked your car. That's easy.

The second way to mark your parking spot requires that you have Bluetooth turned on. As soon as you shut the engine, Maps will automatically drop a pin where your car is parked. Tap on the pin directly to add notes like landmarks or streets.

If you don't have Bluetooth, just drop a pin at the location. When you're ready to go back to the car, press and hold the pin until you see the screen change. Tap on Directions and you'll be navigated back to the car. (Image 10.150)

Android & iPhone Clock App

This is one of the most used apps on my phone. I love it. And the reason I love it is that I no longer miss appointments, because I set alarms. I don't burn my food (as often), and I consistently take my medicine. I would be worried about my memory, except I've had a terrible memory since I can remember. I have always lost things, dropped things, and regularly forgotten eggs boiling on the stove. It seems, though, that I have a very common disease. It's called CRS. Most of the people I know have it to one degree or another. Many others have admitted to me they suffer from it too. CRS disease. It stands for "I can't remember $*-!" Thus, dear reader, alarms and timers are my constant and trusted companions.

Android and iPhone clock apps are very similar. When you open the app, look at the very bottom of the screen. Just as in the phone app, you'll see four different functions this app has. On Androids, from left to right:

- Alarm
- World Clock
- Stopwatch
- Timer

On iPhones, from left to right you'll see:

- A globe for **World Clock**
- An old-fashioned alarm clock for **Alarms**
- **A** stopwatch for **Stopwatch**
- A countdown clock for **Timer**

Android Clock Settings:

Tap to open the clock app. (Image 10.141) You will see existing alarms in Image 10.142. Note if they are toggled on or off. To add a new alarm, you can either edit an existing one by tapping on it and making the changes, or you can tap on the "+" sign and the screen will change. (Image 10.142)

Image 10.143 shows how you can adjust the time (remembering to note AM or PM). You can change the date by tapping on the date. Tap SAVE when you've selected the desired date. (Image 10.43) On this screen you can also customize the alarm sound and vibration.

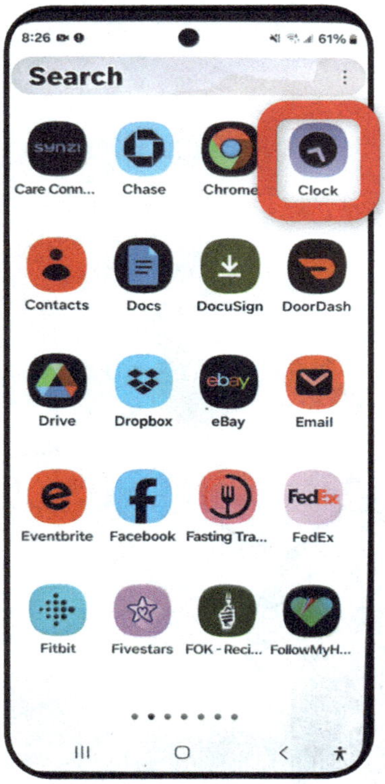

Image 10.141

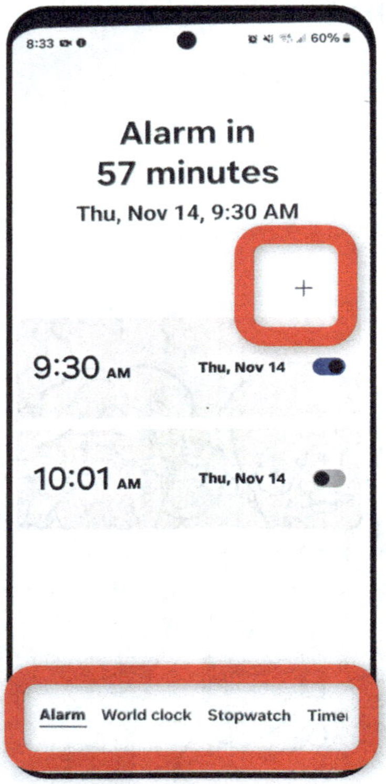

Image 10.142

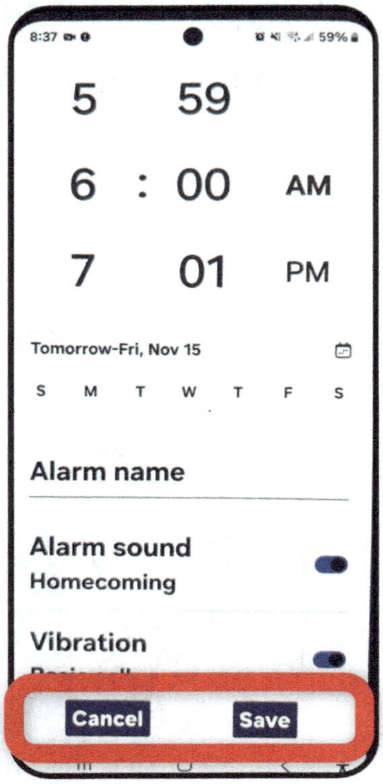

Image 10.143

ANDROID SET SLEEP MODE

In order to set a sleep schedule, edit and sort alarms, tap on the three dots on the right, as shown in Image 10.147. The screen changes. (Image 10.148) Choose the action to take. In this case, Set Sleep mode schedule. The screen changes, Image 10.149. Now you can set the sleep schedule by tapping the desired action. Scroll down the page. There are a lot of choices.

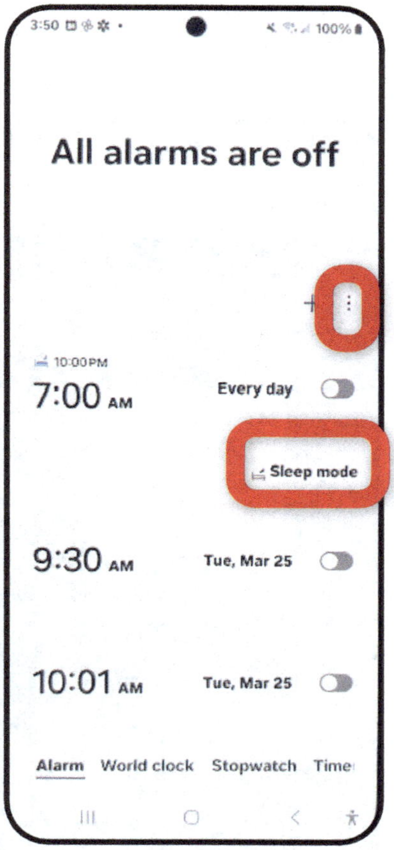

Image 10.147

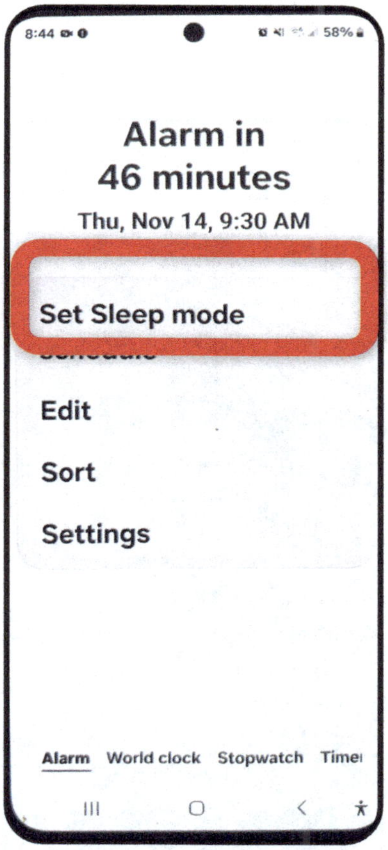

Image 10.148

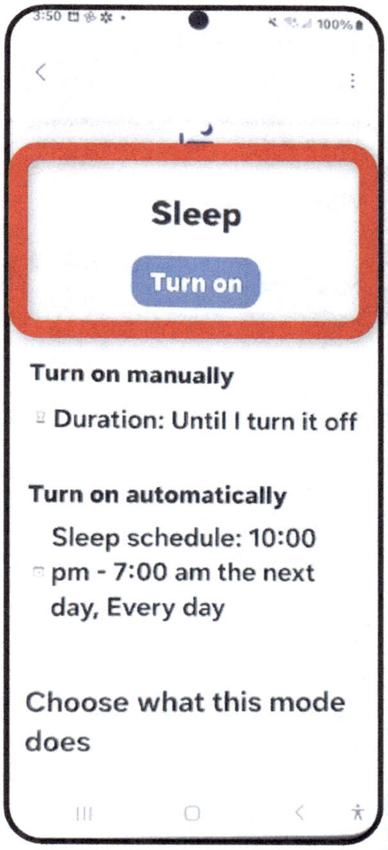

Image 10.149

Android World Clock

When you tap on the World Clock at the bottom of the screen, the screen changes. In this case you see New York. Let's say you want to add California. Tap on the "+" sign, and the screen will change. (Image 10.150) **Using PINCH and SLIDE gestures**, move the map until you find the location to add. Here I used Los Angeles. Tap on location and a little box will open and you will tap ADD to complete the action. (Image 10.152)

Image 10.150

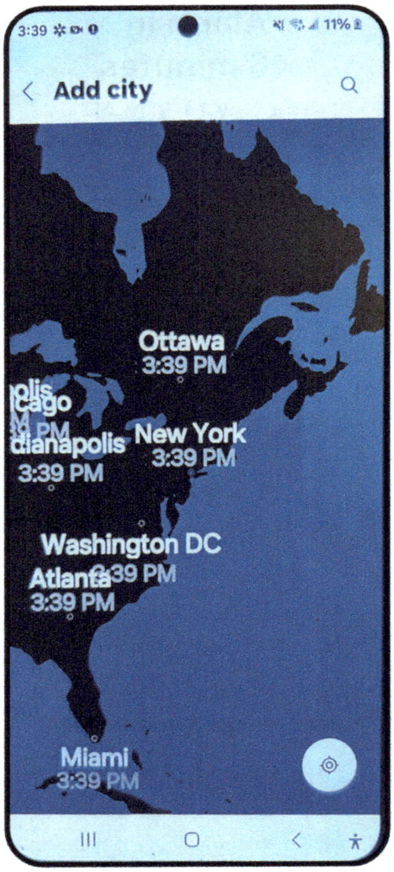

Image 10.151

Image 10.152

There are also three dots next to the plus sign. Tap on those and you will see options to EDIT, a TIME ZONE CONVERTER, and SETTINGS. We are only going to look at settings here. Tap on the three dots. (Image 10.153) The screen will change, and you will see the clock settings.(Image 10.154) Go through them and choose what you do and don't want. (Image 10.155) Scroll down to PRIVACY. This is where you will see how the app uses information. (Image 10.156)

Image 10.153

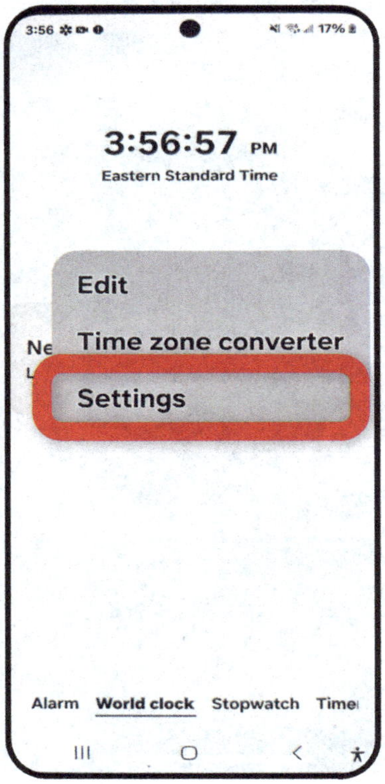

Image 10.154

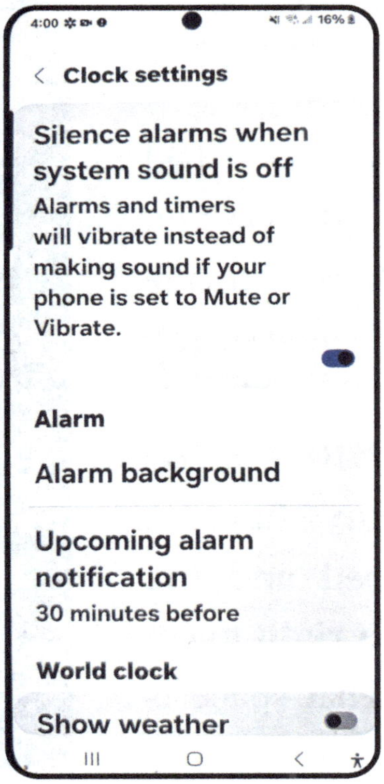

Image 10.155

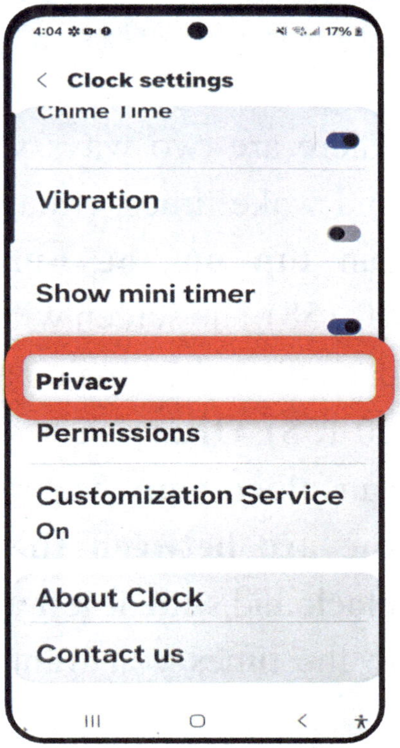

Image 10.156

iPhone Alarms

Open the clock app. If the top of the screen does not say Alarms, bring your eyes to the bottom and TAP on the alarm clock. It's the second from the left. Now the top and bottom of your screen say "Alarms."

You can set a sleep/wake-up schedule. **TAP on CHANGE** (it's orange).

SET A SLEEP SCHEDULE

SETTING A SLEEP/WAKE ALARM - OPEN THE CLOCK APP > TAP ALARM > TAP CHANGE > SET BEDTIME & WAKE-UP TIME > TAP DONE

There are two ways you can set bed and wake times. (Image 10.157) You can **tap on the numbers**. (Image 10.158) The screen will change so you can adjust the time on a wheel (Image 10.158), **OR**, as shown in 10.159, you can **place your finger anywhere on the arc between the bed and the clock** and **slide it left and right** to get to the times you want. That space is

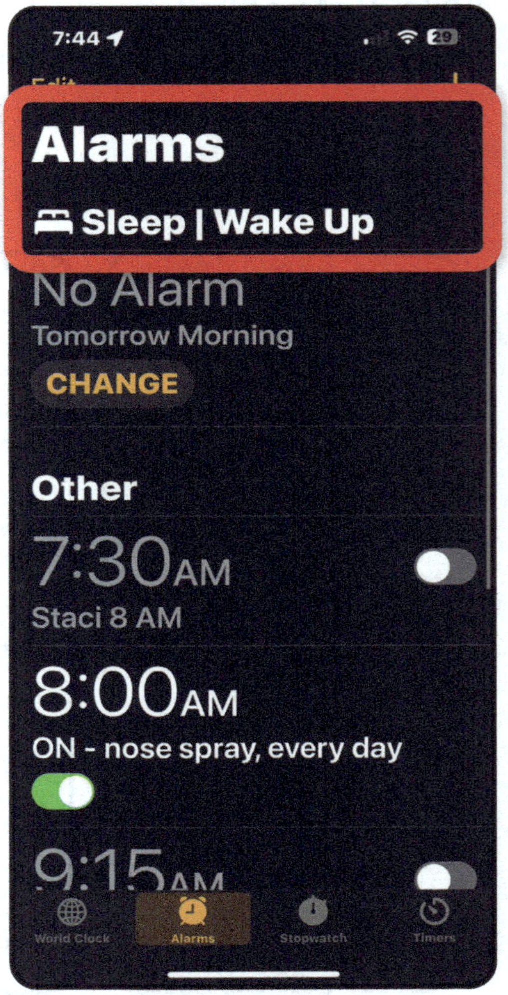

Image 10.157

actually a gold color, but the picture doesn't reflect that.

When you finish look at the top of the screen. Image 10.158 shows **CANCEL** on the left and **DONE** on the right. Tap cancel if you want to go back to the main alarm page. If you've made changes, TAP DONE. You will be asked to change just the NEXT Alarm or Change This

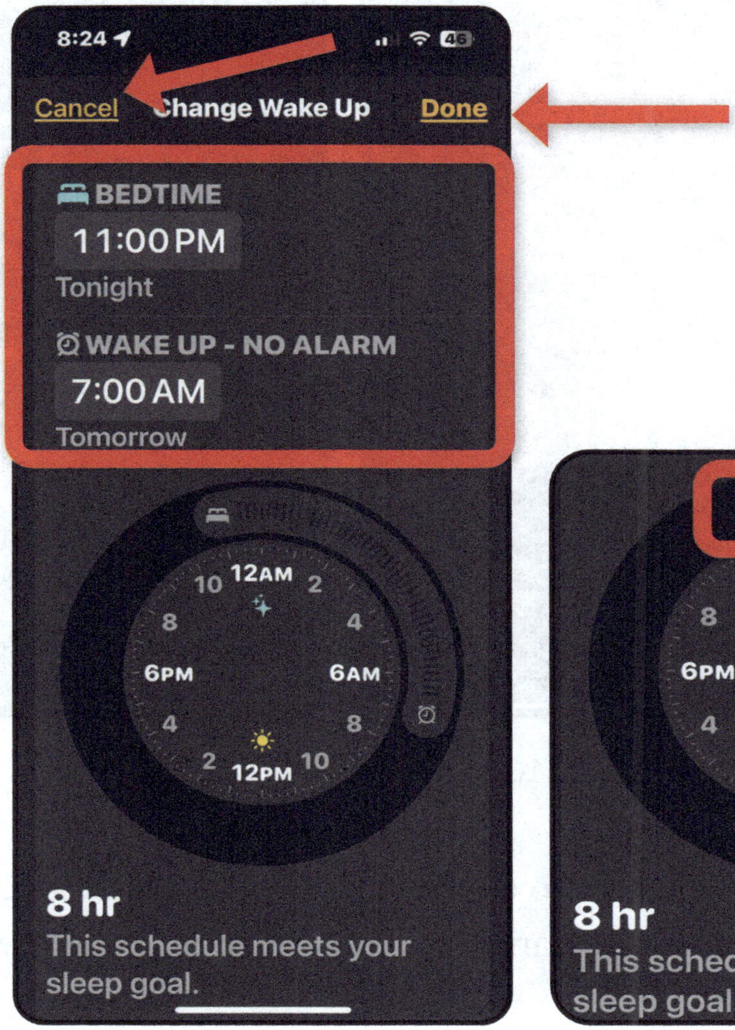

Image 10.158

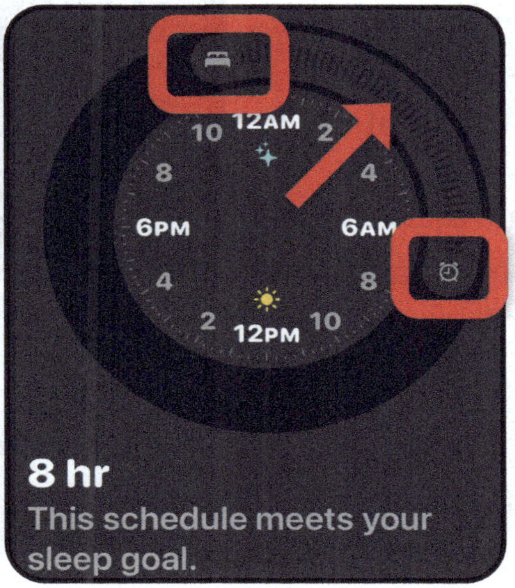

Image 10.159

Schedule. Tap CANCEL if you don't want to do anything.

SETTING ALARMS

Once you select the time (and tap AM or PM) (Image 10.160), it's time to label the alarm. (Image 10.161) **TAP LABEL** and the keyboard will appear. Simply type what you need to remember and tap **SAVE** at the top right.

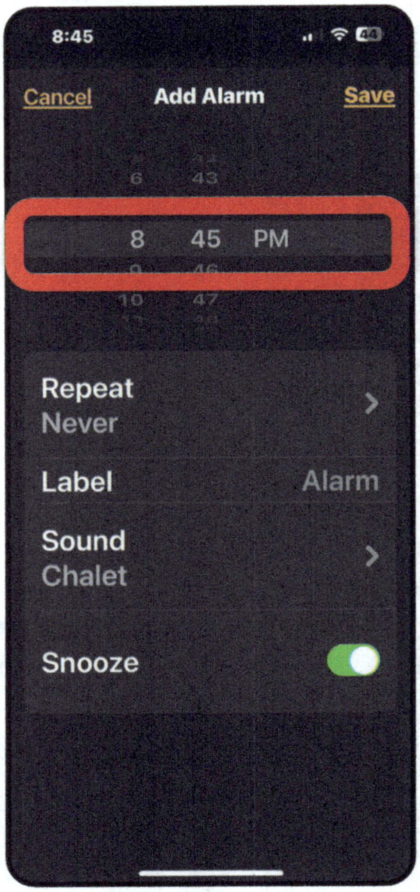

Image 10.160

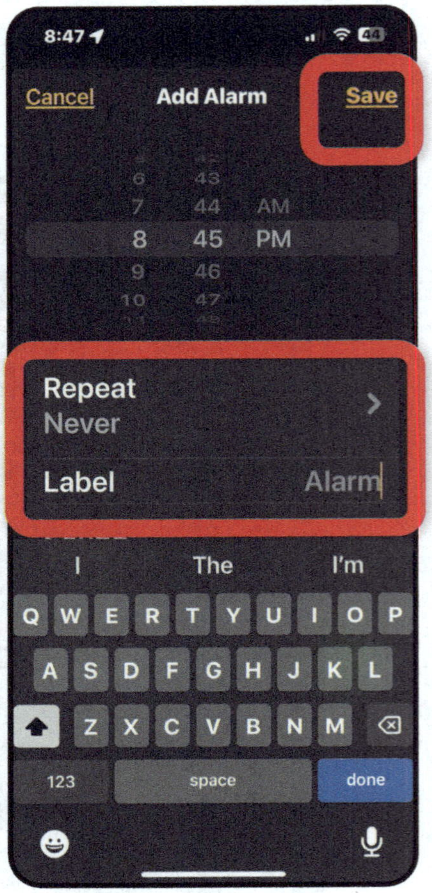

Image 10.161

Some alarms need to be repeated. My 8:00 AM alarm goes off every day (Image 10.162), and it says so on the screen. (The toggle is green, meaning it's on.) Some of my alarms are only once or twice a week.

By tapping on **Repeat**, (Image 10.163) the screen changes and you can choose the days of the week you want this alarm active. (Image 10.164) Once your selections are made, **TAP BACK** at the top left of the screen. (10.164)

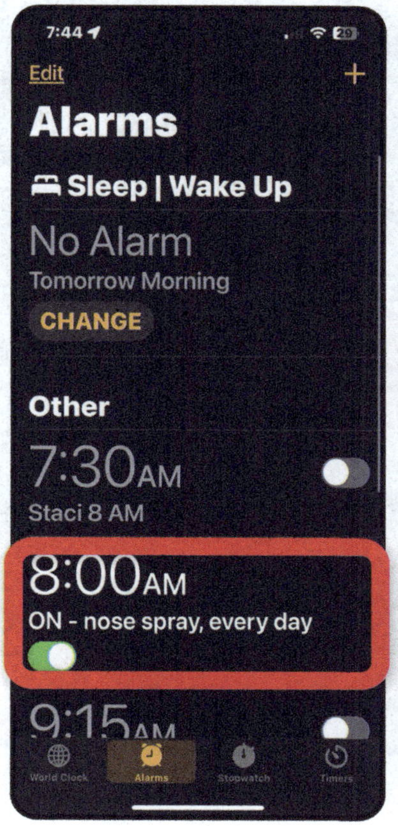

Image 10.162

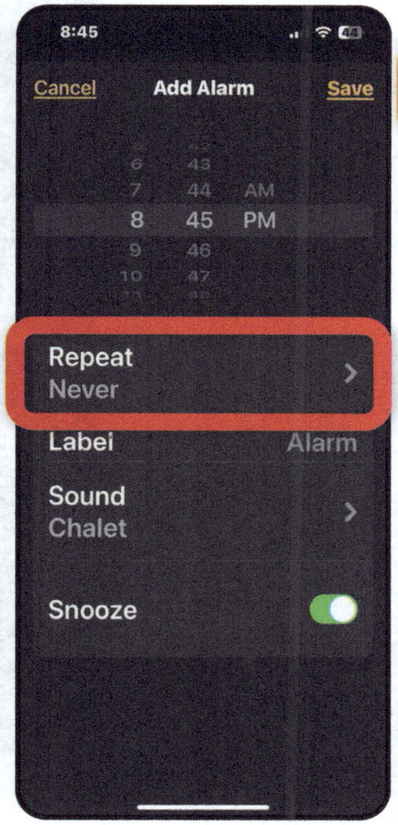

Image 10.163

Image 10.164

Timers

Whenever I put something on the stove or in the oven, I set a timer. When I have to leave in a few minutes, I set a timer to remind me. It's so easy. **Tap on TIMER** on the far right of the bottom of the screen. (Image 10.165) Now just **scroll the dials to set hours, minutes, and seconds. Tap START.**

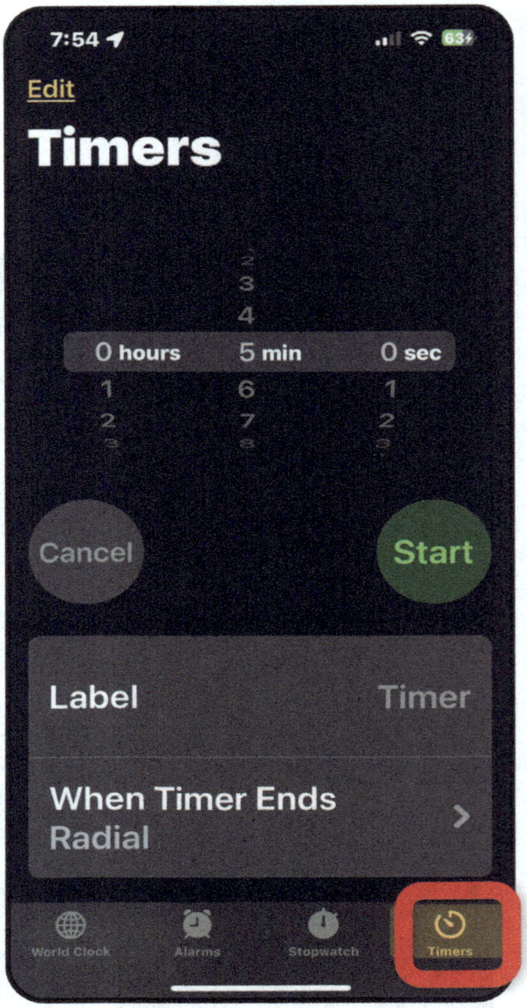

Image 10.165

Use Siri to Set Timers and Alarms

One of the very best uses of Siri is to say, "Hey Siri, set a timer for fifteen minutes labeled 'Time to leave.'" Or "Hey Siri, set an alarm for tomorrow at 10 AM labeled 'Remember to exercise'" or any other message you need to remind yourself of. Siri will handle it, and you don't have to touch your device.

Stopwatch and World Clock

The stopwatch is great if you want to challenge yourself in some way while exercising or playing a game or trying a new recipe. It may be useful to track the time it takes to do the task. Tap Start to start the stopwatch. (Image 10.166) Tap Stop when done. (10.167)

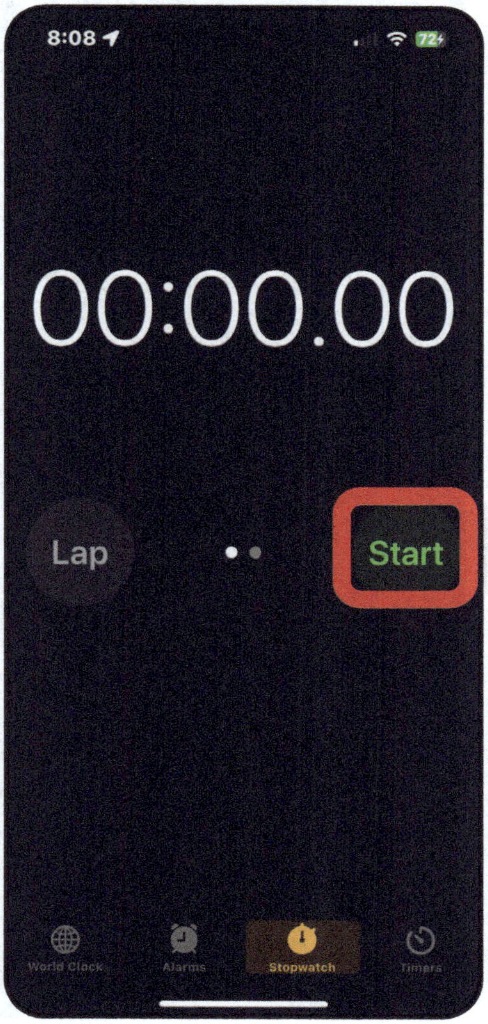

Image 10.166

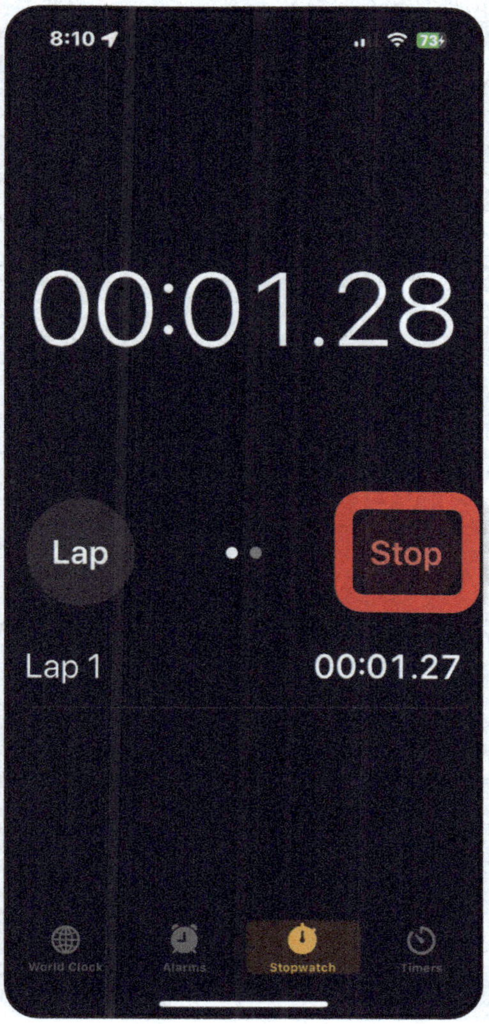

Image 10.167

The world clock is nice if you have family in other parts of the globe. My cousin is in London, my assistant is in India, and my son is in Denver. I keep those on my world clock.

To add a location, tap on the "+" sign at the top right as shown in Image 10.168. Type in the name of the city and country as in Image 10.169. Tap on it and that location will be added to your world clock.

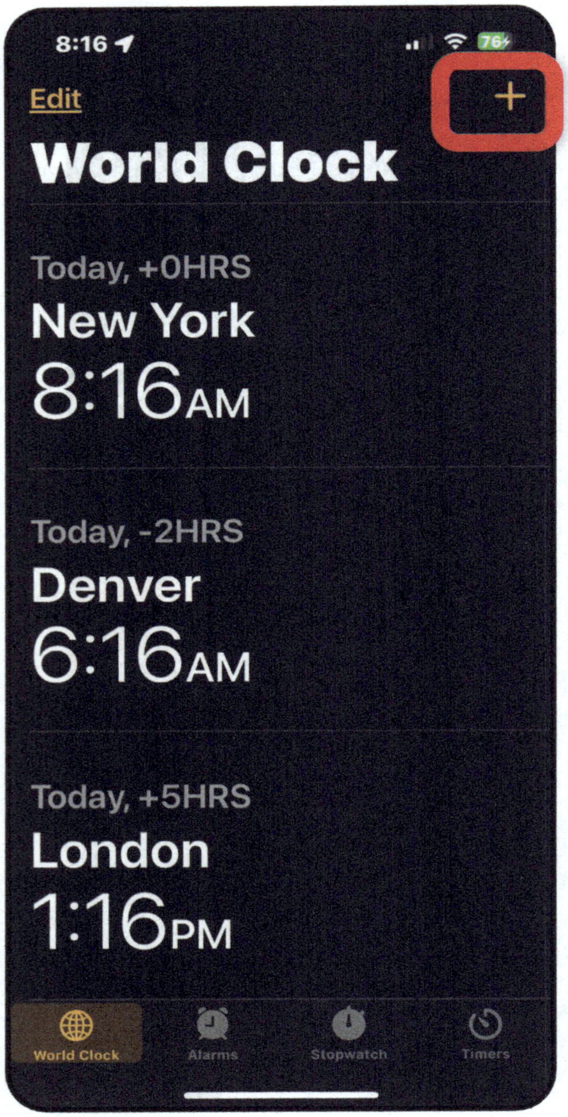

Image 10.168

Image 10.169

Chapter 11

Passwords, Passcodes, and Passkeys

Table of Contents

A hacker called and said he had all my passwords. I ran for a pen and paper and said, "Thank you SO MUCH! Please tell them to me!"

-Anonymous

After eleven years of teaching tech to seniors, I can tell you the one thing every senior hates, and I mean truly hates, is a PASSWORD. Passwords are the scourge of using technology. Keeping track of passwords is harder than keeping track of your socks when you take them from the dryer.

Even if you do very little online, you have passwords to keep track of. Your email, social media, and other apps require a username and password to protect your account information. No normal human is going to remember every password, and reusing passwords is patently unsafe and not a good idea.

You may have heard something about passKEYS. This is another security measure that will likely replace passwords, but only a small percentage of companies are using them, so for now we have to deal with passwords. Later on I will explain in depth what passKEYS are and how to use them when you come across them. For now, let's stick with passWORDS.

The first step to online safety is security. And the first step in security is a password.

You have security at home. You certainly have a lock (or two) on your front door, plus a lock on your car. Maybe you have a vacation property with its own lock and key. Are these keys all the same? Of course not. But why? Obviously, because that would not be secure.

> The password is the key, and the username is the lock.

Think about it like this. You own an Airbnb. You leave the key for your guests. But because all your keys are the same, your guests can easily find out where you live and use the key to get into your house, take whatever they want, and then leave in your car—all because you had the same key for each lock. Imagine if that key also opened your safety deposit box! Now, this may sound ridiculous to you, but many of you use the same password over and over, and it's kind of the same thing—one "key" for each lock.

Here is another reason to have a strong password, using a bank as an example. Criminals break into a bank, and now they're in the building. But they still have to get the keys to the private vaults if they want what's in there. So, getting into the building is only step one. Step two is actually getting into individual vaults (i.e., password-protected accounts). But to get into your specific account, they need your specific key, i.e., your password. If you have a simple password that you have reused, it won't be difficult for the criminals to figure it out. And once they do, they will try that password on every account you have. If you've reused passwords, you are in for a world of grief. They will try that on your investment accounts, utilities, and credit card companies, and they will hack you to goodness knows what damage.

PASSWORDS ARE KEY TO ONLINE SAFETY.

Creating a Great Password

If you are not using a password manager (more on that later) to create passwords, here is a trick to easily create a complicated password. I like to take any word and write it out with spaces. For example, I can use my last name and slip in symbols and numbers between lowercase and capital letters.

Photo by ChatGPT

G.ol/Db64$Erg. Now that's a super safe password. **Your passwords should be at least twelve characters or more** and should seem random. The more characters, the safer the password. The above is random to anyone else but not to me, so it's just easier to use. And, as you will see in a minute, you won't have to remember these passwords anyway.

Passcodes

We sometimes call passcodes personal identification numbers, or PINs. They are the numbers you use to unlock your smartphone, your computer, your home alarm system, your debit card, and more. They are those four to six numbers you use to unlock your phone, your iPad and/or computer. It's that debit card PIN number you use at the ATM. It's the same series of numbers that face recognition and fingerprint replace. If your face is not recognized, the device requests your passcode. I reuse my device passcodes, using the same numbers for my phone, desktop, and laptop. It's just easier that way and I'm not worried.

Photo by ChatGPT

The last four or six digits of a phone number, or an address from your childhood that you will never forget, are great to use as passcodes and passwords on your devices. These should not be addresses and phone numbers from the past thirty years, though. Those might be able to be found online. Use something from your youth that is emblazoned in your brain. Things to avoid in passwords are your birthday, year of your birth, current address, telephone number…essentially anything that people can find out about you online makes a bad password.

Passkeys

According to Adam Clark Estes at Vox.com, passKEYS are the next stage of Internet safety, replacing passWORDS. Without getting bogged down in the technical details as to how they are set up, just know that when you set up a passkey, it allows you to sign into that website using your DEVICE PASSCODE. What that means is that when I sign in from my phone, I either enter the passCODE that unlocks my phone, or the app uses my Face ID, and that's it. No additional password to remember!

Passkey as imagined by ChatGPT

Setting up a passkey is so easy. When you are logging in to certain websites like Google, Amazon, or Facebook, you will be asked if you want to set up a passkey. Say yes. The system does some technical stuff and then asks you to unlock your phone with your face, fingerprint, PIN, or swipe pattern. Now that same login code becomes associated with that account login and is even saved in your password manager, if you have one. (Password managers always ask if you want to save the new password. ALWAYS say yes.) The next time you log into that site, you will get in easily with just your device security.

Don't delete all your passwords yet, though, and follow the safety guidelines detailed in this chapter to keep your accounts safe. Not all websites are on the passkey bandwagon.

Fingerprint/Face ID

This is, without a doubt, the easiest way to sign into your device. Setting up face or fingerprint ID is not difficult. Follow the easy prompts, and the only time you'll have to put your PIN in is after you power down your phone. Otherwise, your login will be easy and secure.

ANDROID —SET UP FACE OR FINGERPRINT ID

SETTINGS > Tap On Search (Look For The Magnifying Glass) Type SECURITY > Fingerprint (Or Face ID)

Photo by ChatGPT

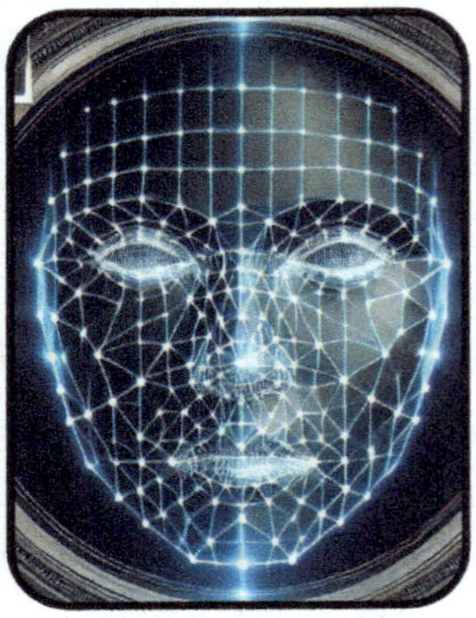

Photo by ChatGPT

Once again, depending upon the make and model of your device, you have options for fingerprint and/or face ID. To do this, open settings. In order to see the search bar in iPhone settings, you have to swipe down from the top of the screen, and the search bar will appear. Tap on the magnifying glass and search for FINGERPRINT. Before you even finish typing, you will see three suggested results. Tap on ADD FINGERPRINT. You will have to put your passcode in to verify it's you. The screen will change. Tap CONTINUE. The screen will change, and you will be prompted to roll your finger around the circle, ensuring all parts of your fingerprint are captured. The phone will tell you when you are successful.

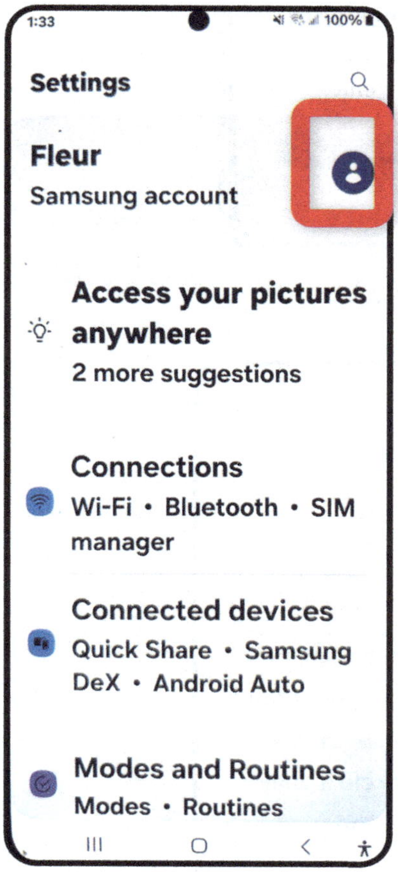

Image 11.1

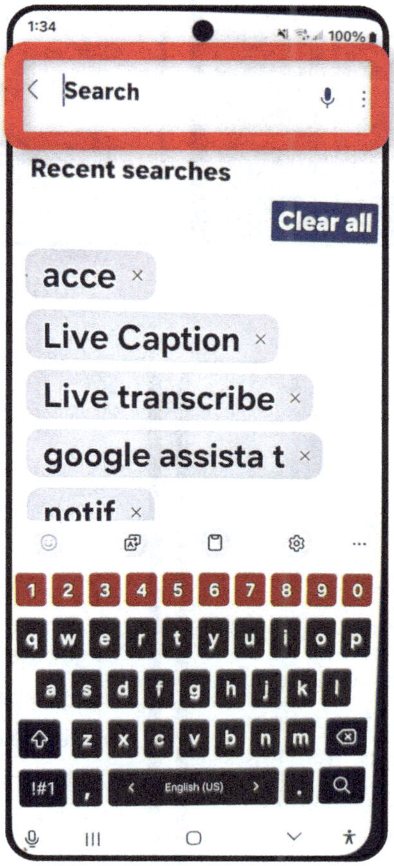

Image 11.2

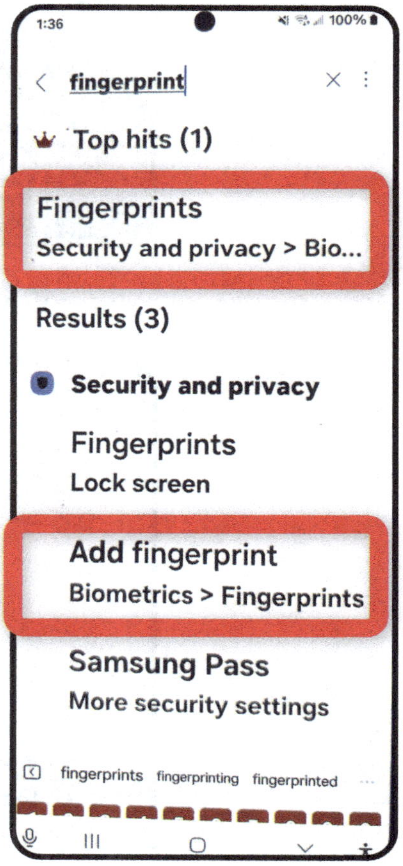

Image 11.3

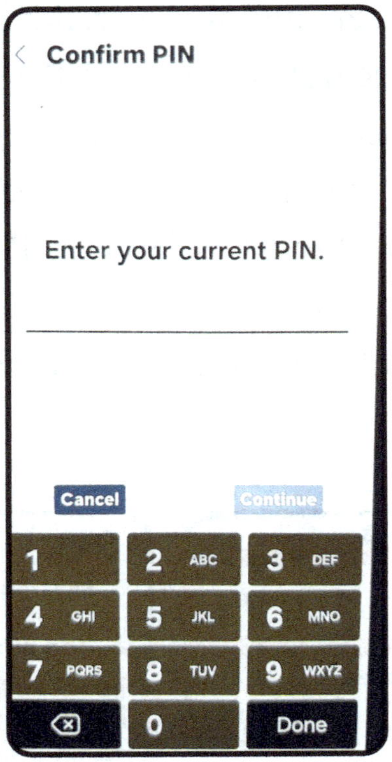

Image 11.4

Image 11.5

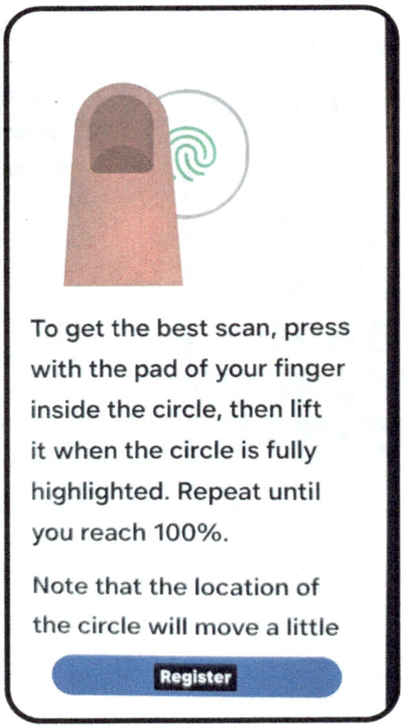

Image 11.6

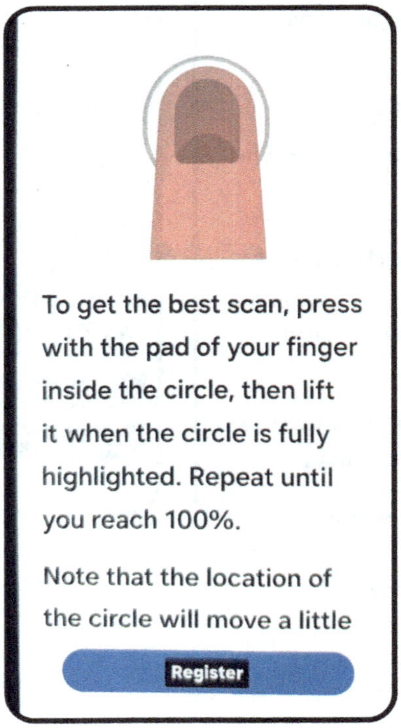

Image 11.7

iPHONE —SET UP FACE OR FINGERPRINT ID

iPHONE—SET UP FACE ID SETTINGS > SCROLL TO FACE ID & PASSCODE > ENTER YOUR PHONE'S PASSCODE > SET UP FACE ID

The newer iPhones only offer Face ID. Some of the older models with buttons (the original iPhone SE, for example) will offer fingerprint ID. If you're not sure that your phone has it, open the Internet and enter your phone's make and model with the word "fingerprint." Your phone will not have fingerprint if there is no physical home button.

The process is pretty easy. First open settings. (11.8) Slightly pull down the page from the top and you will see a search bar appear. (Image 11.9) Begin typing Face ID. Before you finish, the phone predicts what you want. **Tap on FACE ID & PASSCODE.** (Image 11.9) The

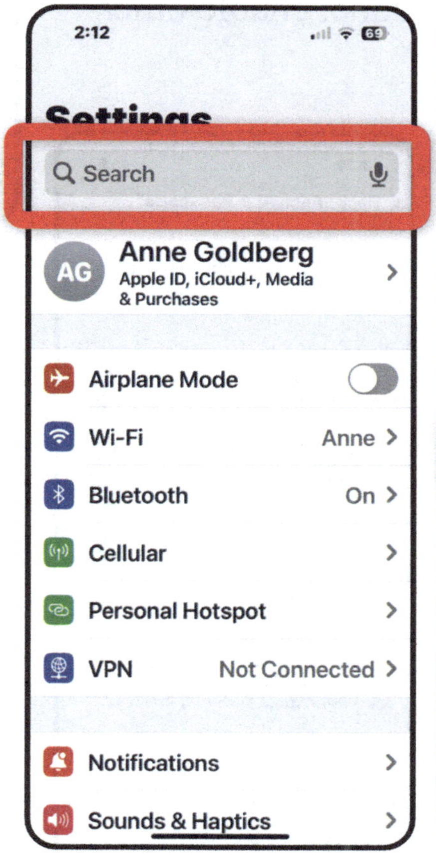

Image 11.8

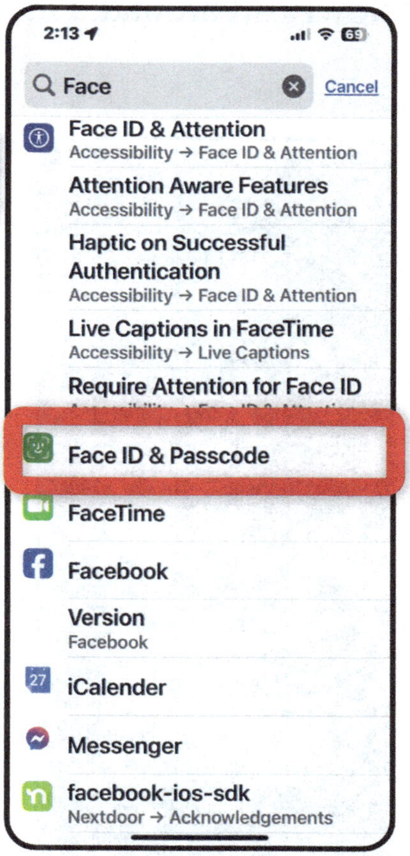

Image 11.9

screen will change. Put in your passcode. (11.10) The screen will change. (Image 11.11) Now you can allow the device to create a map of your face. Follow the prompts and slowly turn your head side to side, up and down. You will see the little lines change size. You will be told when the process has been completed, or it may ask you to do it again.

Make sure that you move your head very slowly all around. Once done, enable other apps to use Face ID (11.12) especially password autofill, your bank, the app store, and any other apps you use all the time that you would like easy access to. Read the screen.

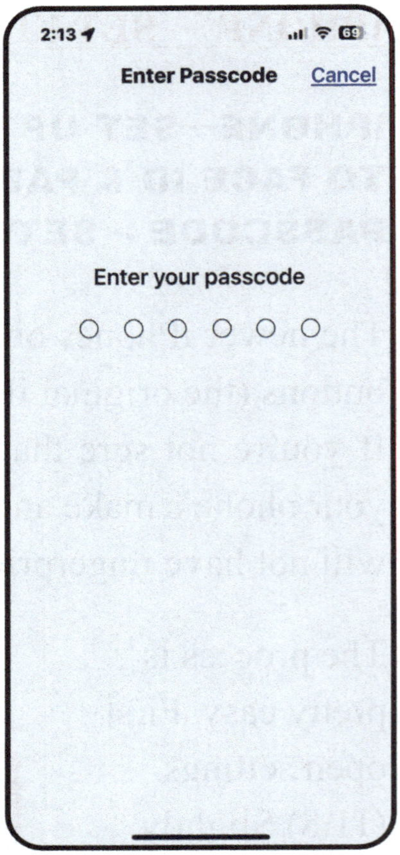

Image 11.10

Image 11.11

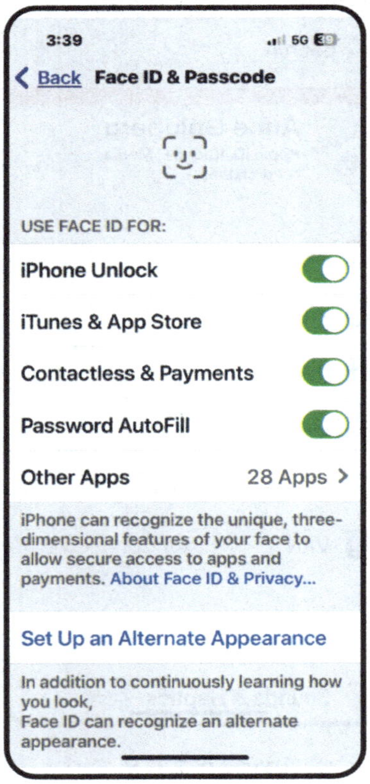

Image 11.12

Tap on other apps to add new apps to face ID.

Fingerprints are more secure but not always offered as it depends on the model of phone you have. With Face ID you do run the risk of someone with very similar bone structure being able to access your phone, but I do not let that deter me from the total ease of using the phone when it automatically unlocks upon seeing my face.

Password Managers

A password manager is like a safe that remembers all your passwords, so no more little pieces of paper or notebooks with scribbled passwords. Some of you have lovely excel spreadsheets with passwords that you may forget to update when forced to change a password. How's that been working for you? Generally, it's a nightmare of disorganization.

Password managers relieve you of the need to keep paper records for all but two passwords. You need to always know the password to the password manager, and it is smart to know your main email account password. (See Saving Master Passwords in Notes further down in this chapter for how to save these two important passwords.)

With a password manager, you set up an account with a master password that unlocks your account. Obviously, this needs to be a very strong, secure password as it is the key to your online life.

The password manager will save every password as you log in, as long as you say yes to the prompt that opens. Now every time you log into that account, the password manager will log you in! OMG, could it be any easier?

Password managers will also create super strong passwords for new websites you log into; save them and autofill the next time you log in.

Some well-regarded password managers are Bitwarden, 1Password, or Dashlane. And you can also use the password managers built into your browsers like Chrome and Firefox. I highly recommend you choose one and use it.

HOW ANDROIDS SAVE PASSWORDS

OPEN CHROME > TAP PICTURE AT THE TOP RIGHT OF THE SCREEN > TAP GOOGLE ACCOUNT UNDER YOUR NAME > SCROLL HORIZONTALLY TO SECURITY > SCROLL ALL THE WAY DOWN TO PASSWORD MANAGER

Google is at the heart of Androids, and it's good to familiarize yourself with your Google account. There are many settings that you want to control. For this discussion, we are only looking at passwords.

Androids automatically save passwords to your Google account. If you want your passwords saved somewhere else, you must make that change in settings.

Finding Passwords Saved in Google

If you want to view your saved passwords on your Android phone, assuming you are using Google to access the Internet, open Google and tap on the circle with your photo in it at the top right of the screen. (Image 11.13) The screen will change. Look down the page and find Passwords. (Image 11.14) Tap on it and the screen will change again, and you will see a list of passwords.

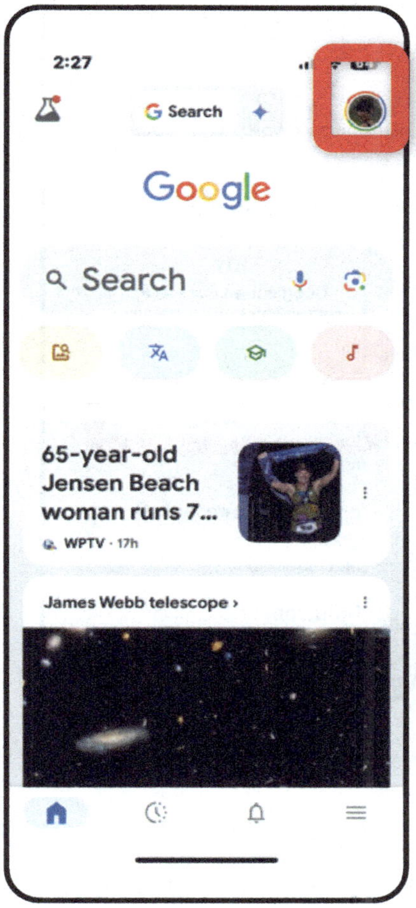

Image 11.13

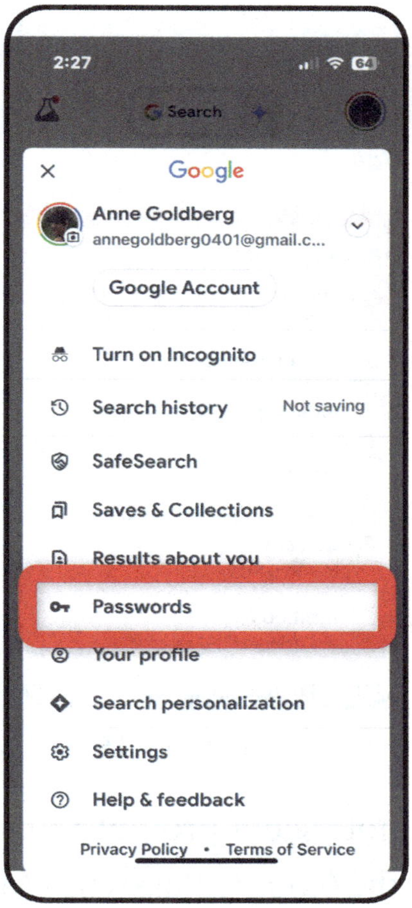

Image 11.14

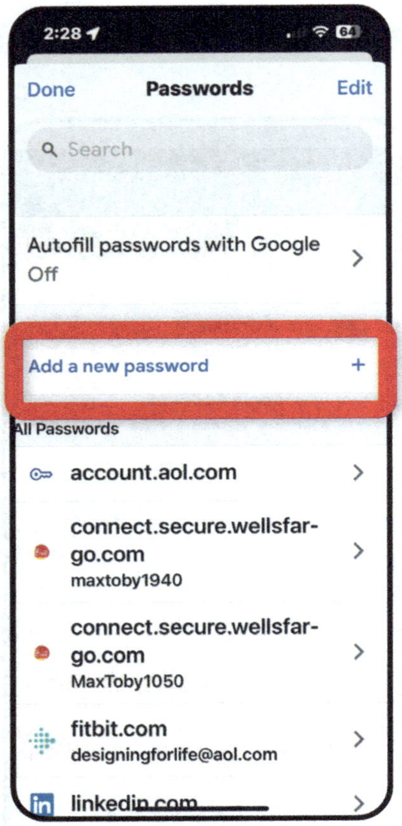

Image 11.15

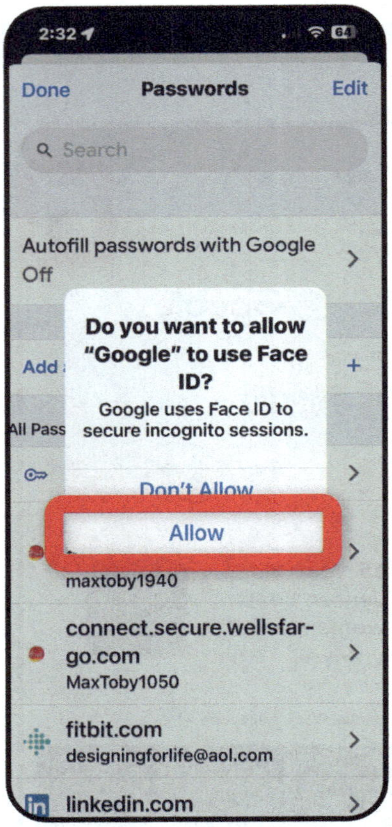

Image 11.16

(Image 11.15)

When you want to see the password of any particular account, tap on it. The screen will change and you will have to input your password or, as you see in Image 11.16, you can allow Face ID (or your fingerprint) to be used instead.

You may (or may not) see a prompt to encrypt your passwords before they are saved to the Google Password Manager. For the purpose of this tutorial, I request you **TAP DISMISS**, unless you are comfortable following the prompts to encrypt (make safer) your passwords. If so, **TAP SET UP** and take this important security step.

If you want to manually add a password to the list, tap on the blue *Add a new password* and fill in the information. Make sure there are no typos!

It is possible that your screen may look different if you have not updated your Android or Google itself. I recommend doing all updates whenever you are notified.

HOW IPHONES SAVE PASSWORDS

IPHONE SAVES PASSWORDS TO ITS NEW PASSWORD APP.

With the iOs18 update, Apple changed its password management. Keychain went away and a new **Password App** was put on your phone. It's gray with colorful keys in the center, and it replaces the entire password section in settings on all phones from iPhone XR to 16. If you can't find the password app, swipe left until you get to the App Library and search for "password."

If you have an iPhone 8, 7, or heaven forbid a 6S, please get a newer phone. You may think your phone is working just fine, but in reality it will get buggy, and it is more vulnerable to cyberattack. Please, believe me when I say you do not want that aggravation.

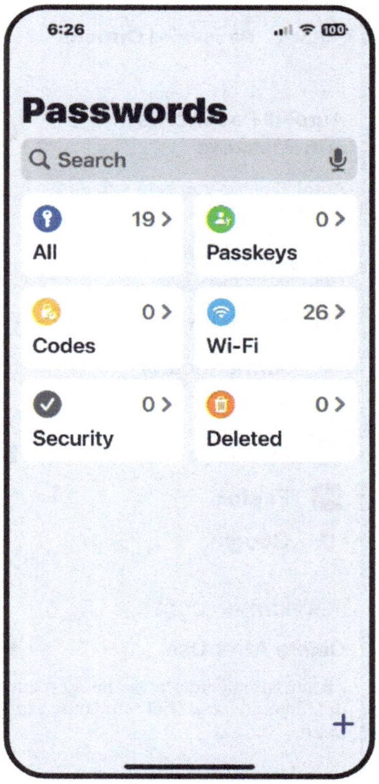

Image 11.17

If money is tight, the various carriers typically offer discounts for seniors. Check your local carriers for details. And, for those of you with a really old iPhone, it may be worth $50 to maybe $100. This would offset the cost of a new (or newer) phone.

As you can see from Image 11.17, the password app contains not only passwords but passkeys, codes (for 2FA Authenticator and QR), Wi-Fi passwords, deleted passwords, and any security notifications you may have. According to Apple, the app is end-to-end encrypted, which means no one, not even Apple, can see your information.

Using this password app is great if you live in Mac-world, with all Apple products. It's a better version of Keychain (which remains on the older phones). This new app can create unique, complicated, safe passwords that you don't have to remember. And it will continue to automatically fill in your username and password. YOU WON'T HAVE TO REMEMBER THEM! The app will also notify you about any security issues like weak passwords.

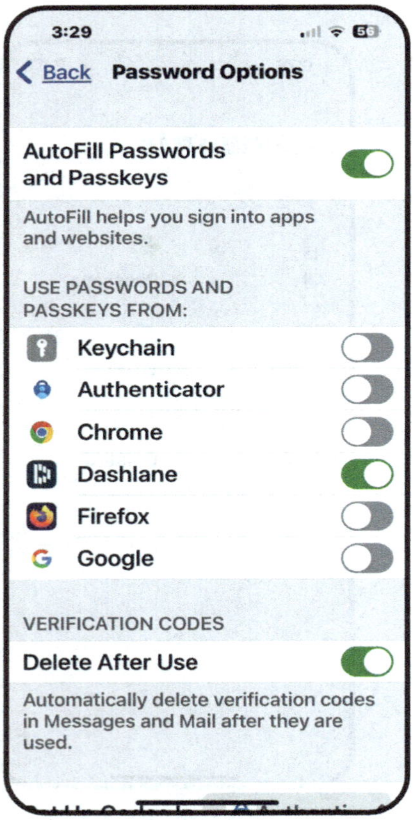

Image 11.18

If you are like me and have a PC and an iPhone, then saving to Apple Passwords is of little value. I need access to my passwords on two PCs and my phone. So, you can see in Image 11.18 that I have my passwords saved to Dashlane. It's easy to change. Just slide the toggle wherever you want to save your passwords. Make sure that you have toggled on "**AutoFill Passwords and Passkeys**" in the Password Options page in settings.

TWO-FACTOR AUTHENTICATION (2FA) AKA MULTI-FACTOR AUTHENTICATION (MFA)

You know how, when you call any big company like a bank, credit card company, or retailer, they ask you for a whole bunch of information in order to verify that you are actually the owner of the account? Well, 2FA is just like that. It is a second way of verifying that it's you. It is entirely for your safety, so just go with it. Use it especially for any companies that store your money or your credit cards.

This also applies to your password manager account. Set up 2FA and store the information somewhere locked away or in a secure site.

SAVING PASSWORDS IN A BROWSER

Browsers like Chrome, Safari, and Firefox are equipped to manage your passwords too. *They are not as good as using a password manager; however, they are way better than reusing passwords and little pieces of paper.* So, if you need to keep it simple (i.e., you're not willing to deal with a password manager) and are willing to stop using the same few passwords over and over again, take advantage of this convenient feature. They're free and there is nothing extra to do.

Choose the browser you use all the time. Chrome, Firefox, Safari, and Edge work on all your devices: phones, tablets, desktops, and laptops. They also will make up complicated passwords that you will never have to remember, making you and your accounts safer online. And they, along with password managers, can autofill your name, address, and telephone number on various forms requesting it online. It makes it so much easier when my name and address are autofilled. Why, it saves me valuable seconds of my time! Seriously, though, it's a cool feature.

Just keep in mind that the **browsers do not have the same security that a password manager does.** They are much safer than reusing passwords, but not as safe as a third-party company whose business is security. Which brings me to the next section.

PASSWORD MANAGERS

Perhaps now you can understand that using some kind of password manager is a wise decision. They store the confidential login credentials you need to use the various apps on your computer, phone, or Internet accounts.

Password managers remember all your passwords so you don't have to. They keep these passwords locked up tight, similar to a bank vault. You need to remember one password for access to all your passwords kept in a password vault.

Using a password manager is much safer than writing passwords down on paper or using the same simple password for everything. According to the New York Times **Wirecutter** newsletter, using a password manager "… (is) the most important thing you can do—alongside two-factor authentication—to keep your online data safe."

Once you've set up the account and logged into the password manager using a "master" password, it will **generate** and **remember** your passwords and passkeys for all your online accounts. Just like the browsers, password managers autofill passwords, name, address, phone, etc. They will also create safe, complicated passwords that you will NEVER have to remember.

A great password manager is easy to use and has outstanding scores on security. Right now, the online consensus seems to favor Bitwarden and 1Password as the two most highly rated password managers. Dashlane and Nordpass are also well-reviewed. Bitwarden is free, and Dashlane and Nordpass have free versions. Of course, with paid versions you get more features. You can't go wrong with these free versions either.

The caveat with a password manager is that if you forget your master password, you will be locked out of your passwords. You have to be careful with how you store it. Let's explore how to save your master password.

Choose a strong master password. *Write down the password before you enter it.* Try to remember it. Use the password formula on Page 190. Write it down somewhere safe. Safe is not in your desk drawer where your computer is if you have strangers in your house for any reason. At the very least, lock the drawer. But there are better ways. Some people keep a log in their Notes apps. Some create a contact for each website and keep that in their phone. But **do not do this if you do not have a passcode** that locks your phone. It's clear that the best and safest way to protect this information is with a password manager. But how do you keep the master password safe?

SAVING MASTER PASSWORDS IN NOTES

If you do this correctly, there are really only two passwords you must know—the password manager master password and your Apple ID or Google password. Why do you need these? A few years back, while visiting friends, my phone died on me. I got a replacement and, with my master password memorized, tried to log into my password manager. It had 2FA that I could not confirm because I did not have my phone, nor did I have access to my Gmail as I did not remember that password. I could not access my email or phone to confirm the 2FA, so I had no access to my password manager until I got home to my PC, where all the information was safe.

To summarize, always have access to your master password as well as your Google Account or Apple ID passwords in a place you can easily access. Believe it or not, I recommend a piece of paper in your wallet with only these two passwords on it. Don't put any other information here, just the passwords. I promise, you will thank me if you ever lose your device.

ANDROID NOTES TO STORE MASTER PASSWORD: NOTES > NEW NOTE > TAP 3 DOTS > TAP ON LOCK ICON

A box will open and at the **BOTTOM** of the box, you will see a series of icons. One will be a **picture of a lock**. **TAP ON IT.**

At this point, you will have to confirm that it's you trying to set a lock, and that's good security. Put in your password but don't squirm if you don't have it. There is an option to VERIFY WITH ONE-TIME

EMAIL. Once verified, the note will lock and only you can unlock it. If you have a phone with face or fingerprint recognition set up, you won't have to put in any passwords.

IPHONE NOTES TO STORE MASTER PASSWORD: OPEN NOTES > TAP THE NOTE TO SAVE > TAP CIRCLE WITH THREE DOTS

Open and tap on the note you want saved, shown in Image 11.20. A box will open and at the top you'll see some icons.

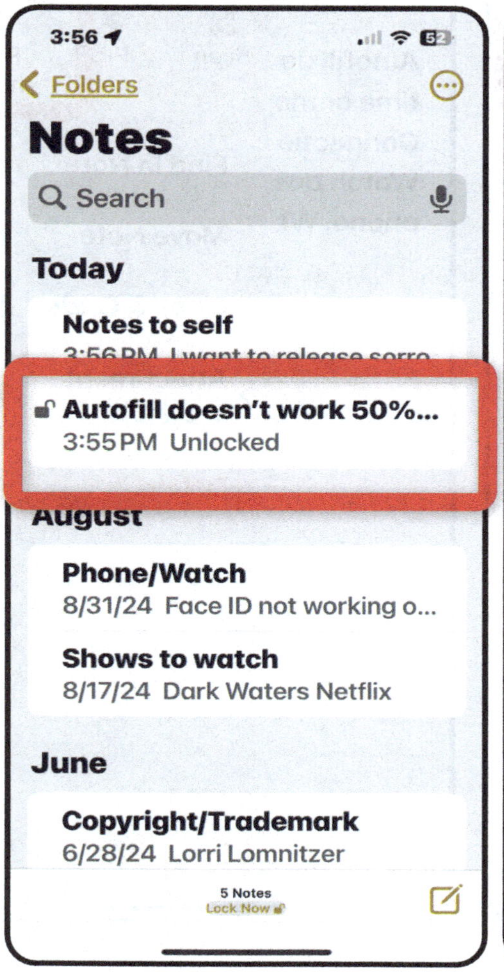

Image 11.19

Image 11.20

The one on the right says lock and is a picture of a lock. (11.21) **TAP ON IT**. The note is now locked.

Unlocking the Note – If you want to unlock it, look at the top of the screen in Image 11.22 and you will see a picture of an "unlocked" lock. **TAP ON IT.** If you have face or fingerprint recognition, the Note will automatically unlock. Otherwise, enter the phone's passcode.

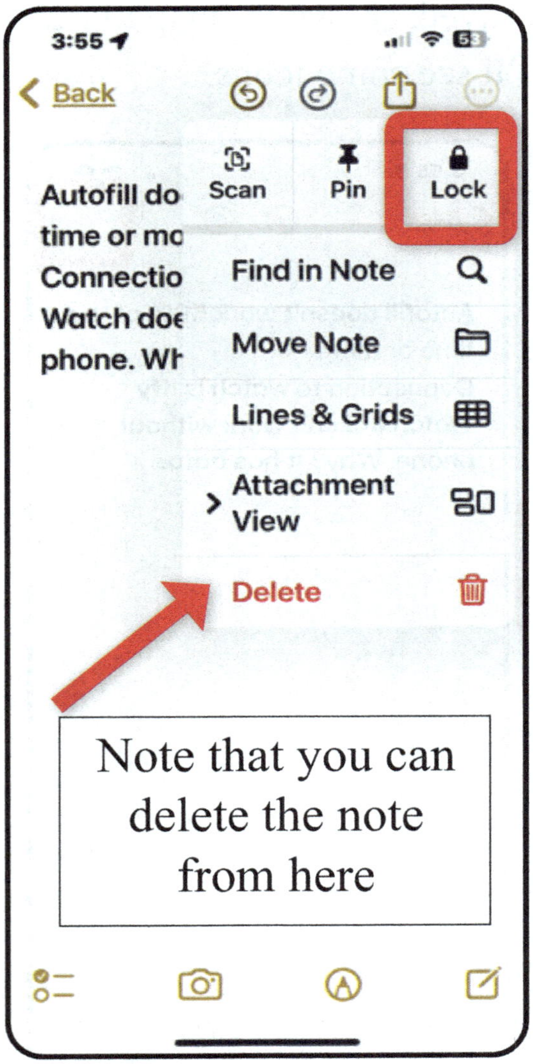

Image 11.21

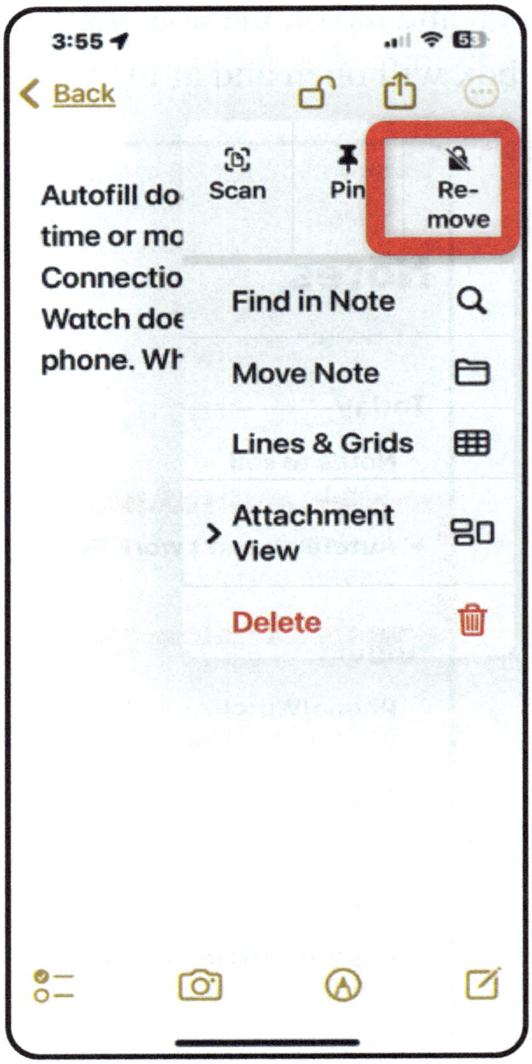

Image 11.22

Chapter 12

Staying Safe Online

Table of Contents

Scams & Spam

Scams and spam arrive in email, texts, phone calls, and dating sites. It's technology's version of the monster in the closet—hiding in the shadows of the Internet are cybercriminals who want your money and will do anything to get it. There is a sure-fire way to know something is a scam. THEY ARE INTENDED TO **SCARE YOU.** Maybe they threaten that you'll be arrested unless you pay, or that someone you love is in grave danger, or you will miss the *chance of a lifetime to make a killing in crypto*. Criminals depend on your fear to cause you to respond. They will create a sense of urgency. Do it now OR ELSE! Do not give in to that. If you get a call, email, or text saying that you owe money to the IRS, or your Medicare card needs to be replaced…or else…that is a scam! To verify your benefits, visit Medicare.gov or IRS.gov. The government does not accept crypto or gift cards as payment for anything. Never give anyone your bank information, which could result in an unapproved ACH transfer of funds.

Photo by Chat GPT

INDUCING FEAR IS THE HALLMARK OF A SCAM—scaring the daylights out of you is their objective! We've all gotten those spam calls. The phone number might even appear to be from the IRS or Medicare. You will know that's false as soon as they say something to frighten you. You owe money! Pay now or suffer the consequences! They are depending on your emotional response. They want you to be terrified. They will tell you to pay with gift cards or crypto currency! Baloney! It's pure, unadulterated baloney. Hang up! Block the number. Go on with your day.

I don't know how many ways I can say this. No matter who is calling; no matter what they threaten you with, NEVER, EVER INTERACT **with them. NEVER give PINs, passcodes, passwords, your social security number, or credit card account access. NO MATTER WHAT THEY ARE SAYING. Hang up. Call or go online to whatever company/agency/police they referenced. You will find out directly if anything is wrong. There won't be.**

If you are on the Internet and a pop-up appears telling you your device has been infected and "DO NOT TURN OFF YOUR DEVICE OR ALL YOUR DATA WILL BE LOST"—**shut down the device and restart it.** Immediately. (Even if you have to pull the plug on a computer!) This happened to me just this morning as I prepared to write this chapter. And I can tell you it is scary when suddenly there's a voice telling you there's a problem. Know this: Tech companies do not monitor your computer. No one in the outside world knows if you do or don't have a virus. What did I do? I restarted my computer, and the problem disappeared.

PHISHING

Fishing is a sport. **Phishing** is a con. Phishing scams come through your email and pretend to be someone you trust (a company or a person) and feel safe giving out personal information like passwords, bank account numbers, etc. There's a blue underlined link they want you to tap or a phone number to call. The writing may be slightly off, with weird language and grammar, and a slightly blurry logo pretending to be your bank or credit card company. With the sophistication of AI, some of these fake sites look very real. Again, NEVER, NEVER, EVER interact with these communications. Make it a policy to never click on any blue links unless the email comes from a trusted friend or colleague.

SMISHING

This is the same as phishing, except the communication is in your text messages. Typically, these are urgent requests for action that want you to tap on a malicious link.

VISHING

This is the term used for when the fraud attempt begins with a phone call. We've all gotten the calls about extended auto warrantees. Often the scammer wants to record your voice saying the word "yes." Never say yes to a stranger on the phone. Respond with a question. For example, asked if I am Anne Goldberg, my answer is "Who wants to know?" The reason they want a recording of you saying yes is to then use it to pretend to be you on the phone to authorize charges or access financial accounts.

If you want to know whether something is phishing, there's a really great way to check.

Image 12.01

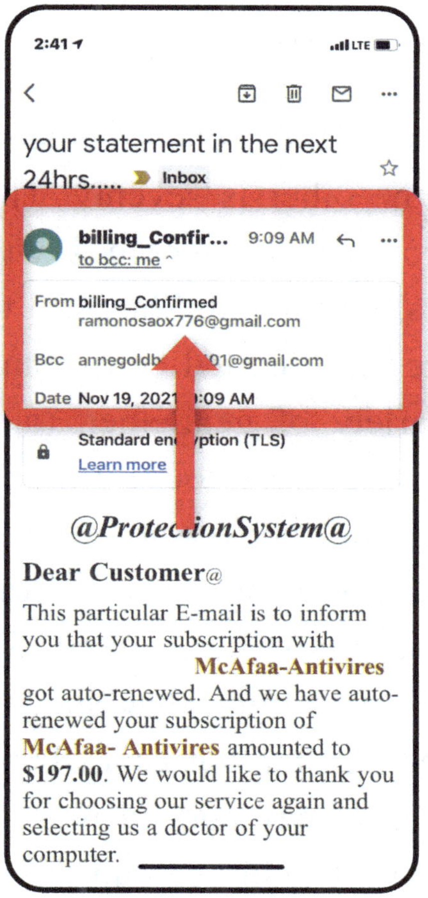

Image 12.02

Open the email and tap on the teeny, tiny down-arrow. (Image 12.01) This opens the field wider, revealing the email address of the sender. (Imge 12.02) This email is allegedly from McAfee, the anti-virus protection software. Notice that McAfee is spelled wrong, and the sending email address is a Gmail address and not from McAfee. That is 100 percent phishing. They want you to engage with them. Even if it's from chase.com, **do not click on any link** in that email. In an abundance of safety, open the Internet and log into your bank.

PIG BUTCHERING

Photo by ChatGPT

I have two friends; one is ninety-two and the other is seventy. The ninety-two-year-old, whom I will call Sheila, was bored. She went to dating sites and started conversing with a variety of gentlemen (and I use that term very loosely here). After a few nice conversations with lots of compliments, Sheila was given a sob story and asked for money. Keep in mind that Sheila knew they were scamming her, so she replied, "I should give YOU money! You should give ME money! I have bills to pay and no one to help! How could you ask me for money!" She would keep up this game until the scammer would stop talking to her. Her stories are pretty funny because she was in control the whole time. There was not a snowball's chance in hell of her parting with $1, let alone $10,000.

Then there's my other friend, whom I will call Terry. Terry was feeling alone and wanted to be in a relationship. She went on dating sites. Almost immediately she started talking with a man who treated her so nicely…for about two months. So nicely, in fact, that she declared him to be her boyfriend, although they never met, and she only saw a photo of him. Sometime along the process, this man started asking her for money…and she fell for it. To make a very long and horrible story short, to date she has lost well over $200,000. The tack they took was "If you deposit $40,000 into an account, we will return $4 million to you." She bought it hook, line, and sinker. At this time, nearly a year later, she is still believing this man cares about her and cannot understand why every single person in her circle has told her this was a scam. **When your dearest friends and family tell you you're being scammed, please believe them.**

Image generated with
Google Gemini

This particular scam is not limited to dating sites. It's called **"Pig Butchering"** because the scammers "fatten" up the victim with flattery, promises of making a lot of money, and nicey-nice talk until they come in for the kill, stealing whatever assets they can.

In a February 2024 article, Time.com reports that over $75 billion has been lost in the past four years globally. The Internet Crime Complaint Center of the FBI estimates that U.S. citizens lost nearly $12.5 billion to criminals in 2023 with $652 million in losses associated with romance and confidence scams. Sadly, most of the perpetrators are victims of large criminal organizations and are actually held by human traffickers and forced to do this under dire conditions.

Pig Butchering happens on all apps, across texts, emails, and even in person as people will impersonate investment experts, romantic prospects, and even UPS & FedEx drivers. It's not just on dating sites. It can happen to anyone. Pig Butchering investment scams promise very high rates of return. Do not fall victim to this. **Trust no one** who contacts you via text message saying they have a great investment for you. **Trust no one** on dating sites or Facebook, WhatsApp, and many other online social platforms. Anyone wanting to "friend" you who you don't know or who is connected through just one of your Facebook friends is not looking to be your friend. **They only want you to make them large sums of money, whether in ACH transfers, gift cards, or cryptocurrency. BLOCK THEM. DO NOT ENGAGE.**

Image generated by Google Gemini

CHARITY & DISASTER FRAUD

With all the natural disasters in the world, charity and disaster fraud are vibrant businesses for the bad guys. There is a great way to know if a charity is not only legitimate, but what percentage of your donation actually goes to the cause and how much is spent on administration. Go to CharityNavigator.org, Give.org, or CharityWatch.org. You will see exactly how your donation is used and if the charity is legit.

There are many other scams out there involving consumer fraud schemes and elder fraud, which targets seniors, such as tech support scams, government impersonation scams, sweepstakes and lottery scams, home repair and, one of the biggest, cryptocurrency scams. Just know that ANY MONEY you send these criminals is gone, likely forever. In the great words of Nancy Reagan, Just Say No!

GRANDPARENT SCAMS

Grandparent scams are pernicious. They pray on your love for family. Here's a great way to avoid a problem. Have a SAFE word with your family. Pick a word that you will all remember, and if you get a phone call allegedly from your kids or grandkids, ask for the safe word. When the caller doesn't know it or hedges in answering, you will know it's a scam.

Remember, the criminals want your money. They care about nothing else. Don't let them win.

UNSAFE APPS

In 2024, Malwarebytes (a premier anti-malware software company that I recommend for all PCs) found more than 22,800 phishing apps on Android's Play Store. Of them, more than 5,000 are able to bypass 2FA (secondary authentication) because they are able to look at your text messages! OMG!

Malwarebytes goes on to say that another 4,800 apps can potentially read your notification screens. This is terrifying. These apps masquerade as legitimate, like Spotify and WhatsApp, and trick users into entering usernames and passwords so the criminals can gain access to your accounts.

So, how do you stay safe from these *phishing* expeditions if you have an Android phone? Well, follow basic online safety.

1. Android phones, like PCs, need extra protection in the form of anti-virus software. It is recommended that you install mobile security on your Android phone. Companies like Bitdefender, Avast Mobile Security, Norton 360 for Mobile, and Google Play Protect are highly rated.
2. Only download apps from the Google Play Store. Never download from a website. You just don't know its safety. Furthermore, when looking at apps to download, check out the reviews. There should be thousands of reviews. Any site with just a few reviews is suspect.
3. Use a Password Manager as described in Chapter 11, page 309.
4. Implement multi-factor authentication. Yes, it's annoying to wait for the code, get the code, copy the code, and paste or type it again. Yes. I know. And it is like having an additional lock on your door in a high-crime neighborhood. So, as Nike says, "Just do it!"

ANDROID/GMAIL – IDENTIFYING & DEALING WITH SPAM

Spam email is junk just like the catalogues and advertisements that used to fill our mailboxes, trying to sell us something, unwanted newsletters, offers, and deals. Annoying, but not malicious. Spam mail is just so much junk. Unsubscribe and delete. There are two ways to unsubscribe from emails and then there is blocking them and reporting them as spam.

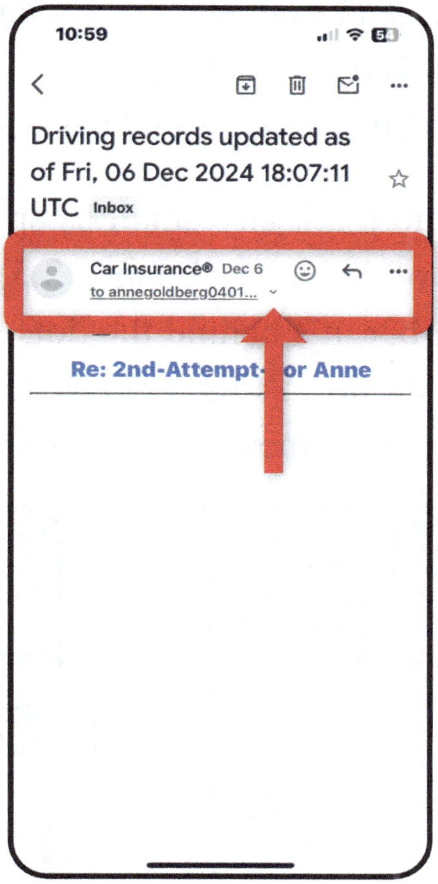

Image 12.03

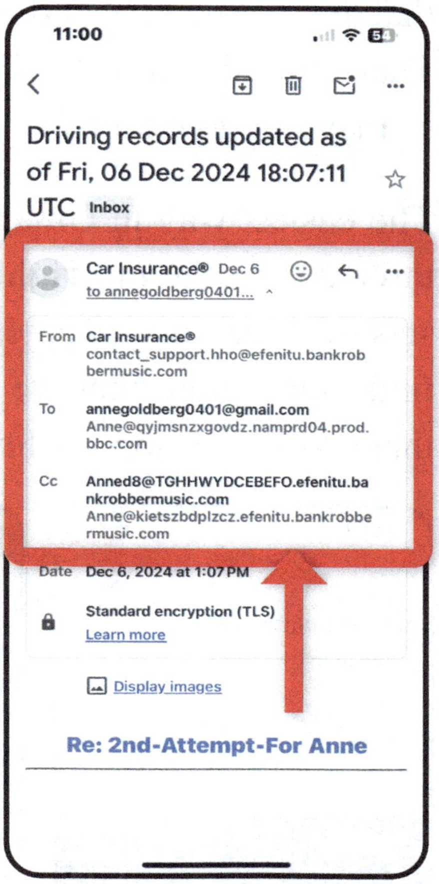

Image 12.04

In Images 12.3 & 12.4, you can see how to identify the sender of any email. By the looks of it, this should come from some insurance company; however, if you tap on the teeny tiny arrow in the address area, you can see the sender's actual address, which in this case is: Contact_support.hho@efenitu.***bankrobber****music*.com. Now there is a sense of humor. The criminals tell us they are bank robbers!

Marking as Spam

Marking an email as SPAM, however, is like telling your email provider that this is junk mail and should be put where you can check it to be sure. That's the SPAM or JUNK folders. Future emails from this sender may or may not go directly to spam—at least that has been my experience.

The easiest way in Gmail to mark any email as spam is to tap on the three dots at the **top right** of the page. (Image 12.5) Yes, there are two sets of three dots. (Remember, it's behind the dots and dashes that we find much more that we can do in this app.) When you tap on these three dots at the top, a whole other menu of actions appears. (Image 12.6)

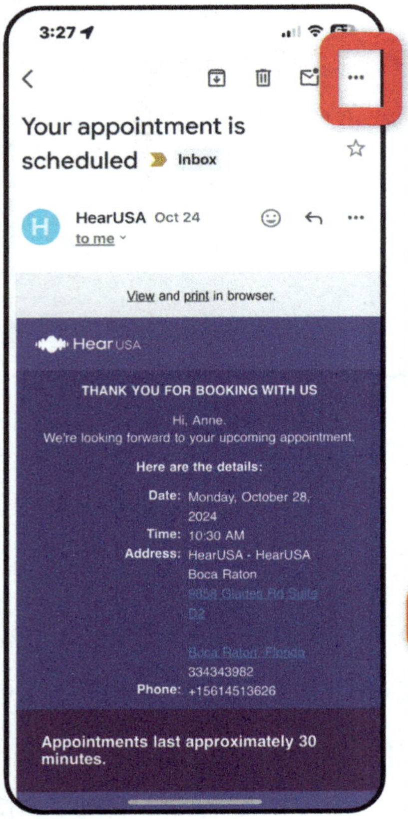

Image 12.5

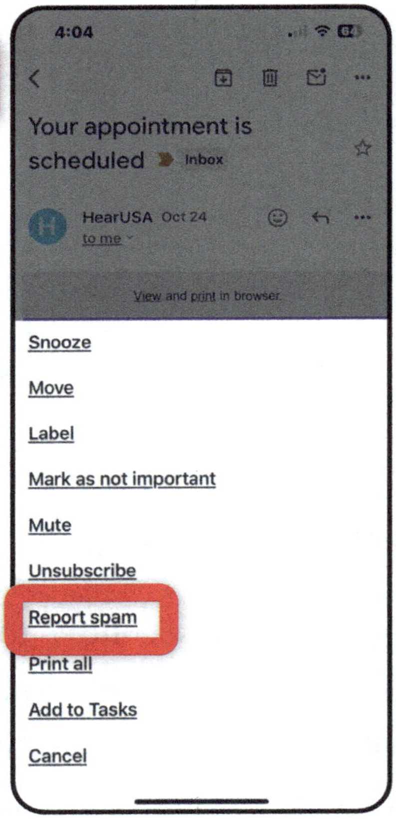

Image 12.6

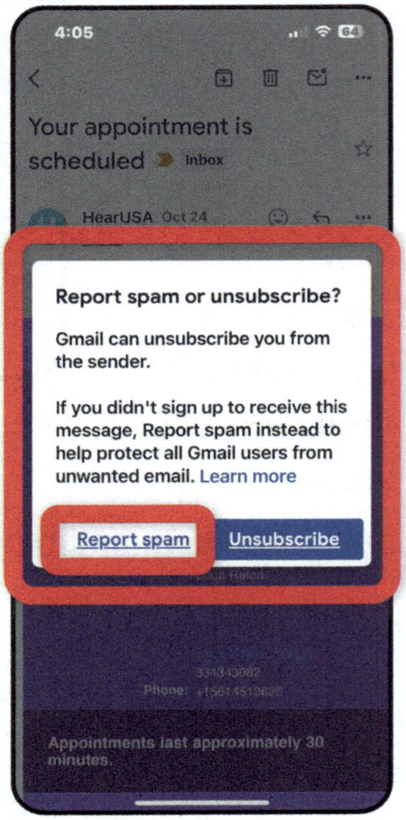

Image 12.7

Fourth from the bottom you will see **REPORT SPAM**. Tap on that. Tap again. Now you are done.

Blocking Emails

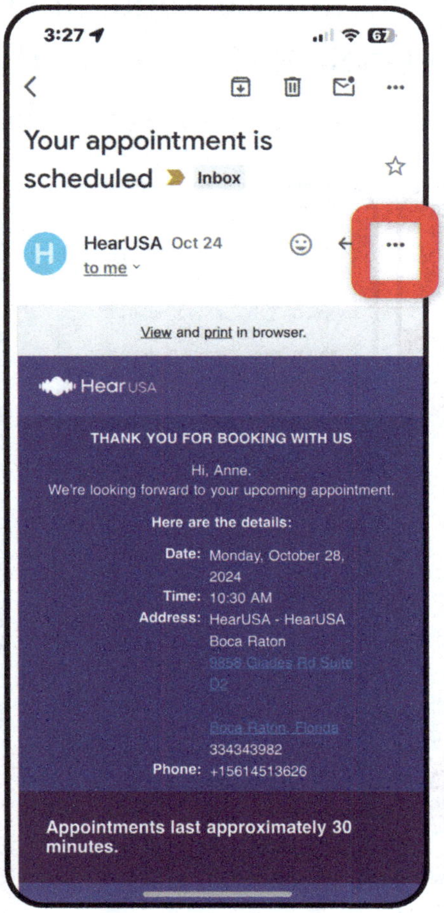

Image 12.08

Blocking emails is just a bit different. Open the email. If you're in Gmail (and most Android users are in Gmail), you will see three horizontal dots right where the "reply" arrow is. This is the second set of dots on the page.

Tap on those dots. (Image 12.8) A white box will open, and you will have choices, among which will be Block (the sender of the email in Image 12.9). Tap on it to block this sender.

(There is an option to UNBLOCK on the screen if you change your mind.) When you block a sender, it's as if you put a "DO

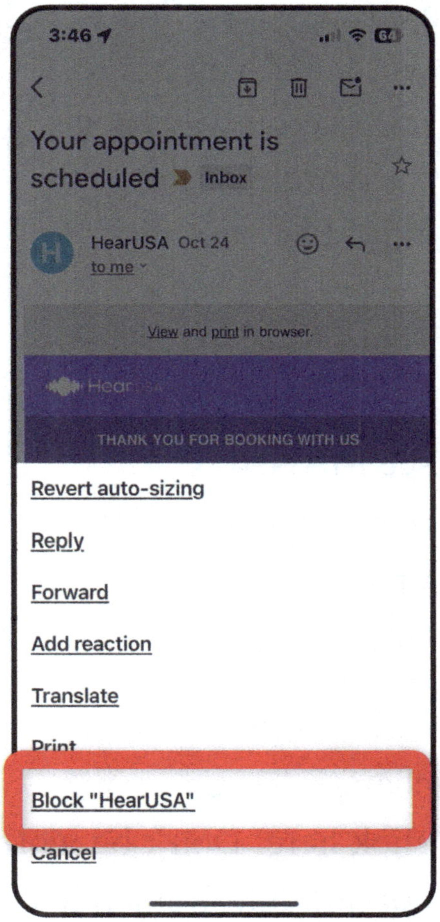

Image 12.09

NOT DELIVER" sign for that sender, and you won't see it again. And remember, if you decide you don't want to do anything, tap on Cancel.

Unsubscribe From Emails

Any legitimate company will offer an easy way to unsubscribe from their email lists. Often, you will see the word UNSUBSCRIBE clearly at the top of the page. (Image 12.10) This is the easiest way to unsubscribe from a mail list.

Sometimes, though, you won't see that word, and you must scroll way to the bottom of the page and carefully look for the word UNSUBSCRIBE, or you may see MANAGE (CHANGE) YOUR PREFERENCES. (Image 12.11)

Image 12.10

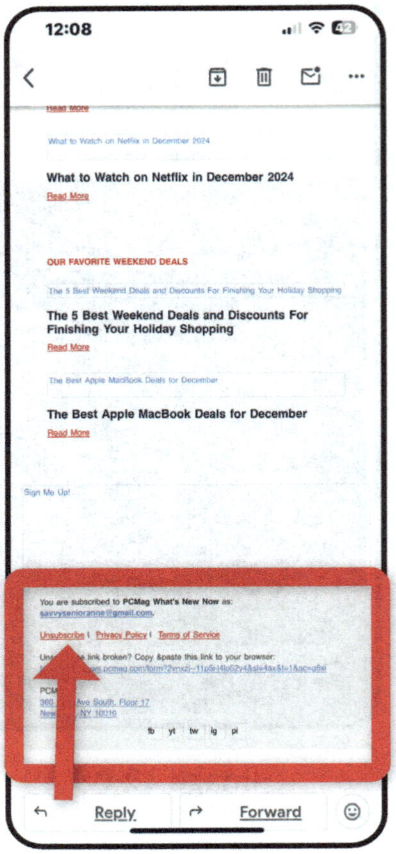

Image 12.11

The screen will change when you click here. Don't be worried. Follow the prompts and you will see it's not difficult. Remember to read the screen.

There is a caveat to this. If the email you want to unsubscribe from is *People Magazine*, by all means scroll down and tap UNSUBSCRIBE. However, if the email is from some company you don't know, don't do this. If you do, you are letting the criminals know they have a good address. Or worse, it's a malicious link that may cause you heartache. In these cases, use the email program to mark as spam, as detailed above.

APPLE MAIL

Now let's see how to spot a fake email in Apple Mail. Tap directly on the "from" email address, in this case, Tech Help Netw… Notice that it's blue and underlined. It is a hyperlink. Tap on it, the screen will change, and you will see that this email has come from a Gmail address and not a company.

Identify Spam Email

If you don't know who sent you an invoice, there's a simple way to see where that email came from. TAP on the address and the screen will change. (Image 12.13) You can see here that this email came from a Gmail address and not a company.

Image 12.13

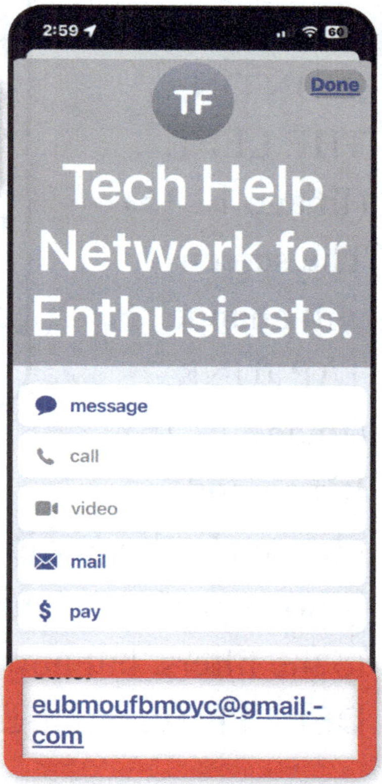

Image 12.14

(Image 12.14) This is a sure indicator of SPAM. Block and delete. See how next.

Mark As Spam

In order to mark an email as spam in Apple Mail, you have to work with the icon at the bottom of the screen. TAP THE SECOND ICON ON THE LEFT. (Image 12.15) The screen will change. TAP JUNK. (Image 12.16) It's a good idea to check your junk and spam folders from time to time as this is not a perfect science. Important emails may be considered Junk to the filters, but not to you. Once you've gone over the spam mail, DELETE everything.

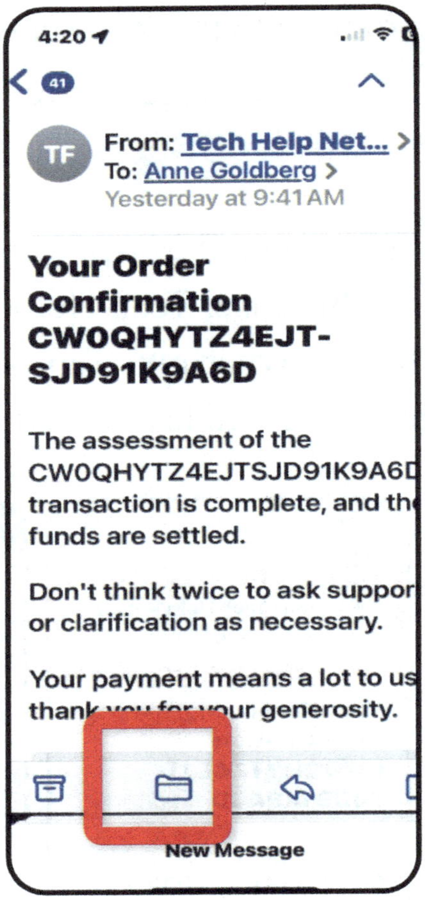

Image 12.15

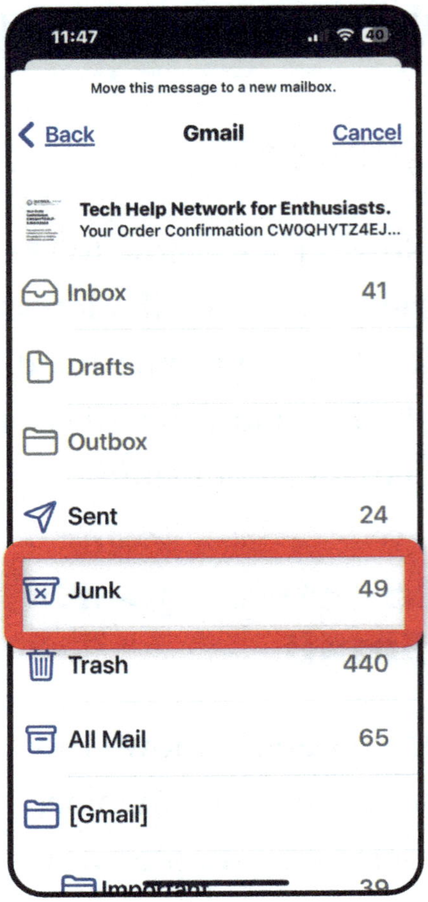

Image 12.16

Block This Email

TAP on the Sender in blue. (See Image 12.17) The screen will change to an information page related to this sender. (Image 12.18) You see the full email address it came from, (Image 12 .18). You will also see options: "Add to VIP," and then "Block this Contact." **TAP BLOCK THIS CONTACT** and confirm the action. (Image 12.19) If you change your mind, tap on cancel. Tap DONE at the upper right corner when complete.

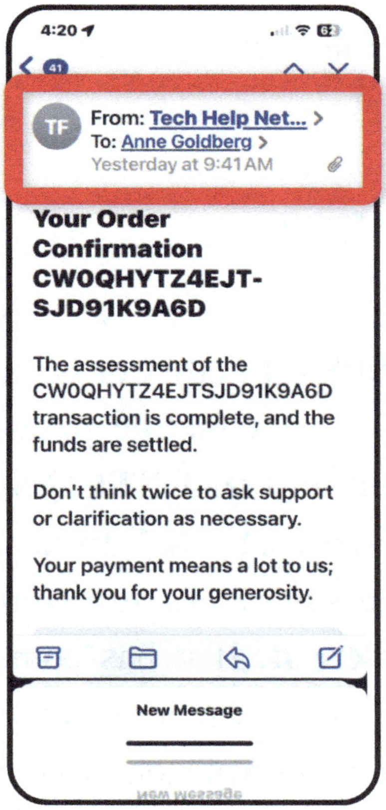

Image 12.17

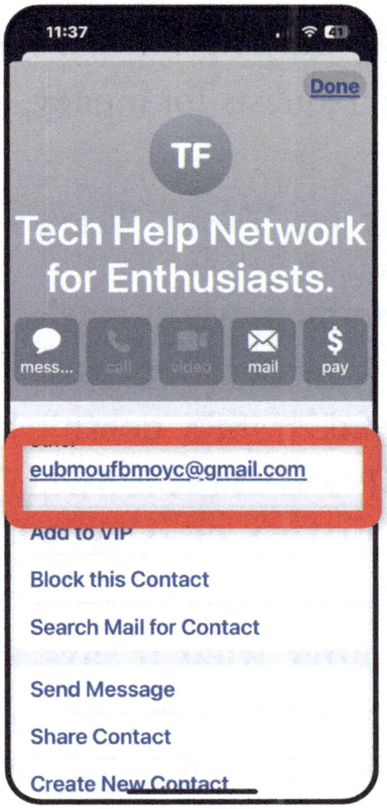

Image 12.18

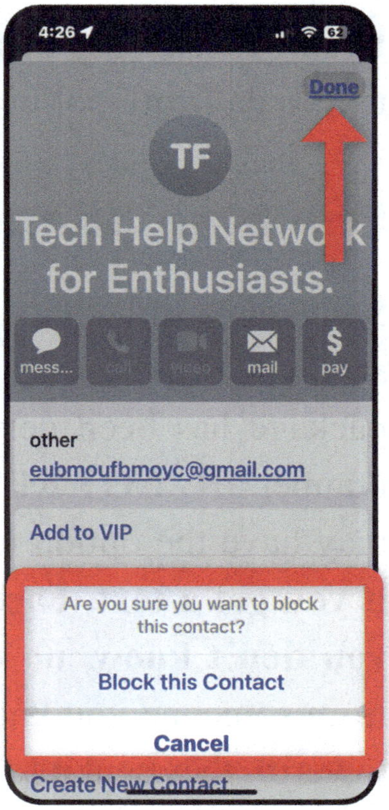

Image 12.19

How to Stop Political and Other Ads

A great way to reduce these junk texts is to simply text back one word: **STOP or UNSUBSCRIBE**. This should stop the communication from that phone number. Of course, the bad guys know this, so they can just substitute a different number. Reply with **STOP or UNSUBSCRIBE** again (and again, if necessary). You should receive one last text acknowledging your stopping/unsubscribing.

I can honestly say this is working for me. I am no longer getting ten texts a day with political requests for money.

Phishing Scams in Text Messages

Sometimes, though, scammers try to catch flies with honey, so they send you a text saying, "You won!" or "Your USPS (or FedEx or UPS) package has been delayed." USPS doesn't have your mobile phone number. **DO NOT RESPOND TO IT. Swipe left and DELETE.** You may have the option to **"DELETE AND REPORT JUNK."** In fact, **if you get a text, Facebook, or WhatsApp message from someone you don't know, no matter what it says, delete it.** If it has come from someone you know, open a new message and text them directly to verify they sent it to you. If you get a message from Amazon or your bank, **DO NOT INTERACT** with it. Call or log into your account online and check to see that all is well.

Then there are voter, Medicare, and IRS scams. Know this. The government NEVER texts or emails you unless you have opted in for Medicare emails. Otherwise, the government communicates via regular U.S. mail. You all know what those envelopes from the IRS, Medicare, and Social Security look like. Any other correspondence is fake. DO NOT FALL FOR IT.

And regarding Medicare, when it's open enrollment season, the scammers have a field day. You may receive a call, text, or email suggesting that you might lose your benefits or that your card needs to be verified. Call 1-800-MEDICARE or go to Medicare.gov to verify.

Apple and any of the Android manufacturers do not monitor your devices for malware. They have no idea if your device is infected or not. If you get notices like that, close your open apps. (See Chapter 8—Closing Open Apps.)

On an Android, tap the three parallel lines on the bottom of the device. The screen will change and you will see all your open apps. Swipe away the offending page.

On an iPhone, swipe UP from the very bottom of the screen to reveal your open apps. Swipe and close the bad one. Following that, it's not a bad idea to shut down the device. Turn it off. Then turn it back on. If the notice is still there, call whomever you call to fix technical issues. Do not engage with the message.

I can't say this enough. Never, never, ever tap on a blue-underlined link when you do not know who sent it to you.

Let me be clear. **NEVER, EVER INTERACT OR GIVE OUT YOUR SOCIAL SECURITY, MEDICARE NUMBER, OR DRIVER'S LICENSE TO ANYONE WHO CONTACTS YOU. PERIOD. END. OF. STORY.**

Protecting Yourself When Information Has Been Stolen

If you've watched any television in the last fifteen years, you've undoubtedly seen shows where some genius hacker can open a digital doorway to the highly prized information to highly secure sites. Well, there is a reality to this. Bank of America suffered a breach in February 2024 which exposed sensitive information like birthdates and social security numbers. United Health revealed a loss of $872 million due to ransomware. This is when you lose access to your computer system unless you pay a ransom. $872 MILLION!

But the biggest and scariest is the 2.9 million records, including social security numbers, that were stolen from National Public Data, reported in April 2024.

So many seniors I know refuse to do banking or access other financial apps from their smartphones because they think it's not safe. As long as you have strong passwords protecting your account, it's as safe as anything can be.

The trick to safety online is to take the steps below that every online expert recommends you do when your personal information has been stolen from a third party.

CHANGE YOUR PASSWORD

If you are notified as to a company breach like T-Mobile, United Healthcare, or Equifax, the first thing to do is change your password immediately. Why? If your keys are stolen, the first thing you'd do is change the locks on your house. Well, changing your password is the same thing. Following the example in Chapter 11, create a long and complicated password or let your password manager create one for you.

FREEZE YOUR CREDIT

Experion, Equifax, and Transunion are the credit reporting agencies that track your credit. Whenever you request to open a new financial account, the institution will look up your credit. If there is a freeze on your credit report, no new loans, credit cards, or mortgages can be taken out in your name, unless you temporarily unfreeze your credit. This is wonderful protection. And let's face it, at this age you're probably not making too many large purchases where your credit report needs to be accessed. It is a small inconvenience with a very big pay-off in safety and security for you.

FREEZE CREDIT: OPEN A BROWSER > SEARCH EQUIFAX FREEZE CREDIT > FOLLOW THE STEPS.

Repeat for Transunion and Experian.

You will have to type in your social security number, address, etc. so the credit bureau freezes the correct account. Do it for all three reporting agencies. It will take about ten minutes or so to do each of them. Do it. You will thank me when some big company is breached, and your social security number is stolen.

Enable 2FA/MFA on all your accounts.

Yes, two-factor authorizations are inconvenient. Yes, it takes longer to do everything in your accounts. That is the world we are in. You can put your head in the ground and ignore it or you can be proactive and protect your assets. It's a small inconvenience that yields a great degree of security. These settings are in the website you are logging into—Facebook or your email account, your bank, etc.

INSTALL ANTI-VIRUS & MALWARE PROTECTION

Yes, even smartphones can be hacked, especially Androids. There are two different kinds of infections, malware and viruses. According to iPhoneLife.com, "Malware is short for malicious software and includes harmful viruses like Trojan horses and spyware apps. Viruses are programs that replicate themselves once they've invaded."

With respect to iPhones, there is some debate. Apple security is top-notch, but be careful about the website you visit and the apps you download. **Only download apps from the App Store.** While iPhones are fairly immune to viruses, they are not immune to malware. **The**

most important thing you can do is install all updates from Apple as soon as they are available. How to check for updates?

INSTALL UPDATES ON iPHONE: SETTINGS > GENERAL > SOFTWARE UPDATE

Now you're in Software Update, where you will see if your device is up to date or there is a new update to install. Follow the prompts. It is not difficult. First you will download the update; then you will install it. Two steps. Easy. We think that these updates happen automatically, but in my experience, you need to check. They do not always automatically install.

For Androids, there are very good anti-virus products out there—Bitwarden is a favorite according to Forbes and techradar.com. Total AV, Norton, McAfee, and Malwarebytes are popular and highly rated as well. If the idea of doing this yourself causes you to hyperventilate, call on family or the Geek Squad or any trusted computer repair person to help you ensure you're properly protected and that your Android has not been infected.

Android & iPhone Internet Safety & Privacy

I absolutely LOVE the Internet. Endless information, movies, books, SHOPPING! OMG, the Internet can be so much fun. Go to YouTube and look for videos to make you laugh. Find reruns of the classic *Tonight Show* with Johnny Carson episodes, and any other show you loved in the fifties, sixties, seventies, and so on. You could spend the rest of your life just on YouTube learning, traveling, and being entertained. But all of this comes with a price. The bad guys are always trying to con us. So here are a few Internet safety tips.

Safety Tip

NEVER, NEVER, NEVER, NEVER EVER click on a **sponsored ad result** when you search for something, especially if you use Google or Chrome. The reason is the bad guys are bypassing Google security by spoofing (i.e., reproducing) known company websites like Macy's. (Image 12.20) These only come up under search results that are **SPONSORED or say AD**. More recently I've noticed the word

Image 12.20

Image 12.21

AD on the right of the search result, where SPONSORED seems to always be on the left. **LOOK FOR BOTH!!** They look like the real thing, but if you make a purchase, you are not paying who you think you're paying, and you will not receive your merchandise nor a refund. Image 12.21 shows the real Macy's search result.

Keep scrolling past any search result that has either the word SPONSORED or the word AD in it. You will find the true result a bit further down on the screen. Feel free to tap and shop safely.

Android/Google Privacy Settings

GOOGLE PRIVACY SETTINGS

Internet safety requires that you make certain changes to Google, Apple, Facebook and Instagram, Amazon settings, and more. For now, I'm going to focus on Google and Apple settings.

We have to face the fact that everyone on the Internet is out to get information on you. They want to know what you think, what you like and don't like, the beer, wine, or soda you drink, the appliances you use, and the shows you watch. They want to know what you buy and how often. They want to know as much as they can about you so they can monetize it. They want this information so they can pommel you with ads for things they think you want and need. Technology is listening and, sometimes, watching.

Do you want that? I certainly do not, and I take great pains to protect my online privacy. How do I do that? First, share as little as possible. When you log into apps, largely on social media platforms, you will likely be asked to *allow access to your contacts*. Wait, does that company want me to let it copy all the information for every one of my contacts? Yes, that's what they mean. Is that okay with you? On the plus side, you can get matched up with family members and old friends on Facebook and Instagram. That's nice, yet there is something creepy about giving a social media platform all this private information. Think twice before you say yes to that or any request for your personal information or contacts.

Image 12.22

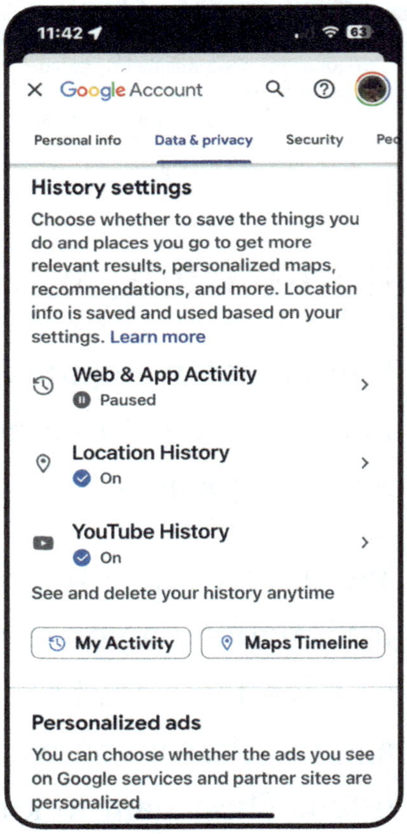

Image 12.23

You also have the option to stop personalized ads. (Images 12.23 &

24) The reason to stop them is to stop the tracking. While the ads you may see are irrelevant to you, that's better than Google knowing every online step you take.

I encourage you to tap on every blue line and read what comes up. Turn off as much personalization as possible to protect your privacy.

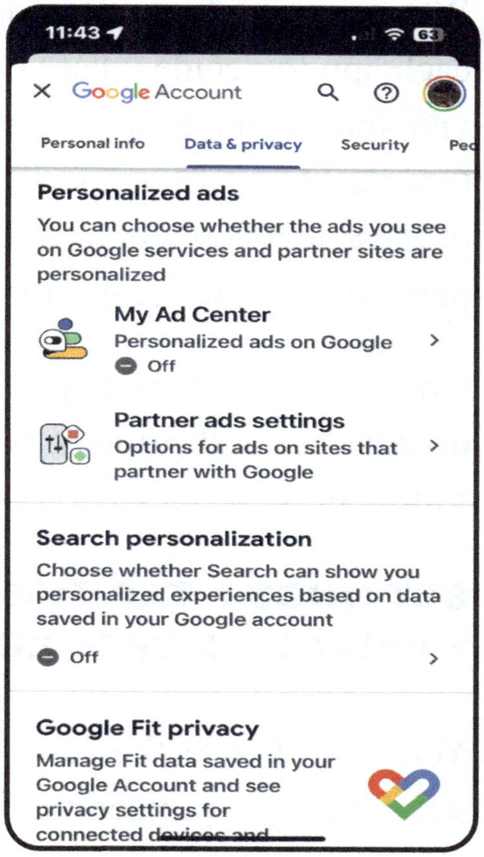

Image 12.24

Google Drive and Privacy

Google's default save location is Google Drive and Google Photos for pictures. According to Cloudworks.com, Google Drive is secure but not so private. So it is less likely to get hacked by outsiders, but Google itself is scanning and "reading" your drive. "Google knows what you are doing while using its apps," the article goes on to say. Google is always capturing your activity and data to support its metrics and analytics.

As a result, don't save anything sensitive or confidential in your Google Drive.

SETTINGS > SECURITY & PRIVACY > PRIVACY > PERMISSIONS MANAGER > REVIEW APPS

When you get to the Permissions Manager, tap on it and read through each app to decide what you want to give permission to. For example, you may want to give Contacts permission to connect with email, Google Meet (if you use it), messages, phone, WhatsApp. Tap on each of those and you will be able to toggle permissions on or off. The fewer permissions, the greater the privacy.

Google Chrome is a powerful web browser, but it does have its drawbacks, and privacy is one of them. To change privacy settings, follow these prompts:

SETTINGS > TAP THE THREE DOTS AT THE TOP RIGHT > PRIVACY & SECURITY > SAFE BROWSING

You can choose the level of "safe browsing": enhanced protection standard or no protection. I use the standard level.

"Do Not Track"

Turning this on sends a message to websites you visit to not track you. Turning this on is not a guarantee that you won't be tracked, but many websites do heed this request, and it's better to be on than not.

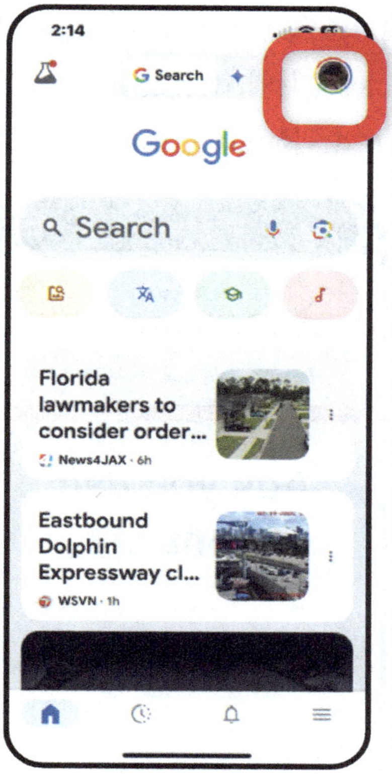

Image 12.25

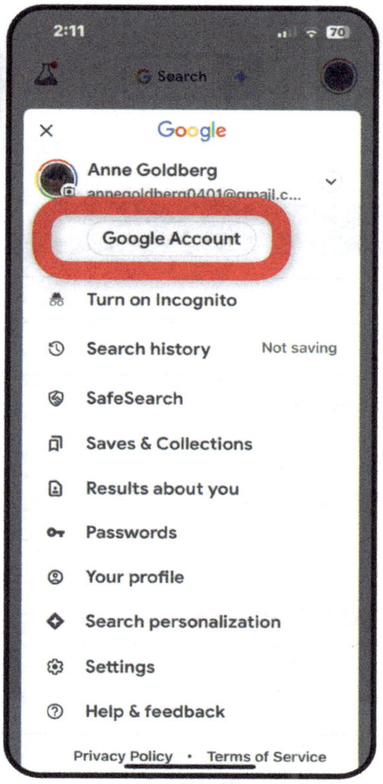

Image 12.26

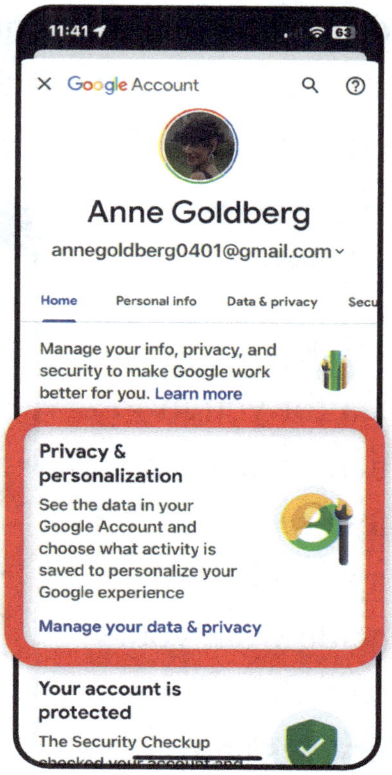

Image 12.27

OPEN GOOGLE CHROME > TAP THREE DOTS ON UPPER RIGHT OF SCREEN > SETTINGS > PRIVACY AND SECURITY > DO NOT TRACK > TURN ON

OPEN GOOGLE > TAP ON CIRCLE AT TOP RIGHT > TAP GOOGLE ACCOUNT > PRIVACY & PERSONALIZATION

Open the Google app on your phone and tap on the circle with your picture in the top right of the screen. (Image 12.25) Tap on Google Account. (Image 12.26) The screen will change and you will see **Privacy & personalization**. (Image 12.27) **Tap on *Manage your data & privacy*.** The screen will change. Scroll down a bit until you get to **Personalized**

ads. Tap on My Ad Center. (Image 12.28) The page changes. I have all personalization turned off. (Image 12.29) If you scroll down the screen, you may find things that you want personalized. Read each section and decide for yourself.

I think it's a great idea for you to click around on these settings. Tap, read, and decide what you want. Location Services and YouTube are the only apps I like to have turned on. The former helps with finding restaurants, pickleball games, and directions.

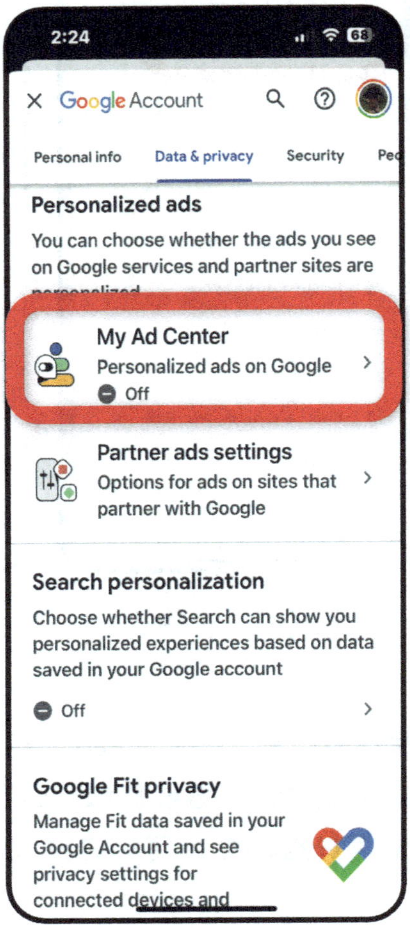

Image 12.28

Image 12.29

The latter allows me to see my YouTube viewing history, which I want as I sometimes want to watch something again, especially if it's exercise related.

iPhone Privacy Settings

iPhone users have a level of protection since iOS 18 was released in October 2024. You'll see a pop-up screen that will ask you to allow or deny access to your contacts. Should you want to share some names, there will be another prompt that gives you the chance to select which contacts to share. That's a step in the direction of privacy. Thank you, Apple. There are things to do to make your device even more private and safe.

iPhone Privacy

SETTINGS > PRIVACY & SECURITY > LOCATION SERVICES

This allows different apps to know your location. Certainly you want your GPS to know your location. But the App Store does not need to know, nor does 7-Eleven. Tap and decide which apps merit access to your location. You can set these to NEVER, ALWAYS, or WHILE USING APP. You get to choose. Typically, I choose "WHILE USING APP" for this setting.

Open Settings and scroll to Privacy & Security. (Image 12.30) Tap on it. You'll see Location Services. (Image 12.31) If you use the GPS or want relevant search results (i.e., restaurants near you), then turn on Location Services. Apps that do need to know your location are AOL, the camera, and voice memo do not need every step I take. The App Store is *only when I ask.*

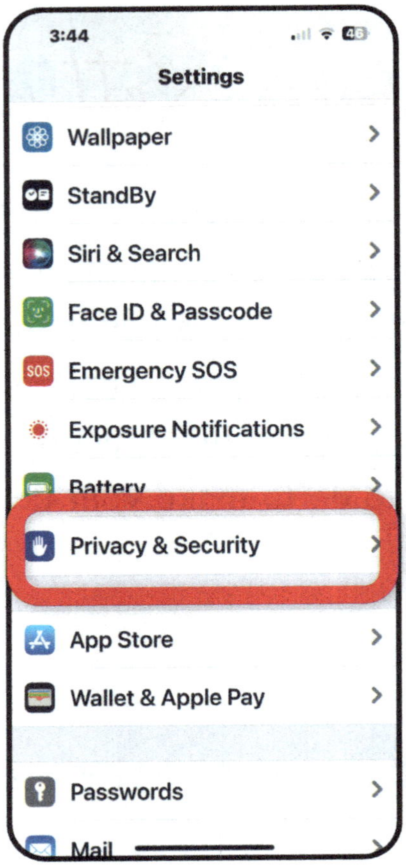

Image 12.30

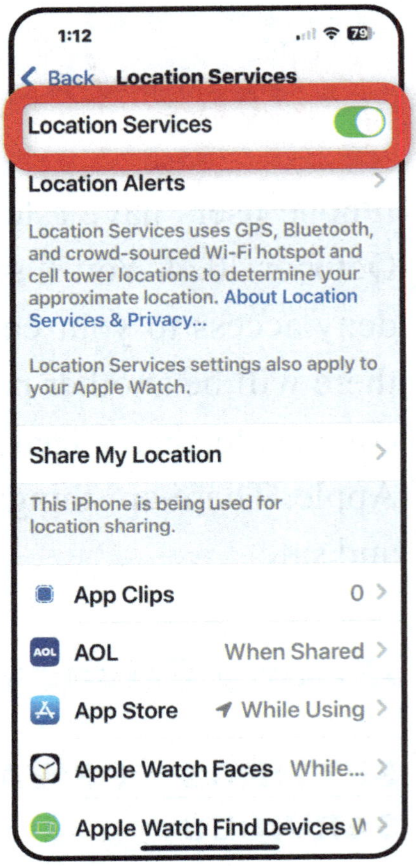

Image 12.31

SETTINGS > PRIVACY & SECURITY > TRACKING

Tracking is a whole other thing. Tracking allows apps to follow what you do, what you search for, what you buy, basically everything you do online. It's beneficial to businesses, merchants, social media platforms—pretty much anyone who wants your attention.

Notice that Tracking is turned off on my device. (Image 12.33) **TURN OFF tracking if you value your privacy**. These strangers do not need to know your habits, likes, and dislikes. It is none of their business!

Image 12.32

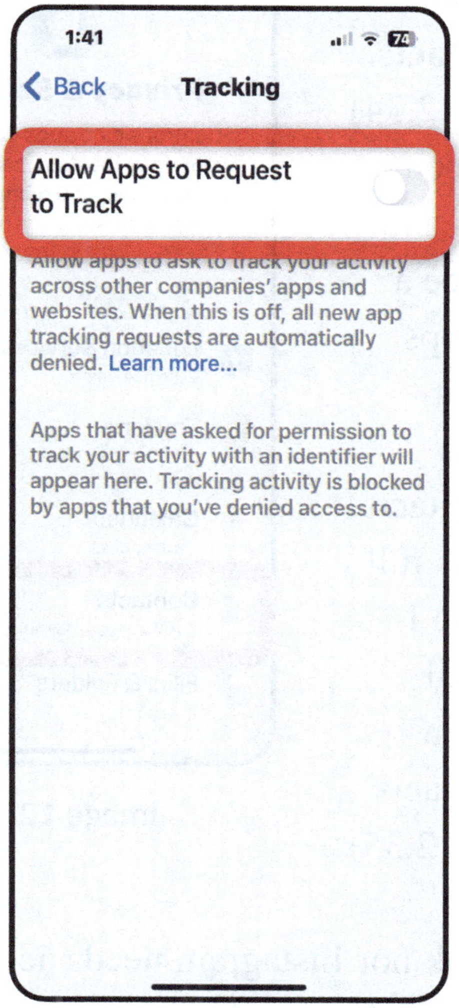

Image 12.33

iPhone Contacts

Looking at the Privacy & Security page, find and tap on **Contacts.** (Image 12.34) The screen changes and you'll see a list of apps that want access to your contacts. AOL has full access so I can email anyone in my Contacts. (Image 12.35) Neither Facebook nor Instagram needs access to my contacts, nor does Messenger. Anyone I contact is already part of their network.

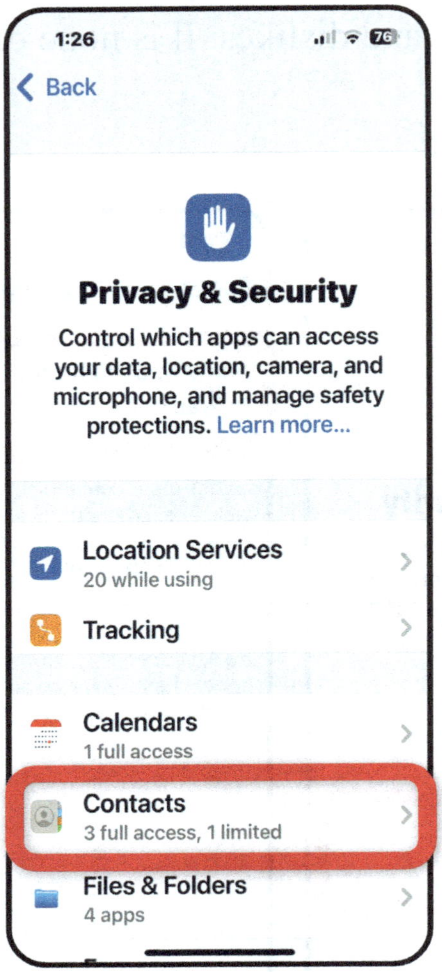

Image 12.34

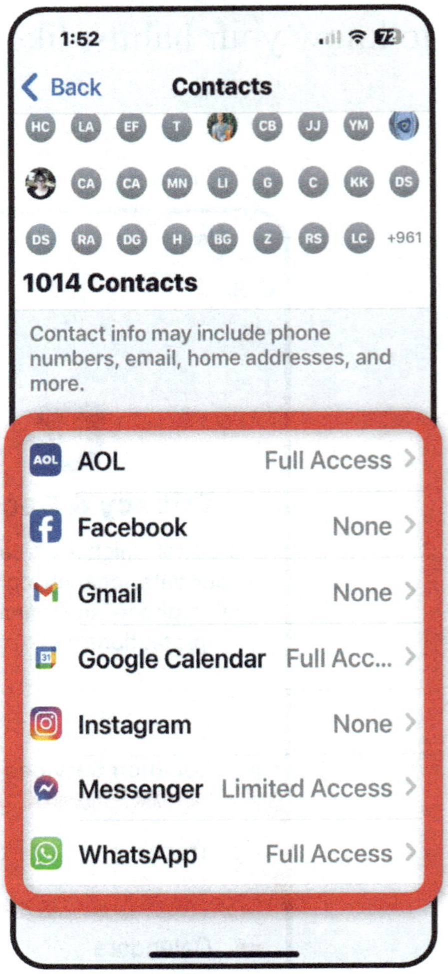

Image 12.35

Gmail definitely needs access to my contacts as I use it daily. So does the calendar and Maps. Why Maps? If you say, "Siri, take me to David Hall home," Maps needs to interact with contacts to get that information. Same with WhatsApp, because you connect with people in your contacts on WhatsApp. Zoom does not require access to your contacts to work. Scroll down and go through the list of apps and turn off permissions. In summary, the less you share, the better off you will be. Privacy matters.

iPhone Microphone

SETTINGS > PRIVACY & SECURITY > SCROLL WAY DOWN TO MICROPHONE

Microphone is another feature that should be allowed limited access to your apps. Music apps broadcast, they don't receive, so you do not need to allow them access to your microphone (i.e., what you are saying). If you want to use voice commands for certain apps, like WhatsApp, Messenger, Waze, or Gmail, you need to have the microphone toggled on for those specific apps so you can give verbal commands. But does Target really need to access your microphone?

iPhone App Store

When downloading new apps, you may be asked to allow that app access to your contacts, your photos, or something else. Use discretion and allow access only if there is a legitimate need for the app to have that information in order for it to work.

Turn Off Ad Topics

SETTINGS > PRIVACY > ADS > AD PRIVACY > AD TOPICS—TOGGLE OFF

Do you want to see ads about vacuum cleaners when you happen to mention one or look at a vacuum cleaner online? I know I don't. I categorically do not want my device listening that carefully. Here's how to block them:

When you get to Ad Topics, look through the various settings and turn off features you do not want.

APPLE STOP THIRD PARTY ADV: SETTINGS > PRIVACY > ADS > AD PRIVACY > AD MEASUREMENT—TOGGLE THE SLIDER TO OFF

DELETE YOUR ADVERTISING ID

Believe it or not, your phone will provide information on you to third-party apps and advertisers. This information is used to personalize ads for you. I don't want any ads, personalized or not. To delete your advertising ID:

APPLE STOP PERSONALIZED ADS: SETTINGS > PRIVACY > ADS > "RESET ADVERTISING ID" > SCREEN CHANGES, TAP DELETE ADVERTISING ID

A Note on Alexa

Did you know… Alexa systems (includes Alexa-enabled thermostats, TVs, etc.) are always listening for the *wake* word, "Alexa." As soon as this system hears it, it records all conversations in its range. **The recordings are kept unless you request they be deleted**. It will also record conversations if it thinks it hears Alexa, with words or phrases that sound similar. According to PIRG.org (a public education group concerned with our health, safety, and well-being), Alexa collects and keeps voice recordings and gathers a lot of other personal information, including your location, contacts, and everything you do on Amazon—think Ring doorbells, Prime books, video and music, plus Kindle. Amazon grants other companies access to your data! That's why you get emails from companies you've never heard of.

DELETE ALEXA VOICE RECORDINGS: OPEN THE ALEXA APP > MORE TAB (BOTTOM OF SCREEN) > SETTINGS > ALEXA PRIVACY > HISTORY > VOICE RECORDINGS > FILTER BY DATE, DEVICE OR PROFILE > DELETE SELECTED RECORDINGS > CONFIRM YOUR SELECTION

These steps will delete your voice history and stop Alexa from saving future recordings.

Another reason to delete your voice recordings is that humans can access your recordings as part of training Alexa. You can stop this by taking the following steps:

If you do not want Amazon to share your information with third parties, you can rescind permissions:

ALEXA RESCIND PERMISSIONS: OPEN ALEXA APP > MORE TAB (BOTTOM OF SCREEN) > SETTINGS > ALEXA PRIVACY > MANAGE YOUR ALEXA DATA > HELP IMPROVE

ALEXA PERMISSIONS OFF: OPEN THE ALEXA APP > MORE TAB (BOTTOM OF SCREEN) > SETTINGS > ALEXA PRIVACY > MANAGE SKILLS AND AD PREFERENCES > TAP TO EXPAND THE MENU UNDER EACH ITEM > TOGGLE PERMISSIONS OFF > TAP CONFIRM

And finally, if you do not want Alexa to share your information with advertisers (which will result in all kinds of targeting ads to you), follow these prompts:

ALEXA DO NOT SHARE MY INFO: OPEN THE ALEXA APP > MORE TAB (BOTTOM OF SCREEN) > SETTINGS > PRIVACY > MANAGE YOUR ALEXA DATA > SCROLL TO INTEREST-BASED ADS FROM AMAZON ON ALEXA > TOGGLE OFF > CONFIRM SELECTION

Chapter 13

Android & iPhone Artificial Intelligence

Table of Contents

ARTIFICIAL INTELLIGENCE SCAMS

For fun, I asked ChatGPT, an AI itself, to explain Artificial Intelligence. It described itself as "designed to understand and generate human-like interactions based on the input it receives." What does that mean? According to MIT Technology Review, "Artificial Intelligence is actually an umbrella term for a (type of technology that) enables computers to do things that are thought to require (human intelligence). Think of recognizing faces, understanding speech, driving cars, writing sentences…"

It means that AI learns by analyzing large amounts of text from books, websites, and other sources to understand language patterns and provide relevant responses. Its answers are only as good as its training. AI learns and makes decisions, a bit like how our brains work, but much faster and with limited knowledge. It understands speech, recognizes faces, and is a formidable chess opponent.

The important thing to remember is that AI is a human-built tool designed to make certain tasks easier or better. It's not magic. It's programming. The more it learns, the greater the range of tasks it can perform.

Using AI while writing this book was fun and a big help. It was great to ensure I didn't miss anything when considering a certain feature or app. I took the information and restated it with my interpretation of the answers given by ChatGPT and Claude AI.

Generative AI has the training to create artwork based on your prompts. I asked for a picture of a senior frustrated with his smartphone, and I got a man with three arms holding a phone! It was pretty funny.

AI Reliability

What does it mean when AI hallucinates? That's a marketing term for "making it up." Yes, AI isn't always right. You have to exercise your judgment when using it and always verify facts from other sources to be sure your AI results are accurate and not a hallucination.

Furthermore, depending on how the AI was "trained," it can have biases and not be objective, so getting political or medical information can be tricky. It's easy to think that the AI you're dealing with has some human element to it. It does not. It is a machine and only regurgitates what it has learned, and what it has learned depends upon who is teaching it.

AI is changing fast. Give yourself time to adapt. Play with it as suggested above. Know that whatever you ask AI becomes part of its learning base and helps to train. So don't give away any personal details. And finally, always double-check any information from AI before you act on it.

ANDROID INTELLIGENCE – HEY GOOGLE

Once again, this is going to vary widely from manufacturer and model. But one thing that is constant over all Android devices is the Google Assistant, which is deeply embedded into the device and is best used for:

- General knowledge web searches
- Google Lens search, which allows you to take a picture of an object and find out what it is, its cost, and where to buy it. So, if you're at your friend's house and see a chair that you love, simply

USING GOOGLE LENS: OPEN GOOGLE > TAP ON THE COLORFUL SQUARE/ROUND ICON ON THE RIGHT SIDE OF THE SEARCH BAR > SCREEN CHANGES > FOCUS ON THE ITEM > TAP ON THE SHUTTER (SEARCH ICON IS INSIDE)

See Image 13.1

- Access via "Hey Google," the Android system of AI
- Includes Live Translate, Advanced AI editing, which removes objects and performs generative edits for phenomenal photos and more.

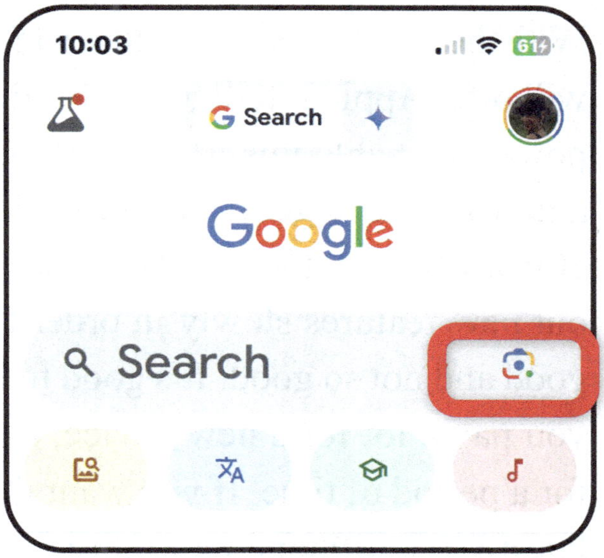

Image 13.1

Additionally, Samsung phones have their own AI called Bixby, which is more useful for hands-free interactions with the phone. For example, "Hi Bixby, lower the volume" or "Hi Bixby, open the photo app." Bixby will also do basic photo editing.

Android also offers Google AI on some newer phones. Voice notes can be summarized, and there is a fabulous photo editor with an eraser that really does take out unwanted people or backgrounds. From what I've read, Android may offer better AI options, but they come with a price, and the price is privacy. More on that later in the chapter.

> Simply stated, search the Internet for information using *Hey Google* and operate the phone with your voice using *Hi Bixby*.

APPLE INTELLIGENCE – HEY SIRI

With the iOS 18 update, iPhones 15 Pro, 16, 16 Pro, Plus and Max devices will offer Apple Intelligence. Earlier devices do not have the computing power to enable this. But should you use it? Or should you upgrade to a new phone to get it? There's a lot of chatter on the Internet about its efficacy or lack thereof. Without getting deep or technical, Apple rolls out new features slowly in order to ensure they work properly. This is good and not so good. It's good to be cautious. It's not so good, because you pay a lot for a new device, and the features are somewhat limited for a period of time. If you want the latest tech, by all means, go for the latest model iPhone or Android. There is wisdom in waiting until the software is fully developed before buying a new phone, especially if you have anything newer than an iPhone 14.

As I become more familiar with these advancements, I will post videos with step-by-step instructions on TakeThisPhoneandShoveIt.com. Being a part of our community means you will always have access to training that you can understand.

AI and Seniors

For us, AI can be a huge benefit. You know those devices like "Alexa" or Google Nest? You talk to them from across the room, and they play music and can perform all kinds of actions, depending on how "smart" your home is. Some people use AI to run lights and AC, music, and their refrigerator. (More on that in a minute.)

These devices are trained to understand what you're saying and respond, as if you had a personal assistant playing the music you want, letting you know the weather forecast, time, day, date, and helping you to shop for the things you need. There is a lot of debate about AI, but this is not the place for that. From my perspective, AI can offer several benefits to us seniors.

VOICE ASSISTANTS – SIRI, OK GOOGLE, AND ALEXA

Early artificial intelligence apps like Siri, Google Assistant, and, in Samsung phones, Bixby. These can help you navigate your phone, as well as open and close programs.

Smartphone AI allows you to make tasks easier. "*Hey Siri*" and "*Hi Bixby*" (or "*Hey Google*") allow you to use the phone hands-free for so many actions. You can make a call. "Hey Siri, call David." You can hang up on that call. "Hi Bixby, hang up." You can write and send texts, open apps, get the time and the weather just by asking. No hands necessary! I set alarms and timers by having Siri do it. When in the car,

I make, answer, and hang up calls using my voice, never taking my eyes off the road.

Is reading hard for you? Your voice assistant can be set to read articles, emails, and texts to you and even summarize what's happening in the story or article. (See Chapter 9, page 143 – Android Accessibility Settings).

For many older adults, typing on a smartphone can be challenging for all kinds of reasons, not the least of which are fat fingers that tap more than one key at a time. There are vision and touch issues. Not to worry. You can dictate Notes, email, and text messages using the AI on your device.

If you are always forgetting birthdays, anniversaries, and other important events, AI can help you by sending reminders and organizing tasks.

If you set up your health apps in iPhones and Androids, smartwatches monitor your health 24/7 with heart rate monitoring and fall detection. The latter will automatically alert emergency services or family members.

I got an Apple watch after two of my friends' lives were literally saved because their watches notified them that they were in A-fib. They did not know they were having a problem. In one case, my friend was rushed to the hospital as her condition was dire. Think about that. This device literally saved her life.

There are two medications I need to take twice daily, twelve hours apart. There is no way in this good green earth that I will remember to take them at the right time, so I use the clock app to set alarms that go off daily at 8 a.m. and 8 p.m. And I label the alarm reminding me which meds to take (not that I need that, but I like the confirmation). I love the clock app! (See Chapter 12.)

But please do not think that AI can accurately diagnose and/or cure any disease. You need a doctor for that. My beloved had a nasty growth on his leg. I used Google Lens (and its AI feature) to see what it was. Well, had we listened to that, we would have been very upset because it was suggested that it was cancer. A trip to the dermatologist determined that it was only precancerous and not any imminent danger to his health. It was treated and removed, and AI was just inaccurate.

AI-enabled security systems that can recognize family members and caregivers have the ability to alert the resident to unfamiliar visitors. Some can detect falls and alert a contact or 911 if a fall is detected.

With iOS 18, Siri introduces Apple Intelligence, a whole new approach to AI, providing you have an iPhone 15 Pro, 15 Pro Max, or iPhone 16. With these devices Siri is being integrated with ChatGPT. What this means is that if you ask Siri a question it is unable to answer, you will be asked if you want ChatGPT to take over. If you say yes, you will be interfacing with the much smarter ChatGPT. It can summarize documents and answer questions about photos. There are many other features of Apple Intelligence. I will address all the new things this newer tech can do on my website in video updates. NOTE: As of publication, Apple Intelligence is being rolled out in small doses. Apple likes to do things slowly.

EMERGENCY CALLS

There's a one-touch emergency call option that you can press if you need assistance quickly. On iPhones, **PRESS AND HOLD** the power button simultaneously with the volume UP and don't let go. The key here is pressing both buttons at the same time. This is also how you power off the phone. After about ten seconds of continuous holding, you will hear a siren from the phone, and if you keep holding, it will connect you to 911 (Image 13.1a). Alternatively, press and hold the power button and volume up at the same time until you see the screen change. There will be an option SOS Emergency call.

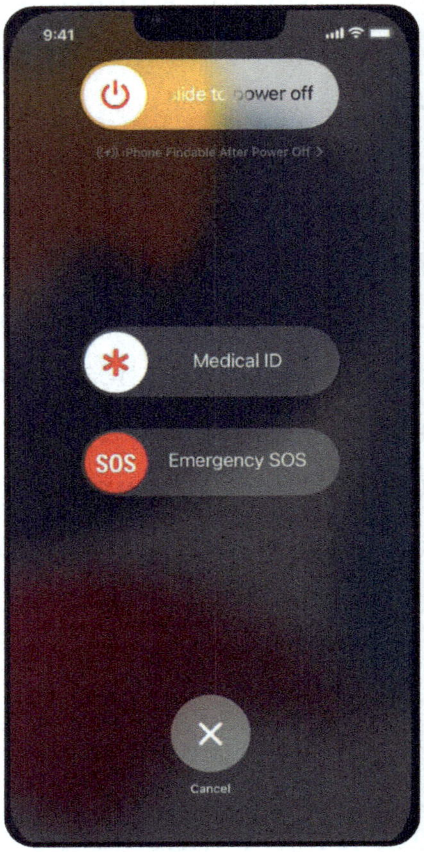

Image 13.1a

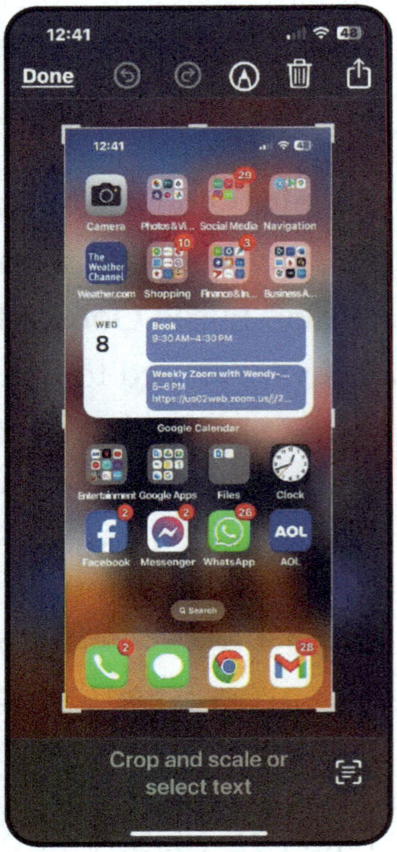

Image 13.1b

Be aware that if you press and **QUICKLY RELEASE** these same two buttons, you will take a screenshot. If that happens, tap on the garbage pail at the top of the screenshot (Image 13.1b) to delete it and try again.

Remember, you have to HOLD the two buttons until the screen changes. If you don't let go at all, then the siren and automatic connection to 911 will happen.

SMART APPLIANCES

A smart appliance has Wi-Fi connectivity and can communicate with the app. Smart stoves use AI to detect if they've been left on and can automatically shut the burner off to prevent fires. You can also turn the oven on or off from an app on your phone. You can even look inside your refrigerator remotely to see what produce you need to buy! Imagine your refrigerator making shopping lists for you! Well, that technology exists as some smart refrigerators track food inventory and suggest grocery lists. The technology exists to even connect a smart refrigerator with credit card payment and the grocery store of your choice so it can order food when you run out! This is freaking me out just a little. I can't fathom my refrigerator restocking itself, but that is what's coming.

I will admit, though, that I LOVE my AI-powered robotic vacuum cleaner. We have two cats and there is always fur on the floor, but our bot vacuum helps maintain a clean living space without any physical effort on my part. I think of it as my robotic maid, never complaining and keeping my floors clean.

AI at home is kind of like having remote control for all the electrical equipment, reducing the need for you to move around a lot, and this can be very helpful to a segment of seniors who suffer with physical impairments. Turning lights and appliances on and off via an app can be a blessing, empowering the disabled to live more easily.

ENTERTAINMENT AND MENTAL STIMULATION

You can access AI-curated content suggestions for books, movies, brain games, or music based on your preferences. AI-powered games are designed to keep your mind active and potentially slow cognitive decline.

If you're having a dinner party and want to use the ingredients you have already, you can tell the AI bot what's on hand and ask for a recipe using those ingredients. Or you can ask for meat or vegetarian, dairy-free or vegan recipes for a party of six. AI can create an entire menu with recipes for you, making planning so much easier. In fact, AI can tell you how to time what you cook so that everything will be ready at the same time. If you're a wine drinker, AI can suggest the perfect pairing for your food, and when it's time to serve dinner, AI can suggest the best music based on your preferences.

TRAVEL

Possibly one of the coolest things you can do with AI is travel planning. Let's say you have a certain budget, and you want to go overseas. Craft the inquiry with all the information you want, such as desired activities (places with great art museums or fabulous food), flights, hotel, and complete travel itineraries. AI can identify places for handicapped travel or adventure travel, summarize what they offer and at what price. The answers you get, just like with any Internet search, are only as good as the questions you ask. Be as specific as you can. If you get results that are close, ask for more of what you want…"handicapped accessible beachfront lodging" or "close to easy walking paths."

RESEARCH

AI is at its best when you are looking for comparative information, for example the pros and cons of particular automobiles or appliances. It's great if you're trying to learn a subject. You can ask AI (ChatGPT, Claude, Co-Pilot) to help create a study aid, step by step. If you're trying to learn a new language, you can ask AI to give you lesson plans and tests so you can evaluate your progress.

It's also great if you want to customize a diet plan based on your health conditions, budget, and taste. Ask AI, "Create a low-sugar, low-carb meal plan for a diabetic with high blood pressure who loves meat and potatoes" and see what comes up.

If you are looking for a local support group for any reason, AI can help find them for you. Just ask, "Looking for a support group in my zip code for (overeating) (helping care for my parent with dementia) (exercising in your eighties)" and so on.

WRITING

Have you ever considered writing your life story, but the idea is overwhelming? Well, AI can absolutely help with that. You can put in specific details and ask it to write a chapter based on your information. Paid AI programs will learn how you communicate and mimic your style. It's very cool and your kids and grandkids will appreciate knowing your story in greater detail.

Setting up AI Voice Control

Android

GOOGLE APP > PROFILE PICTURE > SETTINGS > GOOGLE ASSISTANT > HEY GOOGLE & VOICE MATCH > VOICE MATCH > HEY GOOGLE

G Open the Google app on your phone. Tap on your profile picture in the top right corner. The screen will change, and you will see a dropdown menu with many choices. Tap on Settings. (Image 13.1)

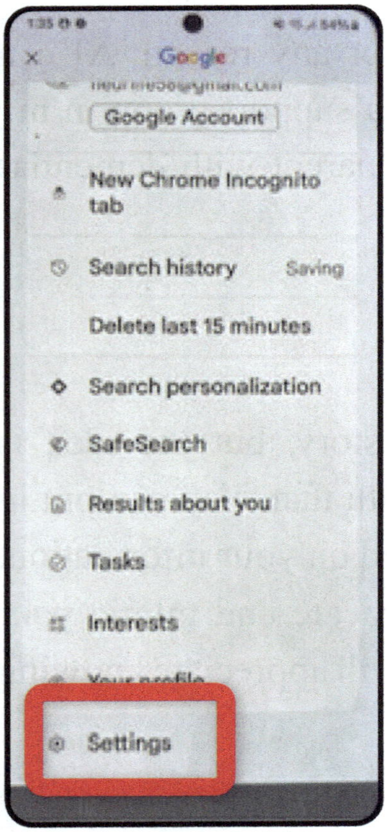

Image 13.1

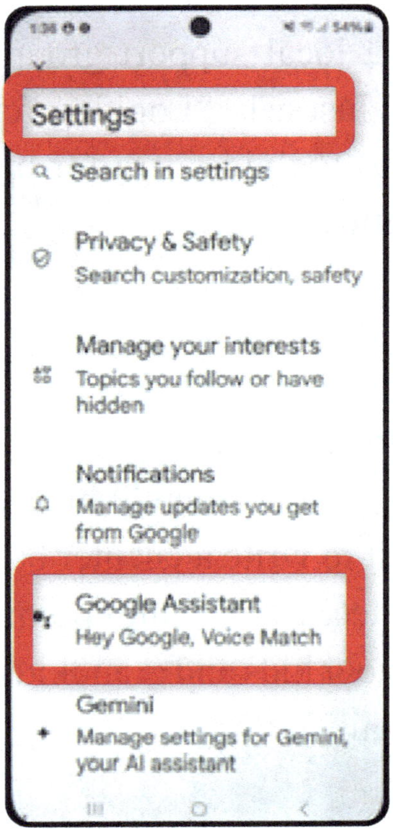

Image 13.2

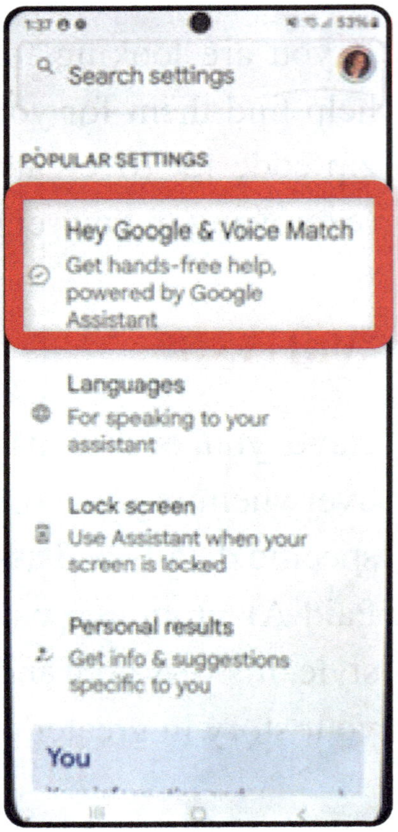

Image 13.3

Then tap Google Assistant settings, (Image 13.2) scroll down, and tap on **"Hey Google & Voice Match."** (Image 13.3) Now tap on Voice Match and toggle the "Hey Google" feature on.

Now Google will want to train it to your voice. (Image 13.4) Follow the on-screen instruction to say "Hey Google" a few times and in a few different phrases so the phone can learn your voice. (Image 13.5)

After setting it up, you can test it by saying "Hey Google" while the phone is awake. This will work even when the phone is charging.

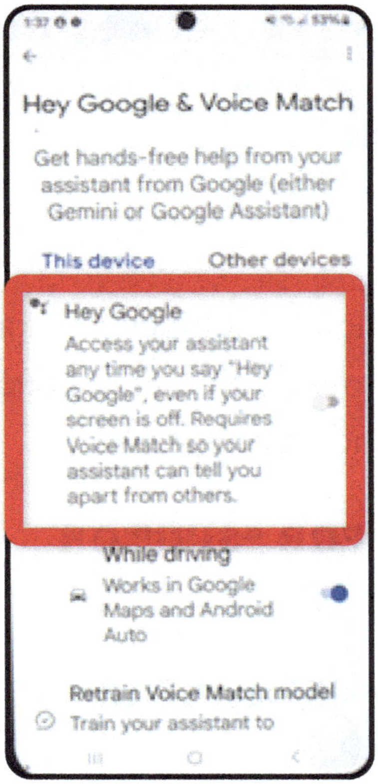

Image 13.4

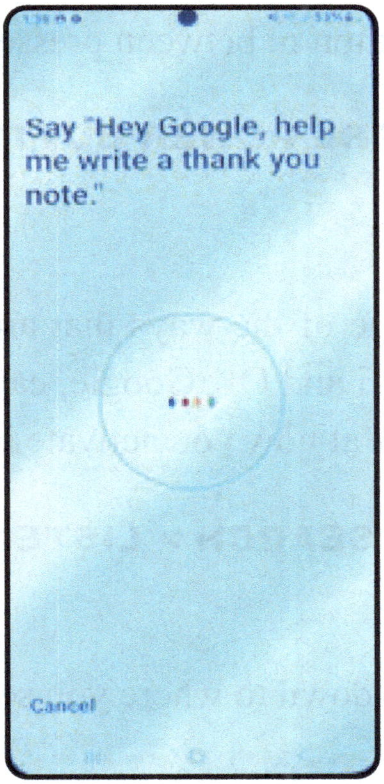

Image 13.5

Image 13.6

You should see the Google Assistant pop up, ready to help you with questions or tasks.

Note: If your phone is in power saving mode, "Hey Google" may not always work.

iPhone

To use Siri with no special settings, simply press and hold the power button until you see the symbol for Siri come on the screen. If you have an iPhone with a home button, you have to double tap the button—that's two taps in immediate succession for Siri to open. (Hint: Don't lift your finger off the button in between presses.)

PRESS AND HOLD THE POWER BUTTON

Using Siri Hands-Free

Now that you know some of the ways that artificial intelligence, aka voice commands, aka Siri and OK Google, can make using the phone so much easier, let's look at how you activate hands-free access.

SETTINGS > SIRI & SEARCH > LISTEN FOR "SIRI" OR "HEY SIRI"

Open Settings and scroll down to where you see SIRI and SEARCH.

Once you've found Siri and Search in Settings, TAP on it. (Image 13.7) The screen changes and you will see a dedicated Siri page with all kinds of settings. (Image 13.8)

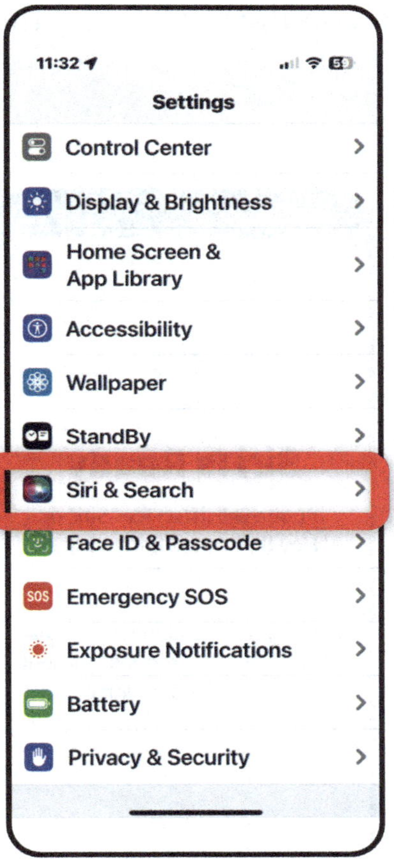

Image 13.7

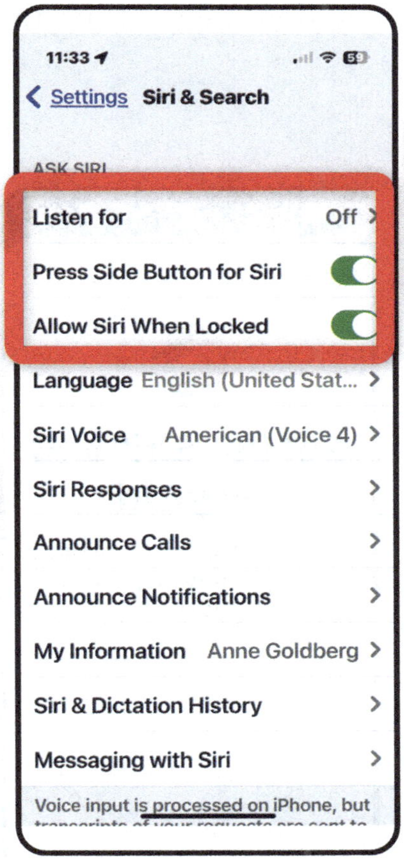

Image 13.8

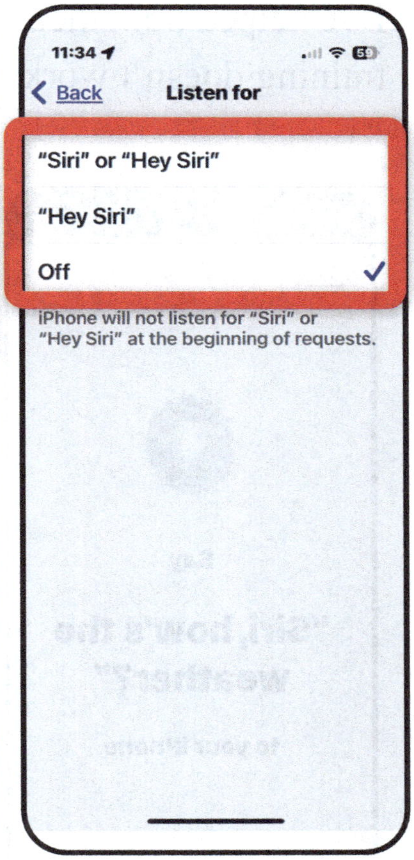

Image 13.9

Tap on "Listen for." The screen will change. (Image 13.9). Then TAP on "Siri" or "Hey Siri" (Image 13.9) The screen will change (Image 13.10) This is where Siri is trained to recognize your voice. Once you begin, you are to repeat, in a normal voice, whatever is in quotation marks on the screen. There are four different screens that you will repeat. Say only the words that are in quotation marks, exactly as it's written. If the screen says, "Say 'Hey Siri, how's the weather?'" to your phone, you say, *Hey Siri, how's the weather?* You do not repeat "*Say Hey Siri how's the weather?*" **You only repeat the words in quotes**. Some may wonder why I am being so specific. That's because most of the seniors I've helped train their voice read everything that's on the screen and the training doesn't work.

Image 13.10

Image 13.11

Image 13.12

Speak clearly in your normal voice. Once done, you can call to Siri from across the room. "Hey Siri, what time is it?" "Hey Siri, what movies are playing near my location?"

THINGS YOU CAN DO USING BIXBY AND SIRI VOICE COMMANDS

- **Make Phone Calls and Send Texts**
- **Brighten or Darken the Screen**
- **Call 911 or My Emergency Contact**
- **Open Apps**
- **Set And End Timers and Alarms**

Hey Siri (Hi Bixby) … Call (name)

Hey Siri (Hi Bixby) Text (name). Follow the prompts

- **Set Reminders.** Voice assistants can help set reminders for important tasks like taking medication, attending appointments, or even remembering to water the plants.

Seniors can say, "**Hi Bixby" or "Hey Siri, remind me to take my medicine at 8 AM**," and Siri will notify you at the correct time. You will get a NOTIFICATION—i.e., your phone will make a sound and/or show a banner with a reminder, depending upon your Notification Settings in Chapter 9.

- **Ask For Information.** By far this is my favorite thing about having my smartphone. I can ask it anything, and I mean ANYTHING. We were watching TV the other night, and I was curious what year Sigourney Weaver was born. My phone was on the nightstand, and I asked, "Siri (or "Hey Google"), how old is Sigourney Weaver?" and I got the answer within seconds. BTW, she's seventy-five! I wonder if she needs help with her smartphone.

- **SETTING ALARMS AND TIMERS**. I would never get to an appointment on time without my alarms and timers. It's so easy to do.

HEY SIRI (HI BIXBY) "SET AN ALARM FOR 2:45 P.M. AND LABEL IT MOVIE AT 8 P.M." OR "TAKE YOUR PILLS," OR "REMIND ME TO CALL LAURA AT 3:45 P.M."

When the phone's AI really helps is in the car. I can say **"SIRI, TAKE ME HOME"** and the turn-by-turn instructions will appear. Or, when I'm desperately low on gas in an unfamiliar place, I say, **"SIRI, WHERE IS THE NEAREST GAS STATION TO MY LOCATION?" ANDROID USERS SAY, "HEY GOOGLE, WHERE IS THE NEAREST GAS STATION TO MY LOCATION?"**

More ways to use voice commands:

SENDING EMAILS OR DICTATING TEXTS.

But be careful! What you say and what the AI hears are often two very different things. This can lead to hilarity when you are telling someone you're going home in a hurry and the text says you have a comb in curry. So ALWAYS proof read what you've dictated to be sure the message you want to send is the message the recipient gets.

OPENING APPS. You can use voice commands to open any app on your phone.

Siri and Apple Intelligence

Image 13.13 shows settings on how to use Apple Intelligence and Siri. First make sure that you toggle on Apple Intelligence as shown. You also want to be able to access Siri even when the phone is locked, so make sure to toggle that setting on as well. It will also turn green.

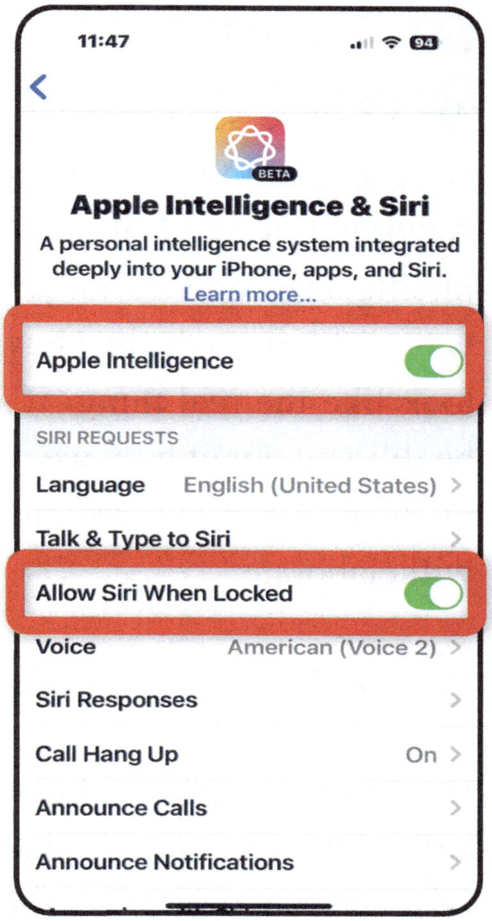

Image 13.13

Further down the screen you can customize Siri's voice to male, female, American, Australian, English, and more. Tap on this and check out the options. Remember that anything you turn on, you can turn off. Look at the **Call Hang Up** setting. When toggled on, you can tell Siri to answer or hang up on any call.

Scroll through the screen. There are many choices. Just look. Make a change or don't, just become familiar with the options.

AI Scams

As we have seen through time immemorial, when something good is developed, the bad guys find ways to use it to your disadvantage. According to the National Council on Aging, AI scams "use artificial intelligence tools to target victims in sophisticated and personalized ways." AI gives the bad guys tools to build website impersonations that look like the real thing. It's the Wild West in Cyberland, so we must be diligent about how we interact online. They gather data from social media or other sources online to target victims. So, what do they do? I will elaborate.

AVOID BEING SCAMMED BY AI

If you were walking down the street and a stranger came up to you and asked for your social security number, would you give it to them? Of course not. That's ridiculous, right? Well, it's no different when a stranger calls you on the phone and asks for personal information, including but not limited to social security numbers. Treat them just like a stranger on the street and say no. No matter how nice, no matter how forceful or pathetic, hang up. Done. Block the call.

Another clue to identifying scams and spam is weird English (or French, Dutch, German, Spanish). That's a sign that the AI has been trained on more formal types of correspondence, not suitable for business mail.

High-pressure tactics are not okay. The bad guys want to convey a sense of urgency… "Act now or you will miss this incredible opportunity to make a fortune!" "Pay NOW or there will be a warrant issued for your arrest!" They want you to make a knee-jerk decision based on fear, without caution or thinking about it.

And finally, no government agency, credit card company, or police department accepts cryptocurrency, wire transfers, or gift cards as payment. None! Any legitimate business will give you several ways to send money, and those three are never choices. The reason the criminals want you to pay this way is because these payments are not traceable. Once you give over your money, you are out of luck and stand almost no chance of recovering it.

> **Think you've been scammed?**
>
> Report it to FTC.gov or your local consumer protection agency
>
> **https://www.usa.gov/state-consumer**

Protecting Yourself Online

- Make sure you have good virus protection, especially on Androids, which are much more likely to be infected than iPhones. iPhones are not immune; however, Apple issues updates for known threats, and that can happen quickly. Updates in the Android architecture are slower to be implemented.

- Don't overshare on social media. If you go on vacation and your house is empty, don't share pictures until you return.
- If you think a relative is in danger, call their phone directly. Likely they will answer.
- Do. Not. Engage. Do not click any links or call phone numbers (even if your screen is screaming that you've been hacked!). This happened to me a few days ago, while writing the book. I had Chrome open, and all of a sudden my screen was taken over and a voice came across saying "Warning! Don't turn off your computer or you will lose everything!" What did I do? I turned off my computer. Immediately. When I turned it back on, the message was gone, and I continued writing.
- **Change passwords** if you think you've been scammed.
- **Freeze your credit.** (See Page 341 for step-by-step instructions.)
- **Report the scam to the Federal Trade Commission (FTC.gov)** or get in touch with your local consumer protection agency (https://www.usa.gov/state-consumer). One last way to address any possible scams is to call Adult Protective Services in your area (eldercare.acl.gov) or 800-677-1116.

Voice cloning

Just a short clip of you speaking is enough for your voice to be cloned, i.e., impersonated. Consider this. You get a phone call from your brother telling you he's been kidnapped. It sounds like him. That's his voice and it's terrifying. They want you terrified. How to combat this? A possible solution is to create **FAMILY PASSWORD** with all of your family and friends.

It's best to do it in person, but if that's not possible, use WhatsApp or iPhone-to-iPhone text messages, both of which are safely encrypted. Once you have a safe word, if you receive a concerning call, ask for the safe word. The AI will not know it. You will be confident it's a fake.

There are scams out there where you get a call and the caller asks if it's you, giving your name. **DO NOT SAY YES!** They are looking for you to say yes so they can record it and use it for nefarious purposes. In fact, don't say your name at all. Whoever is calling you should know who they're calling and not need to ask your name. If they don't know, you don't need to talk to them!

Deepfake scams

This is when a bad guy uses AI to create videos, photos, or audio clips attributing terrible things to the victim. They will take your head and create a nude from that. Now they can try to blackmail you. It's fake. Stories can be planted by foreign governments that are so real, it's impossible to think they are fake. But they are.

Phishing

AI is the hook, line, and sinker when it comes to these malicious attempts to get you to engage with a fake email and text messages. They are very difficult to distinguish from real websites. To be safe, if you get an email or text from your bank (or any other company), do not engage with it. Open the Internet and go directly to the company's site by typing the web address into the search bar. For example, chase.com or amex.com or macys.com, etc. (Note, you do not need to type "www" in any web search. At this point, it's implied.) This is the new way of responding to emails. Don't click on any blue, underlined links.

This is particularly sinister when it comes to investments, particularly with cryptocurrency scams. You see an ad, maybe on Facebook or as you are searching for something online. The ad looks real, so you click on the link and are taken to a beautiful, professional-looking website. You answer questions and provide information, some of it very personal. The problem is that the website is a sham, and the personal information you have provided is now in the hands of criminals. Heaven forbid if you give any money to these sites. It is gone, gone, gone. If you want to invest, ask friends who they use. Or do a deep search on investment firms and look up their reviews. Reviews are everywhere online and are a great indicator of the experience you will have.

According to the Cyberguy (cyberguy.com), the newest forms of phishing are fake legal requests. How do these work? The bad guys get illegal access to police and government email accounts, and the end result is that you get an official-looking email with a fake subpoena. Typically, companies are the targets of this vicious scheme, but it could happen to you too. How do you stay safe? Do not respond to any email that makes you worry or elicits a frightened response. You can verify the sender's email address by following the steps outlined on Page 325

Sponsored Ads

One last comment about searching on the Internet, specifically where Google is used. You will see search results that say "Ad" or "Sponsored" or "Sponsored content." **NEVER, NEVER, NEVER, EVER** click on a sponsored link or ad. Google has had a real problem with phishing in these ads. It is best to **scroll down until you see actual results and not paid advertising.**

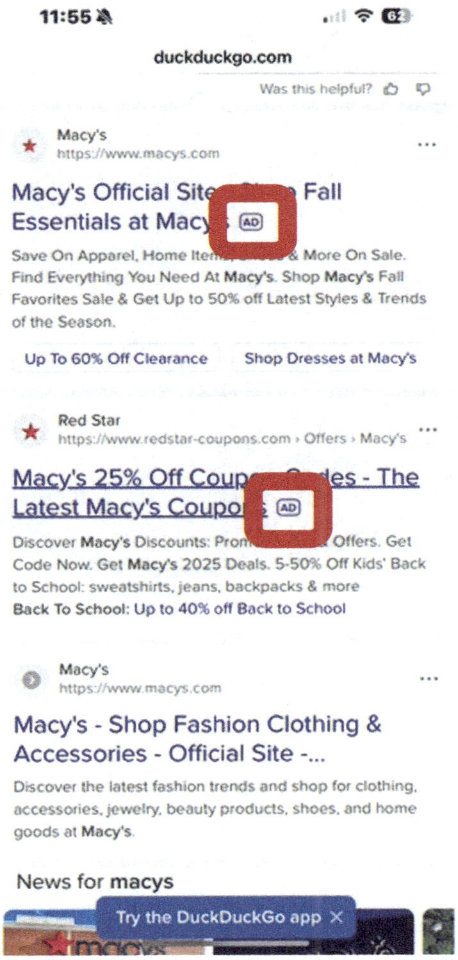

Image generated by LeonardoAI

Chapter 14

Addendum: Why I Wrote This Book

I was born and raised in Sheepshead Bay, an eighteenth-century fishing community in the southeast corner of Brooklyn, very close to the beaches along the Lower Bay of the Atlantic Ocean.

Brooklyn was a small town back then. I took my Barbie doll in her mock black patent leather case and walked to my friends' apartments or to the candy store a few blocks away. I was little, perhaps six or seven years old. It was safe. I especially remember catching fireflies in the summer. We'd put them in glass jars until their lights faded away and they lay lifeless.

In the mid-seventies I settled into a twenty-three-year career as an executive recruiter for actuaries. I lived in New York until 1985 when I departed for a nine-month adventure, solo traveling to eighteen countries, returning to the U.S. (and moving to Florida) in October 1986.

My life got established in Florida when I married and had two sons, who are the joy of my heart. That is, until I had three granddaughters. Now, *they* are the joy of my heart, and my sons can get in line! I continued recruiting until 1999, sold the business and spent time raising my kids. In 2007, I reentered the workforce, again recruiting, only this time with a specialty in Water Resources. Things were going great until everything crashed in 2009 with the recession.

For the next four years, I had a variety of jobs. They were just a thing to do to earn money. They did not fulfill any passion or purpose in my life. Then, one day in 2013, I was jobless, out of ideas, disheartened and discouraged. It was a very tough time, and I was at my wit's end. That's when I surrendered. I literally got down on my knees and completely let go of the idea that I knew what was best for me. I declared that I would not look for a job, but rather I would spend time helping my friends. I committed to paying attention to any signs that might come my way.

It took just under two weeks… Six seniors I did not know called and said, "I don' t remember who told me, but I heard you teach the computer to seniors. Can you help me?" *I never told anyone I was teaching computers to seniors!* In fact, the idea never occurred to me. It became crystal clear with that sixth call that I was to teach seniors how to use computers and other technology. The doors flew open, and I got jobs immediately. Anne Goldberg, The Savvy Senior and Savvy Senior

Services were born October 17, 2013. And so began my career teaching seniors how to use technology.

Since 2013, I have worked with over thirty different senior residences and a few thousand seniors in independent and assisted living, 55+ communities, senior centers, and groups. It has been richly rewarding work that I took to like a duck to water.

After so many years of classes and private lessons, I have come to understand the common issues seniors face when working with technology. I understand what my students don't understand. I know that passwords are the bane of nearly every computer-using senior I've worked with. I get that *fear is the single largest obstacle to learning.*

The sad reality is that today's technology leaves most seniors feeling stupid. Let me be clear about this. You are not stupid. You are simply uneducated as to how to communicate with these new devices.

> *"Fear is the biggest issue facing seniors when it comes to learning new technology."*

I took my knowledge of technology and my love of teaching and put them together to write this book. My purpose is to help allay your fears and give you a tool to help you help yourself when using your smartphone. I want to help you to communicate with your loved ones via email, texting, Facebook Messenger, or WhatsApp.

I wrote this book because I want to empower every senior to advocate for themselves by learning how to look for information on the Internet about health, wellness, and longevity, investments, travel, movie and/or restaurant reviews, and so much more. I wrote this book because I can't be everywhere teaching seniors in person, but this book can.

To your empowerment and independence,

Anne Goldberg
September 2025, Boca Raton, Florida

Chapter 15

At-a-Glance Instructions

Chapter 16

Sources

Chapter 1

https://www.psychologytoday.com/intl/blog/science-of-choice/202401/how-to-create-a-durable-memory

https://neurosciencenews.com/rwpwtition-memory-26114/

https://www.med.upenn.edu/csi/the-impact-of-sleep-on-learning-and-memory.html

https://www.ncbi.nlm.nih.gov/books/NBK557811/

Android history: The evolution of the biggest mobile OS in the world (androidauthority.com)

(iPhone History: Every Generation in Timeline Order 2007-2023 (historycooperative.org)

https://www.gotechtor.com/android-history/

https://doyouremember.com/121138/tv-turned-off-at-midnight

(Android history: The evolution of the biggest mobile OS in the world (androidauthority.com)

https://newretro.net/blogs/main/brick-phones-eighties-mobile-tech

https://www.androidauthority.com/history-of-cell-phones-timeline-3264425/

Android vs. Apple Market Share: Leading Mobile OS (2023) (bankmycell.com)

https://www.techwalla.com/articles/the-history-of-car-phones

https://techbuzz.att.com/explainers/history-of-the-mobile-phone-from-1g-to-5g/

https://www.statista.com/statistics/272698/global-market-share-held-by-mobile-operating-systems-since-2009/

https://www.statista.com/topics/2711/us-smartphone-market/#topicOverview

https://www.statista.com/statistics/1045192/share-of-mobile-operating-systems-in-north-america-by-month/

https://www.digitalspy.com/tech/asixty753959/iphone-vs-android/

https://www.explainthatstuff.com/wirelessInternet.html

What Is Mobile Data? Everything You Need to Know | WhistleOut

https://www.msn.com/en-us/news/technology/router-vs-modem-whats-the-difference/ar-BB1hZBJW https://mcpress.mayoclinic.org/healthy-aging/the-power-of-neuroplasticity-how-your-brain-adapts-and-grows-as-you-age/

Chapter 10

https://www.techradar.com/pro/top-data-breaches-and-cyber-attacks-in-2024

https://www.vox.com/technology/379394/fido-alliance-guidance-passkeys-death-of-the-password

https://www.nytimes.com/wirecutter/reviews/best-password-managers/?campaign_id=9&emc=edit_nn_20240715&instance_id=128795&nl=the-morning&regi_id=124232903&segment_id=172185&te=1&user_id=4227be95bf3762ab8ff15200c87afc6b

https://www.usatoday.com/story/tech/2024/08/15/social-security-hack-national-public-data-breach/74807903007/

https://www.washingtonpost.com/technology/interactive/2022/guide-protection-hackers-viruses/?itid=sf_technology_personal-tech_top-table&itid=lk_interstitial_manual_13

https://www.zdnet.com/article/sick-of-ads-on-android-change-these-5-settings-for-more-privacy/

https://www.howtogeek.com/424624/how-to-check-and-tighten-all-your-iphones-privacy-settings/#how-iphone-privacy-works

Chapter 11

https://www.nytimes.com/2024/10/02/technology/apple-social-apps-contacts-change.html?campaign_id=158&emc=edit_ot_20241003&instance_id=135930&nl=on-tech&regi_id=124232903&segment_id=179541&te=1&user_id=4227be95bf3762ab8ff15200c87afc6bhttps://www.washingtonpost.com/technology/2024/privacy-settings-change-guide/

https://techcrunch.com/2024/06/12/ios-18-cracks-down-on-apps-asking-for-full-address-book-access/

https://pirg.org/edfund/resources/alexa-listening-explainer/#delete-your-alexa-data

https://time.com/6836703/pig-butchering-scam-victim-loss-money-study-crypto/

https://www.fbi.gov/how-we-can-help-you/scams-and-safety/common-frauds-and-scams

https://cyberguy.com/privacy/how-to-change-your-privacy-settings-on-android/

Chapter 12

https://www.computerworld.com/article/1614899/android-contacts-management-ultimate-guide.html

https://www.androidcentral.com/apps-software/apple-ios-18-adds-rcs-support-android

https://www.tomsguide.com/phones/iphones/can-you-get-rcs-messaging-on-your-iphone-heres-how-to-find-out-and-enable-it-in-ios-18

https://techcult.com/whatsapp-vs-texting/

https://www.cnet.com/tech/services-and-software/everything-you-should-know-about-rcs-messaging-in-ios-18/

https://www.macworld.com/article/794705/track-parked-car-on-iphone.html

Chapter 13

https://www.ncoa.org/article/what-are-ai-scams-a-guide-for-older-adults/

https://cyberguy.com/scams/alarming-rise-fake-legal-requests-privacy/

https://www.washingtonpost.com/technology/2024/12/11/apple-ios-182-ai-features-explained/?utm_campaign=wp_post_most&utm_medium=email&utm_source=newsletter&carta-url=httpspercent3Apercent2Fpercent2Fs2.washingtonpost.compercent2Fcar-ln-trpercent2F3fe4439percent2F6759c87b9a856778d402b1cdpercent2F5ee0d5d9ade4e276b38b6sixtydpercent2F27percent2F56percent2F6759c87b9a856778d402b1cd

Chapter 14

https://www.ncoa.org/article/what-are-ai-scams-a-guide-for-older-adults/

The Savvy Senior *Credo*

I am
...old enough to have a past
and young enough to have a future...™
and I **pledge**
to move into that future
with a commitment to **honor myself**,
to stay with the times
and not be left behind,
to learn how to use technology
to improve my life
and **benefit my overall well-being**
and cognitive health
through learning.

I hope I have inspired you to know
you're ...old enough to have a past
and young enough to have a future...™

You can do this!